THEATRE IN YOUR LIFE

Second Edition

Robert Barton
Annie McGregor

Australia · Canada · Mexico · Singapore · Spain · United Kingdom · United States

Theatre in Your Life
Robert Barton and Annie McGregor

Regional Manager:
Todd Rupp

Custom Editor:
Nancy Case

Project Development Editor:
Lisa Sizemore

Marketing Coordinators:
Lindsay Annett and Sara Mercurio

Production/Manufacturing Supervisor:
Donna M. Brown

Production Editorial Manager:
Dan Plofchan

Pre-Media Services Supervisor:
Becki Walker

Custom Production Editor:
Tina Espy

Senior Project Coordinator:
Melanie Evans

Rights and Permissions Specialist:
Kalina Ingham Hintz

Senior Prepress Specialist:
Deanna Sullivan

Cover Design and Image:
Deanna Sullivan

The Adaptable Courseware Program consists of products and additions to existing Thomson products that are produced from camera-ready copy. Peer review, class testing, and accuracy are primarily the responsibility of the author(s).

ISBN 0759390355

International Divisions List

Asia (Including India):
Thomson Learning
(a division of Thomson Asia Pte Ltd)
5 Shenton Way #01-01
UIC Building
Singapore 068808
Tel: (65) 6410-1200
Fax: (65) 6410-1208

Australia/New Zealand:
Thomson Learning Australia
102 Dodds Street Southbank,
Victoria 3006 Australia

Latin America:
Thomson Learning
Seneca 53
Colonia Polano
11560 Mexico, D.F., Mexico
Tel (525) 281-2906
Fax (525) 281-2656

Canada:
Thomson Nelson
1120 Birchmount Road
Toronto, Ontario
Canada M1K 5G4
Tel (416) 752-9100
Fax (416) 752-8102

UK/Europe/Middle East/Africa:
Thomson Learning
High Holborn House
50-51 Bedford Row
London, WC1R 4LS
United Kingdom
Tel 44 (020) 7067-2500
Fax 44 (020) 7067-2600

Spain (Includes Portugal):
Thomson Paraninfo
Calle Magallanes 25
28015 Madrid
España
Tel 34 (0)91 446-3350
Fax 34 (0)91 445-6218

Contents

STUDENT QUESTIONNAIRE

THEATRE IN YOUR LIFE, BY ROBERT BARTON AND ANNIE MCGREGOR

Thank you for sharing your feedback on the draft edition of this textbook! At the end of your course, please complete this questionnaire as thoroughly as you can. If you need more space to write, attach more sheets of paper. When you've completed this questionnaire, please turn it in to your instructor.

1. a. Please comment on the authors' writing style and tone. Did you like it? Dislike it? Did you not notice?

   ☐ Loved it   ☐ Liked it   ☐ Didn't like it   ☐ Didn't notice it

   Please explain your response:

   b. How clearly did you feel the concepts in this text were explained?

   ☐ The concepts were explained clearly. I had no problems understanding the text.

   ☐ Generally the concepts were explained clearly, but occasionally I got confused.

   ☐ The concepts weren't explained clearly at all. I didn't really understand the text.

   Please identify, if any, the difficulties you had understanding the material in the text:

2. Do you think the material in the text is presented in a logical fashion? Do concepts and topics flow well one after the other? Please explain your response.

3. Did this text's approach to theatre help you become more interested in the theatre arts? In other words, when you finish this course, will you be more inclined to attend the theatre or possibly pursue theatre as a major? If yes, why? If not, why not? Please provide specific reasons why you feel the way you do.

4. If a friend asked you about the text, what would you say (in 50 words or less)?

Thomson Wadsworth needs your written permission to acknowledge your assistance with this project. Would you please **check the appropriate responses and provide your signature below?** Please make sure your name is written in the exact manner that you want it to appear in a textbook and in such other forms or formats that Wadsworth desires.

Your attention to this detail is greatly appreciated. Thanks again for your assistance with this project!

I do ☐ do not ☐ grant permission to the authors and Wadsworth Thomson Learning to acknowledge my assistance as a student reviewer by listing my name and school affiliation in the **preface and/or inside front cover** of the textbook titled *Theatre in Your Life.*

I do ☐ do not ☐ grant permission to the author and Wadsworth Thomson Learning to acknowledge my assistance as a student reviewer by listing my name and school affiliation in **marketing materials** (e.g., catalog, brochures) used to promote the textbook titled *Theatre in Your Life.*

Signature _____

Name (please print) _____

School _____

Date _____

INTRODUCTION

Dear Reader,

Theatre in Your Life is currently in development for publication and scheduled for widespread release in 2008. The book you are reading is one of our final drafts before the text goes into a lengthy production process. We appreciate your comments on it and will make every effort to implement your suggestions into the last stages of creating the complete text.

The book will ultimately be lavishly illustrated, with color photos of each of the global theatres described, of actors and others who are quoted, of various theatre spaces, customs, historical periods, and styles, including films and personal or offstage theatre events. There will also be additional columns, tables, and side features further expanding the content of each chapter.

What we are most curious to learn is if you feel the text speaks to you in a direct, accessible and sometimes humorous manner, if you feel the voice of the work is one to which you can relate. And if not, can you help us in any way to achieve the kind of connection where you feel spoken to rather than at and where you feel your own genuine curiosity is satisfied? Even though both authors are two of the "blondest" people on earth, we have made every effort to embrace and explore other cultures, to break through a Euro-centric and sometimes Ameri-centric perspective that has dominated the study of theatre in our country for many years. We would like to know the degree to which you feel we have succeeded in this quest and would be grateful for any suggestions you may have for moving further into inclusiveness.

The student questionnaire that follows asks you to address the clarity and logic of the book, but we would also appreciate any information about how it may have affected your decisions regarding whether or not you want theatre to become more a part of your life.

Thanks again for being part of the process,
Annie and Robert

WHAT IS THEATRE?

ANTICIPATION

CONTENTS

YOU WALK INTO a theatre full of anticipation. Even if the "theatre" is a chair in front of your DVD player and you have just rented a new movie, you hope to be transported for the next few hours. You hope the chair is magic, so that you can sit and watch, yet go on a journey—fueled by energy and navigated by imagination—into galactic possibilities. You hope the show will take you away.

For live theatre, your anticipation may be even greater. This is kind of a special occasion. You may have reserved tickets, and gotten dressed up. Most of all, what you and the other audience members are seeing tonight will be different from any other performance of the show. Things could go wrong. They could go spectacularly right. There is danger and expectation. Great live theatre combines the fun of watching a film with the thrill of being at an athletic event or concert. You get to sit and be told a story, while right there with the storytellers.

Wendy Wasserstein, *playwright*

"There is nothing as human as sharing a laugh with strangers in the dark. We share these worlds and we're acknowledging that we're all made of the same stuff. Unlike reading a book or watching a television show, theatre is communal. Walking into a theater, I always feel a profound anticipation of things to come."

You will be breathing the same air as the actors. You will be highly aware of each other's presence. You will have a special relationship with them and other members of the audience for the duration of the performance. And you will have power.

Author's Insights

Robert: "The last time I was in London, I saw two of the greatest living actors in the world, Judi Dench and Vanessa Redgrave, onstage. Though I had seen both on film many times, their live performances are now forever part of my mental landscape more than their screen work. Why? I was physically present while they demonstrated their phenomenal power, presence, and command. I was there."

The show is not complete without your response, without interaction between actors and audience. Whether you laugh really hard, remain stonily silent, or shift in your chair and cough, you affect the performance. You can *change* the actors, how hard they push, or how relaxed they are. You will make this a different show than it would have been without you. In turn, the actors affect you. A performance might start strong and then lose its way. But then perhaps the actors will adjust to the energy in the room and regain their connection with the audience. Each group brings energy to the event. Each charges and stimulates the other.

The physical presence of another human being introduces variables. You may rehearse an important encounter with someone in your life, but he or she will almost always do or say something that makes it different from the way you planned it, perhaps giving you that look that always unhinges you or an answer you never expected.

Filmed performances, unlike theatre, are unchanging, but our *response* to them can change over time. If you watch the same film at various times in your life, it may seem different with each viewing, because *you* have changed over the years. The performances are the same, locked in celluloid permanence. Live theatre isn't.

This chapter will introduce you to the art of theatre, help you examine various theatre experiences you have already had, or prepare you for seeing what may be your first live performance. It will familiarize you with those who do theatre and with what theatre does for us, as well as offer some ideas to think about how it might become more a part of your life.

WHAT IS THEATRE?

While various cultures have defined theatrical elements in different ways, we can strip our definition down to its most basic elements: **actor, audience, space** and **story**.

Do we need to be in a theatre to do theatre? A big, formal building with an actual stage and a bank of seats? No, theatre is done in warehouses, basements, on street corners, in churches, and parks. It's done in garages, cafeterias, gyms, and playgrounds. Do we need a play script? Not always, because some theatre is based on improvisation and spontaneous suggestion.

> **Peter Brook, *director***
>
> "The theatre has one special characteristic. It is always possible to start again. In life this is a myth; we ourselves can never go back on anything. New leaves never turn, clocks never go back, we can never have a second chance. In the theatre the slate is wiped clean all the time."

What is needed (according to Shakespeare) is "a board and a passion." In other words, we need a place to perform and the overwhelming impulse to do so, combined with eagerness on the part of others to watch, listen, and participate—a passionate engagement on the part of those who present and those who observe. For an event to be called live theatre, we must have the following:

Actor—A performer takes on personas other than those of their normal daily existence. They become others, taking the best of childhood "dress up and let's pretend" into full role playing. Even in a one person autobiographical show, the actor assumes the role of narrator (hopefully more polished and reflective than on an average day) and also assumes characters and selves from earlier times in his own life. There will always be some degree of transformation. Sometimes there is an astonishing transformation—to the degree that the actor is unrecognizable.

Audience—Those who agree to witness the enactment, to take the time to experience it with the actors. Most will make an effort to become engaged, to actually lose themselves by being swept up in what is presented. Whether they have paid a lot and anticipated this event for months or have just had their attention grabbed by a free performance while out walking, there is now a willingness to suspend the distractions of life's details in favor of an imaginative journey.

Space—A place transformed for a performance. If it is a large opera house, empty seats will be filled, lights will be dimmed around those seats and come up on a stage. As actors and scenery move around that stage they will alter the "seeing space" over and over again. At the other extreme, if the space is a street corner, the audience may form a circle around the actors or they may agree to stand near the curb while the actors perform against a storefront. In any case, a place will be temporarily altered to reflect the redefined relationships between those who give and those who receive the performance.

Story—A tale is told about the life of someone real or imagined who has experienced or dreamed something worthy of attention. The story may have a fully developed beginning, middle, and end or it may be incomplete and fragmentary. In some performances, such as a musical review, there is no discernible plot. There are, however, songs that tell small stories or lay out fragments of stories allowing the audience to fill in the details from their own lives. In each of these instances, at the very least the singer says "This is who I am, this is what is going on with me, let me tell you how I feel." Here we get bits and pieces of a larger story. In abstract non-linear theatre, we get snippets of lives, much like walking down a street, catching bits of conversation and glimpses of people in windows, on porches, or in alleys. We then tend to fill in according to our own experience and perceptions. In other performances, we get epic proportions and complete details. But always there is an invitation to enter the life of another.

How do these four elements separate theatre from other public events? If an **actor,** an **audience**, and a **space** are needed, what's the difference between theatre and a sporting event? Well, hopefully no one knows the outcome of the game or how the **story** will end. In sports, a planned outcome is unethical, sometimes criminal. Though theatre is not always scripted, it is also rarely completely spontaneous. Even Improv Troupes, groups of actors (usually comic) who appear to invent their performance before our eyes, have rehearsed and planned for certain desired outcomes and have set ways to check in with each other to move the "discovered" story forward. Their performances are seldom, if ever, completely random. And while some athletes assume a public persona, it is rarely sustained or complex enough to be called acting.

Philip Seymour Hoffman, *actor*

"Sports are like theatre. You do the same play, but it's different every night. There is discipline and creativity. When I used to be a wrestler, I would be on top and think 'Okay if I hit his arm there I can get around here' and you see yourself do it. Same as acting. You have a goal and go after it. With sports, the margin for a different ending is greater."

Sometimes a non-theatrical event becomes theatre. A political rally can become theatre if the ingredients shift. Imagine you are at an outdoor event where people have come to share their feelings about a war. Strongly opposing opinions are presented with speeches, chants, demonstrations, and debates. Then imagine that someone gets up and says:

"This is the character Hector from the play *Tiger at the Gates* by Jean Giraudoux. Hector was the general of the Trojan army and lived over 1400 years ago. At the moment of this speech, his country has just fought one war and is about to embark another, the legendary and bloody Trojan War. Hector has just been asked to speak honoring those who have already died."

This commands attention. It is different from what the audience has heard up to now. In the silence, the speaker's voice carries throughout the space:

> *"You want me to give a speech honoring the dead of war? I don't think so. The speech would be a hypocritical defense of those of us who are still alive, a plea for acquittal. I am not so sure of my innocence. Besides, I have given that speech already. I gave it to them when they were still with me in their last minutes of life, in the aftermath of battle, while they could still give me what was left of their sight and hearing. Want to know what I said to them? There was one completely disemboweled, already turning up the whites of his eyes and I lied, "You're doing better. Going to get you home soon!" and another with his skull split in two and I said, "You look pretty funny with that broken nose, you know that?" And my aide, barely more than a boy, no really just a boy, with his left arm hanging useless and his last blood flowing out of him and I said, "Phew. It's a good thing for you it's the left arm you've splintered." And he smiled. So, what did I do? I gave them one final swig of life; it was all they asked for; they died drinking it. Now I would just ask them to forgive us, those of us who still have our eyes, feel warmth and can see the sun. And that's all there is to say. Let there be no more war."*

(English text by Robert Barton)

Because the speaker has become an actor by assuming the character of another, and because the outcome of Hector's story is known rather than random, the tale of his final encounter with his dying men becomes a moment of theatre in the midst of a political gathering. The actor has become someone else whose story is one of the oldest in Greek mythology. It is no longer just someone expressing an opinion. It is art based on the idea of the unchanging nature of war over the vast expanse of time. It is far more powerful than if he had gotten up and said something like, "You know people have been dying senselessly for thousands of years. It's time to stop." It does not matter how many people present know that Hector eventually died a horrific death in the very war he was trying to stop. There is enough of his story here to bring his ideas alive and to bring theatre to the debate.

WHAT DOES THEATRE GIVE?

What will theatre do for us? What does it offer? In the instance above, the invasion of a moment of theatre gives those present a chance to move beyond the particulars of the debate and into a more universal place. And what do we reap from regular attendance at the theatre, from making a habit of going to plays? What do those of us who attend regularly hope to receive? What, for us, is theatre's *function*?

1. Theatre diverts us and takes us out of our daily grinds. Being told stories is good; having them acted out can be sublime. It can delight, distract, transport, and make us feel entertained. Many plays and productions strive for little more than this and many audiences find it fully satisfying and more than enough, though theatre can be much more.

2. Theatre gives us an "emotional work-out." Many theatergoers report laughing and/or crying more at a performance than they did the entire week before, experiencing more of the big, intense, and often therapeutic emotional releases. Plays tend to take place on the most important days in characters' lives—when enormous changes take place and powerful feelings are present. These feeling are contagious. The same way some go to the gym to work out physical muscles, some go to the theatre to work out emotional ones. Theatre can save us from our tendencies to be indifferent or disengaged, to become emotionally unplugged.

3. At its best, theatre illuminates some aspect of the human condition, tackling either important social/political issues or taking on the major questions about the meaning of life. The great plays can provide us with profound insights into the very act of being alive. Theatre can spur us to take action and bring about change, just as it can lead us to acceptance and peace in our lives. When we can sit and observe others struggling with our major issues and finding resolution, we can sometimes go empathically on the same journey and find inspiration for our own.

4. There is an old saying about books that, "We read to know we are not alone." It could be said that we go to plays to *prove* that we are not alone. Theatre is a way for the community to come together and share essential experiences. In our increasingly industrial and technological world, we become more and more isolated—strangers in our own neighborhoods and communities. We are also an increasingly mobile society in which some of us change location so often that we lose touch with our original community—our tribe of origin—and have difficulty accepting and being accepted by our new tribe. Some of us spend time with others at church, work, and sporting events, but others of us don't participate in such gatherings. So there is theatre, which is all about a live and immediate communal experience. It provides us with the chance to share laughter, ideas, feelings, and wisdom. By sharing, we grow stronger as individuals and we all can become more fully invested members of the tribe. Sometimes sacred, sometimes profane, live theatre is always about our shared humanity.

5. Theatre gives us lasting, indelible memories. Because we were there on a certain night, really *there* in the midst of the magic, we tend to remember, re-hash and relive our great moments in the theatre like no others. If you are new to theatre itself, you may have some concert memories of this kind. It did not matter how many CDs you had of a favorite singer or band or how many times you saw them onscreen. Chances are, if you got to experience them in a space you actually

shared, you will never forget it. If some of the songs were about deep personal journeys, you probably felt something close to what happens when the story envelops us in the theatre.

THREE KINDS OF THEATRE

In this book we will examine the theatrical experience from three perspectives. We will use the term *live theatre* to mean performances with actors physically present and *media* to mean any screen (film, TV, DVD, CD) that takes the place of living human beings. We will also ask you to consider theatrical elements in your own life, your *personal theatre*.

You might be wondering why, if this is a book about theatre, we plan to devote attention to filmed performances. For one thing, many of our formative theatrical experiences are with TV and film. Media theatrical is a crucial part of our private histories and personal mythologies. Many of our ideas about drama and life were formed in front of a screen. And most of us will spend many more hours of our lives there than with live theatre, particularly as home media centers and screening rooms become more common and the cost of live theatre continues to rise.

Are you a video baby? Has your entire life been a theatrical event in the sense that the camera has been your audience? Did you know that others would watch your "performances" at a later time? Did you watch favorite videos hundred of times, memorizing every line and frame? If so, your celluloid adventures have formed who you are and how you will respond to any theatre event. And your experiences as both audience and actor have been very different from those of other generations.

Because cinematic experiences have been such a deep, rich part of our heritage, and because we all have such a powerful memory bank of screen references, we will use these resources throughout the book to enrich your future live theatre and media experiences.

> **Robert Townsend,** *popular culture expert*
>
> "For many young people, life has been documented almost as if it were their own personal movie. Dad had a camera aimed right at them when they exited the womb. Then every time they took a first step or blew out the candles on their birthday cake, somebody was video-taping it. This is very different from those who just have their memories and a few photos."

We will also consider a blended event, *media theatre*, where both canned and live elements are present. Interactive performances of *Little Shop of Horrors* are classic examples of the constancy of the film projected being challenged and enhanced by the variety of live performances and audience participation. There are also an increasing number of plays and performance arts presentations that incorporate media into the overall experience, whether as part of the scenic design or actual dramatic interludes. And the circumstances under which we experience a film can result in a "one half" theatre event, one half (actors and story) constant and one half (space and audience), live and variable. Imagine seeing a film for the first time:

— in a classroom with other students engaged and informed on the subject all eagerly taking notes and looking forward to a lively discussion afterward.

— at the Cineplex on opening night, after waiting in a long line, in a packed house, surrounded by hysterical fans of the leading actor or this series of films.

— in your own living room surrounded by rowdy, imbibing friends, often loudly dishing, talking about, and shouting back at the characters in the film and at each other.

—in the private screening room of your most hypercritical acquaintance, who will stop the film frequently to offer devastating critiques of the work of everyone involved.

—at your parents' home, having just bought them this film, hoping they will love it as much as you do, but a bit insecure and uncertain.

—in a bunker near Mosul (Iraq), with soldiers from two different cultures and some recently rescued civilians, with the sound of explosives going off in the distance. Some here do not understand the language of the film, but all are grateful for the diversion.

—in a village in Uganda where some of the film was shot, with a sheet serving as the projection screen and villagers seeing themselves for the first time, some delighted, others disturbed, some having to be cautioned by the tribal elders to quiet and calm themselves for the duration of the showing.

Think about your actual first exposure to some of your favorite films and expand that to all the other ways it might have happened. You begin to see how variations in space and audience can alter—in a live, interactive sense—your perceptions of the film and even how much of it you actually see and hear.

Unless you have actually acted in a play or worked on a production in some other capacity, you may have only experienced theatre as audience member. But what about your personal theatre? Many of us do not stop to notice that whether a camera is present or not, we are starring in an ongoing event called "My Life," while playing supporting roles and walk-ons in the lives of others. We are all actors from the time we are small. Children act to try on roles; adults act to successfully adjust to circumstances. In some professions, such as law and politics, much on-the-job time is spent in performance. But all of us give everyday performances, perhaps showing off for someone we want to impress or changing our behavior when we realize someone is watching. Sometimes we act so that we don't get hassled, so we feel better about who we are, or so that we are allowed to join in. Sometimes we simply try to act like someone else who seems more graceful, compelling, or powerful. We don't just *act* our lives, we often *direct, produce, design, light, score,* and *promote* them. Personal theatre simply turns what we do all the time into art. In fact, before they were professionals, many actors were learning key skills by simply acting their lives.

As we learn about live theatre and how to evaluate it, we can apply these ideas to our ongoing personal theatre, and gain some awareness, possibly even some control of the elements (actor, audience, space and story) of our own lives. If we learn from our mistakes, if we rehearse in our lives what we learn in the theatre, we can begin to discover how, in the words of Sam, the heroic black South African man in Athol Fugard's play *Master Harold and the boys...*, to "live life like champions, instead of always being just a bunch of beginners at it."

Leonardo DiCaprio, *actor*

"I used what would later be my emotional range as an actor to fake the greatest illnesses or family tragedies to prevent me from exploring algebra."

Derek Luke, *actor*

"I lived in tough neighborhoods and the older boys picked on me so I had to learn how to street fight. That's when I became an actor. I studied the cool guys with their hard faces, hard walk, and hard talk."

> **Julia Stiles,** *actor*
>
> "Even when I was just a kid, I could walk around the city by myself and no one would mess with me. I learned to act tough and use my killer look."

THE RANGE OF THEATRE

All cultures have theatre in some form. People everywhere tell their stories and act out their issues. It is powerful to act out a concern and equally powerful to observe this enactment. Watching someone walk through your experiences clarifies and crystallizes them. At any given moment, all of the following theatre groups may be simultaneously telling tales, raising questions, and in some instances, offering answers.

- **The Bread and Puppet Theatre** may be offering biting political satire in an open field, mesmerizing audiences with the use of gigantic and strikingly expressive puppets.

- **The Spiderwoman Native American Theatre** may be reviving its classic "Women in Violence" at an international festival, using broad comic devices to make serious points.

- **The New Globe Theatre** in London (the replica of the theatre used by Shakespeare in the Elizabethan era), may be staging a performance of one of his plays featuring an all male cast and rushes on the stage floor in authentic historical recreation.

- **The National Theatre of the Deaf** may be touring one of their adaptations of a classic children's book with both sign language and spoken sequences for deaf and non-deaf audiences.

- **The Beijing Opera** may be warming up for one of its gymnastic extravaganzas, demanding Olympic caliber athletic skills and astonishing precision from its cast.

- **The Ridiculous Theatre Company** may be holding auditions for one of their gay literary satires, inspired by the legendary Charles Ludlum.

- **The Access Theatre Company** of Santa Barbara may be rehearsing an original dance piece partnering disabled with non-disabled performers.

- **The International American Indian Theatre Project** of Arizona may be presenting their "Coyote Tails" shows and workshops to military personnel on a base as part of their diversity training program.

- **The San Francisco Mime Troupe** may be setting up in a downtown park right in your city, where they will present broad farcical characters and get huge laughs while seriously attacking our administration's policies regarding personal privacy.

- **The Fidel Castro Theatre** a new and magnificent theatre in Cuba, may at this moment, be presenting a "politically correct" professional production. Simultaneously, a struggling amateur production of a new play goes on in the empty, derelict shell of an old pre-Castro professional theatre, *and* a polished extravaganza is staged in the new Tropicana complex in Santiago de Cuba where only foreigners are allowed to see the show.

- **Ogun's Mysteries**, a tale passed down orally through the generations, may be in preparation outside Dakar, Senegal. The entire community is involved in this annual performance of the story of reunification with God. It is both a much anticipated social entertainment and a deeply felt spiritual experience.

- ***The Silken Phoenix***—a musical theatre work celebrating three of Asia's greatest women poets from past centuries—may be touring the world, questioning stereotypes of passive Asian women and showing what accomplishment is possible even in a repressive society.

These are just samplings of theatre occurring globally and simultaneously. All of these theatres impact lives.

WHO MAKES THEATRE HAPPEN?

It takes a village to put on a show. And often in the final stages of production, we have spent so much time together and so little with others in our lives that we do begin to feel as if we have been and may be together forever. Then the show closes and snaps us out of it. Mounting a theatre production is like a game with teams and elaborate rules (many made to be broken), and like any team effort, players with complementary skills are necessary for the play to be successful.

Kenneth Lonergan, *playwright, screenwriter*

"We live in our imaginations. And the imaginative connection you get between a play or movie and its respective audience is as close as most of us ever get to each other."

Anatole France, *writer, critic*

"To know is nothing: to imagine is everything."

John Keats, *poet*

"I am certain of nothing but of the holiness of the Heart's affections and the truth of Imagination—What the imagination seizes as Beauty must be Truth—whether it existed before or not."

We will try to deal with nearly all the theatre artists and craft persons in the course of this book, all of whom are the Storytellers. Some are involved in preproduction work long before opening, others become involved as the play moves into rehearsal and production, and still others are involved in postproduction after the show closes. All are necessary to make the specific event happen in its own miraculous way. Look at the chart on the next page. It may surprise you to learn that any production can easily involve a hundred people or twice that many. The chart omits important assistants who swell the number even more. If you have stayed at the end of a film to read all the credits, you know that with technicians, this number can multiply several times over. The table on the following pages shows some of those who may be listed on a live theatre production.

There are a few "grunt" jobs in the preceding chart, involving labor without much demand for creativity. For the vast majority of these staff members, however, the job requires a tremendous amount of **imagination** as well as the drive to realize fanciful visions in concrete ways. Play productions involve imagination driven by **impulse**. Webster defines *imagine* as "to form a mental image of something not actually present to the senses." Everyone has an imagination

---

**While these jobs may be filled by separate individuals, many small theatre productions have merely a handful of participants doing the ultimate in multi-tasking. Sometimes the village is very small, with some extraordinarily hearty and versatile villagers.

Preproduction	Rehearsal Production	Postproduction
PLAYWRIGHT (author)	ACTORS (performers)	CRITICS (journal reviews)
COMPOSER (author of music)	GRAPHICS DESIGNER (creates images, lay-out used in ads)	STRIKE CREW (dismantle and/or store physical production elements: props, costumes, set pieces, lights, etc.)
LYRICIST (author of song lyrics in a musical)	DRESSORS (assist actors with preparation)	ALL OF THE ABOVE (memories)
LIBRETTIST/BOOK AUTHOR (author of dialogue in a musical)	MAKEUP DESIGNER (designs actors' makeup)	
PRODUCER (financial and business decisions)	MAKEUP ARTIST (assists actor in makeup application)	
MANAGING DIRECTOR (oversees day-to-day business)	HAIR/WIG ARTIST (designs/ assists actors' hair/wig)	
ARTISTIC DIRECTOR (oversees creative staff)	TECHNICAL DIRECTORS (oversee the construction of scenery and placement of light/ sound equipment)	
GOVERNING BOARD (oversees everything and everyone)	SHOP FOREMAN (oversees craft persons in one of several areas)	
DIRECTOR (artistic guide)	SHOPPER (purchases cloth, clothing and properties)	
CASTING DIRECTOR (assists in actor selection)	PATTERN DRAFTER (transfers Costume Design drawings into working patterns)	
MUSIC DIRECTOR (guides the music performers)	CUTTER (cuts patterns and fabrics for costumes)	
FIGHT DIRECTOR (creates and coaches stage fight choreography)	DRAPER (sews and fits mockups and costumes)	
CHOREOGRAPHER (designs dance and movement-based sequences)	PROP ARTISAN/MASTER (coordinates all items carried by actors)	
VOICE SPECIALIST (designs and trains actors in use of voice, accents, line interpretation)	SET DECORATOR (coordinates the detailing of scenic environment)	
MOVEMENT SPECIALIST (designs and trains actors in physically demanding use of the body)	MASTER CARPENTER (oversees construction of all built units)	
DRAMATURG (research and text specialist)	MASTER ELECTRICIAN (hangs, focuses, maintains lights)	
DESIGNERS	SOUND DESIGNER/ENGINEER (designs and records sound effects and underscoring)	
SCENERY/SCENOGRAPHER (designs visual environments)	CREW HEADS (teach and supervise crew members)	
COSTUME (designs clothing, wigs, masks, etc.)	CONSTRUCTION CREWS (build needed units)	
LIGHTING (designs lighting and often special effects)	RUNNING CREWS/BOARD OPERATORS (make changes during the production to scenery, costumes, lights, etc.)	
SOUND (designs auditory environment)	AUDIENCE (us)	
FX (devices special effects)	CRITICS (newspaper and broadcast reviews of the production)	
STAGE MANAGER (guides production communications before and after opening night)		
PUBLICIST ("sells" the production and/or season)		

and all areas of human effort require the ability to use it. As are the body and the emotions, the imagination is like a muscle; it needs exercise to stay healthy and strong. It requires engagement and willingness to meet the object, event, or idea halfway, to participate in the experience. The ability to imagine is inherent in human DNA, as may be the *impulse* to do more than imagine, to use theatre techniques as a means of stimulating our own imaginations, telling our stories and expanding the imagination of others. Children have tons of both of these—yet sadly are sometimes left unnourished.

The imaginative impulse is traceable to the beginning of recorded human history and seems likely to have occurred in prehistoric cultures as well. Why? Maybe because it is so powerful. Maybe because it brings such joy or release. We often use our imagination to let our minds soar above unfortunate circumstances such as an unpleasant family event or a dead end work situation. For many, imagination does not necessarily mean action. For the artists of the theatre, however, it is all about making imaginative *leaps* and pushing forward to actualization. From the playwright trying to figure out how best to create a story that can be told in a few hours, to all those who figure out how to tell it, all the way to the marketing team who tries to imaginatively connect the play with its intended audience, there is constant envisioning and creative execution. In subsequent chapters we will try to take you inside each of these artists' various journeys of imagination and impulse. Having identified the personnel, let's now turn our attention to the content of theatre. What is it likely to be about?

LIFE THEMES

One of the best things about theatre is its ability to show us both the surface differences and the essential sameness of human experience. It gives us windows into the lives and traditions of unfamiliar others (thereby reducing our fear of the unknown) and builds bridges into those same lives (as we see how much we all have in common).

Sometimes surface differences between us are so strange or exotic that it seems we have little in common with others. But theatre always makes us aware that we are more alike than unalike and that whatever we are experiencing in life, others are as well. Playwrights choose certain topics over and over, within which to explore human experience. Below are six of the most common, along with some film and play titles you might recognize. Since any interesting story includes more than one major idea, don't be surprised if you would put a particular film in a different category; it's all about the experience you had.

1. Love
   It makes the world go 'round and it's never easy. (films: *Brokeback Mountain, Shallow Hal, The Sea Within [Mar Adentro]*, and *Titanic*, plays: *Much Ado About Nothing* and *M. Butterfly*)

2. War
   It invigorates hope. It destroys life. (films: *Jarhead, Braveheart*, and *Hotel Rwanda*, plays: *Arms and the Man* and *Necessary Targets*)

3. Generations
   Parents want their children safe and secure. Children want an exciting new world. (films: *Meet the Fockers, Osama*, and *Million Dollar Baby*, plays: *King Lear* and *Roosters*)

4. Rebellion
   The status quo isn't working. Social, cultural or political upheaval may make things better. Or not. (films: (*Star Wars, Crouching Tiger, Hidden Dragon*, and *The Constant Gardner*, plays: *Antigone* and *Master Harold. . .and the boys*)

5. Dreams

All of us have ambitions, fantasies and hopes. They may barely resemble the lives for which we settle. (films: *A Beautiful Mind*, *Deuce Bigilow: Male Gigolo*, and *Capote*, plays: *The Three Sisters* and *Bitter Cane*)

6. Values

What if your most powerful beliefs about what is true are the exact opposite of those with whom you must coexist? (films: *Good Night and Good Luck*, *Fahrenheit 911*, *Bad Education*, and *The Lord of the Rings Trilogy*, plays: *He and She* and *The Piano Lesson*)

We will explore each of these Life Themes by examining two different play scripts between the chapters of this book. The first script is a Western European classic and source of many of our American theatrical traditions. The second script is a contemporary play by or about underrepresented peoples: women, persons of color, challenged, or disenfranchised voices. Each pair of scripts will give us an effective taste of the best of the old and the new, the long honored and the long overdue.*

OPPOSITES

The universal symbol for the theatre is a set of two masks: one **tragic** and one **comic**. We can take any of the topics above and decide to laugh or cry about them, and many artists challenge us to do both. In the theatre, as in life, balance is the elusive goal. While we will define the extremes of the masks further in later chapters, suffice it to say that a difference comes from the understanding that in tragedy death is nearly inevitable, but in comedy, life is. Characters in both gain self-knowledge, but it often comes just too late to transform what is left of life in tragedy, while in comedy, it is never too late to change perceptions and alter the future. The overwhelming presence of death or life tends to dominate.

> ### Janet Suzman, *actor*
>
> "The regenerative twinkle of life and love gleams in the eye of comedy; the questioning mark of doom crouches on the forehead of tragedy."

The main character in a comedy is likely to make and be around friends, while the tragic journey is a lonely one. Often we in the audience seem to be the only true friend and confidant of the tragic hero. Comedy has a healthy, robust feeling to it as if the actors have really big appetites and cannot wait to devour an enormous banquet right after the show. There's no such stomach for food in tragedy, too much anguish deep in the gut, too many heavy burdens. These contrasting interior landscapes affect the kind of light in the actor's eye, the energy in the body and the overall relationships that occur between characters and between actors and audience.

Two other important components of theatre that seem like opposites but are only two sides of the same mask, also require the search for balance. When we go to the theatre, we choose for that time to believe that these are real people experiencing real life, so we take our tendency to disbelieve and suspend it. This is called **suspension of disbelief**. At the same time, a part of us never forgets we are watching a show and taking in whatever messages are being conveyed. This is

---

*These plays are presented in their entirety along with more detailed introductions in the anthology Life Themes, available as a companion volume to this text.

called **aesthetic distance**. These two concepts intermingle in intriguing ways. One allows us to forget ourselves and project ourselves into the lives of the characters onstage. The other allows us to step back and gain insight into our own behavior.

GETTING TO THE THEATRE

Media and personal theatre are already parts of your life. But you may be less familiar with live theatre. Now, while you are studying the art form, is the perfect time to experience it first hand. Here are some tips for finding information and obtaining tickets:

1. **Listings**: Your local newspaper probably has an Arts and Leisure section once a week where information about play performances appears. Midsized and large cities also have a free, widely distributed Weekly Guide with theatre listings. All theatre departments have a central bulletin board with information about local productions.

2. **Full-price tickets**: Tickets for students at a college theatre production average about $10, while some Broadway shows have top tickets of $100 or more.

3. **Free admission**: Most nonprofessional theatres need ushers and almost always give them free admission to the show. You sign up in advance to work a performance. You need to be there about forty-five minutes before the show to be trained, but it is an easy and enjoyable job. It is fun to be part of the pre-performance energy and to interact with people with whom you will be sharing the show. Also, if your school paper does not have a regular play reviewer and you are interested, you could offer to write a review for a production that interests you, in which case you are almost invariably given a complimentary press seat. This could be the beginning—in a few years you could be the next Ebert or Roeper.

4. **Cheap tickets**: Many productions have preview performances for several days before they actually open. The show may not be quite as polished as it will be, but these tickets are less expensive than regular admission. Most theatres have a student discount, which is often not advertised, so always ask about it. The theatre also often schedules special student performances, usually week nights or matinees. If you are attending a show at your college, chances are you have already had some funding for the theatre included with your student fees and so should receive a standard discount with your student ID.

5. **Rush tickets** are bought the day of the performance, often an hour before curtain, when seats may be discounted in order to fill the house. There are some touring shows (like *Rent*) that have a built-in clause requiring rush tickets for students at significantly reduced prices. In large theatres, tickets in the balcony are less expensive and some sell standing room, which usually allows you to lean on a platform at the back of the auditorium. Almost all theatres have group rates starting at ten people, so if you can organize nine of your friends, it may be worthwhile. If you are attending as a class, your teacher may purchase clusters of tickets at group rates. Sometimes these are built into the course fee.

6. **Ticket Booths** in large cities (called TKTs in both London and New York) offer discounted (often half price) tickets for professional productions available for that day's performance. Even a highly successful show may release discounted tickets if that day's performance looks as if it will fall short of a sellout. For a Broadway show, there are numerous alternatives to those $100 seats. The web site BroadwayBox.com collects discount codes found on posters, mail fliers and other web sites. The Frugal Theater Goers Guide to Discount Tickets (http://home.nyc.rr.com/frugaltheatergoe/) contains dozens of links to discount sites. The Theatre Development Fund (http://www.tdf.org) offers a buying service for students, teachers, and seniors for greatly reduced prices.

7. **Reservations** may well be your best plan if you do not need a super-cheap, same-day-only seat. If you want security, you will probably be happiest if you reserve by phone or at the box office in advance because this allows you (except for general admission shows) to choose exactly the seats you want. Most audience members prefer to be in the middle of the house on an aisle. But if the show is a lavish spectacle or splashy musical, you can sit far back and still get the full effect.

RESPONDING TO THEATRE

A fully realized response to theatre requires time and study. In the final chapter of this book, we will provide guidelines for writing an informed criticial review based on some exposure to the full spectrum of the world of the theatre. Like anything else, the more you know about it, the more you can appreciate its nuances. The power of an abstract painter like Jackson Pollock can be enhanced by learning more about his work, his generation of artists, and his culture. The same is true of an elegant mathematical formula or the magnificent scale of molecular biology. A few of us, touched by genius in a particular area, can see, hear, and understand a great work in that field at first glance. For the rest of us it takes time and study. Nevertheless, you may well be asked to attend and respond to a show early in the term, so it is valuable to have a useful framework for doing so, one that allows an honest first impression without in-depth knowledge. Below are some guideliness for that response.

Theatre Protocol

Appropriate behaviors at a play will vary widely from place-to-place and culture-to-culture as well as by the nature of the production. At some theatre events, an audience sitting quietly in the dark with their hands in their laps would signal to the performers that they were failing to reach the audience. In another, the same behavior is considered to be the only appropriate response. Let your own sensitivity to others guide your general behavior. Remember that you are not alone and that rude, distracting behaviors are not acceptable. You are, by definition, in a space full of people. You can fully subscribe to membership in the tribe by paying attention to their protocol structure.

The following is a brief list of rules that can be thought of as fairly universal. They may seem obvious. Theoretically no one needs to be told about simple courtesies, but unfortunately, this is not always true.

1. Turn off any electronic devices that make noise (better yet, if you can, leave your cell phone in the car or at home) so that all can have an event without interruption.

2. No productions can be recorded on video, camera or any other image capturing system. In most cases, attempts to do so would be not only rude, but illegal.

3. Respecting the work is important. Whether the audience is silent or shouting, attention must be paid. If your personal mood or lack of interest prevents you from engaging in the work, let others around you enjoy their experience by not drawing attention to yourself by eating, talking, or sending text messages.

4. If you have been required to report on the play as a class assignment, try not to take notes during the performance. It is distracting to the actors, the audience around you and yourself. Sit back and experience the event. Trust that you will remember things about the production until intermission or the final curtain.

5. If you are one who does not retain impressions and you feel you *must* jot down notes or you will lose your insights forever, do so briefly, discreetly and quietly. Never show up with a full sized notebook or clipboard. A few notes cards or small pad that fits in your pocket is all you need.

Better yet, just take notes on the program, possibly checking names of those you wish to praise or putting question marks around those who made decisions with which you disagree. In any case, these should be nothing more than brief reminders to help you fill in details later and never enough that writing actually takes you out of the performance.

Organizing Your Thoughts

Your response, whether formally or informally communicated, can be deeper and clearer by thinking through the specifics of your original emotional reaction by having guidelines around which to organize your thoughts. The following are possible avenues to responding to a theatre event.

1. How will your familiarity with the material impact your response? Have you seen this play or film before? Having the exact experience as the first time is impossible. Have you, for example, studied a play by William Shakespeare as literature and are familiar with the text, before you see a production of the play so you already have strong expectations? Or, is the material completely new to you, so the freshness of your response will be unique to this production? You'll not see the same play in the same way ever again. You only get one first kiss in life. Familiarity or the lack of it, affects your experience.

> **Author's insight**
>
> **Annie:** "Be aware of overdoing 'environment' in your report. A few years ago, I read an eagerly awaited review that discussed nothing but the uncomfortable seats in the theatre. Oh, and the writer's sore butt. Noteworthy, I'm sure, but it was as if no production had taken place at all."

2. Your response to a theatre event will more often be "mixed" than all good or all bad. We often "liked but didn't love" or "didn't enjoy but found interesting." Rating an event on a scale of 1–10 can be a useful initial step in examining our experience. Don't be surprised to find that you seldom give theatre a 1 or a 10. We often find ourselves somewhere in the middle.

3. Having established a production's place on your scale of 1 to 10, explain why you feel that way. You should be able to discern and articulate the conditions of both the event and you. We are all willing to critique other people's work. Sometimes we forget to critique ourselves in the event:

   YOU—What mood or state of being did you bring into the theatre space? Were you focused or distracted? Eager or resigned? Physically well? Did you have dinner and a couple of drinks right before, or were you dying of hunger and couldn't wait to "get out" and have dinner? Did the event happen to intersect with things going on in your personal life in either a positive or negative way?

   THE ENVIRONMENT—What factors in the space contributed to your experience? Was the space too hot or cold? Were the seats comfortable or cramped, or did you have to stand? Did you have an obstructed view? Did the people sitting near you share your experience or irritate and distract you? Awareness of the environment and its impact on your response will help you give a fair and reasoned judgment.

The Production

Having critiqued factors beyond the production's control, you can confidently move on to the production itself. The first set of questions can be applied to the specific show you are critiquing.

The second set can apply to both to the culture of origin of the text/event and to the production itself. See Appendix B: Responding to a Production for a useful format.

The Story

1. **What happened?** Sometimes this is clear, sometimes not. In our personal theatre, we often get that befuddled feeling after an encounter of asking: "What just happened?" In live theatre, some stories are downright formulaic, others challenging.

2. **What was the central conflict?** How much was at stake? Which characters took what side in the conflict? Who played on each team? What prize was at stake? Who won, who lost, who gave up, and/or who changed sides?

3. **What was the primary emotional mode?** Tragic? Silly? Intellectual? Hectic? Sly? This is not about the emotions of the characters, but the overall emotional mood of the event, that is, the playwright's mood. Was there indeed an overall mood or did the production shift and alter unexpectedly?

The World of the Play

1. Time: When in history is the play written or organized, set and performed? How far does this production move away from the original time period? How familiar or unfamiliar are you with the time period?

2. Space: How is space defined and viewed? What kind of space did the production use?

3. Values: What beliefs seem most widely shared by characters in this play? Which truths, ideals, traditions are deemed to be self-evident?

4. Structure: What is the social and familial structure? How strictly enforced are the standards of behavior? What is the hierarchy of authority?

5. Pleasure: What is considered beautiful and desirable by these characters? What is the collective attitude toward sexuality and sensuality? What's hot and what's not?

6. Senses: Which, if any, of the five senses are most frequently and effectively stimulated? What is the quality of light, sound and patterns that constitute the play's sensory world?

You will obviously not be able to answer all the questions. But just considering them helps you enter the world of the play more openly, without the tendency to impose your own world on it. What things are so familiar you wouldn't have ordinarily noticed them? Where do your personal and social norms bump up against those in the play? Is the world offering a "homecoming" or an adventure in an exotic alternative world? Let the event tell you what is important. "Loved it!" or "It sucked!" are legitimate immediate responses, but when sharing your response with others, something more thoughtful is needed. Exploring *why* you loved, hated, or felt ambivalent is interesting and illuminating.

IS THEATRE FOR YOU?

It will probably take at least the rest of this book to answer this question but now is a good time to start asking it. You will be introduced to a large number of ways to become involved in the theatrical process. At the very least you will become a more informed and insightful audience member, so going to a play will be a richer, juicier, and more complete experience. You will learn to see more, hear more, and even feel more as an audience member. If you to decide to audition for a play, sign up to work on a production crew, take an additional theatre class, write a play, or become involved in some other way, what will you take away? Those who have spent time, even brief sojourns, in the theatre, often report that they felt they were in very good and lively company, that they got back in touch with what they most valued about the child in themselves, that they experienced enormous tolerance and respect for individuality and eccentricity, that they felt a genuine sense of community and play, and that they laughed a lot. Welcome to the world of the theatre.

SUMMARY

Your anticipation of a theatre experience tends to rise in proportion to the commitment you have made to have it. Though most of our formative experiences as audience members were with media, the interaction of live actor and audience is often the source of our most indelible memories. We all also have elements of theatre in our everyday lives, where we decide how to act just to survive. Every culture has had theatre for as far back as recorded time and probably long before that. There are numerous participants on the producing team of a play, but the essential ingredients are an actor and an audience sharing a space and telling a story. Some themes are so universal that they are chosen for plays over and over. You will probably be going to a live theatre event in the near future. There are ways to attend the theatre at a reasonable cost. You can take your cues from the audience around you, but remember certain behaviors are never appropriate. You may be asked to respond to a particular production, either formally or informally. Familiarity of the material, your mood, the environment, etc., affects your response to the production. Guidelines to think about when forming a response to a production are time, space, values, structure, pleasure and the senses. Ample opportunities exist to explore theatre online.

SUGGESTED ASSIGNMENTS

These questions may be used simply for reflection. They might also be handled as short writing assignments and/or discussion topics shared in small groups.

1. Where have you been in the audience and known that your reaction and that of those around you was actually influencing and changing the performance itself?

2. What is your own earliest memory of an encounter that could become the first scene in the play of your life?

3. As an audience member, what is your most memorable live theatre experience so far? Your most memorable media experience? How do they compare to each other?

4. What, so far, has been the best (offstage, personal theatre) performance of your life? Why do you consider it a personal triumph?

5. What has been the worst? What caused you to bomb?

6. What is your own most memorable experience of seeing someone only on film and then experiencing that person live?

7. Interview an acting student (or, if you can find one, a professional actor) and ask what they love most, and least, about practicing this art form.

8. Pick a movie or personal theatre event and discuss it with friends following some of the guidelines provided in this chapter. Or discuss with friends your shared senses of time, space, values, pleasure, structure and the senses.

9. Examine each of the major topics chosen for dramatic conflict (Life Themes). Which of these have you already experienced in your own life that might someday provide the basis for a play?

10. Survey your own key relationships in life. Which of these people are you more likely to act for or to pretend to feel other than you really do? With which persons are you most authentic and real when you are around them?

SUGGESTED ACTIVITIES

1. Individual—Make a list of five to ten films that have had a profound impact on you at various times in your life., Choose one or two from early childhood, grade school, middle school, high school, and from the current year.

2. Group—Make an entire evening out of going to the theatre with several friends or with classmates you have just met. Agree to have dinner together before the play and dessert/coffee after. Discuss your anticipation beforehand and share your collective responses afterwards

3. Long term—Start a Personal Theatre journal. At least twice a week, note a performance you observed and one you gave. That is, instances where the behavior would have been entirely different if some kind of "audience" had not been involved.

4. Large Lecture—See #1 above. Share your lists in groups of ten, do a quick assessment of the most impactful films for the group. Select a spokesman to share your group results as others in the room do the same.

KEY WORDS AND IDEAS

Theatre = Actor, Audience, Space, Story

Live Theatre

Media vs. Media Theatre

Personal Theatre

Imagination

Impulse

Comedy/Tragedy

Suspension of disbelief

Aesthetic Distance

Theatre Protocol

Responding to Theatre

The World of the Play

ORIGINS

CONTENTS

HOW DID theatre begin? For many years, historians claimed it started in Athens in the 5th century BCE with the "first" playwright Aeschylus, then developed in Europe and spread to the New World. We call this the DEWG (Dead European White Guys) syndrome, a perspective that has afflicted many disciplines. We now know theatre is immeasurably older than 2500 years and far more geographically diverse than one peninsula on the edge of Europe. We also now know more about how early contributions from women and non-Europeans have influenced global theatre.

Why was Western theatre scholarship dominated by cultural chauvinism for so long? Euro-centric scholars came from a patriarchal literary tradition which had little or no knowledge of other cultures grounded in oral traditions. Knowledge was based on what was familiar to the scholars themselves. In all fairness, it is far easier to research available evidence than to pursue less tangible sources. Our intention is not to show disrespect or ingratitude to the DEWGs. They have given us towering genius and profound wisdom. Some of the greatest works of dramatic art and some of the most meaningful insights into the human condition have come out of their tradition and perspective. They were presenting the truth as they knew it. Most of us would have not done any better in their situation. We will turn to them constantly for information and inspiration. We have all been DEWGs in some aspect of our lives. The term is created with affection, gratitude, and just a bit of irreverence. Our goal in this book will be to expand beyond their insights to embrace a wider perspective not available to them, but revealed by more recent research.

This chapter will offer varying cultural perspectives, share some of the very earliest theatrical offerings, identify major theories about how theatre came to pass, demonstrate the importance of ritual in our personal and theatrical lives, and establish the rules of make believe we all accept as part of the theatre experience.

TRANSLATION POWER

Here is a vivid example of how cultural bias can alter meaning. One of the more common shared experiences amongst Christians is recitation of the Lord's Prayer in unison in a place of worship. This event has theatrical elements, where all present usually stand and take part in a public performance of worship. But what exactly are we saying? Here is the version from the King James Bible:

> Our Father which art in heaven, hallowed be thy name.
> Thy kingdom come, thy will be done on earth as it is in heaven.
> Give us this day our daily bread.
> And forgive us our trespasses as we forgive those who trespass against us.
> And lead us not into temptation, but deliver us from evil:
> For thine is the kingdom and the power and the glory forever.
> Amen.

Here is the original Aramaic version:

> Abwoon d'bwashmaya
> Nethgadash shmakh
> Teytey malkuthakh
> Nehwey tzevyanach aykanna d'bwashmayo aph b'arha
> Hawvlan lachma d'sunganan yaomana
> Washboglan khauboyn (wakhtahayn)
> Aykana daph khnan shbwogan l'khayyabayn
> Wela tachlan l'nesyuna. Ela patzan min bisha
> Metol dilakhie malkutha wahayla wateshbukhta l'ahlam almin
> Ameyn.

Author's insights

Robert: "Whenever my some of my students claim to dislike a great classical play that has been translated, I always urge them to look at two or three other translations because of the power of the translator to profoundly change the work itself."

When material is translated, the translator can't help but filter the words through a cultural bias so ingrained that it may not even be noticed. What follows is a careful attempt to translate the words as closely as possible to their original meaning rather than imposing values from another time, place and perspective.

> O cosmic Birther of all radiance and vibration,
> Soften the ground of our being and carve out a space within us where your
> Presence can abide.
> Fill us with your creativity so that we may be empowered to bear the fruit
>   of your mission.
> Let each of our actions bear fruit in accordance with our desire.
> Endow us with the wisdom to produce and share what each being needs to grow and flourish.
> Untie the tangled threads of destiny that bind us, as we release others from the entanglement of
>   past mistakes.
> Do not let us be seduced by that which would divert us from our true purpose, but illuminate
>   the opportunities of the present moment.
> For you are the ground and the fruitful vision, the birth-power fulfillment, as all is gathered
>   and made whole once again.
> Amen.

Not only are the words different. Meanings have changed. It would be absurd to conclude that the original English translators got it "wrong," since what emerged is one of the most powerful, beautiful profound and inspirational documents in Western history. This does not, however, make it any less intriguing to imagine translation with less cultural filters. Time, translation, and perception can transform writing beyond its original context. If the written word, which is at least captured on the page, can change so much with interventions, what about the uncaptured and ever elusive spoken word?

FIRST PLAYS

What really was the first play? The first recorded drama is not from Greece, but North Africa. Fragments of a work called the *Abydos Passion Play* have been traced back at least 2,000 years before Athenian drama emerged. It was elaborately staged on boats, stopping at various locations along the Nile and concerned the murder, mourning, and resurrection of the wheat god, Osiris. It is our first documented production through literary testimony. Plays of the oral tradition go back far more, though that tradition by its very nature resists empirical evidence. Two things are likely to be true about the first play:

1. It was about the changing of the seasons, an explanation of why we have to endure winter in order to re-experience spring.

2. It was about the relationships of gods and humans and how what was going on between them may have influenced these seasonal shifts.

Author's insights

Annie: "When I finally found a superb (by Seamus Henley) of *Beauwolf*, it not only changed my view of the work itself, but I suddenly understood some parts of my family, especially those from Northern Europe. I felt I had discovered a heritage!"

Why? One or both of these issues emerge in every discovered work from times gone by. These are the two overwhelming concerns. Much preliterate evidence has been neglected and now sadly lost. But scholarship is finally finding, recording, and preserving rich theatrical heritages of cultures with sophisticated oral traditions. A growing body of archeological artifacts also reveals contributions from women and non-European artists. A more global and inclusive view of the art form continues to emerge.

One example of ancient drama preserved by oral tradition is *Uzume's Trance*, a Japanese folk comedy that has been performed in one form or another for many centuries and continues today. This theatrical ritual is enacted each year on the winter solstice and is designed to ensure and celebrate the return of spring, regardless of scientific evidence that seasons are brought by annual rotations of the earth around the sun. It features a woman performer known as a *miko*, or female shaman, who plays the title character, a young mischievous goddess named Uzume. What follows is the story in its bare bones outline.

UZUME'S TRANCE

Once upon a time, Amateratsu the sun goddess was so offended by a remark her consort made about her beauty that she shut herself in a cave. Suddenly the sun was gone from the sky. The entire world turned dark. The people began to suffer. Crops died. The village elders tried to coax her out of the cave, but she would not budge. Suddenly a young playful goddess Uzume leapt in front of the cave, danced in a wild and funny way, sang bawdy songs and flung her skirts over her head, making everyone laugh. Intrigued by the laughter of the people, Amateratsu came out of the cave, returned to the sky, and light and warmth were returned to the people.

Your first response might be that *Uzume's Trance* is a story not a play. In oral performance tradition, a narrator has memorized the basic story, without setting the words. Others are selected to enact various named characters. The performance includes the core story presented by the narrator, pantomimed action by other actors, and interludes where improvised dialogue is inserted. Many of these may be spontaneous, while some lines may also be considered important enough to be passed on exactly from one generation to the next. The "script" often does not exist on paper, but in the imaginations and memories of performers and audience.

What follows is an adaptation that might be performed by an American acting troupe. Since the oral tradition continually adapts and evolves, performances—while respecting traditional ideas—may involve contemporary dialogue, and if the story is basically comic, may include slang and pop culture references. The following script would provide a starting place for a contemporary company from which to build and expand.

*Uzume's Trance**

(to be performed by 10 actors)

CHARACTERS:	Narrator
	Amateratsu, Sun Goddess
	Consort/Boulder
	Elders
	Children
	Uzume

NARRATOR: Once upon a time, long, long ago, Amateratsu, the sun goddess was traveling in her usual course across the sky when her consort made an unforgivably rude remark about her beauty. (*Amateratsu and her consort appear.*)

CONSORT: You're looking old today, baby.

AMATERATSU: What????!!!! (*She strikes him hard enough that he falls down, then kicks him, and he curls into a ball becoming a boulder.*) Let's see how you like life as a boulder! I cannot shine under these conditions. I'm going to go in that cave and never come out. (*Two actors form an arch like the entrance to a cave.*)

---

*English adaptation by Annie McGregor and Robert Barton

NARRATOR:	Amateratsu was so angry that she retired to a cave and rolled an enormous boulder across the mouth of the cave.
AMATERATSU:	Get over here boulder and cover my entrance! *(The actor rolls across the stage and fills the entrance created by the other two actors.)*
NARRATOR:	Suddenly the sun was gone from the sky and the people began to suffer. Their crops died in the fields. The children cried from hunger and cold. All the village elders went up to the cave where Amateratsu was sulking, and they tried everything they could think of to coax her out of the cave. *(Villagers ad-lib moaning, pleading, supplicating. Sample dialogue)*:
VILLAGERS:	Please come back and give us light! We miss you so much! We brought you rice and sweet treats! You are so beautiful!
AMATERATSU:	Not everyone seems to think so *(kicks the boulder)*.
VILLAGERS:	Your consort is a jackass!!!
AMATERATSU:	Well now he's just a boulder. OK, maybe a jackass boulder. But I am here to stay.
NARRATOR:	They wept and wailed, but Amateratsu sniffed imperiously and ignored them. The cold and dark continued and the suffering of the people grew. Soon the whole village gathered in front of the cave, begging and praying.
VILLAGERS:	*(Again, largely adlib dialogue such as)*: We will do anything. Anything! We cannot live without your light! Have mercy! Have mercy! You are the most beautiful goddess ever!
NARRATOR:	But Amateratsu, still angry in her cave, only harrumphed.
AMATERATSU:	Go away and stop bothering me!
NARRATOR:	The people were in despair, and they simply sat in a circle in front of the cave and waited to die. *(Actors form a circle and sit.)* Suddenly, a young goddess named Uzume jumped into the center of the circle and began to dance and sing. *(Uzume leaps from offstage into the middle of the gathering.)* At first, the people were too sad to notice her. But she only danced more wildly and sang more raucously until the people stared at her in amazement. She began to twirl in place, round and round, until all were dizzy watching her. She danced and twirled and sang bawdy songs until the people slowly began to smile and a few clapped their hands in time to her song.
UZUME:	*(singing, she may also improvise dialogue between her ventures into song)* "Roll me over in the clover. Roll me over and over and do it again." "I'm just a girl who can't say no. I'm in a terrible fix. I always say come on let's go, just when I ought to say nix!" "I want your sex. I want your sex. I want your sex!" *(Uzume in an inspired state, continues to sing snatches of racy songs, perhaps even encouraging the audience to shout out requests.)*
NARRATOR:	Finally, she picked up her skirts, flinging them over her head, showing Amateratsu and everyone else her underpants … and the people began to laugh. *(Uzume has under her very full skirt, petticoats and bloomers or some other amusing kind of underwear so what she shows is funny and not particularly revealing.)* They laughed and laughed as she twirled with her skirts over her head until Amateratsu heard the laughter.
AMATERATSU:	Alright, what is so damn funny, anyway?? Move it, boulder. Let me take a look. *(The boulder obligingly rolls out of her way.)* Ohmygod, that is hilarious!! *(She doubles over with laughter.)*
NARRATOR:	She laughed so hard she almost missed the small mirror Uzume had placed in a nearby tree. *(One actor "holds" a mirror toward Amateratsu who can't resist her own beauty, and the actor with the mirror begins to tease her with it.)* Finally, Amateratsu left the cave and before she knew it, the other gods and goddesses grabbed her and pitched her back up into the sky, and the warmth and light of the sun shone down on the people again.

	(Some of the actors lift her up and twirl her and pass her around. Finally she and everyone onstage are dancing. The boulder returns to his consort state.)
CONSORT:	You're lookin' good, baby!!
AMATERASU:	Yeah, well I don't need you to tell me that. *(Villagers cheer her on. She ad-libs lines about her own beauty perhaps culminating with a claim like "I am the original bling!")* Come on, Uzume, let's leave this loser and dance!
	(She and Uzume join in a joyous dancing circle with all the other actors doing the same movement in unison.)
NARRATOR:	And so Uzume once again teased Amaterasu out of her cave and twirled her way into the hearts of the people, proving once again that a girl with a mirror and a great pair of underpants can accomplish anything!

Each year as the sun hides herself in the long nights of December, people gather together and let a *miko* (female shaman) play the role of Uzume and make them laugh, knowing that the sun will soon return to her place in the sky. In this early piece of theatre we find the healing power of comedy, the link between sex and comedy, the necessity for female energy in many performance traditions and the satisfaction derived from ancient and enduring traditions.

Another drama, this one from West Africa, transmitted orally between generations for thousands of years, helps us understand the early traditions of tragedy. *Ogun's Mysteries* is part of a large body of works. In Yoruban culture, the Mysteries detailed the many adventures of Ogun. While the culture of ancient Greece identified the first actor as someone named Thespis, in West Africa there is no doubt that the first "actor" played the god Ogun. The following is one of his dramas. (Note: The term "griot/griote" denotes both a storyteller and something much more sacred. The griot is the living memory of the people, the keeper of the communal consciousness.)

*Ogun's Sacrifice**

(to be performed by 10 actors)

CHARACTERS:	Griot (narrator)
	Obatala
	Babalu Aye
	Ogun
	Other gods
	Humans

GRIOT:	In the beginning, there was only the One, encompassing all Creation in divine harmony. One day as he tended his garden, his slave rebelled and rolled a huge boulder down upon him, sending him crashing into the abyss where he shattered into one thousand and one pieces. *(Other actors enact this event in an abstract way, coming tightly together and then bursting apart and collapsing at various points on the stage.)* From these shards of the One came all things, including the gods. One god was Obatala, who became the Creator.
	(Throughout the following, the actors often use large, stylized, dance-inspired movements to represent the eternal qualities beyond everyday behavior, which identify them as gods.)
OBATALA:	I am the fabric that binds the universe together. Each day my hands form new children to be born into the world. *(As he speaks he spreads his legs and moves his hands as*

---

*English adaptation by Annie McGregor and Robert Barton

	various actors emerge from beneath him and are released by his hands into the world.) All the people are made by the hands of me, Obatala.
GRIOT:	Obatala is the essence of passive creation, serene, unchanging and unmoving. Sadly, Obatala's great weakness is drink. (*Obatala mimes rapidly downing huge quantities of alcohol*), and when he is drunk on palm wine, his creations become a little "wobbly" so that some among us are blind or lame. (*He begins swaying. Actors now appear to limp or struggle to find their way when released by his hands.*) Obatala, in his serene composure, goes on making children. Babalu Aye is the god of suffering.
BABALU AYE:	I am the god who teaches the people to cope with misfortune, to learn patience and forbearance without despair. I am calm in the face of all the tides of fate. (*He/she embraces each child as it's born.*)
GRIOT:	Ogun is the warrior god, the first actor, the dispenser of justice both gentle and harsh.
OGUN:	I am the embodiment of force, energy and most of all, the power of Will.
GRIOT:	Long ago, as the ages passed, Ogun noticed discontent and sadness in his fellow gods. (*Other actors mingle around Ogun.*)
OGUN:	What ails you, my friends? What is the source of this overwhelming grief?
OTHER GODS:	(*dividing and ad libbing the lines as needed*) We feel lonely for human men and women. The great abyss separates us from the people. We wish we could have them in our lives. But the abyss saddens and frightens us. It is a place of chaos, terror, and annihilation.
OGUN:	Let us go through the abyss and see our little brothers and sisters. Let's go right now.
OBATALA:	I would go with you, my old friend, but the business of Creation itself is in my hands. It is my destiny to remain unchanging.
GRIOT:	Simple consciousness was all Obatala could manage. Or maybe he was drunk that day. I don't know. What did Babalu Aye say?
BABALU AYE:	Suffering is to be endured. It cannot be avoided, so maybe it would be better to just be quiet.
GRIOT:	Babalu Aye believed one could only wait and endure, that we simply must manage with our lot. But Ogun, warrior and the first actor, felt differently.
OGUN:	I cannot stand it anymore. I will do whatever it takes to bring us all — gods and humans together. I will go to the worst possible place and find out.
GRIOT:	And as the other gods watched in horrified amazement, Ogun poised on the edge of the abyss, and gathering all of his Will, he threw himself in. (*Ogun thrusts himself forward to the ground where he is barely caught by other actors. All the actors continue to act out the chaos that surrounds him, pummeling him, then lifting, even throwing him high into the air.*) The terrors he experienced in the chaos can only be imagined. The pain he suffered was not to be imagined. He was torn and shredded, but he endured and struggled on. At last, one day at the end of long days and ages of pain and hardship, he landed at the bottom of the abyss and shattered into 1000 pieces. (*The actors lift him high above the ground from which point he jumps down and falls to the ground and appears to be dead.*) Then slowly, agonizingly, Ogun began to pull the pieces of himself together again (*The actor performs a painful resurrection*), and he began the long and painful climb up the other side of the abyss, cutting a path through the terrible abyss and called for his fellow gods to follow him. From that day until this, we, the people, live among the ancestors and the unborn. (*The other actors form a wide circle and slowly all go down on their knees to pay homage to Ogun, who stands in the center.*)

OGUN: We will all now live together, the gods and the demons, the good and the evil, the strong
                    and the weak, all living fully in the universe with all that exists available to us if we only
                    have the Will to act.
GRIOT: And we all now know the power of our own will, thanks to the hero-god, Ogun.

This ancient ritual drama holds many essential elements of tragedy: the suffering of a people, the rise of a hero, the willingness to sacrifice for the good of others and ultimate redemption. Many hundreds, perhaps thousands of years later, Aristotle would describe this process in *The Poetics*.

Identifying the first play, while an enjoyable quest, is ultimately a purely academic one. We know that plays existed long before Western tradition and that we can move beyond our known canon to include the world at large. We now understand that we only have theories about the origins of theatre. Here are four of the best:

SPONTANEOUS INSPIRATION

Robert Edmond Jones' seminal work *The Dramatic Imagination*, offers a possible story of the first play:

> "Let us imagine ourselves back in the stone age. It is night. We are all sitting together around a fire—Ook and Pow and Pung and Glup and Little Zowie and all the rest of us. We sit close together. We like to be together. It is safer that way, if wild beasts attack us. (A lion has been killed today, and it is all anyone wants to talk about). The lion's skin lies close by, near the fire. Suddenly the leader of the tribe jumps to his feet. "I killed the lion! I did it! I followed him! He sprang at me. I struck at him with my spear! He fell down! He lay still."
>
> He is telling us. We listen. But all at once an idea comes to his dim brain. "I know a better way to tell you. See! It was like this! Let me show you!" In that instant drama is born.
>
> The leader continues, "You, Ook, over there, you stand up and be the lion. Here is the lion's skin. You put it on and be the lion and I'll kill you and we'll show them how it was. . . . And now these two men—the world's first actors—begin to show us what the hunt was like. They do not tell us. They show us. They act it for us. The lion growls. The hunter poises his spear. The lion leaps. The spear is thrown. The lion falls and lies still. The drama is finished.
>
> Now Ook takes off the lion's skin and sits beside us and is himself again. Just like you. Just like me. Good old Ook. No, not quite like you or me. Ook will be, as long as he lives, the man who can be a lion when he wants to."

Jones theorizes a spontaneous "light bulb" moment when Ook decides to *show* the lion hunt rather than tell about it. Theatre is then born in pure inspiration. The Ooks of the world were unable to send out mass emailings to share their discoveries and are unlikely to have had direct contact with more than a few hundred people during their whole lives. The notion of just getting up and performing stories must have inspired countless actors in different places and times. Could it be that the need and ability to create theatre is inherent in each of us?

IMITATION TO RITUAL

Internationally renowned mythologist and anthropologist Joseph Campbell, inspired by a fascination with Native American culture in his youth, sought to unify all myths. His theory says that human capacity to imitate and fantasize, leads to the creation of myth and ritual.

Campbell observed that children everywhere need to imitate behavior, learning to talk, walk, play, read, and sing by watching and mimicking. As our imitations become more complex, we practice playing "house," "school," or "war." We may then create long dramatic scenarios, like television series, returning to the same game (and exploring behaviors and consequences) in episode after episode.

We then move to complex dramatic situations, beyond our known worlds. Campbell noted that once children are engaged beyond their own living room, tent, or cave, they begin to fantasize about worlds that are partly real and partly invented. Did you play "Ninja Warrior," act out stories with a "My Little Pony" collection, or play in a "fort" in your backyard or under the dining room table? You probably went beyond imitation to playing out roles that only existed in your imagination.

Combining imitation with fantasy is universal. In Dakar, Senegal (West Africa), every boy has a ball, bundle, or tin can with which he plays soccer endlessly, dreaming of one day becoming star of the Senegalese National Soccer Team. Boys may not have player cards to collect or a television to watch the games, but can recite names of current and former team members and their vital statistics. Girls play "house" in courtyards and enclosed spaces, dreaming of being first wife of a rich man (a man can have up to four wives if he can afford to care for them). Less popular girls have to play second or third wives. A favorite war game for all is still "rebellion against the French," who exerted colonial control of the country into the 1970s. An actor who pretends to be Hamlet, Prince of Denmark, existing purely in imagination, is only a more sophisticated version of children playing El Hadji Diuof (the great soccer star), Mom, Fidel Castro, or Sponge Bob Squarepants.

Campbell understood that for the childhood impulse to construct drama to become the art of the theatre, community engagement is crucial. Childhood games explore mysteries of life, but long after childhood we still want answers. The mysteries—our purpose in life, our relationship to higher powers, why we suffer and whether true justice exists in this world or the next—simply grow more complex. We imagine answers through myth, ritual, and community—moving from childhood imitation to theatre art.

The source of all mythology is *need.* Long before science and technology, we depended on autumn harvest to see us through winter, with meat brought home by hunters and roots and plants harvested by gatherers, preserved to prevent starvation during the lean months. But what if one year, the hunters come home empty-handed time and time again? They have roamed far and wide but have seen no sign of the much-needed herds. The community is afraid. We gather together to decide why this is happening. An elder suggests the animals have left us because our creator is angry with us. What could we have done? Can we appease the anger and bring the herds back? Someone suggests an offering of something precious to us. We agree, we make the offering and within days, the hunters return loaded with meat for the winter and we can see the returning herds from our own home. Coincidence? Maybe. Maybe not.

According to Campbell, a mystery like this will cause us to *do* something. If that something has the desired results, we repeat it. To make the mystery plausible, we evolve stories about the creator/ spirit, the people's response to divine anger and about heroes who solved the mystery. We continue the behavior that worked the first time we needed it. Each generation may make the event bigger, developing elaborate stories of life and death, seasonal renewal, plenty and starvation—called myths—our way of comprehending the unknowable. Long after we evolve past the hunter/gatherer stage, our myths and rituals are preserved and passed on. A sacrifice that involved five minutes and minor effort in the beginning may now include elaborate effects and community wide participation with many roles to be cast. Cultural identity is reaffirmed through mythic reenactment with diverse peoples creating drama dealing with the same essential mysteries.

Stepping Out

Our third theory is from Aristotle's 4th century BCE document, *The Poetics*, the first known Western analysis of a body of dramatic literature. His essay is often used to define the very nature of Western theatre. While he wrote of a specific culture, place and time, his theory can be applied to any community. (More about Aristotle and Greek tragedy can be found in Chapter 7.)

Aristotle believed that theatre evolved out of religious rituals known as *dithyrambs*. The *dithyramb* involved the entire community gathering on occasion to sing songs and recite words in unison. One day, according to Aristotle, a man named Thespis stepped forward and began speaking to the community and letting the community respond in unison. This changed the nature of the event. Instead of a group monologue, a dialogue was created between speaker and community. The dynamic of a man standing alone on the stage speaking to the community is changed. Now the man is impersonating a mythological or historical figure (a character), and the community is represented by a group of actors known as the Chorus.

Thespis has been immortalized in Western theatre culture. His name has been adopted to represent not only actors but also members of any dramatic society, who are called Thespians. The likelihood is strong that other performers in other and earlier cultures also one day stepped outside the group and created dialogue. Thespis was the lucky one whose name is remembered.

A DIVINE GIFT

A fourth theory comes from ancient India and encompasses much of the Asian theatre-dance tradition. The Hindu theorist Bharata wrote even earlier than Aristotle about what theatre is and should be. The god Brahma ("the breath of the world") is one of a triumvirate of primary gods, including Siva and Vishnu, and is believed to have commanded the first drama. When humans desired to imitate the experience of the gods, Brahma confided his secrets to Bharata, whose seminal work is *Natya Sastra* or the Canons of Dance and Drama. He was trying to identify the crucial components of Sankrit drama.

Plots for many plays in this tradition were originally based on two epic poems: *Ramayana* and *Mahabharata*, religious and ethical works, which still are primary sources in classical and modern dance dramas, including contemporary film-making in India.

Music and dance are required in much of Asian drama, and according to Bharata, language must be poetic, plots familiar, and narrators must define the outline of a performance while actors perfect gesture and physical nuance to express the writer's intent. The presence of a storyteller is desired, and the use of puppets allows the expression of something beyond the capacity of human performers. The perfection of gesture and physical nuance should be the highest priority of the actor. Drama is believed to approximate the poetic flights of words in ideas.

Acting, dancing, and puppetry, according to the *Natya Sastra*, attempt to reach beyond the natural world, and in this effort, trance states are sometimes induced. The puppet (in some ways akin to a mask) cannot act poorly or tell a lie, but rather represents "the symbol of man in the great ceremony of life and eternity." The puppet can teach the actor simplicity, precision, and a lack of affectation, just as a character may teach the actor how to expand his view of life in general. Appreciation of the divine gift and magical transformative states gives theatre its profound power.

The theories of Jones, Campbell, Aristotle, and Bharata are plausible and compatible. The sudden spontaneous "Ook" impulse is common among adults and children in the midst of discussion or at play. Rituals are often fully communal. Participation in them is a crucial rite of passage. And each culture's Thespis could easily make the inductive leap from stepping up around the fire, recreating the beast, to stepping out of the chorus to create character. The magical components of theatre, its trancelike moments and the fusion of the actor with any and all around him may indeed be divine gifts.

RITUALS OF LIFE

Each of these four origin theories focuses on ritual. Rituals are central to the theatre just as they are to everyday life. A ritual is any act that is repeated over and over in a very specific way. When you wake up, you may proceed to a series of ritualistic preparations for your day, which foot you put in which slipper first, the order in which you brush your teeth, and the way you gather what you need to venture into the world. Rituals center us. The more difficult the day ahead or behind, the more we value comfort rituals.

A ritual with an audience, even an audience of one, becomes a performance. In your offstage life, you may have repeatedly performed private rituals, such as a particular way of putting on your socks or taking off your jeans. When you do any of these in front of a new roommate, it suddenly turns theatrical. Your audience may comment on the "weird" way you do it and make you realize that not everyone else in the world does socks and jeans as you do. So you reconsider your choices. You may decide to 1) only change clothes in private from then on; 2) change how you do it; or 3) enjoy your own individuality; maybe even flaunt it, encouraging other comments from your room-mate, in fact "performing" on a regular basis. If you choose 3) you might consider becoming a theatre major.

We have official rituals from birth to death. Most cultures have some ceremony welcoming and/or naming a newborn child into the village and then religious and secular celebrations, graduations, and other rights of passage, games, pageants, sports events, dances, awards ceremonies, weddings, public hearings, presentations, debates, trials, and finally funerals and memorial services. These all have strong theatrical elements and defined performer and audience roles. Sometimes we skip or reject rituals and then regret it deeply later. Friends often say how much they now wish they had shown up. Why? Because the ritual may have allowed them to let go, gain peace and move ahead.

Theatre people are often superstitious. Backstage rituals abound. Many actors arrive at the theatre at precisely the same time each day, put on their make-up in an exact, perfected pattern and converse with others in the cast in a predetermined sequence. So do many athletes. These rituals are often not done so much out of the fear of consequences for breaking them as for the sense of continuity in keeping them.

The line between the performance of a play and of a community "play like" event is often thin. Below are examples of how theatrical elements outside the theatre itself provide powerful and profound experiences for all those who perform and all those who observe.

RITUAL GROWTH

In the theatre of our lives, rituals can be not only comforting but sometimes our salvation. The following is an example of how the elements of theatre have formed an annual event of great healing:

Wiping Away of Tears

In 1890 at Wounded Knee Creek, the U.S. Cavalry opened fire on and exterminated almost 350 women, children, and elders, all members of the Lakota Tribe. One of their chiefs, Big Foot, was attempting to bring them to shelter after the assassination of their leader and greatest war chief, Sitting Bull, who had defeated the cavalry repeatedly in the past. They had traveled hundreds of miles to seek refuge at Pine Ridge Reservation and were just twenty miles short of their destination before being rounded up and shot. This incident remains one of the most questionable events in our military history in terms of judgment and compassion.

Ron His Horse Is Thunder, *Sitting Bull's great, great, great, grandson*

"This massacre broke the back of our nation and it continues to stand as the most potent symbol of the American Indian genocide."

After this, tribal elder Black Elk predicted "seven generations of anguish and then regeneration." The remaining Lakota were stripped of their lands and placed on reservations, beginning a downward spiral of despair, poverty, and unemployment. Similar conditions permeated the lives of other tribes on the 314 reservations in our country, but no single incident exemplifies total devastation as does Wounded Knee. Many descendants believed such conditions were simply their destiny. An enervating sense of futility pervaded a population that felt stuck and without hope.

Then, as the hundred-year anniversary of the massacre approached, something remarkable happened. Tribal elders decided they needed to break the cycle. They founded a public ritual, called "Wiping Away of Tears," to release the collective grief of their people. In this yearly ritual, tribal members now repeat the long, cold ride of their ancestors with eagle feathers on the staffs they are carrying. Since the wind-chill factor makes temperatures dip well below zero, the ride is grueling. It is observed and assisted by other tribal members at various places along the journey.

Each of the six days of the ride culminates in a specific prayer for members of the tribe: day 1—children and orphans, day 2—the elderly and shamans, day 3—the physically and mentally sick, day 4—prisoners, day 5—women, day 6—the spirits of those who have died and the hope for an end to war. The ritual has gradually focused more and more on the children of the tribe and has been renamed "Future Generation Riders." Those who have taken part report a renewed sense of hope and a greater commitment to education and success.

Vina White Hawk, *tribal elder*

"The grieving helps the children to accept who we are and to grow from that."

It is as if many Lakota felt trapped by a single moment in history and were released by acting it out. It was not enough to tell the story. It had to be fully ritualized. It had to be experienced and felt. It had to be performed. Many of us experience this phenomenon in our personal history, but in this case an entire population felt an identical and overwhelming frustration, ritual absolution and release. Sitting Bull's direct descendent, Ron His Horse Is Thunder, not only serves as one of the leaders of the ride but is president of one of 37 tribal colleges, spearheading a campaign to build a new educational and financial future for young and newly ambitious tribal members. A new generation of American Indians is turning the event into one of healing and redemption.

Melanie Kuntz, *teen-age rider*

"I didn't really want to do it but my Dad wanted me to so I did. Then I got to talk to the older people who know the history of this place. They told me our ancestors were watching as we rode through the hills—and you know, I truly felt it. Now I'm interested in learning more about my heritage. And I feel like maybe I can do a lot more things with my life than what I thought before."

Alex White Plume, *tribal member*

"This journey has helped us rebuild in the seventh generation. It has allowed us to find the peace within ourselves and to extend that peace to others, even those who have hurt us."

You may ask if this is a theatrical performance or a spiritual event. Is it theatre? We believe, that yes, this is theatre functioning at its most serious and spiritual level. We have performers playing the roles of their ancestors, audiences participating fully in the event, a designated space (vaster than most conventional theatres but still a performance space), and a story. As *Uzume's Trance* is performed as a comic expression about serious issues of survival, so "Future Generation Riders" is performed as a tragic expression of regeneration and renewal.

Embracing Womanhood

Rituals may include an entire culture or be focused on life-stages of an individual. The transition out of childhood is honored by Jewish bar and bat mitzvahs for 13-year-old boys and 12-year-old girls as does the Vision Quest embarked on by some Native Americans on the brink of adulthood. However, there is probably no more vivid ceremonial transition than *Quinceanera*, which celebrates the fifteenth birthdays of young Latina women. This event often involves formal wear and up to eight young men in attendance, men designated as guardians—or *chambelanes*—for the honored young woman. It may also involve a court of young female attendants called *damas*. Events move from the solemnity of Mass, prayers, ceremonial gift giving and vows, through a formal procession, to festive banqueting and dancing. *Quinceanera* starts with deeply spiritual ritual and ends with vibrantly secular fiesta celebration.

While the specifics vary among communities, traditional elements include a special headpiece, called a *diademia* (much like a tiara), worn by the honoree, ornamental altar pillows, pastel colors, a birth stone ring, and a *libro y rosario* (missal and rosary).

Dan Wojcik, *folklore scholar*

"Most Caucasian Americans fail to recognize this key rite of passage, making a challenging life transition even more difficult and confusing for all involved"

Pancita Davila, Quinceanera *planner*

"From this important day on, the sweet fifteen girl can find a good path to become a better person with new ideas."

Marlowe Velez, *recent quince celebrant*

"It's an opportunity to express your maturity and to be thankful. Every girl should have that whether she's Hispanic or not."

The *Quinceanera* can be traced all the way back to the first encounters between Spanish explorers and Aztecs in Mexico over five hundred years ago. Both these cultures already had ceremonies recognizing the coming of age of young women. The two traditions intermingled and evolved into a day-long celebration. While not all elements of *Quinceanera* are readily understood by those outside the culture, at least two of the key rituals can be universally appreciated. The honored young woman at one ritual point gives away a doll to a younger girl and accepts the gift of a pair of high heels.

Both the "Ride for Future Generations" and the *Quinceanera* have the basic elements of theatre—performers and audience, costumes and/or props and a definite progression from a beginning to a symbolic final curtain. And most importantly, lives are touched by the event.

Because of the profound connection between ritual and theatre, the question inevitably arises "What is the difference?" When is one not the other? While there is some disagreement among theatre practitioners, our bias is in favor of not quibbling. We would say that it is possible to argue that a ritual is not theatre if it is private or unobserved (no audience), if the participants remain entirely themselves with no hint of dressing up or role playing (no actors) and if the ritual act is functional and/or utilitarian rather than narrative (no story). We would say theatre may not be ritual if it is a single- one-time-only event, particularly if presented with largely improvisational elements. Repetition of the kind that occurs in rehearsals and multiple performances is essential. The one-shot ritual is an oxymoron. The "Young Rider" will extend its run with new casts. While each young woman will only experience her own *Quinceanaera* once, the ritual, with many of the same participants shifting roles, will occur over and over again within the community.

It is often said that theatre is built on illusion, on things not being what they seem. It is also based on an agreement to pretend, to choose to see or not see, which we will now discuss.

CONVENTIONS

In each piece of live theatre, we are asked to accept theatrical *conventions*, which are conditions of make-believe that demand our willing suspension of disbelief. Some conventions are so familiar to us, we don't even notice them. We often use the term "realism" to describe a play in which people act much the way we do in life and "style" or "stylized" for those in which they do not. In a modern realistic play, presented in a traditional theatre space, the setting, the performances by the actors, and the way the story unfolds might seem very like our own everyday experiences. But the most "normal" performance is still subject to conventions. We may look through an opening called *a proscenium arch*, the frame (much like a picture frame) that defines the acting space. The space within that arch is called the *fourth wall*, which has been left open so we can peek through it. We act as if this fourth wall has magically opened for us or that we are flies on that wall. In either case, we're going to pretend the wall is there and that we are not.

Onstage, everything represents something else. Ice tea may stand in for bourbon, a blinding light for God, a specific hand gesture for love, a sharp light and sound change for a character's emotional distress, a wild dance for a character's ecstatic inner thoughts, or ketchup for blood. Blood may also be a red ribbon suddenly revealed, a scarlet sheet dropping over a victim or a wash of crimson light on the back wall. These we accept.

The more unfamiliar the style of a play, the more we are asked to say "yes" to new conventions. The actors are playing "dress-up and let's pretend" and we are joining in the "let's pretend" part. In less realistic plays, we accept the convention that the actors may ignore us for much of the evening and then occasionally turn to us and comment (called *asides*) or speak their thoughts aloud with no one listening (called *soliloquies*). In some plays, we accept a constant interweave of actors speaking directly to the audience, acknowledging our presence for a time, and then going into intimate, private scenes where they ignore us. And we have no problem being there and then not being there. In theatres around the globe, audiences readily pretend that masks are faces, men are women, extravagantly be-wigged and painted actors are animals, precise synchronicity among many actors is natural, percussive instruments are the human heart beating and that mortals are gods.

If conventions of other cultures are challenging to us, we need to remember that our own theatre can be as "strange" as any in the world. Musicals are widely believed to have originated in the U.S. and yet musical theatre is a feast of outrageous conditions of belief, readily accepted by the audience. When we go to a "madcap" musical, we agree to pretend, for example, that it is perfectly normal to wear tap shoes and even sequins to the office, to totally color-coordinate your shiny outfit with that of all your co-workers and that the most reasonable behavior in the world, when someone says "I've got an idea!!" is for everyone on the office staff to lean way into him suddenly and shout in unison "What???" We accept that his idea (perhaps for improving sales for the company) will naturally be expressed in song. And if his idea goes over, the whole office staff will of course join in that song and naturally start dancing on the desks and file cabinets to express their joy and relief at the brilliance of the plan. As an audience member, you agree to pretend that this is reasonable behavior, even though you would (and should) have serious second thoughts about trying it in your own workplace. In subsequent chapters, we will deal with the variety of conventions from different cultures and time periods.

EXTENSIONS

How do these conventions extend to media? As we watch a film, we pretend that life has a musical underscore that swells up to stir our emotions. We pretend that everyday people by our favorite superstars can naturally wear the hottest designer clothes to their minimum-wage job and rent a huge Manhattan or Parisian apartment without any predictable, constant source of income. We adjust our sense of reality to serve our desire to be swept away. Have you noticed the haircut transformation phenomenon? In almost any film, if a character decides to change her hair, she or a friend will just cut randomly away, perhaps with a kitchen sheers, and the result is always fabulous. Has anyone ever had this experience in life?

And in personal theatre? How often have you laughed politely at what was supposed to be a funny story or joke , but just didn't get it or got it but found it lame? How often have you and whole roomful of people done this? We accept the convention of responding as we *ought* to rather than as we want to. And you may live with family conventions which dictate how you are always expected to respond to any news. In some families, only polite reserve is acceptable, in others, unbridled, gushy enthusiasm or confrontation is the norm.

We usually adjust to our space being invaded and pretend it's OK. When on a crowded elevator, personal space at a premium, a common choice is to pretend the other people aren't there, avoiding any kind of eye contact to compensate for the fact that some stranger may actually be pressed physically against our privates. The art of "public privacy" is highly developed in parts of China, where masses of people push together when a scarce commodity like transportation becomes available. The more crowded the space, the more intense the rules of make-believe. When someone says or does something reprehensible in the grocery store, the most common choice is to pretend it did not happen and hope the offender will just go away. This will go on for some time as the offensive behavior escalates, and the patience of someone expires, at which point the convention is dropped and confrontation occurs.

The conventions of daily life are as many and varied as those in a theatrical production. We all pretend in order to make life better. If it is disappointing, we pretend to make it bearable; if it is good but not great, we do so to make it full of magic, passion, and wonder.

SUMMARY

For years the origins of theatre were believed to be a distinctly Western male, literary phenomenon. Now scholars are looking to other cultures, both sexes, and oral traditions to find universal impulses that lead and have always lead to theatre everywhere. Four major theories of how theatre began include: **spontaneous inspiration**—acting out the day's events to make them come alive again, **imitation to ritual**—the impulse of children acting like adults evolving into repeated acts and expanding beyond the home to embrace the community in an act of communion, **stepping out**—someone taking part in a group activity, emerges from that group one day and turns a choral monolog into a dialogue, where ideas are not merely expressed but also exchanged and a character emerges, and **divine gift**—accepting magic, trance and communion with inanimate objects as a reality far beyond ordinary life. Theatre grows out of an intense desire for ritual in all aspects of our lives, from the mundane daily comforts to life changing ceremonies. In performance, something always represents, stands-in-for, or symbolizes something else. Performance is defined by ritual conventions, which are the rules by which we all play make-believe at the theatre and in everyday encounters.

SUGGESTED ASSIGNMENTS

For reflection, short writings and/or discussion:

1. How does the image of the deity being addressed and the specific requests being made alter between the English King James version of The Lord's Prayer and a more direct translation from Aramaic? What shifts in values appear to have occurred?

2. What are the most crucial rituals in your life? The ones you could not possibly live without?

3. Now that you're learning more about how theatre started and starts, what was the biggest misconception you brought into this course? How is actual theatre most unlike what you expected?

4. What was the most memorable moment in your life when you found out that your ritual choices were not those that very many other people make? What was your response?

5. What is your strongest superstition, and how does this influence your behavior? How does this become a ritual? Are any of these done with observers? How do they then become theatre?

6. In your personal theatre, what is the most consistent performance you give? Where are you most in the pretense mode?

7. Where in your own public life is there the largest set of conventions? At what kind of occasion or group gathering is there the most agreement about what is real and what we are going to pretend is real for this event?

8. Does your family have any rituals that are unique to them? When did you find out this and how did you react?

9. As a child, when you play-acted based on TV shows or movies, what were your most popular choices?

10. How did you take the basic details of the shows above and embellish them into fantasy?

SUGGESTED ACTIVITIES

1. Individual—Go back and look over the list of childhood game enactments shown earlier in this chapter. Make your own list of what you acted out most often.

2. Group—In groups of five, agree on a role playing childhood event that several of you took part in earlier in life. Take ten minutes to "cast" the roles, play it out and present it as close as possible to your best memory of how you did it back then.

3. Long term—Start a ritual journal, with sections such as private, public, theatrical, ceremonial, and communal. Observe and record the degree to which ritual is a crucial part of life.

4. Large Lecture—Identify and perhaps even change a ritual annoyance in your community. Find a ritual that the class can identify with, such as standing in line at the registrar's or dealing with nasty roommates. Figure out together what your specific goal is and what is blocking you from that goal. Get four or five volunteers to act out the usual response. Is it passive or self-defeating? Have the whole class shout out alternative approaches. Act them out to discover the results. Continue until a truly viable alternative is found. If you have an idea, join the volunteers. Work as a community to solve a problem.*

KEY WORDS AND IDEAS

Abydos Passion Play

Oral tradition

Miko—*Uzume's Trance*

Griot—*Ogun's Mysteries*

Origin theories:

    Robert E. Jones—*Dramatic Imagination*—Spontaneous Impuls

    Joseph Campell—Imitation to Ritual

    Aristotle—*The Poetics*—Stepping Out

        Dithyramb

        Thespis/thespian

    Bharata—*Natya Satra*—Divine Gift

Myth

Ritual

    Conventions:

    Realism/Stylization

    Proscenium arch

    Fourth wall

    Asides/Soliloquies

---

*This exercise is adapted from the works of Augusto Boal, who is featured in Chapter 11.

WHO DOES THEATRE?

STORYTELLERS AND STORIES

CONTENTS

O NE OF THE most powerful human impulses is to tell stories: from our own lives, the lives of others who have touched us in some way, or simply from our imagination. Those who are skilled storytellers are honored in any culture. In this chapter, we will look at the people who create theatrical stories in Africa, Asia, Europe and America, examine differences between oral and written traditions, and provide methods for analyzing plays in all forms.

GRIOTS/GRIOTTES, SUTRADHARAS AND BARDS

In all likelihood, the first "authors" of plays in every culture were masters of oral tradition. In Africa, this tradition continues today as a primary means of communicating stories of the people. Storytellers there are often called *griots/griottes* (or "praise singers"), and they are legendary for their musical skill, dramatic intensity and endurance. One famous oral narrative from West Africa, called *Ozidi*, is an epic narration of the communal history of the region's people. *Ozidi*, or parts of it, is still used as a foundation for some emerging new theatre in Africa. Griots who tackle *Ozidi* must be true masters of their art: The epic lasts for 24 full hours, and the griot plays all of the parts.

Most performers of the oral tradition needed to master the arts of music and dance as well as characterization and narration. In China, early influences came from Buddhist monks who spread the teachings (the *Sutra*) of the Buddha through memorized song. Later, secular artists added verses, dance, movement, and more songs influenced by contact with Indian and Central Asian Sanskrit dance/drama. These narrators are sometimes called *sutradharas* (or "string pullers" from the tradition of puppetry, since the narrator also "pulls the strings" of the story and sometimes guides or manipulates other performers). Not only did the *sutradharas* have to memorize long, intricate texts, but also interpret the work for audiences who did not know Sanskrit as a language, yet could appreciate the beauty of its sounds. The *sutradhara* was also required to play at least one musical instrument and to guide dancer/actors into correct visual presentation of their work.

Steven Spielberg, *film maker*

"I consider myself first and foremost before anything else to be a storyteller."

In numerous ancient cultures, including Europe and the Middle East, the presence of a *bard* was an essential part of existence. Often associated with the ruling family, the *bard* was expected to capture the events and stir the emotions of the people, just as Ook did with his recounting the story of the lion. Working with a single musical instrument, playing male and female characters and sometimes employing song, chants, and narrative poetic forms, the *bard* would help inspire and excite the people for an upcoming battle or long journey. At the end of a difficult or significant event, at the end of an evening's meal, the *bard* would put what had happened in perspective and shape it into meaning through theatrical means. For many, it was as if the events had occurred but they were not finalized until the *bard* captured them.

Each of these storytellers could function as creator and memorizer, entertainer and communal historian. Some twentieth century recordings have captured the artistry of the oral performer. While not live, and therefore losing something in translation, these recordings nevertheless reveal multi-dimensional performance skills and give us a glimpse into the selection and training of oral storytelling masters.

For example, in Europe, after the fall of the Roman Empire, our best guess is that professional actors/entertainers, having been banished from Rome, spread out across the wilderness that was Europe and made their way beyond the reach of Catholic Rome. If they were lucky, they found patrons to protect and nourish them and became vassals of their liege lords. Displeasing your lordship was a risky business, and many of our most beloved stories, plays, and films are romanticized versions of events created by *bards* in honor of their chieftains/lords. Training was by apprenticeship, and it is likely that minstrelsy or court performing ran in families as did other trades.

In Africa, the *griot/griotte* was trained by the elder storytellers, and selection was based on both suitability and a sacred spiritual calling. A few years ago, Habibu Selemani, one of the masters of the art in Tanzania died, leaving no trained survivors to carry on his work. He had learned the art by watching his masters from the time he was five until he started performing himself at age fourteen.

His passage without a successor is felt as a great loss in his culture despite leaving many performances captured on audio tape. Some of the stories have survived, but no one now knows everything he remembered, including his mastery of the music, movement, impersonation and character. One of his eulogists declared that the griot tradition is dying out in post-colonial Africa, but others believe it may simply be changing. Contemporary playwright Ngugi wa Tiong'o of Kenya, for example, has been imprisoned for his plays which are critical of the dictatorial government of Kenya. Today his plays are being spread across the country by griots and griottes who enter the town, recite the script and shape the performance elements, then slip away to avoid arrest and prosecution.

In India, young girls were dedicated to religious communities where they were raised and initiated by the priestesses into the mysteries of dance/drama that was learned through exhausting repetition of each tiny gesture and sound until perfection was achieved. Into the twentieth century, in some Asian cultures, the tradition of adopting very young children into a sacred or theatrical house continued, sometimes with painful and cruel deprivation part of the training. In ancient Persian and Arab cultures, female bards were considered essential to the well-being of the empire and of individual clans.

Though earliest dramas were developed in the oral tradition, with each culture's stories taught to succeeding generations, the transition to written narrative was inevitable. The balance between written and oral narrative today will vary, depending on the traditions of a region or country. Some believe the emergence of rap and hip-hop represent a renaissance of the art in a new form.

Nelson George, *author, Hip Hop America*

"Hip-hop is all acting. Some are more gangster than others but it's all about the creation of narrative persona. That's why every rapper uses a fake name. It's an inherently theatrical form."

More traditional storytelling has experienced a revival in part due to the International Storytellers Festival in Jonesborough, Tennessee, which attracts 10,000 visitors each fall and features such renowned performers as Emmy winning contemporary storyteller Mark Lewis. It is a gathering place not just for those wishing to listen but for those very much committed to keeping the form alive.

In most parts of the world today, some form of playwriting is the starting point for most productions. We will identify those elements of the playwright's work which are common to all engaged in the effort and ways that we can analyze those works to understand them better.

PLAYWRIGHTS

Most productions start with plays, but how do plays start? Some are commissioned, in which case a theatre picks a theme, an occasion or an issue on which to take a stand and then hires a playwright to produce a script. This process begins with those who manage the company itself, so the playwright is second on board.

But far more often the playwright is first, working in isolation, creating something on paper that may or may not end up as theatre magic and which, in fact, may or may not ever be produced. If a theatre company decides to mount a new play, the script can go through a long evolution process, ending with an opening where critics pass judgment and audiences may flock to the theatre or stay away. The play can close after a single performance or run for years.

What about the weird spelling? A "wright" is by definition "a construction worker, a carpenter, mechanic, or manufacturer, a skilled craftsman." Throughout history there have been boatwrights and also book-, cart-, coach-, gate-, house-, mill-, plow-, ship-, wagon-, wheelwrights and others. What does the person who makes plays have in common with these? Another definition is "one who makes or contrives, a deviser or inventor." The playwright is different from the novelist, poet, essayist, short story writer, biographer, or other literary figures because what is being "wrought" is the first step in a crafting process where these words will not stay on the page for silent reading but will be molded into a living, breathing performance. The playwright makes a play as the plowwright makes the plow, crafting ingredients sturdily, readying the product for years of use by others. The playwright shapes words to be spoken by people in costumes and makeup, lit a particular way, walking on a stage, in the presence of other actors, crews and audiences, in places where the playwright will never visit in any way except through this script. The playwright does not create words to be contemplated exclusively in cozy solitude or the occasional public reading, nor taken in parts at one's leisure and put aside for periods of reflection. The playwright prepares for an event that, once it starts, will proceed with or without intermissions, until it is over.

Most writers need to consider only the reader. The playwright needs to consider all participants and other elements of theatre as the script evolves. The "wrighter" needs to envision a finished product that will be used, that will in fact *move*, like a boat, a plow, or a wheel. What goes on at her desk at home must project forward through collaboration and evolution. She needs to hear the words spoken and to see them enacted. Many brilliant writers from other literary backgrounds fail as playwrights. Their words do not leap off the page and across the stage. Their texts have not been built to be used and used hard by others.

Steven Dietz, *playwright*

"There's no fast way to make plays. It takes just as long and is just has hard as it was a thousand years ago."

Arthur Miller, *playwright*

"What I'm doing is helping reality out. To complete itself. I'm giving it a hand."

In early theatre models, the playwright (including Kanami Kiyotsugu of Japan, Sophocles of Athens, and Shakespeare of England) was often the primary production guide, coaching and cajoling the actors, structuring the event, steering the play toward opening. The creator of the script continued to create through performance. Nowadays, playwrights are often excluded from the final process except when the director needs advice or script changes. So, while they are in some ways the most central figures in the theatrical process, they can also be the ones who feel most outside that process in its final stages. At this point, others may change what they had in mind, perhaps shifting the emphasis of their words, minimizing their themes, even seeming to sabotage their ideas. What they experience onstage may be far from what they envisioned at their word processor or legal pad back home.

It is sometimes difficult to separate a play from its production. Let's examine what constitutes a strong script, which is very much what makes for a good story, no matter how it is told.

A Good Play

A successful theatre script must have five essential ingredients:

1. *Action* moves the play forward. A script needs to move. Something important must happen in a play. Sometimes what happens is physical and sometimes it is psychological. Even in Theatre of the Absurd, a style of Western theatre particularly important after the Second

World War, in which characters may wait endlessly for something that never happens, it is likely that this is the most compelling day in their wait, perhaps the one in which they realize that indeed things will never change, and they have to deal with it. Plays take place at crucial life moments.

2. *Suspense* keeps us wondering. In some plays it has to do with twists and turns of plot. In many of the great classical plays, the audience knows the entire story, so suspense is about smaller surprises and discoveries, the original variations that pop up along the journey. A good play keeps us engaged by the possibility that what we think will happen might not.

3. *Believability* makes us accept the world of the play and its inhabitants as enough like us that we recognize their struggles, successes, and failures. No matter how unfamiliar the situation (a well-known Nigerian play features the King of the Cockroaches trapped in a bathtub), we must feel that it is true to its own conventions. Each person (or metaphorical being) should be fully realized, whether a man, a goddess, or a cockroach. Many of us can write about people very much like us, but to write with empathy and truth about those beyond our comfort zone is a true gift.

4. *Fluidity* allows the events to occur smoothly from beginning to end. The playwright considers where actors will enter and exit, where there will be breaks between scenes, where acts will end and intermissions occur. The playwright considers how the evening will shift and turn through various handlings of the text. She must be aware of audience and cultural expectations as to length, tempo, and rhythms in the style of play "wrighting." Even the seemingly rough, jagged moments should be consciously and wisely chosen. The best scripts are clear roadmaps for the actor in terms of what is essential to the author's vision and what is open to creative interpretation.

5. *Compression* transforms events into condensed and compelling forms. Because the story needs to unfold publicly over the course of an expected period of time (whether that's 90 minutes or 24 hours), the playwright has to edit and reduce details to what is essential. She needs to constantly consider the mechanics of the theatre and whenever possible, streamline and make choices that focus our attention on the exact part of the story that is important.

David Henry Hwang, *playwright*

"You're under a lot of pressure. If you've spent a year with a play, there's something absurd about rewriting the whole thing in four weeks."

Freedom and Influence

When a new play is being produced, the playwright may be expected to do revisions as the show passes through readings, rehearsals, and even previews. This can be electrifying and frustrating.

This is, however, the only time the author is entangled and obligated daily to meet the scheduling needs of others. For the rest of the earlier process, the trade-off for being isolated is that the playwright is the most free of all theatre artists. Unlike the rest of them, she can work when she wants. She can pick the time of day, place and circumstances, without concern for inconveniencing an army of collaborators. The playwright also has the freedom, if a script gets published, to not be involved in any way with subsequent productions and yet still earn an income from royalties because the script is the only lasting tangible element in live theatre. When shows close, most participants' experiences can be put in a single envelope: opening night notes, telegrams, reviews, maybe some pressed flowers, a souvenir program. This huge experience leaves almost no lingering evidence.

Every other person connected with the show needs to go on to a new job when the play closes. After closing night and strike (the process of tearing down the set) they just have memories. But if the play is successful, it may be published and produced for many years in many places without the playwright even knowing about it, except through royalty checks. Just as you are reading this book without the authors having direct contact with you, so someone is mounting many playwrights' work without their direct involvement, though their sphere of *influence* continues.

Playwrights also have the power of being listened to. Their ideas are shared, discussed and passed on. People pay attention and pay to pay attention. They can have profound impact on the thoughts and actions of others. For this reason, we revere our successful playwrights as highly as any artist in the theatre. And while the fame of others fades, the playwright has a chance at genuine immortality as scripts live on long after their deaths. Sophocles of Greece, Shakespeare of England, and Zeami of Japan are alive again in theatre after theatre and in the pages of this book. Tennessee Williams, Eugene O'Neill, and Thornton Wilder have long ago passed on, but they are at the center of our culture. The recently deceased Arthur Miller, August Wilson, and Wendy Wassterstein have joined them. Living legends like Wole Soyinka of Nigeria, Augusto Boal of Brazil, Marie Irene Fornez of Cuba, and Ngugi wa Thiong'o of Kenya are only steps behind. You may not recognize all these names, but you probably recognize some of them, which would be unlikely for other theatre artists. Playwrights change lives and re-invigorate cultures.

Some claim that the playwright has become less central to the theatrical process as more and more scripts are evolved through improvisation and games or created by entire performance companies instead of a single writer, and as texts have sometimes been altered through *deconstruction* (taking the play apart and reinventing it in a particular way) or *problematizing* an isolated issue (making one possibly minor problem in the script, major in the production). But these processes and the scripts resulting from them are simply redefining what it is to have "wrought" a play. Even in a work *devised* through group play (where a topic or non-theatrical work may be collaboratively evolved), the entire gang is essentially functioning as collective playwrights. Rather than diminishing the role of the playwright, these theatre groups are sometimes renewing oral and collaborative traditions that long preceded written text.

Screenwriting

How does the role of the live-theatre writer compare to that of the media-theatre writer? The screenwriter (notice the difference in spelling) has far less need to address how transitions occur and can actually have events juxtaposed in wildly different settings without concern for the limitations of a stage. Many sequences in a screenplay are merely suggested, particularly action scenes involving battles, explosions, aerial shots, and extended chases. Entire scenes where a character reflects silently on what has happened or is observed going on a journey are common. There may be no dialogue at all. Most of the time, film scripts will have fewer words than plays.

Those words that do exist will be far more vulnerable. While The Dramatist's Guild (essentially the playwrights' union) requires as part of its standard contract that no changes are made in dialogue, no such protection is afforded the screenwriter whose words may be altered by almost anyone involved, on or off the set. The screenwriter is also less likely to achieve legend status. In the medium of film, actors and directors achieve immortality. The cinema is indelibly, even profoundly, visual and less tied to text. Unless screenwriters are auteurs (think Clint Eastwood) who also direct and even perform in what they write, they tend to be relegated to a backseat behind their more glamorous colleagues. For how many films can you name the author? The American Film Institute asked critics to select the 100 best films of the past century, and only six of the winners had started as plays. This may be about how plays are often too talkie for "the talkies" and about how the entire experience of primarily listening vs. watching is decidedly, blessedly, vividly different.

You the Playwright

In this epic called *My Life*, when do you tend to write script? For most of us, it is in preparation for an important encounter with an authority figure (boss, parent, or teacher) or companion (friend, lover, or potential lover) where we do not want to "mess it up" and therefore may even write out what is to be said. Or we may just write it in our head and practice speaking it over and over. Unfortunately, the other person, the recipient of these brilliantly crafted words, often does not respond with the lines we have written for them. If only we could control *their* script as well as ours.

Would you perhaps like to move beyond composing a seduction-of-your-new-sweetie speech or a telling-off-your-bastard-boss speech into real scripts? Let's explore how to proceed.

Getting Started

The oldest and wisest advice in the world is "write about what you know." Playwrights need to dig into their own life experiences and imaginations to find what they *know* that might become electrifying theatre. What you know does not have to be what you have experienced firsthand in an autobiographical sense, but it should be about what you know deep inside, so it may reflect a powerful fantasy or an imaginative journey that you have traveled so much that it is as much a part of you as the mundane details of your life that actually happened. It should have happened in your mind and heart. You may just start hearing words in your head. Ten other possible springboards are listed below:

August Wilson, *playwright*

"I generally start with an idea, something I want to say, but with *The Piano Lesson*, I just started writing a line of dialogue and had no idea who was talking ... at some point I say, 'Well, who is this?' and I give him a name. But I usually have no idea what the story line of a play is. It's a process of discovery."

---

1. a character who fascinates you, real or imagined

2. a family or group whose interaction intrigues you

3. a startling event in the news or the transcript of an actual trial

4. a real or imaginary world or place that seems exotic to the degree that you want to set a story and imagine life there

5. a controversial issue in which you wish to explore various positions and points of view

6. a life-changing event that happened to you or someone close to you

7. a famous person or fictional character whose biography or story intrigues you

8. a brief encounter you overhear on the street or in a store, which keeps replaying in your head so that you are fascinated enough to create the back story and the rest of this relationship

9. an imaginary encounter between two famous people who probably never met, but what if they did?

10. a personal encounter you wanted to have but never did, but now could happen as drama.

Other Writers: Composers and Lyricists

In musical theatre, the play script is traditionally called the libretto and the playwright the librettist or "book" writer. While spoken words are important, no one leaves the theatre humming the book. And in some musicals, it may be just a way to get from song to song as swiftly as possible. In many parts of the world, the entire play is sung and/or chanted to musical accompaniment. While all composers conceive music that will be performed by others, the musical theatre composer, like the playwright, needs to envision and hear (in his head) the collaboration of a range of soloists and chorus and to imagine what is on paper being taken to another level by aggressive participation. The lyricist essentially writes poetry, to be set to music or to match music already written, with a particularly necessary flair for expressing ideas that rhyme and are revealed through a character, just as Shakespeare has characters suddenly rhyme when they are making a particularly crucial point at the end of a scene or speech. When characters are so full of emotion that mere speech will no longer suffice, they break into song. Both the words and the tune they perform should reflect who they are, how they function in the world and capture a huge emotional wave to be shared with the audience.

These positions are usually filled by two different artists, both of which need to virtually personify the word *collaboration* by being in sync with each other. When we think of the legendary partnerships of the American musical theatre (Rodgers and Hammerstein, Lerner and Loewe, Kander and Ebb), it is as if they are one unit. And Stephen Sondheim, perhaps our most revered living writer for musical theatre, does both.

John Patrick Shanley, *playwright*

"Theatre is a safe place to do the unsafe things that need to be done."

STORY ANATOMY

All artists use available tools to find a way to tell their truth. "True" is not the same as "real." Many use fanciful variations of the "real" world to communicate their ideas. Their truth may move far beyond facts or evidence. Plays can be realistic or abstract. They may be simple or complex. They may speak in poetry or prose. They may be a combination of any of these. Playwrights make choices, each one opening some doors and closing others. By trying to be aware of the choices made, by analyzing the playwright's construction process, we can better understand each script, starting with the choice of medium, mood, and dramatic action.

Medium

The first choice any artist makes is *medium*, the raw materials (such as oil or watercolor for a painter, clay or marble for a sculptor) or method of presentation (such as media or live theatre). The playwright choosing live theatre accepts both benefits and challenges. For example, large epic visual events like the opening scene of the D-Day landing in *Saving Private Ryan* or almost anything in the *Lord of the Rings* are not suited to the theatre medium. On the other hand, live theatre gives the playwright a personal connection with the audience, allowing intense and active interaction. Finding such a sense of communion and connection in film medium is challenging, in part because of the technology that stands between the performance and the audience. We are not unaffected by film events, but we cannot influence them.

While both mediums allow intensely intimate glimpses into the lives of characters, live theatre will more often demand more dialogue by its very nature. In the award winning film, *Lost in Translation*, Bill Murray's character, in Tokyo, receives constant faxes from his wife. Both the content of these messages and his reaction to each are shown in subtle silence. In a live performance of a play, a similar action would require that the actor read the messages out loud or for them to be projected on a giant screen, changing these moments altogether.

The playwright can expect the play to be produced by living, breathing human beings, in a special space designed or designated as a theatre. He also knows that while fabulous visual effects and computer animation may not be available, his audience will probably expect to listen carefully in return, experiencing the event in a more auditory, less visual way. Since playwrights do not work in water colors or marble, but with words, they have a number of decisions to make about those words. Will some of them be set to music or will it be a straight text? Will some of them rhyme, appear in some other form of verse or will it be prose? Will the words be elevated and formal or street talk colloquial? Will the language be sacred, profane, or both? Will the characters have the gift of gab or struggle and stumble to say what must be said? Will speakers generally be allowed to finish or will characters continually interrupt and unsettle each other? Will the language choices be widely shared by all in the play or represent startling diversity? Here is tremendous power and responsibility.

Tina Howe, *playwright*

"I have my white glove plays about aging WASPs recalling better times and my bare hands plays about women blasting into the light *now*. I tend to alternate my WASPy plays with my frisky ones."

Mood

Storytellers must decide early in the process whether they are working in a comic or tragic space. This single decision will affect every other choice the writer makes. The comic mood assumes that while something is wrong in the world, the characters are going to struggle through to a new and better place—or at least find a way to tolerate their lives with less strain. The most common plot in comic mode is the love story. Two people fall in love, obstacles make their union seem impossible, but love triumphs in the end. What is wrong is not insurmountable.

Though Chekhov's plays are seldom laugh-out-loud funny, he calls each of his four masterworks comedies, including *The Three Sisters*. The designation "comedy" suggests that by the end of his play, the world will be different, fresh, maybe even better, but Chekhov's plays have a tendency to end with a sense of melancholy as few of his characters are able to overcome inertia, social restrictions, or their own natures to succeed brilliantly. But they endure; they go on with their lives; they do the best they can with the little they've got.

Tragic mood assumes that the world (or cosmos) is thrown out of order by the actions of an individual or group. Tragic drama frequently involves characters who have and use their power to make others' lives miserable. In *Antigone* (a classic Greek tragedy), a young woman challenges the authority of the new king of Thebes, her uncle Creon, and his reactions will disrupt the lives of the entire community. He doesn't intentionally bring pain and suffering to his people, but his goal (maintaining an appearance of control no matter the cost) causes the known world to careen out of control for a moment. Only when he realizes and attempts to correct his errors can the community, the world, the cosmos return to balance and order. In the tragedy, characters must alter their behavior and relationship with the cosmos in order to survive and thrive. Sometimes (*M. Butterfly*, *King Lear*, and *Antigone*) a character must die in order to restore the natural balance of the universe, but sometimes (*Roosters, The Piano Lesson*, and *He and She*) a character can learn and change his or her behavior before the final reckoning.

The same actual story can be told in either comic or tragic mood though the choice will alter the end result beyond recognition. At times, the two are kept distinctly apart from each other. During the fourteenth century, the venerated, classical Japanese playwright Zeami divided drama into serious or tragic—known as *Noh*—and comic or romantic called *Kyogen*. To this day, the two are performed in different types of theatres, use different conventions, and rely heavily on different styles of theatricality. French neo-classicism of the seventeenth century equally dictated strict divisions in content, style and production venues.

These two still tend to dominate the playwright's range. Comedy is found throughout the world, from biting satire to gentle romance. Tragedy also thrives as we try to make sense out of our complex and dangerous world. However, increasingly, contemporary playwrights blend and distort mood to create tragi-comedies or "dramedies" within a deconstructed, rediscovered or simply absurd universe. Often works will switch gears and even layer one mood on top of another. The comic/tragic contrast is simply a starting point, for increasingly complex, overlapping and still evolving forms.

Dramatic Action

The playwright decides on the action of the drama, guided by three major principles:

1. All dramatic action involves **conflict**. Human interactions are most interesting when we do not agree. On a normal day in real life, we may be able to avoid conflict in every interaction. But no one writes plays about normal days. Plays are about days when something of critical importance is being confronted. Identifying the central conflict is crucial to understanding the play itself.

2. Dramatic action always occurs in the **present tense**. The play must occur before us *as if* it were happening right now. If a playwright needs us to know something about the past, the characters may talk about previous events or actually experience a "flashback," where the characters are experiencing the past as "now." They are not reminiscing; but living the earlier event as it happens.

3. Most stories are told using the same basic **structural elements**. In *The Poetics*, Aristotle's claimed that each play must have a "beginning, middle, and end," which may seem either obvious or vague. However, if you write a play or if you are the great storyteller in your family or tribe, knowing where to start, building intensity for exactly the right amount of time, and then ending it with the only possible outcome or the most surprising one is half the battle. Finding the structural beginning, middle, and end helps us learn the craft of the playwright.

PLAY ANALYSIS

The arts share a peculiar place in the human heart. Many of us are drawn to them, and some of us want to *be* artists, but few of us have both the genius and the luck necessary for a successful career. So those who choose this path must have a very strong need that overwhelms uncertainties and failures. For the playwright, that need might be to give voice to ideas, feelings, or important events. Comedy may offer a chance to satirize idiots and oppressors; tragedy to help us cope with suffering. The playwright leaves a legacy for us to experience here and now. The text is that legacy.

In the following section we to offer two avenues for analyzing script structure and character. We analyze structure to help us understand the playwright's vision and meaning. We identify a character's motivation to understand the play better and to "hear" the playwright's voice more clearly. We start with the common elements.

Dramatic Structure

Ten basic elements define the structure of a dramatic work. While some playwrights may twist or exclude some of them, the act of searching for them gives us insight into the work as a whole.

1. **Point of attack:** Where in the larger story of a life does the playwright choose to start this work? The story of Ogun has many episodes starting from the moment of his creation and continuing into the present. A playwright working in Nigeria today might want to write a new play that will inspire people to continue the work of moving past the colonial era. He could look at the entire Ogun epic, then choose one episode to retell, updating to current and local events. The point of attack is that choice of where in the longer story to start this play. In Greek tragedy, Sophocles wrote of Oedipus the king of Thebes, part of a story many generations long. The story started when Poseidon married Lybia and started Oedipus' family. Long before the birth of Oedipus, one of his ancestors offended the gods; the family was cursed through all generations and Oedipus is the recipient of a fate he did nothing to deserve. Likewise his children are cursed, and their misfortunes carry through generations to come. Many plays continue to be written about this family and each playwright chooses a point of attack. Sophocles' *Oedipus the King*, starts on the last day of Oedipus' reign. The same playwright wrote *Antigone*, a play about the daughters of Oedipus in which the point of attack chosen is long after the exile of their father and a civil war between their two brothers. Both plays tell the same big family story, but different points of attack focus the audience on specific incidents of the playwright's choosing.

Some consider the following three elements more about content than structure, though determining them helps reveal how the work as a whole is constructed.

2. **Protagonist:** Who is the central character in the play? In some forms of playwriting (like Noh drama and Elizabethan tragedies), the protagonist is the tragic hero defined as a well-born, good man who commits an error from which catastrophe ensues. In modern plays, men and women, high born and low, good and flawed, function as protagonist. Ask which character does the playwright wants us to follow? Who changes the most in the play? Which character would you want to hire a top-dollar movie star to play him or her in your movie? Who wins the contest/conflict or loses most spectacularly. More importantly, who does the playwright think ought to win?

3. **Antagonist:** Who is the character most actively trying to prevent the protagonist from achieving his goals? Antagonist does not equal "villain" or "bad guy" except in a more simple form of storytelling, called melodrama. Maybe the antagonist is trying to protect the protagonist by blocking his actions. Maybe the protagonist's goal is one the playwright believes needs to be challenged.

4. **World of the play:** What are the basic facts about the characters and particular universe given to us by the playwright? *Much Ado About Nothing* is set in Messina, a vague, exotic, romantic locale in the home of its governor, Leonato. His estate is large and luxurious. The season seems to be spring or summer. The characters are well-to-do and are experiencing a period of leisure. We identify what is known, without immediate judgment. The basic categories first introduced in Chapter 1: Time, Space, Values, Structure, Pleasure and the Senses are always worth investigating. (Note: Appendix A offers extensive questions within each of these general topics.)

The playwright may also need to tell us about the past or warn us about the future in the next two structural elements.

5. **Exposition:** Information about past events is given by the playwright through character conversation. If we do not go back into the past as a "flashback," one of the challenges of performing exposition sequences is for the actor to make telling the story active and alive. "Telling" is inherently less compelling and legitimate than a character's "doing" or "acting" to relate information. *Master Harold ... and the boys* is an example of a play that relies heavily on exposition. Characters Sam and Hally spend their afternoon together relating stories about the good old days when they lived in the Jubilee Boarding House. The exposition tells us critical information about Sam and Hally's past experiences together and the evolution of their relationship. But for the characters, these are not simple reminiscences. Sam uses the stories "to calm Hally" or "to encourage Hally" or "to help Hally cope." In the hands of a good actor, exposition serves an active function in the present tense as well as cluing us into a past. In contrast, Shakespeare uses little exposition in *King Lear*. We learn nothing about the history of the family, about the mother, childhood, or recent behavior of the daughters. By not sharing the characters' history with us, Shakespeare forces us to concentrate on their present behavior. We may learn a tidbit such as that Lear always loved Cordelia best, and we may make connections between that and the current anger of Regan and Goneril. But neither we nor they are allowed to spend much time justifying their harsh treatment of their father. Shakespeare seems to want to make them (and by extension us) accountable for each choice made in the present, focusing on *what* they do rather than *why* they do it.

6. **Foreshadowing:** Does the play contain a warning about something in the future? In film, foreshadowing is often accomplished by soundtrack music. In *Jaws*, the heavy heartbeat sound, "Baaah-dum, baaah-dum," signals the approach of the shark (or teases us into tensing up only to release us with a fake cardboard shark fin). In our personal theatre, a friend may casually mention that "so and so might be at the party tonight" or "your mom called, she didn't say what about," and in your head you may hear the traditional "uh-oh" music soundtrack. In live theatre, characters who receive warnings are less likely to be supported by ominous sound cues. More often they and the audience don't realize the significance of the clue until later in the play when a jolt of recognition goes through them and us.

Both exposition and foreshadowing can occur at any point in a play. The writer chooses when to reveal or conceal, when to tease or fulfill, in order to build suspense and sustain conflict.

7. **Inciting incident:** Which event changes the life being portrayed in the play? At some point near the beginning of the story, an inciting incident gets things rolling. In *M. Butterfly*, David Henry Hwang reveals one possible inciting incident in Gallimard's life through a flashback to the first time he laid eyes on the "perfect woman," when Song performed at an embassy function. Until that moment, Gallimard's life had been depressingly ordinary. Only through his involvement with Song did his life become interesting enough for someone to write a play about him.

Sometimes the inciting incident is more difficult to identify. In *The Three Sisters*, a play characterized less by dynamic than reflective action, the inciting incident, which "makes this day different from every other day," occurs in the first act, but exactly where? Different directors, actors, and designers may debate and ultimately choose various moments. It might be Irina's birthday party and the fact she turns twenty (thereby feeling a need to "grow up"), or when Masha meets her future lover Vershinin for the first time or when the unsuitable Baron Tusenbach declares his love for Irina. At first glance, any of these might function as inciting incident, but careful study is needed to ensure that the chosen event leads to rising and falling actions and eventually to the climax (see number 9 below) when performed. One method for finding or confirming the inciting incident is to identify the climax of the play and then work

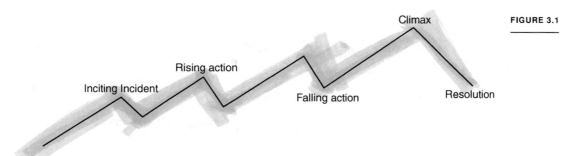

FIGURE 3.1

backward from there, tracing the plot back to the beginning to see if the chosen incident is the triggering mechanism to the climactic outcome.

8. **Rising and falling action:** Where does tension build and release in the text? Good storytelling always involves this alternation. Rising action is an event that increases tension while falling action temporarily decreases it, allowing characters and audience a moment to breathe. Identifying rising actions is particularly critical as the central conflict is intensified and complicated. Falling actions relax us and give us a moment of respite, but they don't drive the action forward. A much-used diagram of basic storytelling structure looks like Figure 3.1

   In some plays, the playwright challenges the "normal" storytelling structure pictured above, and finding rising actions or a traditional climax becomes difficult or impossible. That is the point of analyzing structure. If a playwright does not use traditional techniques, we strive to discover what the organizing principle is.

9. **Climax:** What is the moment of peak struggle or encounter in the central conflict of the play? It is often the final confrontation between the protagonist and the antagonist, when one of them will win and the other lose. The climax is often the place where we learn the purpose in telling this tale. If it was comedy intended to create a new and better world, the climax will usually lead to the victory of good over evil. If it was tragic, good may triumph but only at a tremendous cost. Particularly in contemporary drama, if the "wrong" side wins, the meaning of the work may be showing us something about the struggle itself or the strength needed to even attempt to overcome evil. Sometimes the meaning of our lives is not found in our victories, but in our willingness to fight unbeatable foes.

10. **Resolution:** At the end there may be a new world, circumstances or understanding created by actions of characters. In a standard television drama, the resolution takes place after the last commercial break, when the characters wrap up loose ends, ponder the outcome of the conflict or move on to a new adventure. In live theatre, we may celebrate the victory of love with a dance (as in *Much Ado About Nothing*), or we may try to make sense of the suffering of the characters (as in *Antigone*). Some playwrights refuse to give clear, comfortable resolution. In *Master Harold . . . and the boys*, Athol Fugard denies us the "ahhh" scene in which Sam and Hally repair their relationship with a hug. Instead, Hally exits before they can "make up," and we are left with an uneasy sense that nothing is ever going to be the same for them, but we don't know if that's going to be a good or bad thing. All we are given, perhaps as an antidote to despair, is the vision of Sam and Willy dancing, attempting to keep their hopes alive despite the ugly, destructive climax of Sam's fight with Hally. Fugard refuses to give easy answers to racism and apartheid as complicating factors in loving relationships. But he also refused to leave us without any hope at all.

Character Analysis

While the ten elements of dramatic structure help us comprehend the play as a whole, another tool, character analysis, helps us understand the individuals who inhabit it. The following is one method, designed by the influential acting teacher Constantin Stanislavski (see Chapter 6). These five inquiries help reveal the *who, what, how* and *why* of each character.

1. **Given circumstances (who):** What are the facts given by the playwright about this character? As we work through a small ocean of opinions offered by one character about another, we keep seeking facts. We might be told that a character is named Chata, a female, in her late twenties, of Mexican-American heritage, sister to the husband of the family, living in New Mexico in the present day, and that she has lived a rough-and-tumble life as a prostitute among migrant farm workers (see *Roosters*). If we take any of this further and start making judgments like "she's a slut," or "she's immoral," we are no longer in given circumstances, but only opinions. Another character calls her a "tramp" but that too is opinion, not fact.

2. **Values (who):** All persons have values, those things we believe to be true and important. Conflicts often arise in life and art because of opposing value systems. In *Necessary Targets*, the conflict in values between a privileged American aid worker (democracy, freedom, education, material possessions) is inevitably going to conflict with the values of Bosnian refugees (survival, food, clean water, shelter). One person may value peace at any cost, another winning at any cost. One may value the family or community first, another only himself. A natural human tendency to find opposing values unacceptable may lead us to mistakenly assume a character (or a real person in our lives) "has no values." This almost always means they have values that we don't share. With a character whose values are different from your own, try not to dismiss— but work to understand. Our most important life lessons can come from exposure to value systems of others.

3. **Super-objective (what):** Most of us have a driving ambition that determines our day-to-day choices. You may want to get married, start a lucrative career, or simply graduate on time. This would be called your current super-objective. In a play, the character's super-objective drives her through most of the play. In *Necessary Targets*, a young American aid worker in a Bosnian refugee camp wants and needs "to make a name for herself" or "to teach the Bosnian women how to heal themselves." The actor would wish to choose one of these or seek another. In *King Lear*, Lear wants to retire from the pressures of ruling the kingdom, but he's accomplished that during the first scene of the play, so we must continue searching for his overriding need or want, which might be something like "to shed the burden but keep the privileges of kingship." In some plays, super-objectives of main characters reveal the central conflict. Two or more people may have diametrically opposing wants. In *The Piano Lesson*, Boy Willy wants to sell the family piano in order to buy the farm he is sharecropping. His sister, Berniece, wants to preserve the family history which is carved on the piano. They can't both get what they want.

4. **Actions (how):** What are characters willing to use to get what they want, what strategy and tactics do they employ? Search for verbs that describe each character's "tool bag." Small specific behaviors like "drinks a cup of coffee" or "talks to her husband about her son's problems," don't count. Examples might include arguing, whining, sulking, killing, waiting, observing, or accusing. In *He and She*, both Tom and Ann want to succeed at their careers while maintaining the health of the family, so actions reveal the central conflict. While he asserts his superiority, rejects his wife's efforts, ignores his child, and assumes his male prerogative; she hides her work, struggles to balance work and motherhood, supports her

husband, and finally gives up her chance to succeed. He proclaims, she questions. They want the same thing but use different and conflicting actions to achieve that goal.

5. **Motivation (why):** We often must engage our intuition to determine why a character makes the choices he does. Characters seldom discuss motivations openly, and frequently seem unaware of them. So we must delve deeply into their behaviors and words. Why would a king divide his kingdom into three parts? Perhaps he's motivated by a desire to weaken the authority of each child thereby setting himself up as the better ruler. Perhaps he is motivated by an urge to prove to the world that he is the most fair and honorable father/king ever known. Perhaps he is insecure about his children's love and wants them to make public statements of adoration and loyalty. Applying psychological motivations that were unheard of in the world of the artist and/or characters is dangerous. We now have a tendency to attribute almost all "bad" or "self-destructive" behavior to a "lack of self-esteem." To an Elizabethan, filled to the brim with self-esteem, the idea of a king making a world altering decision because he wasn't feeling very good about himself would be incomprehensible. In Shakespeare's world, concepts as a subconscious mind or unloving parents as motivation hadn't been invented. Seek "whys" that they, the characters themselves, would understand.

THE PLAYWRIGHT'S PLAN

For many artists, we can never be absolutely sure what they were trying to communicate. Playwrights themselves frequently can't identify in objective language what message they hoped to send. August Wilson said he often started a new play because of a song he happened to hear, or a phrase overheard while passing someone on the street. The artist has a burning need to communicate truth, but may be the last person to ask what that truth is. Her plan may come from some other place than consciousness. Art is born deeper in the heart and mind of the creator than language can articulate. But our work as audience members and as participants in the pageant of life is to try to understand what others are trying to tell us. Identifying the playwright's plan is part craft, part art.

Professional critics, though paid to write or talk about the work of artists, all too often are untrained or too lazy to focus on their plan. We have all read movie or play reviews that are mere plot summaries and personal opinion. Frequently, critics simply stop short of true exploration by listing topics found in the play, such as "this is a play about love, family and suffering." We would like to challenge such critics to find a play that is NOT about love, family, or suffering. The following is a process for articulating more specifically the playwright's intended meaning. The plan can be broken down into:

1. **Issue:** The issues are the real subjects being dealt with, sometimes below the level of the simple story, and questions that may emerge out of these subjects. Love, family and suffering are universal. Questions about them recur in all times and places. In *Master Harold . . . and the boys*, racism and apartheid are central issues, but so are love and the pain we cause those we love the most. A play may ask lighthearted questions such as "What is the very best way to spend your free time?" It may also ask "How much abuse should you tolerate from someone you love?" Or, "When is it justified to take someone else's life?"

2. **Point of view:** What is the artist's specific take on the issue identified? On any day, any of us may create a work of art in which we declare that love is a miracle worth any sacrifice. On another, we might declare that "love stinks" and disavow any desire to ever again experience the chaos and struggle of falling in love. Equally, one artist might explore enduring and loving bonds of family, telling us that we should always put the needs of our family first, but another might share the awful things family members can do to each other and encourage us to leave

our family "baggage" behind and build a new community with others more like us. To the serious questions asked above, one play might answer "None" or "Never" to the issues of abuse and murder while another might offer a far more complex answer such as, "As much abuse as you can take without having your heart broken or losing hope for change," or "To protect those close to you, but never simply for revenge."

3. **Support:** Check if the conclusions drawn in categories 1 and 2 are supported by the words and actions of characters. Refer specifically to events, words, images, characters in the text. Earlier analyses can help: super-objectives, climax, and major rising actions of the play are all crucial. Examples of well constructed and poorly constructed arguments follow:

> In *Master Harold . . . and the boys*, one of the ideas explored by Athol Fugard is the issue of fatherhood. What makes a good father? (issue) Fugard seems to be saying that a good father is one who is sensitive to the feelings and needs of the child, someone who spends time caring for the child and worrying about his or her well-being. The biology of parenthood does not necessarily make one a good father. (playwright's point of view) This is supported in the play by the consistent contrast between Hally's biological father and Sam. Hally's father is absorbed in and consumed by his own needs. He is in fact absent from the play as he seems to be absent from his son's life except as a problem. In contrast, Sam is the man who makes sure that Hally eats, does his homework and grows toward being a strong, proud man. As Sam relates in the "kite story," he was the one who carried Hally's drunk father home from the bar and then built a kite so that the boy would look up and find something to be proud of after the humiliating behavior of his father. Throughout the play, Sam is actively engaged in raising Hally, while the boy's biological parents are busy dealing with their own problems.

You may or may not agree with the conclusion reached by the writer above, but crucial elements—issue, point of view and support from the play—are all there.

> The play, *M. Butterfly*, is about a French diplomat who falls in love with a Beijing Opera singer and pretends he's a character in an opera called Madame Butterfly. He is in jail for treason at the beginning of the play. It turns out that his lover is actually a man, not a woman, which would seem to be impossible to not notice. It makes one wonder if the diplomat was really gay or what. I think he was both wrong and stupid to pass government secrets to a Chinese man pretending to be a woman. It also seems like a very unlikely story to me.

This is an oversimplified plot summary and personal opinion by the author of the argument. Only objective analysis should be included. Personal opinion is best saved for later. Anyone may find a playwright's plan boring, stupid, or even offensive. Such response, while legitimate, does not belong in the description of the plan itself. In a critical review, it is essential to identify what the artist was trying to do *before* evaluating how well it was done or if it was worth doing.

Work with an open mind and heart and try to understand the playwright's ideas. Avoid imposing opinions. Understanding another's heart makes us more aware of our own beliefs and ideas, allowing us to stay open, without losing those parts of ourselves that we cherish and wish to sustain.

SUMMARY

Much unscripted storytelling tradition continues to thrive around the world. In scripted work, the playwright is usually the first to struggle in isolation, creating words that must survive the collaboration and intervention of countless others. The more we understand the decisions made by the writer, the better we comprehend the work itself. A medium, mood, and course and pattern of dramatic action are chosen. Decisions are made in: point of attack, protagonist, antagonist, world of the play, exposition, foreshadowing, inciting incident, rising and falling action, climax, and resolution. A storyteller may intentionally scramble the order, leave out structural elements, or create unexpected outcomes to conflict. We assume every choice has a reason.

We can understand the work more fully by analyzing characters asking the who (given circumstances and values), what (super objective), how (actions) and the why (motivations) that define and drive each of them. While some writers cannot identify their intentions, we can make every effort to unearth the playwright's (sometimes unconscious) plan by looking at issues, point of view, and textual support for any conclusions we may draw.

SUGGESTED ASSIGNMENTS

1. When have you been faced with a challenge to create something artistic and had to choose a medium? Consider not only classroom assignments but social events. What influenced your decision to go with one medium as opposed to another?

2. Consider the comic vs. the tragic mood in your day-to-day existence. When have you chosen the one over the other? Have you gone through phases where your life was a tragedy and others when it was a comedy? Or others where it was a hysterical blend? How much of this was caused by external events and how much was due to your choices? If you could go back and do it all over, how might your choice change the events?

3. Both media and live theatre have the potential for overwhelming spectacle and extraordinary intimacy. In a media event, what was your experience as an audience member that simply blew you away with the scope, majesty, and detail of the spectacle or the deep, personal connection of the intimacy?

4. Answer the above question for a live theatre or personal theatre event.

5. Since dramatic action requires conflict, consider your own life. If someone were to create a play or film based on your experiences so far, what would be the primary conflicts that would provide them with an immediate inspiration? What were the main moments in the journey that brought you to who you are now?

6. In this event, Your Life, what would be the answers to fill in the ten elements of dramatic structure? To tell your story most effectively, for example, what should be the point of attack, how much foreshadowing is needed and who (assuming you are the protagonist) is the antagonist?

7. Take a recent film or play and answer these same questions for an event created by a writer.

8. Since foreshadowing is such a key element in analysis, as you examine your own history, what were the primary clues (alas, minus the hints given by the *Jaws* soundtrack) that, if you had recognized them earlier, would have saved you from grief and regret later?

9. Compare yourself to a character in a play or film in terms of the five basic elements of character analysis. Come up with a brief answer for each. How have your insights about the character changed as a result of doing the analysis? What new insights do you have into your own character that you might not have noticed before?

10. Try to find an example of an instance where a critic has successfully examined and revealed a playwright's plan before going on to make judgments about it. Also find an example where the writer limits himself to identifying the issues and quickly jumps to personal opinion regarding the work itself.

SUGGESTED ACTVITIES

1. Individual—Try your hand at writing dialogue, picking two of your friends and creating a conversation that to your knowledge they have not had, but they could have. Be sure to capture the way each of them uses or hesitates to use language.

2. Group—Pick a very familiar story and discuss what it would take to clearly define the event as comic, tragic, and some surprising blend.

3. Long term—Using the list of starters on pp.53–54, start a play ideas journal, each day jotting down something from your imaginary life, real life, or the news that could be the beginning of a script.

4. Large group—Have someone who considers himself or herself a skilled storyteller volunteer to be narrator. Let the class vote on a fairy tale or other universal story. Divide the group into four parts: 1) sounds of nature such as wind; 2) interior sounds such as doors slamming; 3) repetition of key phrases in the story to emphasize them; 4) overt active audience sounds such as gasps, shrieks, giggles to accompany key plot moments. The storyteller will point to each group during the telling of the tale, at which point the group provides the sound supplement to make it come fully alive.

KEY WORDS AND IDEAS

Griot/Griotte, Sutrahdhara, Bard

Playwright

Problematizing

Deconstruction

Devising

Medium

Mood

Dramatic action

Structure Analysis

Point of Attack

Protagonist

Antagonist

World of the play

Exposition

Foreshadowing

Inciting incident

Rising and falling action

Climax

Resolution

Character Analysis

Given Circumstances

Values

Super Objective

Actions

Motivations

ACTORS AND DIRECTORS

CONTENTS

I N THIS CHAPTER we will explore the work of two of the most intimately related members of any production team. They are bound, for good or bad, in a symbiotic relationship of great intensity, which may include shared laughter, tears, discoveries, and challenges. They create theatre together. We will examine the details of that process and try to answer, "What does it take to be an actor or a director?" We will explore their preparation, skills, and challenges.

PUTTING A SHOW TOGETHER

The following chart shows the most commonly employed steps of the actor and director in production. Some shows will include additional steps and others may skip some listed here. The procedures outlined are traditional from Broadway to your local community theatre.

The Prologue—Our chart begins once both participants are involved. Long before this (months, sometimes years before) the director is involved in script analysis and development, historical or style research, brainstorming sessions with various designers, and subsequent design conferences as the preliminary look of the show evolves. The director is also involved in putting together a core staff for the initial rounds of casting and rehearsal, and generally doing enough homework to move confidently to the point where actors will be welcomed into the process.

The Director	The Actor
1. Casting calls—producers or directors notify agents and actors of upcoming auditions for single productions or seasons.	1. Audition notices—working professional actors are notified by their agents; novices will see posted notices, posters, newspaper ads for events sometimes called "cattle calls."
2. Casting, Round 1—directors see actors, performing prepared monologues, usually in 3–4 min. intervals.	2. Auditions—actors perform prepared monologues for director(s) and producers.
3. Casting, Round 2—directors see only those actors who have sparked their attention, may work with the actor on a prepared piece or a reading from the text. **Note**: For musicals, the Music director and Choreographer/Dance director will follow the same steps as above.	3. Callbacks—Actors may have been given a piece of text to work on or advice on preparing for the next round. They can generally expect some kind of direction or interaction with director(s). **Note**: For musicals, the actor must be prepared to audition in all three disciplines: acting, singing, and dancing.
4. 1st Company Meeting—sometimes a "meet and greet," sometimes a first reading, often the director reveals the approach to the play.	4. 1st Company Meeting—actors meet the people they will be working with. May include a first reading of the text and the director's approach to it.
5. Show and Tell—an exciting meeting where the director's vision is explored and the designers' work revealed.	5. Show and Tell—where actors learn what the environment for the play will be, what they'll be wearing, and what world will be created for this production.
6. Read-throughs—work done at the table with the text or script ideas. May last for a week or more with a complex script, or one day for a more accessible one. May involve work with a finished text or evolution of unscripted materials.	6. Read-throughs—hearing the full script aloud and exploring ideas. Length of table work varies, as does the role of the actor who may be reading or developing scenarios.
7. Blocking—stage movement and action developed and carefully orchestrated.	7. Blocking—stage movement and action must be written down, learned, justified, and frequently adjusted.
8. Design Meetings—throughout the rehearsal process the director meets with designers for detail work and problem-solving strategies. Blocking choices must be discussed for safety and ease of movement as well as time frames for quick costume or location changes.	8. Costume fittings—the actor is fitted for clothing, hair, prosthetics, etc. and must be able to envision blocking to discuss safety issues and ease of movement with design staff, as well as strategies for any needed quick costume or location changes.
9. Actor Coaching—work focused on assisting the actor in any aspect of their performance, may be individual or ensemble.	9. Character/ensemble development—being guided by the director toward the desired character or ensemble work.
10. Intensives—focus on critical details or problem areas, i.e., a fall, a love scene, a difficult entrance.	10. Intensives—same as for the director.
11. Promotion—selling the production, getting the word out, photo shoots, TV, newspaper and radio interviews, etc.	11. Promotion—same as for the director, possibly also performing preview excerpts from the show.
12. Technical Rehearsal—incorporating all technical elements to the production, including lights, sound, special effects, scenery changes, etc. A very busy time for the director.	12. Technical Rehearsal—adjusting to all technical components which can effect blocking, stage position and "scale" of performance such as light, sound, and stage changes. Can be a very slow time for the actor as technical problems are solved.

13. Dress Rehearsals—add costumes, hair/wigs, make-up, and hand props. Most directors try for one clean dress rehearsal without stopping for adjustments.

14. Opening Night—an electric moment of birth as the "baby" is brought before the audience for the first time. In professional theatre, this is the end of director's involvement.

15. The Run—the stage manager generally becomes the authority figure who works to preserve the director's vision. In some community and educational theatre, the director may attend performance and give notes all the way up to closing night.

16. Closing Night—the end. The stage will be cleared (called the "strike"), costumes cleaned and stored. A new show will move in and the process begins all over again.

13. Dress Rehearsals—actors are called in early to add make up, costumes, hair/wigs, etc. The process of "make-believe" goes up a notch as the actor is transformed physically into another character.

14. Opening Night—same as for the director except that it is just the beginning of the run and the actor will repeat this performance for the days, weeks, or months to come.

15. The Run—the actor works to balance on a fine line between keeping the work fresh and open to discovery, while not ambushing fellow actors or the director's vision.

16. Closing Night—same as for the director. For successful actors, a few reviews, photos, and mementos are stored and they are off to another theatre, perhaps in another country, state, or city to start a new production.

The Timetable—The average nonprofessional production rehearses four to six weeks, five days a week for three to five hours. A professional production may have fewer weeks and longer hours. It is commonly estimated that plays rehearse at least an hour for each minute of performance time, so a two hour play would rehearse 120 hours. The length of rehearsal expands based on the size of the cast, scale of production, and new skills required of the cast, so a big musical or Shakespeare may easily rehearse twelve weeks. A contemporary, realistic, small cast, simple set show may rehearse less than the standard minimum, whereas a period piece in which women actors need to, for example, learn to work with fans, corsets, bustles, and trains would take longer due to the need for extra rehearsals devoted entirely to these skills.

THE ACTOR

The actor is the heart and soul of theatre. Without actors we have no theatre. They tell us the story, take us out of indifference, and stir our feelings. They are emotional warriors who put themselves on the line and often take great risks to provide a rewarding—even life changing—evening at the theatre. No one is more vulnerable in the performance because no one is more subject to the approval or disdain of the audience and the critics. In less "civilized" times, actors were targets of not just boos and hisses, but of thrown objects like tomatoes. In places where critical social or political changes are taking place, actors sometimes risk imprisonment, torture, or even execution for doing their work. In far less extreme circumstances, actors have been the objects of suspicion or awe, disdain or acclaim, either the "stray cats" or "national treasures" of their society's pecking order.

Despite the vulnerability of their position, actors are often awarded the gift of envy and adoration. When acting works, when the magic happens, it is so exhilarating that almost everyone wants to do it. Many people find ways to make acting an important part of their life as an avocation. Tens of thousands find outlets for the actor in their souls while maintaining another viable career and source of income. They may be "re-enactors" who you've seen at many historical celebrations, fairs, and festivals across the country. They may be participants in Korean folk drama, in which, once a year, they get to put on the mask of a frog and leap around the newly planted rice fields chasing pretty girls. They may be active participants in a local community theatre group, working not for money but for love.

Author's Insights

Robert: "Almost always when I meet people and they find out I am an acting teacher, their eyes kind of glaze over and they talk about an acting class they once took or a show they once did and found unforgettable, or how much they wanted to do one of these but somehow never got the courage, either a high point in their lives or one they wished for but never got."

For most of us, it is a good to choose something besides acting as our primary means of support. The famous "waiter/actor" who auditions during the day and waits tables at night is not a myth. In much of Western culture, so many people want to make acting their life that no profession has a higher rate of unemployment. In any give year, no matter what state the economy is in, boom times or bust, most actors are always under- or unemployed. It is a profession bound by the motto "many are called, few are chosen." Talent, charisma, training, and a wide range of skills are not enough. One also has to be lucky, confident, and able to tolerate rejection. Still, most actors would pay for the chance to perform, and any kind of remuneration thrills them. Their union (Actor's Equity Association) is the only union to negotiate *lower* wages for its members in order to secure them more work opportunities!

Yet in some other countries actors have no choice but to be actors, the decision having been made for them in childhood. Their livelihood is assured, but their choice in the matter limited. In the Noh drama of Japan and the Sanskrit dance drama of India, only those chosen and trained from a very young age will ever be allowed to perform and no "uninitiated person" would dream of auditioning for a part. In other places, theatre is so communal, such a social requirement, that all are expected to participate and the "auditions" are a life long demonstration of developing narrative, musical, dance, and interpretive skills.

So, what exactly do actors do? That depends very much on the tradition one is pursuing. Looking at all global possibilities is beyond the scope of this book, so we will focus on the more universal aspects of the actor's life in the West (Europe, North America, and the world influenced by the colonial era) and the same general aspects of the actor's life in the East (South and Southeast Asia, China, Japan and Korea). The theatre of Africa, Micronesia, and parts of South and Central America is just beginning to throw off the yoke of foreign domination. There, the actor's life is rapidly changing with dynamic new theatres blending colonial influences with traditional, indigenous forms. New companies and actor-training programs are being formed where oppressive puppet dictatorships followed colonial occupation. During difficult times, the actor was strictly controlled by censorship and the need to toe the party line. Those who didn't or couldn't conform were persecuted, driven underground to "hit and run" performances in towns and villages, and then fleeing ahead of the authorities. During the 1980s, Augusto Boal of Brazil had his actors wear firearms under their costumes in order to defend themselves if the police burst in during the performance of one of his many projects critical of the government. Now, emerging nations are demanding a people's theatre. We wait and watch to see what new theatrical world will be invented.

Evolution in the West

The status, training, and financial and physical security of the Western actor has swung on a pendulum of extremes. A brief survey will take us from ancient Greece into modern actor training.

In Greece, the original actors were the playwrights, but by 449 BCE competitions were held for tragic actors. They were probably semi-professionals paid by the state as part of festivals like the City Dionysia, which included a tragic playwriting competition as well. Only three actors were allowed for each playwright. Men played all roles, and wore masks and costumes to indicate character. All needed fully developed vocal skills (in the use of chant, declamation, poetry, and song) to be considered for a role. What scant evidence we have of the tragic actor's status, points to a respectable position in society, and for a few, fame and fortune. The tragic chorus, probably made up of amateurs, performed song and/or dance interludes. They were rehearsed to move and speak in perfect unison while masked, and represented the citizens of the polis. One source speculates that they trained eleven months of the year in addition to their day jobs, much like community theatre actors today.

Russell Crowe, *actor*

"Acting is storytelling. Its roots are age-old and part of who we are as humans. It's the same job as the bloke that used to hold the talking stick aloft and about when the first canoe arrived."

The comic actors were distinct and separate from tragedians, most likely professional entertainers, sometimes bards of noble families, sometimes street performers and always granted greater license than their tragic counterparts. The Greeks were serious about drama, but they also had a lively sense of the bawdy, risqué, and funny. As the comedies of Aristophanes show us, sex farces and buffoonery were part of the Greek temperament. Comedies might come at the end of a day of tragedy, like a dessert. Little is known about the societal status of comic actors.

Martha Fletcher Bellinger, *historian*

"Dill [the historian of Roman society] describes them as showing 'an inhuman contempt for a class whom humanity doomed to vice, and then punished for being vicious.' Legally the position of the acting class was never essentially changed; but in time the social standing was somewhat improved, and gifted artists, such as Roscius in comedy and Aesopus in tragedy, occasionally rose above their station and enjoyed the friendship of men of high standing."

Although much of Roman tradition (c. 250 BCE–100 CE) copied Greece, Roman actors were generally a despised, expendable commodity—often slaves—bought and sold like gladiators and exotic animals for use in huge outdoor theatres. The free Roman actor usually inherited his position (women were still not allowed to perform except as dancers in private performances) and was required to learn a detailed map of gesture and pantomime to indicate actions when dialogue could not be heard over the milling of the vast audiences.

When the Roman Empire converted to Christianity in the late fourth century, theatre was banned from the Roman Catholic Empire, and the profession of actor/entertainer was outlawed. Some changed professions; others fled or were imprisoned and killed. The professional actor would not be seen in Europe again until almost a thousand years later. During that long millennium, actors were amateurs working on religious dramas sanctioned by local church authorities, where guilds, or trade unions, competed in annual religious festivals.

In the fifteenth and sixteenth centuries, professional drama revived. Shakespeare (1564–1616), was first an actor, then a playwright, and eventually part owner of the company with which he made his start. Talented performers, while not high society, could once again make their living performing in the theatre for appreciative crowds. Although women performed as members of Commedia troupes on the Continent, all actors in England were still men. The first women actors would not appear on the legitimate stage in England until the 1660s. Boys were apprenticed to professional companies before puberty and learned by working closely with adults, first playing all female roles, and later when their voices changed, moving up into male parts. The boys might be sons of actors, or they might simply be gifted youngsters with no other livelihood available. Like actors today, some achieved enough financial security to retire to the country. Some did not. Some became stars and others were always in the background.

The status of an actor in Elizabethan England and the status of an actor in the contemporary West is highly similar. The actor was, and is, an odd duck to those not smitten with the acting bug. We revere our favorites, sometimes granting them more authority than they deserve. At the same time, we are not entirely without suspicion because they are different from others. We adore them, give them license to misbehave, and forgive them their public sins again and again.

Next we will look at the entirely different world of acting in the Eastern theatre, which has seen less extreme swings of the popularity pendulum and where tradition is the foundation upon which actors build their life's work.

Evolution in the East

Acting in the East is far more steeped in tradition and repetition than in the West. Many precepts guiding status, training, and performance style were established many hundreds, if not thousands, of years ago and did not significantly change until the twentieth century. The influence of India and the Sanskrit drama was, and is, felt throughout a vast region in Asia, where details articulated in the *Artha Sastra* (c. 300 BCE) has helped shape the perception and training of actors up to the present day.

The *Artha Sastra* was the last of five basic guides organizing all aspects of Hindu life. It defined the status of the actor as near the bottom of the caste system, despite the fact that the art form itself was a gift from the god Brahma. According to the *Artha Sastra*, "The same rules shall apply to an actor, dancer, singer, players on musical instruments, a rope dancer, a juggler, a bard, pimps, and unchaste women." In addition, traditional Eastern social custom enforced strict segregation of the sexes more profoundly than most Western societies. A social hierarchy separated performers from more favored classes and segregation of the sexes caused theatre to develop as either an all male or all female enterprise.

As Sanskrit drama and Hindu distinctions of caste and gender bias spread through South and Southeast Asia during the third century BCE, their influence was absorbed into local customs and beliefs. The spread of Buddhism and Confucianism reinforced status and gender segregation of the actor while regional and local traditions shaped specific schools of performance. Though the actor was officially low person on the totem pole, some still achieved fame, fortune, and fanatically loyal admirers. Status, training, and performance demands of actors didn't change with new governments or the rise and fall of empires. Being a social outcast and idol at the same time went with the job. The actor might never have been admitted to high society, where male actors playing women were suspected of being homosexuals and female actors of being prostitutes. Nevertheless, a male actor in the East might have caused the heart of many respectable matrons to flutter, while a female actor might have been the only literate, well-educated woman in the community, and possibly chaste or married as well.

We can look to ancient Imperial China for examples of the impact of the stratification of society into strictly controlled groups. Confucius (551–479 BCE) taught that family and social hierarchy were the primary stabilizing factors in life, placing the actor outside the pale along with criminals, bandits, scavengers, slaves, prostitutes and other entertainers of all kinds. Actors and their families were forbidden to apply for the much coveted examinations (in literacy and respectability) that were the only route to success for the Chinese family. Without exam access, actors were not allowed valued stations of conformity and the result was isolation. No family would accept an actor as a son- or daughter-in-law. Theatre became a closed corner of society, and the actor was born into a family of his own kind.

Segregation of the sexes has also shaped the life of the actor. Inescapably, when men and women were strictly forbidden to appear together on stage, sexuality and acting became entangled.

In Japan, the kabuki theatre, though originally an all female form, quickly became all male and remained so well into the twentieth century. Young boys born or adopted into theatrical families were chosen at an early age to play male or female roles in their adult careers. Some were trained in the art of impersonating an idealized female called an *onnagata*. The *onnagata* actor did not rely not on any inherent femininity, nor was his sexual orientation at issue. He underwent meticulous, painstaking training in every nuance of gesture, posture, and vocal intonation to create the magical appearance of a perfect woman. (See the play *M. Butterfly* if you doubt the possibility of this.)

C. Scott, *scholar*

"In effect he [the *onnagata*] says to his audience, here is an interesting character, now watch how perfectly I can act it for you, as my father did and my grandfather before him."

Men playing women is not the only form of "gender-bending" in Eastern theatre forms. The Shanghai Opera, as popular and enduring a tradition as is the Beijing Opera further north, all women played both male and female roles. Some critics imply that the popularity of the Shanghai Opera was not based in the talent of the performers, but rather in their beauty and assumed promiscuity. But many talented women achieved star status for the brilliance their work, not their faces.

Bound together by ostracism and segregation, actors in the East have built enduring traditions that transcend time, race and the influences of Western imperialism. The minimal period of training is about seven years, and begins in childhood. The actor then begins playing bit parts and walk-ons, learning from masters of the art who play the leading roles. The work is deeply symbolic, combining familiar stories with dance, music, and movement abstract in form. Innovation from young actors is discouraged. They learn to do it "right," and under no circumstances do they ever correct their master's definition of right. If they are among the fortunate few who gain the prestige and skill to play leading roles, they may then begin to—ever so subtly—leave their own signature on traditional roles.

The great masters (male and female) of Sanskrit dance and drama, Kabuki theatre, the Noh drama, and the operatic forms of China achieve a fan base to rival anything in Hollywood. Few achieve legendary status, and these few often become the head teachers at the intensely private schools that train the next generation. The revered masters select promising apprentices, and the great life's work begins again as another young boy or girl begins years of labor and training. Sometimes history comes full circle. At present the most popular form of Kabuki is Ona Kabuki performed entirely by women.

STANISLAVSKI AND CHARACTER

While Eastern actor training remained prescriptive and traditional, one Russian theatre artist created a revolution in the West. Constantin Stanislavski (1863–1938) created a complete system for constructing a character, now used in some degree by most reputable acting programs. A brilliant actor, director, and teacher, he co-founded the Moscow Art Theater in Russian in 1898, and changed the way actors worked forever. He wrote four famous books (*An Actor Prepares, Building a Character, Creating a Role,* and *My Life in Art*), which establish the basic principles for relaxation, concentration, imagination exercises, warm-ups, improvisations, and rehearsal experiments used in classes and rehearsals. When Stanislavski started acting, he was not a "natural." He was awkward, ungainly, and ill at ease. As such, he was motivated to study what all the great performers did to calm and focus themselves and then to report the results in a systematic way. He came up with a method to deeply comprehend a dramatic encounter.

Authors' Insight

Annie: I was surprised to learn that two of the lead actresses in *Memoirs of a Geisha* are not only Chinese actors with no familiarity with Japanese culture, but also trained at the two Stanislavski Conservatories in Shanghai and Beijing.

The System has two sets of ingredients. Some may be familiar to you from earlier chapters. The first ten are questions actors ask themselves for any scene they are in:

1. Relationship—What is this other character I am acting with to me and what am I to him?

2. Objective—What do I want?

3. Obstacle—What is stopping me? What's in the way?

4. Strategy—What kind of plan do I have to get past the obstacle and obtain what I want?

5. Tactics—What individual maneuvers or changes do I make within my strategy? (*Strategy* is sometimes compared to the "overall game plan" and *tactics* to "single plays" used in sports.)

6. Text—What are the words we speak?

7. Subtext—What is really going on behind these words and between them?

8. Interior Monolog—What is the tape that is running in my head as I constantly and silently talk to myself?

9. Evaluations—What do I consider doing but don't do? What alternatives do I reject?

10. Beats—When do my partner and I change tactics or topics? How does our encounter shift internally?

Richard Brestoff, *acting scholar*

"Stanislavski's System lays the groundwork for inspiration. Doing this work is like erecting lightning rods to attract lightning. The more rods you build, the more likely the bolt will strike. The System is a magnet for the subconscious, our major source of inspiration."

You can see that any life situation could be analyzed and further understood by answering these questions—especially if you come away reeling from an experience with someone and not really knowing what happened, or if you tend to always have the same run-ins with someone in your life and would like to break the pattern. Stanislavski used analysis of human behavior to enlighten any scripted encounter.

Like most brilliant discoveries, it seems like common sense once you think about it. If an actor does each of these things, his attention will be fully engaged, his instrument will respond honestly, and he will be *compelling* to watch. Tension, stiffness, and self-consciousness tend to fall away because the mind can only hold so much.

The elements above help actors enter an *isolated* encounter. For the entire play (or an entire life) the actor adds ten more:

1. Given Circumstances—What are all the major relevant facts that influence your character's behavior?

2. Magic If—Place yourself in your character's shoes asking. "What would I do IF I were this person in this situation under these conditions?"

3. Super Objective—What does your character want most in life?

4. Through Line of Actions—What is the *connection* between all the behaviors of the character?

5. Score—Write down results of previous questions and mark the script into workable units.

6. Endowment—Project onto other actors and objects imaginary qualities which will be helpful when you perform opposite them.

7. Recall—Use your five senses to awaken physical and emotional memories of your own that can be filtered into the character's experience.*

8. Images—Add photos or a film to the interior monolog in your head to "see" what the character does.

9. External Adjustments—Change your own tendencies (physical and vocal) to suit those of the character.

10. Creative State—Use all the previous research to become free, open, and experimental.

The core of all this work is creating a profound empathy for characters so that entering their world is natural and spontaneous. A lot of this is done in private, but the director may guide the actor into incorporating discoveries being made. The System offers great potential for a convincing, compelling performance.

Unfortunately, Stanislavski's ideas have suffered from poor translations and unfortunate delays in the publication of his books so, as often as not, a distorted version of the System has been used. Nevertheless, his system led to the whole idea of actor training as a curriculum rather than something only learned in apprenticeship conditions.

Strasberg, Adler, and Meisner

Much of what Americans know about Stanislavski has been filtered through three famous acting teachers who picked up bits and pieces of his process and left out others. In the early 1920s, the Moscow Art Theatre toured the United States for a year and a half, stunning this country's theatre community with the depth, power, ensemble, and detail of their work. American companies tried to emulate them. The first and most influential of these was the Group Theatre, founded in 1931. Three members eventually became teachers of great consequence.

Lee Strasberg (1901–1982)

Probably the most famous acting teacher of the twentieth century and mentor to film stars from Monroe to De Niro, Strasberg called his work a "reformulation" of Stanislavski. He developed The Method based on a small part of the System, placing emphasis on emotion memory.** Ironically, he defended and widened its use even as Stanislavski moved away from it. He differed vividly from Stanislavski, however, in changing the "magic if" to include one's own response without the necessity of sharing the character's background, allowing what he called a "substitute reality." Strasberg's actors have sometimes been accused of displaying emotionalism and of violating a core of privacy within each performer.

---

* We use the term "Recall" to encompass memories of physical sensations (which Stanislavski always supported) and emotional ones (which he grew more skeptical of with time). Also note what a small place (just one tool in an entire tool box) it had within his total system right from the start.

** You may have heard the term "Method" acting. This is Strasberg's invention, a corruption of a much larger concept, The Method of Psycho-Physical Actions developed by Stanislavski and not to be confused with the totality of his System.

Strasberg developed relaxation processes and ways to help concentration. Many believe his techniques work better on film than theatre because they help actors achieve "moments" that may not be sustainable. A film actor can take time to reach high, personal emotion just before the camera rolls and then, unlike the stage actor, does not need to snap out of it when the take is over or repeat that moment over and over again another day.

Stella Adler (1901–1992)

The most successful actor in the Group Theatre, Adler was frustrated with Strasberg's classes, so she went to Paris to visit Stanislavski in 1934. He led her away from emotion memory because it had led to hysteria in some actors. He provided her with less direct ways of summoning emotion. While Strasberg opened up the actor's own emotional life, Adler focused on character through evidence in the script. She taught that emotion should come from the given circumstances and that a clear and deep understanding is critical for an actor's truthfulness. She trained actors to do research into the text and the world surrounding it, not unlike an anthropologist. One of her most significant contributions is "Paraphrasing"—trying to do lines that are similar to but not the actual lines, thus creating a sense of newness when speaking the text. Adler emphasized the value of the actor becoming the character rather than subduing the character to his own emotionality.

Sanford Meisner (1905–1996)

Founder of the Neighborhood Playhouse, Meisner was the most respected acting teacher of the past century. He wanted acting to come from the heart not the head, for actors to always find a connection with each other instead of indulging in their own private emotional reveries. All of his work is between partners—based on Stanislavski's concept of "communion"—while most Strasberg and Adler exercises are done alone. He emphasized "Preparation"—creation of off-stage emotion, coming onstage with something going on, with a full inner life, and "Impulses not Cues" working not with the end of your partner's line, but the place within speeches or silences where the *will* to respond comes. His teaching builds trust between actors and he succinctly defined acting as "behaving truthfully under imaginary circumstances."

Internal vs. External

The great, ongoing controversy in Western theatre is whether it is better for actors to approach their characters *internally* or *externally*. Should you burrow into the thoughts and emotions of the character and let the performance emerge from this immersion or should you plan and calculate your performance, making vocal, physical, and psychological choices based on observations and carefully accumulated details? Should the actor be a deeply intuitive artist or one who constructs his performance? This is sometimes called the argument between *truth* and *technique*.

The international stereotype of the American actor is of a deeply internal performer and of the British actor as a consummate external professional, one is all instinct, the other all craft. In the East, where technique seems so central, passion and emotive power still determine whether a performance is "good" or "great." In the great Eastern schools of actor training, the actor doesn't choose between the two. First you learn the technique, then the truth will be found in the most subtle flick of the actor's hand. In the West, too, the reality is that most great actors combine the two. They work to get inside the character emotionally but also design the performance technically. The goal is the same whether you are an actress or dancer in one of India's dramas from the *Mahabharata* or an American actor playing your first role in a college production—find the truth and support that truth with technique or more importantly, let them support each other.

No matter where or when the actor is working, given the challenges, it is a true labor of love.

Denzel Washington, *actor*

"Acting is a both craft and a privilege."

THE MODERN ACTOR

Although acting in Western and Eastern traditions may seem more different than alike, the processes of casting, preparing, rehearsing, and performing are similar. Whether it takes years or days, all actors do the same painstaking work, analyzing, their characters, taking notes and ideas from the director, memorizing lines and blocking (stage movement), experimenting with different ways to become the character, trying to make brilliant discoveries in rehearsals then trying to solidify all this preparation so they can repeat the performance with consistency from night to night. Actors should be fit, athletic, and expressive, with fully developed vocal and physical instruments. One of the major tasks of any acting class and rehearsal process is to get the actor back to a childhood sense of wonder and magic. The actor must always be ready to play.

Author's Insights

Robert: "When my son was about four years old, I overheard him talking with friends and asking them, "Don't you love to visit your Daddy's office?" They all responded, "No!" So he asked, "Don't you like to play with all the masks and stuffed animals and swords and balls and...," the list went on and on. I was reminded that most daddies' offices don't have this stuff, that my job requires toys and I am blessed for that."

Finding the balance between the sheer joyful playfulness of acting and the grinding hard work can be challenging. Many novices to the theatre are blown away by the amount of time a show demands. Not only are you committed to rehearsals for at *least* fifteen hours a week (and many more in professional theatre and many, many more in some Eastern forms), you are also expected to do a great deal of your work outside of rehearsal. This is what most actors are required to do between formal rehearsals *on their own*.

1. In-depth analysis of the character

2. Memorize lines, blocking, and script changes

3. Research the role and the world of the play (both as written and as conceptualized by the production)

4. Apply the director's notes and suggestions from the last rehearsal

5. Experiment with character approaches

6. Develop the vocal life of the character

7. Develop the physical life of the character

8. Brush up on material that hasn't been worked through recently

9. Attend costume fittings

10. Participate in publicity photo sessions and interviews

For the media actor, the last item of the list above can become a life-consuming part of the job.

Ralph Fiennes, *actor*

"The theatre is quite grounding. You can't cheat an audience. You can't cut away. You can't have another close-up"

Media Acting

The first feature film, *Birth of a Nation*, came out in 1915 and regular television broadcasts began in 1948, so the Stanislavski System has profoundly affected the relatively short history of acting in front of a camera. In early silent films, the intimacy of the camera makes the non-realistic acting seem melodramatic and over-the-top. What early media actors needed to learn and most contemporary theatre actors must as well, is that the primary difference between acting for stage and camera is scale.

Judi Dench, *actor*

"I'm a stage creature more than anything. You have no control over what happens in film ultimately. In the theatre, you go in and do your bit and come off; you create the evening."

Cynthia Nixon, *actor*

"Doing a film, someone picks you up, they get your food, tell you everything you have to do. To be childlike, to be in that place at the spur of the moment—that's what you're responsible for. The business of life, other people do for you. But for a play, you take the subway to the theatre, put on your own make-up, listen for your cues. Onstage you're responsible for the play."

Stage actors need to project vocally, physically and emotionally to the very back of the house, sometimes all the way up to the third balcony, with much of the audience at a considerable distance. In contrast, the camera can scrutinize you in extreme close-up, and the boom or body mike can pick up your subtlest sound. There is rarely any need to raise volume and diction, to find gestures that clearly delineate reactions. Even in a small, intimate live theatre, no one is as close as a close-up.

A stage actor can calculate an effect and pull it off impressively, while film exposes your technique and effort. Film acting tends to support internal work, while stage acting demands at least some external attention to detail. Some advise film actors to just "be" because anything more can be too much. The stage actor has to sustain and repeat a performance for two or three hours and then again the next day and sometimes twice on matinee days and again the next week. The film actor needs to be able to do "takes" over and over, but that is usually over the course of one day and then it is on to something else. The stage actor gets run-throughs and work-throughs, moving through the story in the exact order it is written. The screen actor shoots wildly out of sequence, sometimes starting with the ending or the most intimate encounter in the whole film, long after the characters have gotten to know each other in the actual story. The stage actor gets constant audience response, while the camera is neutral. Though it loves some actors more than others, it never utters this love. In movement and proximity, screen performers are often asked to move closer than would be normal for everyday interaction because the camera creates space. Finally, the stage actor at some point fully memorizes the text and sets it. The screen actor arrives having to know only today's lines, but prepared for re-writes and text adjustments on the spot.

Acting and Personal Theatre

People sometimes say they are suspicious of actors because they must be great liars to be good at their jobs. In fact, the actor must be truthful, emotionally available, and thoughtful. We all act our lives. We audition for important roles. We decide whether to rely on internal or external techniques or both.

We are auditioning whenever we are in a circumstance that is now temporary and indefinite but may become permanent. So a first date is an audition for a second date, just as flirting is an audition for the first date. Meeting the parents of your partner is a challenging audition to possibly join the family. At each audition, you are deciding whether (or how much) you want the part.

One of the more profound life acting tips is offered by award winning author Toni Morrison who says we should all ask, "Does your face light up when your child enters the room?" For years she was fussing over details of how clean, healthy or prepared they were, thinking her love would naturally be perceived out of this concern. Then she learned otherwise and always vowed to show in her eyes how glad she was to see them. Try this with anyone you love. You may not always be absolutely ecstatic to see them, but you can still send out light.

Whenever we anticipate unfamiliar or uncomfortable events, we prepare ourselves for the event by rehearsing, analyzing the other characters in the event, and accepting or rejecting the advice of someone who might or might not be on our side. Acting isn't about being a better liar than the others around you—it's about being alert and aware, thoughtful and engaged, and making and rejecting choices from moment to moment.

Job interviews can be a high-stress audition, very much like auditioning for a play. One of the largest employment agencies in the country has reported their greatest success is in placing theatre majors—in non-theatrical jobs! Why? They have skills valued by every organization. They have learned to have social poise, self-reliance, to be self-motivated, perceptive, and adaptable. Actor training teaches these things by necessity. It teaches fundamental survival and advanced marketing skills as well.

Analyzing your life choices using the Stanislavski system can be revelatory. You may be surprised to find rehearsal, clear objectives, and focus can change the outcome of life encounters in significant ways. Let the actor inside you search for truth, then figure out how to share that truth with others.

THE DIRECTOR

While the actor and audience are the essential ingredients for theatre, the director has been in many instances the vital link in their relationship. In Western theatre, the director is now regarded as so crucial that it is hard to imagine that no such designated position existed 150 years ago. The director, after months of research, consultation, and preparation, guides the event from rehearsal to opening night. She is responsible for envisioning how the show will be done and for realizing that vision. No one is more directly involved in every aspect of production. No one will be held more responsible if it does not come off, though many others may be more honored if it does. This is because the director's work will often dissolve from consciousness if all artists shine and the show glows. The director molds a final product that may or may not receive acceptance from the critics and public at large. The producer is the one person who can take control away from the director.

Without a hands-on producer supervising (and perhaps interfering) at rehearsals or filming, the director is the leader.

Now we believe the director to be essential, yet no such creature really existed until the late 1800s. The need for a director who was not a playwright or actor doing double duty came about with the advent of a movement called Realism, which emerged in the mid 1800s. For the first time, plays were expected to be believable, not just fanciful. Someone who could coordinate the whole event, modulate the performances, and layer in lifelike touches was needed. The director became even more essential in clarifying presentation for any show.

While the director is a relatively new phenomenon in Western theatre, in non-Western theatre the position is still somewhat rare. The master teacher, author, elders, or *griot/narrator* control the development of the production. Tradition also dictates decisions assigned to directors in the West. Today, those working as directors in other parts of the world are often trained in European or American universities and conservatories.

Prior to the late nineteenth century, we can find no evidence of a member of the company charged with the responsibilities of the modern director. Historical evidence points to the playwright as the primary source of production aesthetics from the classical Greek period (c. 500 BCE) through Shakespeare's era (c. late sixteenth century). For nearly 2,000 years, the playwright was the deciding voice, but we have evidence that actors were active participants in decision making as well. By the mid-seventeenth century, the person in charge of production was the theatre manager/owner, who hired actors and designers, scheduled and supervised rehearsals, arranged promotion or advertisement, and managed the finances of the company. In terms of artistic guidance, the owner/manager had better things to do. Each new play was rehearsed for a few days. Old plays were revived with one quick run-through. Actors were told to memorize their lines and step into the light to talk. Costumes, props, and scenery were pulled from stock and used over and over again in different plays.

During the early nineteenth century in England and America, the star-system developed, placing artistic control in the hands of the lead actor. Successful actors could buy the rights to a play in which they would play the leading role. They then toured, arriving in each new city with a trunk full of their own costumes and props. They hired a hall, secondary actors, and bought advertisement, and staged the show. Actors would arrange the production to suit their own egos. Often, the "star" was the only person on stage allowed to stand in the light. The play could be cut and shaped to emphasize the star's role and de-emphasize others.

After a nearly a century of this, live theatre had become smothered in repetitious, star-oriented melodramas. Something had to change.

Saxe-Meiningen and Unity

Many historians credit George II, Duke of Saxe-Meiningen "the first director," with creating the position as we currently define it. Born in 1826, to wealth, education, and travel, he developed a great passion for theatre. In 1866, he assumed control of the Duchy of Saxe-Meiningen after the forced abdication of his father. When he came to power, the Duchy had a Court Theatre that had long suffered from neglect and mismanagement, and had a well-deserved reputation for mediocrity. He immediately instituted programs to improve the theatre. He named himself *Indendant* (chief administrative officer) and took direct control. As both the Duke and *Indendant*, he wielded authority over the company that became known as the Meiningen Players.

Between the years 1874 and 1890, the Meiningen Players became the most admired company in the Western world. Their repertory was not particularly unusual, but their methods were highly innovative and became influential. Meiningen was able to institute four practices that have become the model of the modern director.

1. He insisted on play-specific costumes, scenery, and props. The design team was expected to do extensive research into the time period of the play and to build detailed replicas of whatever else was needed for each production. This may sound like a relatively obvious choice today, but we have to remember, prior to the Duke of Saxe-Meiningen, scenery, costumes and props were pulled from storage and often had nothing to do with the play being performed. A leading lady might select from stock the most stylish and flattering nineteenth century dress available, and wear it no matter which role she was playing. The Duke refused to allow anything incongruous or anachronistic onstage. If the play was set in ancient Rome, everything onstage would be appropriate to that culture. The designer was expected to research and create a specific set appropriate to the nationality, social status, and economic class of characters. Designers became a vital aspect of the artistic whole and answered to the director.

2. The Meiningen Players abolished the star-system. The Duke fired the old company and hired a group of fresh young actors he could train and shape. He made sure all actors played both major and minor roles and the entire company participated in the realistic crowd scenes, for which the Meiningen Players became famous. The long-term effect of this system was that the company became an ensemble working together without ego for the good of the production. It also established the authority of the director over the actor.

3. Meiningen insisted a production should be rehearsed for as long as necessary, occasionally for a year, though normally for several months. Few modern companies can afford to stay in rehearsal so long, but this innovation influenced theatres around the world to expand preparation periods.

4. A unified production concept, grounded in research and analysis, became the domain of the director, who now does necessary research, analyzes the script, and evolves an interpretation of the playwright's themes. The director must find a means of communicating these clearly to the audience. Sometimes a production concept will be constructed around an image or metaphor, a color or texture, or changing the time period of the play. If a unified concept is important to communication, the simplest way to ensure unity is to have one person responsible for developing it. Most modern directors find this both the most difficult and the most rewarding aspect of their art.

The Modern Director

Nowadays, directors often prepare for months—even years—before rehearsals begin, researching, meeting with other staff members, exploring the text and their own ideas for bringing the script to life. A ton of analytical homework *hopefully* unleashes inventive, intuitive discovery. This combination of careful planning followed by open-ended creativity makes directing enthralling.

Zelda Fichandler, *director*

"I do at least six months of advance research because knowledge releases my imagination. Without knowledge, one's imagination may be too thin."

In some ways, directors are also designers and playwrights. They design all the stage pictures that are created, dissolved, and recreated throughout the evening so no matter how imaginative the design work, it will fall flat unless these moment-to-moment visual creations are compelling and varied. A director needs to be a spatial artist. While the playwright provides a score of words, the director determines how that score will be "sung," how it will sound, so he is an auditory artist as well.

Today there are two major kinds of directors: Traditional and Conceptual. While all directors honor some traditions and all productions have concepts, we capitalize these terms to represent a contrast in basic philosophy and approach. The Traditional director sees his job as serving the script and aims to realize the playwright's vision, hoping to enhance that vision. He seeks the best way for the audience to experience the script as written with any alterations aimed at taking that appreciation up several levels. The production aspires to illuminate and expand the experience beyond that of a silent reading without violating the intent of the text. While the Traditional director attempts to serve the text, he is not necessarily subservient to it. There may be many original touches, but none assault the script.

Jonathan Miller, *director*

"A director should have common sense, tact, and literary sensitivity."

George II and Stanislavski provided models for this style of directing. For others, the challenge of directing involves a more free and personal approach. This second type of directing is Conceptual. The script is simply a vehicle to express an idea, explore a problem, serve a cause, achieve something more (alas, sometimes less) or far different than may have been intended by the playwright. The script may be radically cut, rearranged, interspersed with bits of other text, ignored during improvisational interludes, altered from night to night, and generally made subservient to the director's intent. A script may be deconstructed or problematized to place the emphasis on a formerly minor area of concern. Sometimes the script may not exist but will be evolved through games, experimentation, and group effort.

Peter Brook, *director*

"The great feature of the theatre is that the audience can enter very deeply into contradictions, contrasting points of view. Unlike media dominated works, theatre has the potential to offer visions that are messy and conflicting, full and complex."

One director thought to be the major pioneer in this area is Jerzy Grotowski, whose work with his Laboratory Theatre in Poland, beginning in 1959 influenced the freedom with which subsequent directors have "altered" the text. Grotowski trained his actors to be "uber" athletes, physically and emotionally tuned to survive great demands of stamina, open to finding the shock, terror, and danger in any moment of a play, always moving beyond mundane everyday behavior into the extraordinary. He would also rearrange the relationships of actor and audience so the latter might be looking down into a pit at the former, or surrounded by them, or countless other nontraditional configurations. Other famous directors in this mold include Elizabeth Le Compte, Robert Wilson, and Anne Bogart.

Directing Process

So what do all directors do? They study the play and then they develop ideas about how best to prepare and present it. They cast the roles, guide actors, create a productive working atmosphere, and oversee the work of a very large team. They serve as both managers and artists, which means they have a wide range of skills from attentive supervision of others to wide-open imaginative, creative impulses.

How directors accomplish these basic tasks varies wildly, but they are all likely to do the following:

1. Analysis—Many research intensively, others prefer to come to the script fresh and respond instinctively. All directors at some point examine the text for interpretive clues.

2. Scheduling—Some directors provide casts with a complete breakdown of each rehearsal at the first one so all know when they will be called and what will be done each day. Others feel the need to reconsider each day what might be done at the next rehearsal and post the call that day based on that new perception.

3. Blocking—Some directors spend many hours with a model of the set and figures (sometimes chess pieces) standing in for each actor while they meticulously work out movements of the performers before passing these decisions on to actors. Others work organically, encouraging actors to explore how they wish to move and not setting the blocking until well along in the process.*

4. Organization—While most directors have highly developed skills in this area, a significant number are "spontaneous artistes" who compensate by hooking up with assistants who do the structure work for them.

5. Coaching—Helping actors develop their performances in close, careful sessions with experimentation, repetition, and attention to both freedom and detail is a crucial task. A director who has also trained as an actor will be more likely to achieve this and one who has not will be totally lost.

6. Atmosphere—Some directors are autocrats, making all creative decisions and setting up guidelines for all rehearsals. Some expect actors to warm up on their own and devote no rehearsal to building ensemble. Other directors include group warm-ups, sharing exercises, games and other activities designed to get each participant relaxed and at ease with others in the cast.

In live theatre there is always tension between the autocratic and the more group-oriented director. Much depends on the personality (and success) of the individual. The Duke of Saxe-Meiningen model is one extreme and the ensemble team is the other. A number of theatres today are structured so that as many voices as possible are heard from in the process of putting a show together. The director may chair meetings, solicit and summarize input, and serve as a "tie breaker" when there is not a consensus, but make few decisions without consulting the team. The advantage to this process is that each participant is likely to feel valued and involved. Great minds working together can achieve greater results. The disadvantage is that it takes time, requires more meetings and can sometimes lead (like some political elections) to compromised rather than inspired choices. Some directors feel that while their power is lessened in such collaboration, their accountability is not. They believe their clout or the authority "to do what needs to be done" has been taken away yet they are still held responsible by critics and the public if the reaction to the show is negative. Commercial productions have been less eager to embrace the system because it is so hard to tell where the buck stops. Nevertheless, we will probably continue to experience a trend toward less autocratic and more collaborative leadership. While many directors will not relinquish the right to make the final decision, more and more are wisely finding a more inclusive way of encouraging the best ideas to float to the surface.

---

*Directors and actors use a code or shorthand to write down movement in the quickest way possible and to recognize blocking later at just a glance. Some of these include: US (for upstage or away from the audience) DS (downstage or toward the audience), and such variations as DL (near the audience but to the left side of the stage from the performer's perspective.) or UC (very far away but in the exact middle of the acting area's width). Scenic elements, entrances, exits, platforms may be assigned letters or numbers.

> ### Marc Lamos, *director*
>
> "There is no collaboration if you come to the table and say 'I have this idea—and this is how you will assist me in presenting it.' Collaboration is saying 'I have certain potent feelings about the work, but I don't understand everything.'"

The United States is unusual in that both acting and directing classes are incorporated into college curricula, whereas in most other parts of the world actors train at an academy or conservatory, keeping academics and art as separate institutions. Alternatively, the custom of apprenticing with a master or a company still survives.

Media Direction

While all directors carry tremendous responsibility, there are five striking differences between live and media directing:

1. Focus is a major challenge for the stage director, since each audience member can look anywhere they choose. The media director, on the other hand, has the flexible power of tight close-up to long-shot, bird's-eye- view to below-sea-level, and a myriad of other camera options to literally control exactly what an audience sees at any given moment.

2. Theatre directors have a rehearsal period, for experimenting and developing. Any media rehearsal is rare and costly, so it is far more important to cast actors perfectly and expect them to arrive on set ready.

3. Theatres are relatively controlled spaces. If a film is shooting exteriors, or on location, the potential for natural or physical disasters and surprises (from weather or the local populace) multiply radically.

4. While a theatre staff can be large, media technical demands can double staff size and complicate the coordination efforts even more. Things move fairly rapidly in live theatre except for technical rehearsals where there are huge pauses while adjustments are made and cues are set. In a film, every day is tech day, and there are always huge gaps between times when the camera is rolling.

5. The stage director has to let go of the show as it is gradually turned over to the cast and crew who will be on their own after opening. The film director can continue to tinker and refine the product, often re-shooting, re-editing, scoring and tightening, long after filming has ceased and even after initial showings. Some claim films are largely created in the editing room. While the stage director cannot stop an actor from altering a performance as the live show runs, a film director has that performance in the can and can control and transform it by the way it is cut.

The Director in You

Do you like to plan events? Do details fascinate rather than overwhelm you? Do you love the challenge of molding people into some creative, cohesive whole? Do you love having others ask you how to do it right? Do you love to be in charge? You probably already direct personal theatre events for those around you on a regular basis.

Oddly enough, considering the potential power, authority, and satisfaction of this job, many theatre artists would not touch it. They prefer having their own niche and a tightly defined area of accountability instead of being responsible for the whole theatrical event. Directing requires knowledge of all areas of production, so if you are interested, your best first step is to study every position on your potential team so you can communicate with each member clearly. It also requires major time-management skills because you are taking up the time of so many other participants. You need a strong sense of the visual, timing, analysis, interpretation, management, composition, and a general capacity to get people to work hard for you. Probably the most significant requirement is an elusive capacity to cross brain hemispheres from logic to wonder and back again, to do scholarly research but not get trapped in detail, and to take imaginative leaps but remain grounded. So if you love to be in charge, can attend to details but always see the big picture, can produce on deadline, and do the left/right brain shift on a dime—this may be your destiny.

There are many actors who just want to be told what to do (usually at the beginning of their careers when they do not have many ideas) and plenty of directors willing to tell them what to do (perhaps control freaks that enjoy the power too much). But the best actor/director connections are based on enormous mutual respect, affection, and engagement. Each time they meet they share, exchange, and laugh. They each bring in their individual ideas and emerge with something far more than their isolated solo impulses. They come into the rehearsal with expectations, but leave with discoveries beyond what they expected. In the best of these interactive relationships, the actor gets deep support and stimulation from the director and vice versa. The director gets an, "I trust you and am willing to let you guide me almost anywhere" promise from the actor. The director in turn promises, "I will take you on this trip with the best help I can give." The director will give the actor the skill, belief, and will to fly and then watch that flight with deep, profound satisfaction and some regret that the interchange is now over. Both will be richer and ready for the journey—and ready to move on to the next one.

SUMMARY

The actor and the director engage in one of the most intimate of adventures when they join their talents in production. The actor must bring talent, charisma, and strong training to the relationship. In the East, technique is taught in exacting detail from early childhood to adulthood. In the West, most actors have been influenced by some of the Stanislavski System. In either tradition, the actors are the emotional warriors, putting themselves on the front line figuratively and sometimes literally.

The actor in the West works closely with the director, a relatively recent addition starting in the late nineteenth century with George II, Duke of Saxe-Meiningen, who insisted on appropriate design elements for each specific production, abolished the star based vehicles, lengthened rehearsal periods, and established the director as responsible for a unified production concept.

The modern director is responsible for analysis, organization, blocking/focus, scheduling, and the rehearsal atmosphere. Some directors are Traditional (serving the text) and others are Conceptual (using the text as a springboard). Some are autocratic and others collaborative.

SUGGESTED ASSIGNMENTS

1. When have you had an experience closest to that of an actor auditioning for play? What did you want and how effectively did you present yourself?

2. Were you ever on the line for something you really wanted and you knew the competition? What did you do to win or fail to do?

3. Would you say that you would do better in an audition where you were asked to present polished, memorized material or in one in which improvisation and cold readings will take place?

4. Since theatre involves constant collaboration, how do you measure up as a collaborator? Are you more autocratic or group oriented?

5. In the theatre, it is unacceptable to drop out of a project once it is launched. In other contexts of your life, when are the best and worst times to withdraw?

6. How much do you rehearse your life and how much is improvisation? Do you run speeches you intend to give to someone important in your life over and over until they are perfect? Do you prefer to never prepare and go with the flow? What does this say about you and those with opposite preferences?

7. How does the protocol of your current workplace differ from that in the theatre? What does this teach you about the ways in which theatre is very much like your offstage life and the ways in which it is a whole new world?

8. Since the actors are your direct link to the play's content, when you attend a performance, ask yourself how effectively they accomplished this goal? Could you feel empathetic and connected to them? If not, what was missing?

9. Take either an improvised or written dialogue and ask two of your friends or classmates to rehearse with you. Ask them to make adjustments in their physical relationship, movements, line readings, and attitudes to make the scene work better. Did it work? How does it feel to do this?

10. Choose a play that you have seen or read and try to come up with a unified production concept. What ideas do you want to emphasize? How would you use space, color, actors, etc., to realize your ideas on the stage?

SUGGESTED ACTIVITIES

1. Individual—Identify two famous actors, one with whom you believe you have some connection, who is perhaps the same type as you, and one whom you consider as far removed from your own tendencies are possible.

2. Group—Attend an audition together and observe what you learn from the preparation level and behavior of various actors.

3. Long term—See if you can get permission to visit a play in rehearsal, sit in on the very first company meeting, then return once or twice a week up until opening. Keep a journal of what you particularly notice about how the production develops.

4. Large group—Identify a crowd scene such as a party where someone asks for a date or a crowded terminal where two old friends re-discover each other. Pick the two people with real lines and have a large number go onstage and begin milling about as if it were the real event. Let the teacher guide both the crowd and the featured characters so there is variety, focus, interest and clarity. Try as a group to achieve satisfactory results.

KEY WORDS AND IDEAS

Casting calls

Auditions

Callbacks

Show and tell

Read-throughs

Blocking

Intensives rehearsals

Polish rehearsals

Run-throughs

Artha Sastra

Sanskrit drama

Onnagata

Shanghai Opera

Beijing Opera

Constantin Stanislavksi

Stella Adler

Sanford Meisner

Lee Strasberg

Stanislavski's System vs. The Method

Internal vs. External Acting

George II, Duke of Saxe-Meiningen

Jerzy Grotowski

Star system

Unified production concept

Traditional vs. Conceptual Directors

DESIGNERS

CONTENTS

T HEATRE IS possible without design. It can happen with no sets, lights, costumes, make-up, or sound and it can be magical. Such performance relies on the power of the actors' skilled concentration to transform and enthrall. Audiences want to be transformed and transported. Actors *can* manage this without backup if they are so compelling and imaginative that we give ourselves up the same way we did when being read to aloud as children, when words could metamorphose us through our limitless imagination. Sometimes though, we want the magic—without necessarily working that hard for it to happen.

Designers are wizards who take us out of "same old" into some special other. They jump-start our imaginations. When we are less than resourceful and need recharging, they give us the juice. The world they hand us may be more exotic, spectacular, mysterious, threatening, satisfying, complete, or romantic than the one in which we hang out. It may be so dark and dirty that we are stunned and appalled but compelled. On the other hand, it may be so exactly like some world we know that we lose ourselves in unexpectedly familiar territory and amazing detail. The experience will not be what we got on the ride to the theatre, in the parking lot, the box office, and the lobby. All of that will dissolve, and, hopefully, the experience will give us indelible memories.

This chapter offers glimpses into the world of those who design sets, costumes, make-up, masks, and sound. We attempt to understand more about how each makes the magic happen.

Designers work with five key ingredients and five basic principles. The ingredients are:

1. Line—Are the primary lines going to be horizontal or vertical, and within that domain how straight, curved, angular, zigzagged, or scalloped are they? What does each of these suggest to an audience? What shapes will communicate meaning?

2. Mass—How much and what kind of space will be filled? How thick and how shaped will it be? What kind of bulk, weight, and size will fill the stage?

3. Color—What hue, intensity, or values will be used? Will they be light, dark, warm, cool, tints, shades, primary, or secondary colors?

4. Texture—What will the surfaces be like? Will they be rough, smooth, shiny, matte, or grainy?

5. Decor—What will be added within the overall scheme in terms of furniture, trim, moldings, fringe, and general ornamentation?

All visual artists outside the theatre—architects, home decorators, painters, sculptors, and clothing designers—consider these same elements. Sound designers take visual ingredients and translate them into auditory components. Basic principles include:

1. Unity—How will individual components be tied together in a coordinated, harmonious whole?

2. Variety—Within this unified whole, how will interest, suspense and enjoyment be created (and boredom avoided) by diverse and lively choices?

3. Balance—How will the weight and size of elements be distributed? Where, between completely symmetrical and asymmetrical, will the pictures be? What will be the scale of each part in relation to others?

4. Focus—What will be disguised and what enhanced? Where do we want to draw the eye and emphasize an element? What will be strong or weak?

5. Progression—Will each of the preceding elements and principles stay constant or shift throughout the performance? Which will be repeated, altered gradually, or changed altogether? How will the timing of the event move, segue, or flow?

THEATRE SPACES

The type of staging space used affects all design work and all designers learn to adapt to the variables inherent in each. Five of the most common styles are *proscenium, thrust, arena, environmental,* and *black box* or *flexible staging.*

Proscenium Stages

From approximately the seventeenth century well into the twentieth century, European and American designers were working in theatres with proscenium stages. As you can see in the line drawing, the proscenium stage looks like an opening in a wall through which the audience looks. That hole, known as the proscenium arch, creates a picture frame that controls the point of view of the audience. All audience members are facing the same direction. Designers face both limitations and rewards with this type of space.

The obvious advantage is the ability to control focus. Scenery, lighting, costume, and sound are designed toward the audience, while many of the mechanics of the magic remain hidden. When scenery was made primarily of canvas painted to create the illusion of depth with two- and three-point perspective (seventeenth through the nineteenth century), the starred locations on the chart were known as the "ducal seats," those reserved for the most important audience members. Even today, these seats are set aside for reviewers, major donors, and other VIPs. The proscenium stage works well for large, complicated projects and for creating and sustaining the illusion of reality. Proscenium houses also tend to be larger than some other types, serving more patrons, and all in the audience can see most of the stage at all times.

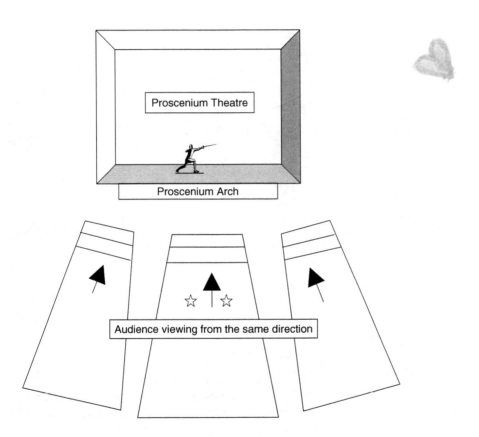

The term "sight lines" refers to how much the audience can see and what the arch or other masking blocks from view. While this type of space controls those elements to a degree, audiences sitting at the outside walls will not be able to see some action at the far sides of the stage.

The primary limitation of the proscenium stage is achieving a sense of intimacy with the audience. The great European opera master Richard Wagner (1813–83) called the space between the arch and the audience the "mystic gulf." Sometimes getting past this gulf is difficult. For lighting and sound designers, the challenges include finding ways to model visual and audio elements into three-dimensional experiences. If all the lights point from the same direction, people on stage tend to blend into the scenery. Equally, if all sound emanates from one direction the effect can be flat. During the second half of the twentieth century, a strong movement away from the traditional proscenium stage occurred.

Thrust (3/4 Round) Stages

In moving away from the proscenium stage, focus issues increase and design detail becomes more important. In the thrust or 3/4 round stage drawing, you can see that the audience sits on three sides of the stage. Only one wall and the stage floor are available for scenic design and they become essential elements of focus whether left completely blank or filled with ornate detailing. Audience members can also see each other. Performers and space have to compete with the unpredictable behavior of human beings.

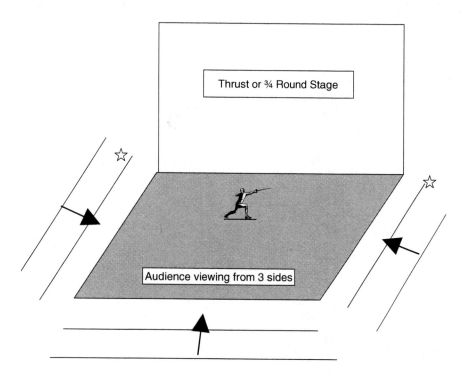

Thrust or ¾ Round Stage

Audience viewing from 3 sides

The single remaining wall in a thrust stage may be architectural, painted, or draped with one or more exit/entrance points for actors. The stars on this diagram indicate not ducal, but "cheap seats," usually sold last because the view of the wall and frequently the performers is reduced. For costume designers, thrust stages allow more intimacy with the audience, so attention to costume detail must rise. Audience members will generally be closer to the stage than when the "mystic gulf" allows a few shortcuts.

For lighting and sound designers, the thrust stage allows a fuller artistic palette. Light thrown on the stage floor becomes a visual focal point, and creates space, time, mood, and patterns as realistic as sunlight through trees or as abstract as swirling blends of color. The challenge lies in lighting all parts of the stage and each actor anywhere on that stage without spilling light onto unwilling audience members. Sitting in stage light spill can be embarrassing, uncomfortably warm, and can distract focus.

The thrust stage similarly challenges and frees sound designers. They have the opportunity to wrap the audience in sound coming from multiple directions. They must, on other hand, control and balance that sound so that half of the audience isn't blown away while the other half barely hears it.

Arena or Full Round Stages

In some ways, theatre architecture has come full circle with the arena or full round stage. As with Ook (see Chapter 2) gathering his clan around the fire to perform his lion hunt, the arena stage gathers the audience in a circle around the stage. In the diagram, the first thing you might notice is that no place exists for walls, drapes, or large units of scenery because the audience is looking at the stage from every direction. The stage floor becomes more central as a design component as many scenic elements are hung above the stage or very strategically placed. The audience tends to be even closer than in thrust stages. The challenge becomes a need for brilliant simplicity in design. Anything of any mass or height blocks sight lines. For the costume designer, the intimacy increases the need for detail. For lighting and sound designers the challenges of balance and focus become even stronger.

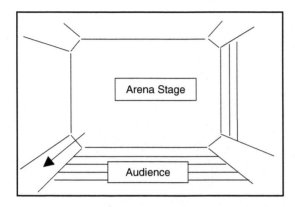

However, increased communion with the audience, a strong sense of being close together physically and psychologically, rewards all of these challenges. The audience member can't help but see other audience members on all sides, and this can powerfully increase a sense of community.

Environmental Stages

The fourth stage is as ancient as theatre itself and as cutting edge as today's news. The environmental stage is any space designated by an agreement between audience and performance as a theatre. In fact, in some *avant garde* theatre, the audience is left out of the agreement. An environment space may be as intimate as a private living room or a big as the wide-open prairie. Street corners and alleyways, churches, town halls, market places, warehouses, ruined buildings, mountaintops, and clearings in the forest can all serve.

The level of design challenge is dependant entirely on the level of control desired, sometimes with nothing altered and sometimes with an intricate creation built in the found space. Environmental stages can provide some of the most magical theatre experiences. They are certainly the kind of stage used by our primal theatrical ancestors. They are the most fleeting and delicate of the five types of stages because as soon as we leave them they disappear, reverting back to what they were before we came to see a performance. If the environmental stage is in the town square, just about anyone passing by can see it, so it can be the most egalitarian and communal of stages. On the other hand, if the stage is someone's private home, it may be the most elitist (designed to keep the riffraff out) or the riskiest (if the authorities are watching). Look for theatre staged in non-traditional spaces, as they are sometimes brilliant, and always intriguing.

Black Box Theatres

By far the most popular choice for contemporary production is the black box or flexible staging space, which is essentially a large box shaped room, usually painted all black.

If equipped with versatile, moveable, flexible seating, lighting, and sound, this space can become whatever the production team wants. It can be (with a frame inserted) proscenium, thrust, or arena by simply reconfiguring the audience/actor proximity. It can become a stadium or corridor theatre with audiences on both sides of the action, like in a football field. The audience can be subdivided in countless creative ways or even moved from stage to stage rather than having the scenery change. For many, the black box is an almost limitless theatrical toy for those conceiving a production, and an ever-changing adventure for audiences who arrive not quite knowing what to expect.

The two basic approaches in live theatre are to design each element from scratch for each new production or to design elements that will be re-used again and again. We will look at the basic processes of show-specific design and discuss one example of permanent design in each section below.

SET DESIGNER

History

For thousands of years, the position of set designer did not exist. Throughout the world, productions occurred in spaces that varied little from show to show. Today, show specific scenery is still rare in traditional Asian and African theatres.

In Europe, it was not until production moved indoors that the responsibility of creating an acting space became constant. Pioneers included Italians Sebastiano Serlio (1475–1554) and Bastiano da Sangallo (1481–1551), followed by their countryman Giacamo Torelli (1640–1719). Jean Berain (1640–1711) of France, and Englishman Inigo Jones (1573–1652) experimented in their respective countries. In fact, credit goes to Inigo Jones for introducing the proscenium stage in England.

When the theatre moved indoors in Europe, it became the plaything of the privileged classes and lavish proscenium theatres sprang up under the patronage of royal or aristocratic families. The designers worked in two dimensions, creating intricate sets of canvas scenery, using two- or three-point perspective to create the illusion of depth. They often used and discarded these magnificent works of art after one evening's entertainment, despite the outrageous expense.

Later, when theatres became more commercial again, even the most heavily subsidized theatre could only afford a set of stock scenes: perhaps a formal interior, an informal interior, a street scene, and a "pastoral" or outdoor scene. These four designs would be used for each production until they wore out or burned up (a frequent event—canvas plus oil paint plus candles for lighting equals flammable scenery!).

By 1800, the scene designer became essential, and during the nineteenth century with the influence of the Meiningen Players (see Chapter 4), play-specific scenery was expected. The box set, or one which is built like a box with the one side open through which we look, dominated the nineteenth century proscenium stage until the legendary scenic artists Adolphe Appia (1862–1928) and Edward Gordon Craig (1872–1966) moved the art further forward into imagination.

Probably the three most widely renowned artists of the present day include the late Jo Melzeiner (1901–1976), Josef Svoboda (1920–2002), and Ming Cho Lee (b. 1930). Each of these five designers moved design away from a realistic, detailed box set to more abstract and metaphoric settings that carve space fluidly and evocatively without literal limitations. They have moved out of cluttered detail into minimalist, spare, and elegant creations.

Post-modern designers (a movement starting in the early twentieth century) now think nothing of combining realistic and abstract scenic elements in the same space. While the box set remains popular because so many "domestic" plays are set in someone's living room, even in these plays we are now more open to experimentation, fragmentation, and scenic surprise. Some designers who describe themselves as "post-modern" experiment with "random" design, attempting to avoid pattern, meaning, and concept by literally scattering pieces of scenery on the stage. These designers represent one extreme of the design pendulum. In contrast, some forms of theatre don't use scenic designers at all, because tradition defines the space. The stage itself is pre-designed to give symbolic meaning to every aspect. At this end of the pendulum, we find the traditional Noh stage.

The Noh theatre of Japan exemplifies tradition that does not embrace the idea of show-specific scenic design. Few stage designs are more firmly rooted in tradition and symbolism than this elegant style of presentation. The stage design was "set" during the fourteenth century, and the only changes are found in the tiniest details where individual artists disagree on "correct" and "incorrect" designs. Few Noh stages have been constructed since the early twentieth century, and one Japanese authority speculates that it may be impossible to build one today—the right woods and materials would be massively expensive, if they are available at all. Above is a diagram of the Noh stage. Each Noh play fits the space, not the other way around.

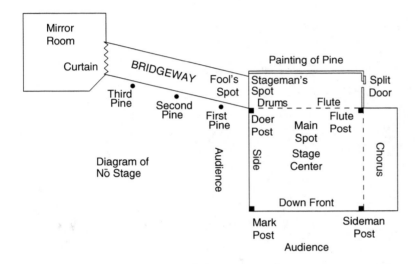

The mirror room is the actors' dressing room, and each character makes a first entrance across the bridge of three pines. The entrance is a critical moment, and it can take minutes for an accomplished actor to make the short journey. The audience is on two sides, making this a type of thrust stage, and the chorus, usually composed of eight people, is in full view. The chorus supports the primary actor, narrating the story, singing in accompaniment, sometimes even speaking the character's thoughts aloud. Most Noh plays feature two characters, and the stage space is relatively small to accommodate them. Clay jars hang under the stage (in exact locations dictated by tradition, those exact locations being an insider secret) at 45 degree angles, functioning to amplify sound. Each image, each board in the stage floor, even the style of roof tiles used to house the stage is deeply symbolic and aesthetically unified. The Noh drama and the Noh stage link inseparably so that one doesn't happen without the other.

In the following section, we will look at the basic processes of the scene designer in theatres that produce shows designed somewhere between the extremes of post-modern randomness and Noh stage immutability.

Scene Design Processes

The set is the first thing the audience sees. If the front curtain remains open in a proscenium theatre, they may see it for as much as a half-hour from when the house opens until the show begins. This first look can set the tone of the production, reveal the time and locale, set the basic style, establish mood and atmosphere, and introduce the concept. It can suggest a lot about the kind of people who will inhabit this world, even before we meet them.

Set designers need a strong sense of the history of art and architecture and of the theatre itself to be able to draw on past elements or recreate these eras. They also need to understand construction, carpentry, and all the methods needed to build their creations. Unless they specifically specialize in historical artifacts, designers need to stay on top of developments. Scenery is no longer based just on wood, canvas and paint as it was for many years but may involve thermoplastics, Styrofoam, molded Plexiglas, expanded polystyrene (EPS), urethane, vacuforms, and an ever increasing use of metal alloys. It also may involve projections. Designers need to be computer savvy and up to speed on technology. Designers also need to have strong analytical skills, the ability to read a text or imagine an evolving production, and to "see" the event in the space provided.

Clearly, the configuration of the theatre itself will strongly influence design. These questions will as well:

1. What number and kind of scene changes will be needed for shifts in locale?

2. How many entrances and exits will be needed, and what will their placement be? How many windows, doors, or any other openings will be needed?

3. Will the set require levels or platforms or will all action be on stage level?

4. Will there be isolated items such as trees, columns, or rock formations? Will there be furniture, if so how much and what kind?

5. Will exits and entrances require escape-step units leading offstage for the actors to return to stage level or to prepare for entrances, and how will this effect backstage space?

6. How will masking block the audience's view of backstage areas beyond the set itself, if at all?

7. Will the set be built right on the stage, in a shop a few feet away or (as is the case for all Broadway shows) will it need to be transported from a studio across town and reassembled onstage?

8. Will the show be playing in repertoire or going on tour so it will need to be taken down and put back up repeatedly or will it be permanently ensconced?

9. Will set changes need to be done by stage-crew members or will they be motorized? Which will need to be done by hand, by flying set pieces in and out of the space above the stage or by moving them via elevators, wagons, treadmills or turntables?

10. How much, if any, of the set can be pieced together from units already in stock and taken out of storage? How much built from scratch?

Three Kinds of Scenery

It helps to break down all the myriad forms of scenery into three components. Much of it is cloth or some variation on a curtain. Some are solid but still one-dimensional units, requiring backing or support of some sort. Finally, some scenery is about mass.

1. **Soft Scenery**

Much of what you see in a theatre is drapes or hanging fabric. In a proscenium stage theater, at the very front may be the "act curtain" which might pull in from the sides like standard drapes at home or be raised and lowered from above the stage. As this opens you will note "borders" and "legs." Borders hang horizontally at the top of the opening to mask the fly space (where lighting instruments and scenery live when not in use). Legs hang vertically at the sides of the stage to mask the backstage area. They are often called "blacks," because of the usual color of choice. They define the stage in terms of what you can and cannot see. At the very back of the stage and covering all of that area, possibly even curving around the sides, may be a "cyclorama," a huge, white or light gray, tightly stretched curtain attached to pipes at its top and bottom. The "cyc" (pronounced "sike") receives light or other projections. As a play progresses and locales change, various "drops," stored in the fly system above the stage may lower onto the stage to represent a new location and fly out when the next change occurs. A "scrim" is a gauze curtain, which seems opaque when lit from the front but becomes transparent when lit from behind. These are popular for dream sequences, appearances by ghosts, and other abstract moments. The act curtain and any of the drops may also be scrims, seen as solid at one point in the play, yet transparent at another.

Any of the items above may be stock scenery pieces in a proscenium theatre, used in show after show. However, the designer might create them for a specific production, such as an act curtain that has a painted mural of the town in which the play is set, legs that are trees instead of simple blacks, and borders that are clusters of leaves.

2. **Hard Scenery**

Some set pieces are constructed more solidly so they can stand and support themselves or be stood upon. Traditionally these are "flats," frames of wood covered by stretched canvas. Increasingly flats may actually be lauan (pronounced "lew-an"), a thin sheet of wood or some other solid, hard-surfaced material instead of just a canvas so that the entire piece is hard. These have the advantage of not damaging as easily as stretched canvas and not shaking on contact. Flats are put together to create walls, doors, windows, fireplaces, arches, castle walls, prison cells, anything that must sustain the illusion of a constructed surface. Whenever something needs to appear absolutely solid, but still needs to take up very little deep space, a hard set unit is likely to appear.

3. **Dimensional Scenery**

The first two types of scenery are flat. Some settings may also use staircases, ramps, and platforms or they may require freestanding, three-dimensional forms such as columns, hills, rock formations, tree trunks, porches, or any other "island" formation that may be approached from various sides, and need to be constructed with considerable support. These units may be light and fragile if they primarily are used for scenic effect, or they may require great stability if actors will perform on them.

Sketches to Models

The set designer draws—first in rough sketches—to enhance discussions with the director and other designers. She may bring in artwork including drawings from other sources for discussion as well. At some point, these will evolve into perspective sketches that begin to look like the actual set, and then, once approved, into renderings that will look like a painting of the set as it will appear upon completion. Accompanying these will be floor plans, which are essentially blueprints drawn to scale with the exact measurements to guide the construction crew. The combination of these blueprints and elevation drawings (rear, front, side, painters) are needed for each of the three-dimensional set pieces under construction. Often the designer will create one or more scale models of the set, which are small replicas like dollhouse versions. The director may use a model to work on blocking the play or it may live prominently in the shop as a reminder of what this thing is supposed to become when it's done.

If the designer will be constructing her own set, the precision of these drawings is less crucial than in those instances where a professional designer may only visit the "construction site" a few times in the process, and the paperwork needs to speak for itself. In these latter instances, where the designer may be out of the country and not available, clarity is crucial.

While some set designers assume responsibility for everything in the acting space, if there are special needs such as a very particular piece of furniture or any hand-held item, an artisan with specific skills may be recruited. Therefore, a production may have a separate prop designer and set decorator.

Media Set Design

Except in science fiction and fantasy, Western film seldom embraces theatricality where sets look like sets (as in *Moulin Rouge* or *Chicago*), so media design is for the most part much less abstract and fanciful. Films often shoot on location using the real thing instead of a set. When that is not possible, the set is often a recreation of the real thing down to the last detail. Sitcom sets on the other hand, filmed before a live audience, are often like old-fashioned box sets where we peek into someone's living room and kitchen. The creation of such sets is not unlike that for domestic plays.

In most media settings, detail, texture, and surface treatment become far more important than overall look since the audience rarely sees the whole thing in long shot and often sees it so close up that it must pass scrutiny. Because of the cost of moving from set to set, movies are filmed wildly out of sequence. Anything taking place in one location is filmed before moving on to the next, no matter how far afield that is from the progression of the story. Sometimes they create a set in miniature for what ends up looking like a long shot on film. Increasingly computer effects enhance or entirely replace spectacular sets in place of major construction.

Personal Set Design

In the theatre of your life, to what extent is setting crucial? You have designed your living space whether you are consciously aware of it or not. Look at your current home environment and see what you discover about the scene designer in you. You may find that you embrace post-modern randomness, and you tend to throw stuff around without thought. You may find that you have re-constructed a space based on memories of an earlier time and/or place in your life. If you were to propose to your beloved, declare your freedom, honor a memory, or declare a significant change in your lifestyle, diet, addictions or connections, to what extent is it important that this occur in the right setting? Do you envision events in their settings? Do you have ideas all the time about improving a place with some imagination?

COSTUME DESIGNER

Costumes are like scenery that constantly moves, but they are far more than that. Costume design is the most personal and intimate of design challenges because the audience experiences the actor and costume as one. In a production-specific design, a costume is created for a particular actor playing a role in a particular production. It is inextricably interwoven with the performer who inhabits it. The evolution of this costume requires complete collaboration and trust between performer, director, and designer.

> **William Ivy Long, *costume designer, formerly a set designer***
>
> "I feel I need psychodrama in my life. I found there's more interaction with people in costume design than in set design ... there's nothing more basic and more right on the line than the fitting room. There's the mirror and there's the actor and there you are."

History

Costumes have always been part of theatre though the earliest ones in any culture were likely to be ceremonial robes for rituals, often religious in nature or found items such as Ook using the lion skin to become the lion (see Chapter 2). Until the advent of realism in the nineteenth century, costumes in Western theatre were generally more about making a spectacular impression than reflecting the actual life of the character. Actors pulled costumes from the theatre's stock of clothing (perhaps donated by a wealthy patron).

Flamboyance was not restricted to Western theatre. In the *kathakali* school of Indian dance drama, a tradition some 300 years old, costumes thrill and transport the audience from the world of everyday life to one of magic, mystery, and eternity. *Kathakali* divides characters and their costumes into five types rather than specific individuals. The types are "green," "knife," "beard," "black," and "polished." The costumes and makeup reveal the internal nature of the mythic character and have no connection to realism. The scene design for *kathakali* theatre is absolutely minimal: a half-curtain used to delay the impending arrival of certain dangerous character types, a lamp, and a stool. But the costume designs more than make up for the sparseness of the stage.

It may take as long as four hours to get into these costume and makeup combinations and as many as two hours to take them off. The *kathakali* traditionally happens outdoors, beginning at dusk and continuing through the night. Actors are mute, the costume tells the audience who and what they are. The chorus, unassumingly costumed in dark colors, sings, chants, and performs the dialogue, while the actor uses the costume to embellish mimed action as the chorus speaks it. Although bound by tradition, each *kathakali* master is responsible for his own costumes. One contemporary master confessed that one of his costumes could run as high as $25,000! Not surprisingly, when a new costume is required, he sends the old one to the construction artists to salvage any usable fabric or ornamentation.

Processes

Today, it is rare for any production to ignore the impact of costumes. Even a very casual improv troupe is likely to share some unifying element (all may wear black, Hawaiian shirts, or company T-shirts) to separate performers from audience and to create a company identity. Costume designers must consider the practical as well as artistic needs of the production. In addition to all the design elements discussed so far, he needs to ask:

1. Is the play going to be true to its period of origin or an "interpretation" of that period with some contemporary elements? Will it move to another period altogether, or perhaps become a collage where characters from various historical periods meet? To what extent will the same be true of place and style and how will this influence the costumes?

2. What should the costume reveal about each character's job, status, style, age, sex, and the degree to which this person is unique or like others in the play? How will it define her personality and relationship to others and how might that change as the story progresses?

3. Is the costume going to take focus or blend with others? Should the costume appear to be shiny new or does it need to be aged in some way? Will it need to look worn and faded and require paint, dye, bleach, staining, brushing, tattering, or other distressing techniques? Will it need to seem to start one way and end the other?

4. Will all audience members view the costume up close in an intimate space or from a considerable distance to the actors?

5. Does the costume need to alter the actor in some way? Does it need to emphasize or diminish some feature? Should it make this person more or less attractive or ugly, thin or heavy, old or young, or distinct or universal? Or, is a major alteration needed since the character is flora or fauna, or some other fantasy creature?

6. Was this costume chosen by the character or imposed in some way as in uniforms, sexy outfits chosen by one's "sugar daddy," or adaptations made to be allowed to join or be accepted?

7. Are there particular movement demands? Do characters dance, squat, fight, faint or fall? Do they run up staircases or leap off parapets? Should they be restricted—as in a skirt too tight to walk in, or an outfit so oversized the character is overwhelmed and can barely make a gesture?

8. Are rehearsal costumes needed to help the actor learn to work in unfamiliar garments such as corsets, trains, capes, or other variants from standard contemporary clothing?

9. Can any items be rented, borrowed, or drawn from costume storage? Can any be bought at new, used, or vintage clothing stores? Or, will this show be built from scratch?

10. Will the actor need to change costumes? If so, will these be quick changes or will they require assistance?

Basic attributes needed by the costume designer include a strong historical background, rendering skills, knowledge of cutting, draping, patterning, and sewing, as well as the ability to show in drawing form the placement of seams, darts, pleats, and other details. While staff may include pattern drafters, drapers, cutters, tailors, stitchers, fitters, wardrobe supervisors, and dressers as well as hair and make-up specialists, it may also include few or none of the above, so the designer has to be able to do it all. In the same way, the designer attends to details like undergarments and shoes rather than just the major garment, attention also goes to the look of the actor from the neck up. The design may include a specific hairdo or wig and make-up for each actor, particularly if the show is extremely stylized and/or actors will look nothing like their offstage selves.

The costume designer's medium is primarily fabric. Swatches (small samples of fabric) are crucial in early conferences, and shopping is a major part of the process. The texture and bulk of the fabric, whether it is sleek or rough, wrinkled or smooth, shiny or flat, supple or stiff and how it reflects or absorbs light, how it drapes, how it clings to or hides the body, all matter. Even the sound it makes (think taffeta vs. corduroy) affects performance.

The process is likely to go from rough sketches through various evolutionary stages to full-color renderings. The fabric is purchased, patterns are drafted, material is cut, parts are basted together, and fittings begin. Once stitching is completed, trim or ornamentation (fringe, feathers, lace, ribbons, etc.) and accessories (purses, hats, belts, umbrellas, gloves, muffs, scarves, and jewelry) are finally added. The actor is rarely called in for less than two fittings and may be involved in many more. A costume chart will finally be prepared to guide changes throughout the performance.

Contemporary Asian theatre often follows the Western model and professional set and costume designers study in England or America. In the more traditional theatre forms, because "start from scratch" design is infrequent, key positions such as prop master and wardrobe mistress take on significant status, with many years of training, in history and culture as well as theatre. These highly respected experts are often as much archivists as designers. In the Beijing Opera or *Jingju* (see Chapter 8), for example, construction companies may produce the same costume in ten colors plus black and white as a part of stock and then selectively re-use them. Working even as a *Jingju* dresser (several steps down the ladder from the "mistress") requires two to four years intensive training, because costumes have so many layers and ways of being presented. Dressers then specialize in headgear/jewels, inner garments, or outer garments. Until late in the past century, dressers needed to keep hundreds of costume plots in memory because all detail was passed on in the oral tradition. Written documentation of this information occurred only in recent years. The wardrobe mistress oversees everything from costume production to storage. The storage system is elaborately codified with costumes placed according to the status of the character and as if the garments themselves have attitudes. For example, tradition requires that the emperor's yellow *mang* is stored third from the top under the red and green *mang* robes so that it (the costume) does not become too self-important.

Media Costume Design

The intense scrutiny of the close-up influences the work of the media costume designer as it does the set designer. In fact, partial costuming, like partial nudity, can look complete by the clever use of camera angles. Stage designers may select many fabric patterns that look a certain way from a distance of a hundred feet or more. Some of these would seem overstated, even garish, viewed up close and personal through the lens. The texture and detail of fabrics become crucial on camera, and here subtlety of design works well—though such costumes transferred to a large theatre might seem hopelessly bland. A costume designer wishing to work in both areas needs to quite effortlessly dial up and down.

Media stars often have their own designers who are not infrequently from the world of fashion rather than costuming. The designer for everyone else will then need to work around, adapt to these very visible garments at the center of the film, and make the whole thing appear somehow unified. Contemporary films are often entirely shopped, so the designer's skill involves finding what's out there that will work rather than in creating it. Because many highly successful modern films are not contemporary realism, the opportunity to create fanciful, elaborate, stylized, and period fantasy ensembles is becoming more frequent than in live theatre. Period films like *Vanity Fair* and *House of Flying Daggers*, and fantasy films like *Lord of the Rings*, *Star Wars*, and *The Village* are giving media costume designers fun opportunities to strut their stuff.

Costuming Yourself and Others

To what extent do you plan your outfits and put together all the accessories as opposed to just throwing something on? Do you change styles and master each new one? Or have you developed a distinct look that does not vary until it is time for a major change? Do you make wise and informed predictions about peoples' behavior based on how they dress? Do you see some people on the street and deeply covet their outfits or feel like the fashion police about to make an arrest? Do you look over any group and make silent judgments about fashion faux pas? Do others tend to seek your advice before making a major garment purchase? Or do all these questions leave you somewhat speechless, even clueless? Are you someone who is just glad to find something clean and not too wrinkled as you face each new day? Either way, you are designing yourself each day by your choice of attire.

Make-Up Designer

Make-up helps communicate age, condition, and attitude of an individual character as well as the general style of a production. In large spaces where lighting can wash out facial features, make-up helps restore color and form to individual faces and aids the actor's expression. As vital as make-up design can be, this is one staff position that many productions do not include. Actors must to learn to do their own make-up and to purchase their own make-up kits whether that means creating the effect of realistic street wear or the stylized extravagance of *kathakali* makeup. A specialist is likely to be employed for extreme alterations in appearance. In film, in part because of the intense scrutiny of the camera, make-up artists are essential.

Jerry Williams, *make-up designer*

"A skilled make-up artist has tremendous power to transform actors, sometimes making them totally unrecognizable. It's like giving them extreme plastic surgery for a few hours of disguise each day."

The basic categories for stage make-up are:

1. Straight—Getting the actor's face to "read" at the back of the house without actually altering his features.

2. Corrective—Making the actor generally more attractive and vivid in appearance, much like the purpose of street make-up

3. Age—Adding years to an actor's appearance. This is a challenge far more common in educational than professional theatre. Directors cast students in roles beyond their years while pros are more likely to play close to their own ages.

4. Character—Changing the actor in a significant way to suggest an entirely different background and personality than that of the performer. This is the most fun category as false noses, beards, scars, warts, jowls, temporary tattoos and the entire range of prosthetic devices (think Austin Powers' bad teeth) may be employed for a stunning transformation.

5. Stylization—Creating a visual impression outside of the natural where characters may be supernatural, animal, mythical, or abstract rather than real. Non-western theatre employs this last category at great length, but we can also see it in Broadway hits like *Cats*.

The basic make-up implements are: a base to cover the face; highlight and shadow (lighter and darker tones) to punch up or recede features; liner and mascara to bring out the eyes; rouge to give the face some color; an eyebrow pencil to define brows and create shadow; brushes and sponges to help apply all of the above; powder to set it and cold cream and tissues to remove it at the end of each performance. These elements would be in any actor's basic kit but may be supplemented by hair whitener, hairpieces to be converted into facial hair or extensions of such, spirit gum to attach hair and an infinite variety of plastics, rubber, and latex materials to exaggerate features beyond what is possible through highlight and shadow. Items such as noses and jowls may be pre-constructed or designed specifically for a performance. False eyelashes, colored eye shadow, lipstick, and all the other ingredients employed in offstage "glamour make-up" may also be included.

If an actor's make-up is particularly challenging, the designer or an assistant apply it at each performance. Far more often, specialists instruct the actor during various dress rehearsals, and provide a make-up plot, then the responsibility moves to the actor for the actual run of the show.

The designer may provide a kit with the non-standard items the actor needs and possibly a chart with a drawing of a face to remind performers of the specific details. Often photographs are taken of actors in full make-up and these are mounted on their dressing room mirrors to provide guides during the run.

MASK DESIGNER

Early Western theatre and many forms of Asian and African theatre to this day use masks instead of make-up or some combination of the two. For many years actors had no "papparazi" or crazed fan problems because their offstage appearance differed so radically from their onstage look. Transformation was the goal, not self-merchandizing. Sometimes this is still true today. The American performance group Blue Man Group has played to rave reviews and packed houses on Broadway for over fifteen years, and now have on-going productions in three other American and several foreign venues. Yet few of us would recognize any of the cast members: three bald men painted entirely blue. Their makeup has become a mask, which hides their identities and transforms each performer into a creature of myth.

In mask theatre, whether classical Greek tragedy from the fifth century BCE, ancient Yoruban masked plays about the god Ogun, or the 300-year-old tradition of the Noh theatre, one thing binds the work of the mask designer—the mask itself is seen as a transformative talisman. When the mask is "off-duty," the owner treats it with care and reverence because it contains within it the spirit of the character conveyed. When combined with the power of the actor, the two join in a sort of communion that empowers both mask and actor to leap into the mythic realm.

Most mask designers are artists who learned from masters who came before them. Some discover on their own that they have a gift for creating inanimate objects that can seem alive when worn by an accomplished actor. Masks may be designed based on long-standing tradition or created for a specific production. They may be constructed from any number of materials and may cover all or only part of the actor's face.

> **C. Scott, *theatre historian***
>
> "As both a sacred object and a means for making the wearer sacred the mask has a long history. The actor wearing a mask is no longer a prisoner of his own ego or inhabited by the conventions of everyday speech and movement."

In live theatre, the mask designer remains the closest tie to the ancient idea of magical transformation. The creator of a mask must combine artistry with craft to create the illusion of life in wood, paper, clay, or any other material.

Most of us have experienced the work of the mask designer in events that call for some kind of festival atmosphere—like Mardi Gras, Halloween, and costume parties. In our culture, the mask is sometimes used to take advantage of the anonymity granted the wearer. You may have attended a Halloween party and been amazed and dismayed at the behavior of a friend who thought they were hiding behind a mask. We may associate masks with dark characters in horror films like *Halloween* and *Scream*, or with license to misbehave in films like *Eyes Wide Shut*, or with super powers like in *The Mask*.

In most live theatre traditions, however, the comic, the lewd, the evil, the heroic, and the virtuous come to life by combining the spirit of the mask with the artistry of the performer who wears it. The actor may remain anonymous, but the mask designer creates the means and the tool, that lets us transcend day-to-day life and experience something larger and more universal.

LIGHTING DESIGNER

"Remember me in light!!" cries the Old Actor in the famous musical *The Fantastiks*. This could be the rallying cry for all actors and everyone else who works in the theatre. No matter how brilliant our work, if it is not lit or is lit badly, we're dead. Lighting designers have the godlike power to plunge us into darkness, to distort, dismiss, or destroy our best efforts—or to enhance, enrich and enlighten them.

> **Jennifer Tipton,** *lighting designer*
>
> "Light can change the world in a mysterious and compelling way that is not true of directing, set or costume design. Lighting can confuse or clarify. It is the audience's guide to the story."

History

There have always been lighting effects. From the earliest moments in history, rituals and ceremonies have been timed to coincide with the rising or setting of the sun, the shape or size of the moon and resulting light. Fire has always been used to create light and shadow. Bonfires, torches, lanterns and candles have been crucial to the desired effect since the beginning of time. No matter how much technology has intervened, we seek these nature-sourced effects in our lives now as much as did the ancients.

In performances during the Middle Ages, shiny metal surfaces were used so that fire could reflect off them. In the Renaissance, stained glass was employed so light could be seen shining through it. At that time, fireworks became a crucial part of major celebrations. For many years, theatrical productions were mounted outdoors in the daytime just to capture and preserve the light.

When Western theatre moved indoors, about 1600 (though sometimes earlier in Italy), candles and oil lamps were employed. When gaslight came along in 1803, lighting took a major step forward. Alas, the combination of spaces crowded with people and flammable light sources ended in tragic consequences often enough to create alarm.

With electricity, stage lighting turned into a major art. Not only was it now possible to control effects, but incandescent lighting was clearly safer than open flames. Theatre artists jumped on this new and miraculous development. In fact, electric stage lighting first appeared in American theatres in 1879, the same year Thomas Edison invented the light bulb—many years before municipal power plants made it available to commercial buildings and private residences! When the spotlight came on the scene in the twentieth century, the art form came into its own, and computer technology has recently made it soar. In the 1980s, automated lighting emerged, and by the end of that decade, the invention of Intellabeam lighting instruments made it possible for lights to change their focus and color and to move without a person running each of them, requiring instead a single person at a control board.

Throughout the years, lighting has always benefited from new technology—even while much of the labor in other design areas is still painstakingly done by hand. Almost 1000 instruments may be used for a big Broadway show, but even a college production may use hundreds. A thousand light cues is not unusual, yet, if accurately wired into the right circuits, these can all be handled easily by one person at the control board.

Lighting design involves determining the following qualities:

1. Intensity—How many instruments will there be, and how high will the wattage be? What will be the distance between the lights and their "targets"?

2. Direction—From what angles will light hit objects and characters?

3. Spread—How focused or diffused will the light be? How is it distributed across the stage?

4. Color—Which filters will be used? Which color sources will be mixed and in what proportion?

5. Movement—How will lights be raised and lowered and when? How will various areas of the stage be illuminated or cast into darkness, and in what rhythmic pattern?

While the large number of women costume designers is not surprising, given their association (at least in public consciousness) with dressmaking, it is noteworthy that some of the most revered lighting designers have been women: Jean Rosenthal, Tharon Musser, Jennifer Tipton, and Peggy Eisenhauer.

Chris Parry, *lighting designer*

"I can't paint or draw so this is how I do it. I use what I call light paintbrushes."

A lighting designer can turn technology to art and paint without paint. Questions the designer considers:

1. How much light will need to seem "real," coming from believable sources such as streetlights, sunlight, moonlight, headlights of cars, lamps, or fires? How much will be about mood and style?

2. How much will light suggest time, weather, or season? How important is this to establishing basic information and moving the plot forward?

3. How will the light change as the fortunes of the central characters do?

4. How much will be direct and how much will be broken up by gobos (filters that carve light into casting patterns like those created by leaves and branches for "dappled" sun or moonlight)? When will light need to achieve focus and when can it primarily create atmosphere?

5. How much front-, cross-, back- and down-lighting will be used and how bright or intense will each of these be?

6. To what extent do the light sources need to be hidden, or does it even matter that they and perhaps their operators are in full view of the audience?

7. Is the light going to carve the space or will it be used mainly for general illumination?

8. What, if any, are the special effects needed or wanted? Is there lightning, a fire, fireworks, or a snowstorm? Which projections are constant and which need to move, as in changing rains, clouds, flames, and/or smoke?

9. Will lighting areas generally have sharp, crisply defined edges or soft, undefined, diffused ones?

10. How will the rhythm of light be used? When will changes be rapid, abrupt, and sharp with sudden blackouts and equally unnerving sudden full washes of light? When will they be slow, languid segues in which light fades in and out with gentle, gradual deliberation? Lastly, when will they be in and out as opposed to cross-fades, where light declines from one acting area as it emerges in another?

Jules Fisher, *Lighting designer*

"Often my job is as much to remove light as to provide it."

Lighting designers need to know something of physics, electronics, principles of optics, the working capacity of the existing system, limitations of available instruments, lamps, electrical cable and connectors, what can be done with spotlights, striplights, floodlights, reflectors and what is possible within an existing budget. They need to master all three kinds of dimmers: resistance, autotransformers, and electronic. They need to command preset, master-control and memory banks. They need to keep up and to know when less is more.

Presenting and discussing lighting design with other members of the team provides unique challenges:

1. Drawings are particularly problematic for the lighting designer when consulting with the director and other designers because it is difficult to draw light. Computers have assisted in this process because one can, to some degree, play with light while in discussion, but many designers still refer to paintings because one can identify a quality of light from such sources, enhancing discussion.

2. How does the quality of light change things? Pure blue may convey cold or night, red may suggest heat or passion, green often radiates illness or panic. Glaring stark white light may convey interrogation or clinical sterility. A warm golden glow conveys warmth, security, or coziness. An important entrance of a major character might bathe that person in light in a doorway, so that her silhouette is vivid, but her actual appearance kept a shadow. In a confusing crowd scene with many people running every which way, light may pluck out the person to whom we should be attending. As a relationship changes, the quality of light may reinforce personal transitions.

Tharon Musser, *lighting designer*

"Lighting is such an intangible thing. Art books are a great way to demonstrate to a director the kind of color or texture you're thinking about."

Dawn Chiang, *lighting designer*

"Lighting design requires insight, innovation, and motivation. You need to rest and rejuvenate between projects. You cannot fully accomplish this work on an overtaxed schedule and too little sleep."

In the design process, values sketches, lighting scores and computer simulations, light plots, and instrument schedules may be employed. While lighting designers begin preparation early, work stops by necessity once initial consultation, research, and drawing is done, until the set and costumes are ready to be lit. It is impossible to set lights based on sketches; it is crucial to see how light hits that wall or pillar or that hat or gown before finalizing it. The designer cannot blindly proceed based on an impression of fabric for ball gowns or texture of columns but must experience the results of the other designers' work.

Media Light

Camera lighting is strongly connected to the work of the cinematographer who creates a film's visual canvas. Because the audience sees what the camera sees, focus is not as much of an issue. If filming takes place outside a studio, lighting equipment is constantly transported, and every day involves a new set-up. Except for action sequences, there is generally less actor movement in film. The camera is more likely to move, so this shifts emphasis.

In addition to the vast knowledge required of the stage lighting designer, the cinematographer (sometimes called director of photography or cameraman) needs to understand everything possible through the lens, in the developing lab and increasingly in post-production where lighting for a scene may be changed radically after the fact. New Super 35 cameras require fewer lights so the process is getting faster and less cumbersome, and more and more "digital doctoring" is taking place.

Cinematographers create an entire lighted world as in the sepia-tone settings of past *Godfather* films (now an almost standard period-piece convention) or the painterly light used by the renowned Conrad Hall in *Road to Perdition*. A highly qualified cinematographer is often considered essential to give a film weight and power.

Lighting Your Personal Theatre

Are you someone who does a hundred candles around the tub or candlelight dinners for romantic encounters? Are you the one with a dimmer switch or wish you had one? Do you select soft or tinted light bulbs and savor the glow of the fireplace even if it's not cold outside? Do you make every effort to avoid harsh overhead neon lights in favor of softer mood and area illumination? When you think of an idealized circumstance, is the quality of light always part of the picture? Do you try never to miss the sunset if you can catch it and savor it? Do you crave light to the degree that you always open the curtains in any room or space under your control? Or do you never even think about or notice such things? Some of us are constantly designing our life light whenever we can and revering what we can't, and some of us barely register it as part of existence.

SOUND DESIGNER

There is a whole auditory world of the play supporting and supplementing sound coming from actors. The sound designer is responsible for:

1. Mood music—from pre-curtain tunes that play as the theatre house opens through intermission musical interludes, possible curtain call music, and even potential post-show melodies that carry the audience out of the theatre at the end, the sound designer creates, sustains, shifts and controls mood. His work may also involve underscoring certain stretches of dialog and action (a convention far more often used in film) to enhance emotional response.

2. Sound effects—the script may require cues such as a car driving up and stopping outside, a thunderstorm, a gunshot, explosion, or siren, all of which need to be believable. Specific plot events and shifts in conditions need to be supported through sound.

3. Ambient sound—other effects, such as background sounds that can run continuously throughout a scene. The constant noises of big city traffic or rural crickets and birds may establish and sustain a sense of place.

4. Internal life—sounds may reflect the troubled state of a character—a throbbing heartbeat for nervous anticipation, discordant percussion as a character becomes unsettled or undecided, the sound of children in delighted laughter when someone experiences childlike euphoria on receiving great news. Sound can punch up a shocking revelation as in a door slamming (and the slam reverberating over and over as the character realizes that door will not open again) or the sounds of a storm intensifying outside as a relationship grows more "stormy" inside.

5. Amplification—in large theatre spaces, particularly for musicals, the sound designer may need to body-mike or hang amplification so that those who need to be heard can be. In some shows, a ghost or any other unearthly figure may be amplified to help separate them from the mere mortal characters.

Author's Insight

Robert: In Shakespeare's *Two Gentleman of Verona*, a major problem is how this guy (Proteus) who has always professed love for his childhood sweetheart (Julia) could drop her on the turn of a dime when he meets a new woman (Silvia). A recent production, besides using costume, make-up, and lighting effects to make Silvia seem like a goddess, also used sound. As soon as her name was mentioned, hot bluesy music started with other characters onstage undulating to it. When she made her entrance, others gasped. Proteus took one look and the clear sound of an arrow piercing a target told us all that his heart had been shot. (These sounds were invaluable in reinforcing his character transition from loyal boyfriend to besotted stalker.)

The designer's sound system includes at least three recorder/playback units for mixing from variable sources, digital or cassette recorders, equipment to alter sounds, microphones, turntables, a high quality speaker system, patch bay for interconnecting sources and amplifiers, computer memory storage and a control console for efficient operation.

Shannon Zura, *sound designer*

"I think my design work is stronger for having explored and practiced every other area of theatre as well. It is important to secure the broadest range of experiences possible."

Oddly enough, sound designers have only been allowed in the club for a very short time. It was 1986 before IATSE, the professional stagehands union, added a sound design chapter and 1993 before designers received standard labor contracts for Broadway shows.

Personal Sound Design

How sound sensitive are you? Are you part of the group who gets asked to leave a restaurant or bar because you are getting so boisterous and too big for the space you inhabit, or are you one of those who ask to have that group over there to shut up or be thrown out? Are you bothered by background noise while you study (unless it is exactly the music you have selected), or are you indifferent, even preferring the white noise of a radio or TV while you work? Are you very fussy about the quality of your sound system and the condition of your CDs and unable to comprehend how others can survive with low-grade systems and careless use? Or are you pretty much satisfied with that bargain unit? To what extent is the soundtrack of life important to you? Do you like your life supported by sound, and how important is it that you decide what that sound is? Or do all these questions make you ask what the fuss is all about?

DESIGN FOR THEATRE OR YOUR LIFE?

Until they are successful enough to have others execute their creations, all designers need to have both vision and the mechanical skill to execute that vision in concrete, practical ways. They are both artist and craftsman. Are you a scene designer? Have you always been interested in buildings and decor? Do you have some natural aptitude for drafting, construction, sculpture, architecture, conceptual space, or projections? Are you a costume designer? Have clothes always fascinated you, and can you identify the main differences in clothes from various decades and periods in history just because you have always noticed such things? Do you have knowledge of, or interest in, fabrics, dying, cutting and sewing? For both of the above, can you draw and paint? Can you show your ideas to others before they are finalized? Are you a possible lighting designer? Have you always been interested in mood lighting, levels, and the effect of light on any space or event? Are you light sensitive? Do you understand electrical work, control boards, and programming? Or are you maybe a sound designer with knowledge of music, sound effects, recording equipment and amplification, and a general fascination for mixing just the right party CD? Do you have a highly developed auditory awareness of the world around you?

Review the "are you" sections describing the work of each of these artists. In the theatre of your life, how important are any of these elements to you, and how much skilled attention do you pay to them? Is your apartment furnished with great care and skill? Do you sometimes sketch your future dream house? Does your wardrobe reflect an artist's sense of personal presentation? Do you always adjust light levels and produce background music for any social occasion from a wild open house, to private seduction, to even a casual gathering of pals?

If you have the intense fascination, but not the skills for execution, consider taking a few courses in your area of interest. Many skills can be trained. Some find out that they cannot make the leap from their head to their hands, but the most important ingredient is extreme interest.

Believe it or not in many theatres, one person does almost all the jobs described in this chapter! High school, small college, community and struggling professional theatre companies often have a single, dedicated (and frequently exhausted) human who drives the whole program and shapes each production. If you connect in any way with these one-person theatre phenomena, recognize and honor all that they do.

SUMMARY

Some theatre artists start their work long before the show goes into rehearsal. The designers (set, costume, makeup, masks, lighting, and sound) create the world in which all the directing and acting will occur. Their work is heavily influenced by the kind of theatrical space (proscenium, thrusts, arena, and environmental) in which they work. There are basic design principals (unity, variety, balance, focus, and progression) they all share yet each is unique in the process. They each must be both artist and craftsman with a unique capacity to envision and the practical skill to accomplish.

SUGGESTED ASSIGNMENTS

Questions for reflection, short writings and or discussion topics:

1. Examine the living room in your apartment or your room in the dorm and imagine it as a stage setting. Which wall should become the open fourth wall? What shifts in location of furniture and other props should occur for this to become a set?

2. On what occasions have you so altered your own or a friend's appearance that it could actually be called costuming and make-up? What was it like to have others respond to it?

3. Try to identify who in your life are the idea people and who are the can-do people. Do you know anyone who combines these qualities? What alignments make the vision and application possible? Do you know anyone at either position who is looking for that collaborative hook-up?

4. After examining the work of all these designers, what was the single event in your personal theatre where you filled as many of these jobs as possible in order to make it all happen?

5. Which design position intrigues you most as one you might consider for pursuing further training and experience? If you chose to have a life in the theatre, which of these would you wish to be?

6. Take any play being read but not viewed as part of your class. Do one or more of the following and write a justification for the choices you have made. Create:

   A. a costume for one male and one female character, drawing the clothing on the models provided.

   B. make-up plots for the same.

   C. a floor plan and/or a sketch of what you believe the set might look like, giving attention to staging and movement requirements.

   D. a sound design with a listing of essential effects, music to underscore, precurtain and post-curtain interludes.

   E. a description of how the light might be generally and how it might shift, including any special effects and moments when a transition in character development and story can be reinforced through light.

SUGGESTED ACTIVITIES

1. Individual—Pick a famous designer identified as a leader in the profession in this chapter. Google the person and write a brief report on his career and ideas.

2. Group—Choose a play and have each person in the group design a floor plan for a different type of theatre space. Discuss the challenges and how the sets adapted to the space.

3. Long term—See if you can get permission to sit in on the production meetings for a production, where each of these designers and their staff check in with each other weekly. What did you learn about how their work progresses?

4. Large group—Take a production or film the entire class has seen. Divide the class into five groups each of which is charged with coming up with a strong argument why sets, lights, costumes, make-up, or sound was the most important element. Have the teacher select the team with the strongest argument.

KEY WORDS AND IDEAS

Proscenium stage

Thrust stage

Arena stage

Environmental stage

Design ingredients—line, mass, color, texture, décor

Design principles—unity, variety, balance, focus, progression

Scene design—sketches, renderings, models

The Noh stage

Costume design – sketches, swatches, renderings

Kathakali costumes

Makeup Design—straight, corrective, age, character, stylization

Mask design

Lighting design—intensity, direction, spread, color, movement

Sound design—mood, sound effects, ambient, internal, amplification

THE PRODUCTION TEAM

CONTENTS

A HUGE production team may be behind a show. The past few chapters have been about those who, if they do well, receive attention and acclaim. Most theatregoers can name some playwrights, some directors, and many actors. While designers are not exactly household names, we can, when we see a show, identify their choices and respond to their contributions. The work of all these team members is in the foreground and they are, for better or worse, highly accountable.

This chapter is about the background team, unsung heroes who make vital contributions without public acknowledgement. Their work is crucial, but they labor almost entirely in obscurity. If you can name three people in any one of these professions, you are far more knowledgeable than the theatergoing public at large. These positions are found in some form in all the theatre traditions of the world. Job titles and duties shift with time, place, and custom, but in Brazil, Nigeria, England, or Japan, the same "behind the scenes" artists create, produce, manage, build and hold theatre together.

Some would argue that these theatre-makers are the ones who have the most fun, getting to take part in theatre magic without overwhelming scrutiny. They seldom receive reviews. They get no cheers, standing ovations, or raves, but also receive no jeers, pans, or public humiliation. Theatre production cannot function without them. Some are involved long before a show goes into auditions, some as late as opening week. They carry the play on their shoulders. We present them in the order in which they generally come on board. The simple chart below indicates the usual hierarchy of university and professional theatres in the West:

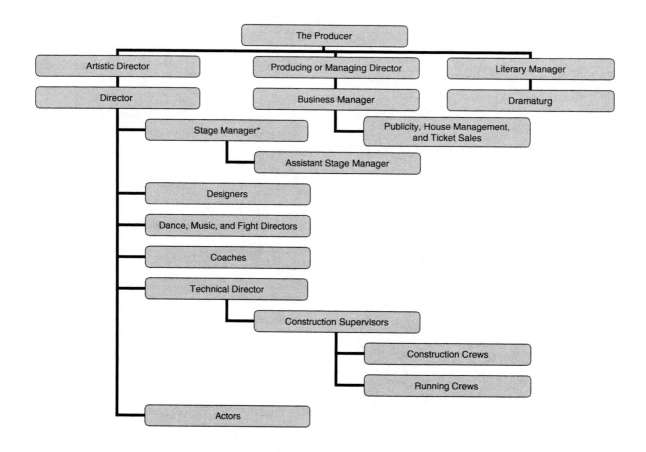

THE PRODUCER

The song says, "There's no business like show business!" and the producer is the business side of the show. While others may be more immediately involved in the artistic process, the show will not happen unless funds can be raised, contracts negotiated, script rights secured, royalties paid, staff hired and supervised, budgets set and enforced, rehearsal space rented, weekly payroll accomplished, investment reports made, performance space booked, promotion and publicity assigned and executed, posters and fliers printed and distributed, media ads designed and booked, tickets sold, and bills paid. In professional theatres, the producer may need to negotiate with eleven different unions and individual agents to iron out employee salaries and contract details. The producer is everything that is pragmatic about the art, and yet great taste is essential for picking the right project.

Daryl Roth, *producer*

"Producing is like an important birth as a new play is brought into the world. I advise producing only the works that speak to you, not the work that you think will speak to someone else. This is too hard a business not to feel deeply passionate about your show." (Ms. Roth is producer of five Pulitzer-prize winning plays.)

There have always been producers because there has always been a need for money. In various contexts, the producer might have been or may still be chorus leader, guild, royal patron, actor/manager or government agency. A producer may now be a single, freelance entrepreneur (in the commercial theatre), a whole board of directors (in a regional repertory company), a set of faculty members (in a university) or elected officers (in a community theatre). In these settings, usually someone is still lead-peer in the decision-making process. This job can be done solo or shared by an entire collective, but more and more often, it is shared. On Broadway, in recent years, it has been rare for there to be one producer, more often, there is a team of co-producers with a retinue of investors.

The producer needs strong artistic instincts and intuition, even if she is always one level away from direct participation, because the choice of the right show, the right staff and the day-to-day decisions about whether any element is worth the investment requires taste and aesthetic judgment as well as an ongoing sense of what will sell. The ability to balance bucks and beauty, vision and practicality is crucial. Common management wisdom is to hire the right people and then leave them alone to do their job. How alone the producer can leave them depends on how right she was to hire them.

Theatres may be commercial for profit or not-for-profit resident companies, which receive some tax breaks. These are roughly comparable to TV networks vs. PBS. For a freelance producer crucial costs involve the rental or booking of a space and raising backer capitol. For a resident theatre owning its own space, these costs shift to building and equipment maintenance, and the wooing of donors, grants, and endowments. Otherwise their responsibilities essentially remain the same. Many artists have dreams and great ideas for starting a theatre or mounting a show. The producer has the job of grounding those dreams in the fiscal world of facts, figures, and fund raising.

Artistic Director/Managing Director

In many resident theatre companies, the Artistic Director and the Managing Director (sometimes called the Executive Director or Business Manager) share producing responsibilities. In these situations, creative and fiscal components are sharply divided.

The artistic director is responsible for the overall image and vision of the theatre, for selecting the season of plays and the artists who will mount them and perform in them. The artistic director chooses directors, designers, actors, and other creative personnel. He offers guidance as each of these artists makes decisions along the road to opening night, and he often directs at least one play per season.

The managing director is involved in determining budgets and making sure everyone stays within them. She may be involved in determining salaries and production expenditures for scenery, costumes, lighting, props, or music. She is ultimately the supervisor for all business, promotional, box office, and front of house staff.

These personnel may intersect, for example, when the artistic director believes that a costume or set piece is not working and needs to be replaced. This creative judgment has to be processed by the managing director who must decide if the artistic change is worth the investment or if the show can survive relatively unscathed with the original choice. Often negotiation is involved.

Producing-Media and Life

You may have mounted a few major events in your time: some big parties, fairs or celebrations. Perhaps you have been involved with fund-raising. But very few of us have much in our offstage lives to prepare us to produce live theatre or media beyond understanding finances, investments, and budgets. There is no official training program or degree in producing, and those who succeed come from a diverse set of backgrounds. Clearly, training in business and in all aspects of theatre is useful. Because the producer needs to filter requests from all other staff, it helps to have walked in their shoes at one time or another, so taking classes and gaining production experience in each area helps. It gives you a stronger sense of the validity of each request or complaint. It also helps if you are known for your objectivity, for not getting swept up in volatile emotional or inconsequential causes. The producer needs to be a solid voice of reason, even when surrounded by extravagant "artistes" who may be just the opposite.

Media production is expensive. Staff sizes can quadruple for all the increased technical components. While many concerns are the same for live and media production, everything escalates for the latter. The film producer needs a more complex understanding of marketing since the target audience is not a specific, geographic cultural market but potentially the whole world. This also means that marketing costs alone may match the film's budget. While some Broadway musicals have major costs and financial risks, it dials up for almost any film.

Are you a regular producer of life events? You probably know this already because if you are, everyone always asks you to help put together the next big shebang. Do people who want to do things ask you if they can afford it or if you have any tips? Are you constantly recognizing where your friends' ideas have no back up, but instead of telling them to forget it, you are interested in exploring ways to make it happen? Are you simply good at cutting corners but still producing an impressive display? When others sink in despair in preparation for occasions, do you step in and offer concrete solutions that get them all back on track? Do you simply have an understanding of how art and commerce must always balance and co-exist without getting bent out of shape over that simple fact? You may be a producer.

Jeannine Woo, *dramaturg*

"As a dramaturg, you have a wonderful opportunity to take the script from a piece of literature to something that breathes with dynamic life."

THE DRAMATURG

Dramaturgy is often traced back to 1767 Germany when Gotthold Lessing became an "in-house critic" for the Hamburg National Theatre, and the position has gradually become standard throughout Europe, particularly in government-supported theatres. This is by far the newest member of the U.S. team, not a standard position here until near the end of the twentieth century. This staff member is least likely to end up praised or panned in reviews because the work is largely invisible. It involves doing research, asking questions, and trouble shooting in order to help the script reach its full potential in performance. A dramaturg may:

1. Explore different translations or adaptations of the script (if it first appeared in a foreign language) to help the director select the one most suited to this production's concept, or possibly assisting in creating a new translation and in cutting the text as well.

2. Research the author's life and other plays to provide background and perspective for the script.

3. Help the director with script analysis and the actors in character analysis by providing challenging questions and background information.

4. Conduct historical research on the period and country in which the play is set and the culture surrounding the play to create a rich context for the work.

5. Summarize critical essays written about the script and reviews of previous productions, so past responses can be scrutinized by the company efficiently while the production moves forward.

6. Attend rehearsals periodically and take notes, mainly with questions for the director about decisions that may appear unclear and interpretive choices that may not be those the director actually intends.

7. Prepare a study guide that will be sent out to instructors if school groups will be attending a performance to provide background and generate excitement prior to the field trip.

8. Provide program notes that will help educate the audience with a framework that will allow them to get the maximum experience out of watching the show.

9. Organize question and answer sessions after some performances and/or visits by the actors to classes and organizations to discuss and present excerpts, extending the influence of the ideas of the show.

10. Prepare and supervise site visits for director, designers and actors when a play deals with unfamiliar circumstances.

Author's insights

Annie: I was dramaturg for a production of *Death of a Miner*, a play set in an Appalachian coal community. We made arrangements to tour a working coal mine. It was so dark, cold and stifling; I know none of us were unchanged by the experience. The lives of the characters were much more real and visceral to us after spending time in their environment."

The role of dramaturgs as educated observers is frequently their most valued contribution. Having someone on the team who knows the play as thoroughly as the director, but who is not involved in every moment of every rehearsal provides much-needed objectivity. The real danger in any rehearsal is that we forget the audience member who was not there when we discovered all the glorious stuff we love, which may or may not be worth keeping. An informed observer who was not there for all those work sessions helps the company stay clear-headed. A good dramaturg does not get caught in the loop but keeps coming back from the perspective of a first-time audience member and asks those kinds of questions.

Author's Insights

Robert: I call these the Mertz questions after Fred and Ethel on *I Love Lucy*. I want a dramaturg who will constantly challenge the clarity of the production from the point of view of people who do not come to the show with a lot of intellectual baggage and may turn to each other at any moment and ask "Fred, why did he do that? I thought he loved that gal so why is he putting his boot on her face? And by the way, don't you ever try that with me!" I want the dramaturg to keep the show as clearheaded and accessible as possible."

In many theatres, the dramaturg is too expensive a luxury for the budget. In an academic setting, a director often selects a play more than a year before production and may choose to do the dramaturgy work herself. Since a campus is a hospitable setting for scholarly research, however, this is also the best environment for nurturing a student dramaturg in training. But in a professional repertory company, where a director may be hired weeks before rehearsals start and then be so busy that he has no time for outside research, the resident dramaturg is a tremendous aid. For example, when doing a period play, the question may arise "What were the courtship rules of the time?" "At what stage in the relationship can a man be alone with a woman, when might he first attempt to kiss her, when sit in her presence, and when embrace her publicly, without supervision?" If the production aims to be historically authentic, answers to these questions are important, and the dramaturg's contribution crucial.

Author's Insights

Annie: "The questions and challenge of finding answers are often the most fun for me. I have been asked "Who won the World Series in 1946?" and "What is 'bathtub gin'?" These may seem like miniscule details, but for the actor and/or director, knowing the right answer can lead to a whole new train of thought."

Sometimes a company will also employ a Literary Manager who may share some duties with a dramaturg, but will focus primarily on reviewing all the play scripts submitted for consideration, preparing analyses, and forwarding those believed to have potential for production. In some instances, the literary manager may also be involved in varying community outreach projects.

The Dramaturg in You

Do you have dramaturg potential? If the list above sounds appealing to you and you like to do research in general, in fact prefer it to production activity, you may be suited to this position. It is also essential that you be good at doing the research without getting caught up in it, allowing you to recognize what will and will not be noticed by an audience. It helps if you have a knack for asking questions rather than telling people what to do.

Are you the person who always does the research on a project while others will just jump in without it? Do you feel compelled to learn as much about the history and facts of any new undertaking, not just to protect yourself from rash choices, but because this adds pleasure and depth to your experience? Do you actually enjoy going to the library on a treasure hunt, delighting as one piece of information leads to a clue that leads to another? And when you share this information, do you tend to do so with contagious enthusiasm without inhibiting the less scholarly among your friends? Are you more comfortable behind the scenes than onstage? Do you have a keen sense of detail? Are you genuinely satisfied if you can make any event better by the research you did and do not really care if others get the glory? Do you always tend to ask probing questions others may not even have considered, but once they do, they realize how valuable these may be? Are you able to provide insights and alternative points of view without making others feel threatened? When you become fascinated with a person or period in history, do you almost automatically collect clippings and memorabilia to create lasting images? You may be the dramaturg of your group even if there is no "drama."

SPECIALISTS

Often experts with special skills are brought in to guide actors. These may involve coaching actors in skills not normally required for most productions.

J. David Brimmer, *fight director*

"Violence is a part of human nature. If we can examine it safely in the theatre, maybe we can process it without resorting to it in life. If people want reality, they can ride the subway. We're looking for the truth of the violence, not the reality."

Other Directors: Music, Fight, and Dance

The production's director may lack specific skills to stage portions of a production, or he may have the skills but not the time. These "extras" can require enormous rehearsal time and, for time management, employing specialists to work with some actors while others are rehearsing scenes in the play is advantageous. Each of these activities involves much to learn, coordinate, and make precise. A 30-second fight sequence may require at least that number of hours to make it clean, electrifying, and safe. A five-minute dance may require endless rehearsals to coordinate the moves for everyone onstage. Whenever basic human interaction stops or escalates into song, dance, or combat, the tension and exuberance of the production soars, but each of these have so many risks and possible pitfalls that they require skills, precision and time to be set and solid.

A **Music Director** may research possible underscoring for any show, including non-musicals, find appropriate choices, and recruit a composer. In a musical, this person will map out the orchestrated and/or sung sequences and take over the guidance of singers and orchestra so that all songs will basically be under his direction in consultation with the director. For productions such as those mounted by the Cirque de Soleil where music is a constant and vital part of the performance, such a position becomes crucial.

If there is any kind of combat, a certified **Fight Director**, with mastery of weapons and safe usage, may be employed. Tasks may include basic hand-to-hand moves such as slaps and punches, as well as the entire range of weapons from guns to swords. For period plays, it may involve rapiers, daggers, broadswords, halberds, or a host of other dangerous, historical weaponry. The fight director may also assist with risky physical maneuvers such as fainting or taking a fall where no contact is involved but the actor needs to be able to respond as if a blow has been struck, even if the source of that blow is internal.

At the point of emotional overload in musicals—when characters cannot contain themselves with mere words so they break into song—and when that uncontrollable impulse may escalate so far that they "gotta dance," the **Choreographer** needs to make this explosive expression seem inevitable and finally rewarding. Non-musical plays may have interludes requiring dancing, such as a ballroom scene, where the action continues but requires finesse through smooth and expressive movement. While music, dance, or fight directors are standard positions, the needs of a production may be more specialized.

Coaches

If you were playing the title role in *M. Butterfly*, you would probably work with someone trained in the arts of the *onnagata* (Japanese theatrical female impersonation) and *Geisha* in order to master countless details that would be outside the knowledge range of most directors and male actors. If you were playing a boxer, you would probably work with someone who coaches fighters. Auditions may test how much you already know or how comfortable you are with these performance modes to determine whether bringing in a coach is necessary.

Movement and voice or speech coaches may also help a cast achieve accomplishments that have not been part of their previous training. If a play takes place in a historical period with particular etiquette and movement conventions, a coach will be brought in to help everyone appear to have lived in another time. There may be instruction in how to breathe in a corset, how to maneuver a hoop skirt, how to keep a sword elegantly at your side (and not accidentally injure fellow cast members), how to hold a staff in the way of an experienced shaman, and a whole range of other adjustments out of your immediate comfort zone in another world.

If a director has no experience in classical speech, a coach may be brought in to help actors speak in a timeless, elegant fashion or just the opposite if actors cast as farmhands have no sense of how to sound genuinely rural. Probably the most common use of a speech coach is for dialects. Mastering how to sound Irish, British, Jamaican, German or Zimbabwean and then teaching them to others in ways that are comprehensible to audiences is a highly specialized skill. Stage dialect-coaching amounts to choosing evocative changes rather than recreating authentic accents that could result in performances few could understand. In both movement and voice, it is not enough to know what is historically accurate; history must be converted and modified into theatre. In traditional Eastern theatre, every syllable, every step, every movement of the eye, hand and foot are rigorously trained, bringing a single actor into perfect alignment.

At this point in the production process, we shift from those who started it to those who are compelled to continue it. All of those identified up to now (except for the actors!) can and sometimes do leave town on or before opening night. Everyone who follows is essential in seeing the production through to the end. There is a tremendous shift in energy and responsibility as the planners of the event phase out and the players of it step forward. The Technical Director (TD) who has been involved in nearly all phases of production represents the major transition.

TECHNICAL DIRECTOR (TD)

The most crucial and least acknowledged participant in the whole event is the technical director. Usually this person runs the scene shop, sets schedules for design and construction deadlines, coordinates communication between design teams, troubleshoots every emergency, assigns crew heads and crewmembers, trains backstage personnel, and generally guides all production activities surrounding the actors. The crews do not get curtain calls and applause, and the TD will get little or no acclaim if all goes smoothly—beyond the satisfaction of knowing that it did. In educational theatre, the TD must often train crewmembers with virtually no experience. In these settings, she is responsible for the safety standards for the entire theatre and is often present at rehearsals and performances to troubleshoot any emergencies.

> **Janet Rose, *technical director***
>
> "A TD needs many construction techniques, but most important is the skill to plan ahead, knowing what pieces are needed for rehearsals first, the painting schedule and the logistics of how the pieces go together. This has to be balanced with the variety of skill levels found in construction crews."

While connected to all designers, the TD is most strongly associated with the set designer, and the TD's duties include planning and managing construction, installation, running, and striking of scenery. The TD also needs to keep track of all stock units in storage and of those needing to be drafted. Often this position involves drafting of working drawings, setting a construction schedule, purchasing equipment and supplies and supplementing the master schedule with daily shop work lists. The TD will supervise load-in (moving the scenery from the shop to the stage), load-out (also known as *strike*), and keep strict accounts of scenic expenses and supervision of all shop personnel. In educational theatre, the TD is likely to be involved with assigning and training personnel in props, lighting, and sound as well. Because of the huge technical component of media theatre, no direct parallel to the TD exists as those duties may be divided between half-dozen positions such as location manager, unit production manager, key grip, foreman, and post-production supervisor.

Personal Theatre and the TD

Are you someone who builds things and likes to do so? Are you the person your friends always call upon to help them realize their dreams in a tangible way? Do you actually know how to make and fix things? Are you the person who, once everyone gets done brainstorming, begins to question, explain, examine, and explore pragmatic solutions? Are you perfectly willing to tell the fanciful, high-flying visionaries in your life that what they want cannot be done on what they've got, that the money and resources will not match their vision? Do you generally thrive in organizing work parties to do construction and actually enjoy the practical challenges of galvanizing a group of non-skilled workers to create and sustain a project? You are the TD of whatever group in which you are a member, if after their breathless ecstasy over discovering the idea, they, often in the cold light of the next day, come to you to ask if and how it might be done.

Stage Manager (SM)

The stage manager (SM) will eventually take over from both the director and technical director and run the show. No one is more crucial once a production is in dress rehearsal and performance. The SM usually "calls" the show from the light booth or a place just offstage in the wings, on head-phones, communicating electronically with crews, alerting them to cues coming up and calling each cue when it is time. A modest production can have hundreds of cues as each change in lights, sound, scenery, costumes, and actor position must be carefully timed and coordinated for the show to run smoothly. The SM makes countless judgment calls from determining when the house manager should start flicking the lights in the lobby to beckon the audience to be seated, to when the house lights should come up at the end of the show to signal that it is time to leave—and everything in between. The traditional symbol for the SM is the "ghost light"—a single bare bulb on a pole, which stands onstage in an otherwise dark theatre, providing the only illumination in the cavernous space. This "ghost" beckons the SM into the theatre, often before anyone else arrives. Sometimes called "Stanley," the ghost light has often been replaced with just turning on a breaker switch for ambient low light. For those theatres still employing it, however, the final ritual of the day will be the SM returning this sole light to its spot before plunging all else again into darkness until tomorrow.

Martha King, *stage manager*

"You will get more work as a stage manager than as an actor. This is a good job for someone who really likes being in the middle of everything. Keep track of all the details and know how long it is before the next break, because that is the most asked question!"

Most SMs join the production team just before casting take place, often running the auditions themselves, handing out, collecting, and collating forms, calling actors' names when it is their turn, timing and cutting off those who run overtime, answering questions in order for the director to remain free to concentrate on each audition. Sometimes the SM will be asked to read with an actor when no scene partner is present. Professional stage managers are actually members of the same union (AEA, Actors' Equity Association) as actors.

After casting, the stage manager will then be responsible for the physical details of each rehearsal, making sure the space is unlocked, lights and heat or air turned on, necessary rehearsal furniture and props are set up as well as making sure all who are supposed to be present are. She creates a daily sign-in list and will be in charge of tracking down those not present when they are due. She will create something called the promptbook, which will include the script and all relevant printed material including notes on blocking and cues as they accumulate. She may prompt actors as they are struggling to memorize and to correct errors in lines. Eventually this book will become the guide by which she calls the cues.

Throughout rehearsal, the SM is liaison between the director, cast, and each of the shops, setting up costume fittings, communicating special needs to designers as they arise in rehearsal, sometimes booking actors for interviews or other sessions where their presence may be required outside actual rehearsal. The SM will help determine actor call times, scheduling those with extensive hair and make-up demands early and gradually working in the timed arrivals of others.

As crucial as this position is, in educational theatre a student often fills it. This person needs to have enough respect among peers to be able to lead and coordinate them. Self-confidence, high organizational skills, tremendous diplomacy, and the willingness to "kick butt when butts need to be kicked" are all crucial. The SM will deal most directly with actors who have been late, missed cues or fittings, or have jeopardized the coordination of the production in any way. In the professional theatre, the SM is responsible for enforcing union regulations, which include the need for a break every 55 minutes, food delivery, if a rehearsal runs past a certain length of time, standards being upheld, and a whole book full of additional rules that keep actors and crews from being taken advantage of. The professional stage manager will also conduct rehearsals for understudies or replacement casts.

There is usually at least one assistant stage manager (ASM) who is often the eyes, ears, and legs of the SM backstage during performance when the SM needs to stay in the booth on headphones. For example, the SM may communicate to the ASM that it is time for actors to take places, and the ASM in turn will make that announcement backstage. The ASM may communicate via headphone that an actor has completed a quick costume change so the SM can go ahead and call the next cue. The ASM provides a vital connection to onstage and backstage activity. Often he is incorporated into the rehearsal process, sometimes being on book, calling latecomers, sharing other tasks with the SM. Both these positions require organizational and people skills. Many of the same questions about whether or not you are suited to become a director determine if these jobs are for you. The crucial difference is that you would have to feel rewarded with just the work and knowing you did it well because SMs, like TDs, remain largely unacknowledged—no glory—just the satisfaction of a job well done.

Musicians

For much of Eastern theatre, and most particularly for Kabuki and Noh, the presence of live musicians is an essential part of the theatrical event. Musicians also play an important role in American Indian performances and of course traditional Musical Theatre where an entire orchestra may be employed. The decision to use recorded or live music may be part of a production plan. Some shows even have performances with both kinds of musical support, generally with reduced ticket prices for the former. In Eastern theatre, the coordination of movement with music, especially the use of percussion, is so vital that the musicians are likely to be an integral part of the rehearsal process. For Western musicals, a rehearsal pianist will be employed in all stages of rehearsal, but the rest of the musicians will not be brought in until very close to opening. These may be musicians for hire, with no particular interest in theatre. So the level of involvement in the process can vary from complete integration to last minute adjunct participation.

Wing Long, *pit musician*

"Playing for a theatre production is way different than playing at a concert. The fact that you are usually hidden from the audience should give you a clue. It is not about you or even the music. It is about how the music supports the acting."

The orchestra for a Western musical is often not seen or only partially visible in the pit. Only the conductor can be seen by the audience, and only she is the potential recipient of a curtain call acknowledgement. Conducting the orchestra for a musical requires exceptional skill and sensitivity. Coordinating the singers and musicians who have been rehearsing separately into a cohesive whole is a great challenge. In general, a theatre musician is a distinct artist from one who just creates music. Each moment is about supporting the actor's performance rather than expressing the musician's personal interpretation. Just as a male ballet dancer primarily presents, lifts, and enhances the presentation of his ballerina partner, this art is about supporting someone else.

Musical underscoring is sometimes used in non-musical live theatre though less frequently in Western theatre than in some other traditions. In media however, the musical score is a major tool in shifting mood and attention. A musician employed to play a film score may have no contact of any kind with the production. Rough cuts of the film might be projected during the scoring session, but that will be as close as the musician gets to the core action. You could play on the score of a film and have little idea of what it was actually about until you saw it in a theatre with everyone else.

At the other end of the spectrum, an Asian production may involve musicians as extensions and interpreters of each actor's every movement and shift in emotion. An actor's entrance may be punctuated by percussive accompaniment, pointing up each step taken. Key shifts in awareness and expression may receive similar treatment. The actor's movement into dance or stylized reactions will have powerful and interpretive sound support. A combat scene may involve unrealistic weapons that never actually make contact with each other or with actor's bodies, stopping just inches short of such contact when a percussion artist produces a sound that represents the contact that might have been made. There is a full integration and communion between musician and actor.

There may be no other area of theatre with a wider degree of involvement from central to peripheral than that of a theatre musician.

CREWS

Just as there are those who plan a show and those who actually play it, there are also staff members who *coordinate* the technical elements and others who *execute* them. In educational theatre, during the day, there will be crews making costumes, building sets, searching out and constructing props, hanging lights, recording sound—putting together the show. These people may or may not stay on board once the show opens, or they may in fact be replaced by a whole *other* group of people who work each performance, in which case the distinction is made between *construction* crews and *running* crews. In any theatrical setting, there are shop supervisors who oversee the implementation of designs. These positions require extraordinary skill in interpreting what the designer has presented and coordinating the efforts of all craft persons who will be engaged in achieving it.

Christine Smith-Mcnamara, *costume shop manager*

"I find management as fulfilling as any part of the costume world. I remember back in high school, I would listen to Broadway recordings and long to be part of that world. Twenty-five years later I am. The more you understand about how the technical work gets done, the more it will help your relationship with a shop."

The costume building crew does the sewing, fitting, trimming, and construction of all costume elements while running crews inventory costumes each day and may serve as dressers for actors with fast or difficult changes. They may also then repair, replace, launder, and iron costumes as needed after each performance. An electrics crew, often under the supervision of a **master electrician**, hangs and focuses lights while the light board operator actually runs them during the show, usually from a booth at the back, which is shared by the sound operator and SM. There may also be special lights such as follow spots which are operated by individual crew members from the back of the theatre or in the grid. The set is built under the supervision of a **shop foreman** and perhaps a **master carpenter**, but then a **key grip** may supervise the changing of scenery, props, and furniture during the show. This pattern follows through each of the other design elements. Ironically, running crews often have no idea how the construction process was accomplished. One of the great advantages for participants is that those who are employed at another job, whether during the daytime or at night, can still take part in the theatre process because it goes on all day long.

PUBLIC RELATIONS (PR) OR PROMOTION

You cannot do a show and know that "they will come." The word needs to get out. There are few experiences more depressing than to put forth all the effort that goes into a production and then have the cast outnumber the audience. While an individual production may have a publicity director, a permanent theatre company is more likely to have a Director of Promotion or Development. The most visible parts of promotion are posters and print ads, which need thoughtful design to catch attention and reflect the production concept while staying within a limited budget. Other standard tasks are writing press releases to submit to local publications and supervising photos to accompany these articles. Developing a positive working relationship with the local press is essential. The posters and perhaps smaller flyers need to be distributed, displays and signs created, businesses contacted to sell program advertising, and the theatre's web site constantly updated and maintained. This person may also keep production records, including preview and review articles as well as archival materials. They may also organize special performances for schools, senior citizens or other special interest groups. Countless details are involved in just preparing the program given to audience members. Cast and staff members' bios, and possibly photos, need to be included, and each cast member's home town newspaper contacted as part of the process.

Adam Maynard, *publicist*

"I feel as if I am the force that releases the show from being a private, intimately shared experience to becoming one that includes countless others. If a tree drops in the forest and is not heard, did it happen? Well, a show that isn't seen and heard did not happen."

A great deal of the promotion process is not about calling attention to a single production but rather gaining long-term support. In educational settings, this involves keeping alumni happy and interested in giving back as well as reaching out to parents of students currently enrolled. It includes wooing new donors or "angels" as they are sometimes called. A theatre's support base includes getting and expanding season subscribers—those who buy a season of tickets and provide a measure of financial stability—so each season's campaign is crucial. Subscribers usually receive reduced price tickets in return for purchasing the entire season and are considered a substantial support base. Making contact with each support group may involve planning special fund-raising events, reunions, and workshops as well as writing and distributing a newsletter to make everyone feel part of that theatre's extended family. Increasingly, on Broadway, publicity is being handled by marketing agencies such as The Marketing Group and Situation Marketing and group sales by companies such as Group Sales Box Office.

Media and Personal PR

If you are alive and well in this country today, you almost can't avoid the extensive PR used in media to boost ticket sales for every new movie, TV show, and video game. In fact, if you start to pay attention, you'll begin to notice that some media is awash in publicity for weeks and even months before opening day. Other new films receive very little commercial attention, and some even go "straight to video" without a whimper. Someone is deciding exactly how much money to spend on promotion. They decide, based partly on the cost of the project and partly on the producer's judgment, whether or not you will hear about it. Pre-opening hype may not mean a quality product. Many aggressively marketed films are mediocre, and films that appear quietly with little fanfare may be some of the best of the independents.

Author's Insights

Annie: "I read a film review in *Rolling Stone Magazine* that said 'we have been led to expect terrific stuff from this director, but this piece is just a tired re-hash...etc'. The very next day, the ads on TV for the same movie quoted *Rolling Stone* as saying 'Terrific!' The coincidence reminded me that advertising can be very deceiving."

Are you a promotion person? It requires a healthy, positive aggressiveness. Your show or theatre is competing for print and media coverage with countless others. You need to prepare convincing publicity packages and be able to follow up with even more convincing personal (often phone) pitches. You must believe in what you are promoting and be constantly inventive in how you get others to share your enthusiasm. And when the houses are packed, you need to feel enormous satisfaction just seeing all those people because chances are others involved in the production will not notice your efforts. Getting them to show up ("butts in seats" is the promotional mantra) is your goal—and ultimate reward.

HOUSE MANAGER

The stage manager finds a counterpoint in the person who runs the theatre's public areas. The House Manager handles those parts of the theatre space that the Stage Manager does not. He is primarily responsible for the safety of the audience and the smooth functioning of all Front of House (lobby, box office, public restrooms, lounges and auditorium) activities—all that is not onstage or backstage. The House Manager organizes ushers to seat the audience in the most efficient way and works closely with the Stage Manager to coordinate the event. The job requires skill in organizing others and in being assertive yet friendly. It may involve checking in at the box office regarding ticket sales and accessibility problems, coordinating lobby and rest room cleanliness, picking up items left on seats or in aisles, adjusting seating, supervising the folding and organizing of programs, putting out parking signs, training ushers, setting up lobby display panels and checking on the hearing assistance system.

> **Beth Carltan,** *house manager*
>
> "I feel almost like a mother tucking her children in and making sure they are comfortable. If the house does not run smooth, the experience of these 'children' will be unsettled. We want them to bask in the warmth of the show."

The house manager is in contact with the Stage Manager to coordinate opening the house and starting the performance, determining, for example, if there needs to be a delay because someone will be late or because the show may be sold out with many tickets not yet picked up. These two managers also consult about intermission length and procedures for starting each act. A few minutes before curtain, the HM may be asked to count empty seats and organize stand-by ticket holders, close the doors at curtain time, turn off the hall and inner lobby lights, then return to the outer lobby to meet with any late-comers or deal with any other problems which might come up. Once the play is started, he may count tickets and arrange the seating of late arrivals as unobtrusively as possible. This process repeats itself for each intermission.

The HM blinks the hall lights when it is time for the audience to enter or return. At the end of the play, he may coordinate ushers for general clean up, store ticket stubs, close up the outer space and turn out interior lights as well as the marquee lights outside the theatre. Being an HM requires being very good at trouble shooting, diplomacy, and finding quick solutions for such issues as disgruntled or suddenly ill patrons or extended delays.

While specific employment statistics are not available for the positions above, there is general agreement than unlike acting, one has a reasonable chance, if sufficiently trained, to find and sustain work in these less flashy, but vital areas of employment.

AUDIENCE

Is the audience, who joins the production last, actually part of the team? We would say they are, because without them there is no game. The actor is one of the two core ingredients for theatre and the audience is the other. No audience, no theatre. Who are these people who attend? For media, the audience embraces entire cultures. In our culture, the number who attend films is vast. It is difficult to find someone who "never watches movies." And despite the dire predictions that the video, DVD, and home theatre phenomenon would destroy the cinema, the cinema continues to thrive. Clearly, watching a film in the cozy seclusion of your home offers a different type of satisfaction than venturing into the darkness of a movie house among strangers. Media, in all forms, is so omnipresent that its audience does not really have a clear identity. And this is true in most areas of the world. In 2004, media artists from both Iraq and Afghanistan began making films again almost before the wreckage of war settled. In India, famous for its "Bollywood" style of extravagant film making, hundreds of millions of people flock to movie houses regularly.

Lois Lebon, *regular theatre audience member*

"I go the theatre to be taken out of my own life. I want to be transported. I don't mind if the play is about a life like my own, but I at least want to learn something and still feel like I have left my own home for some reason. I want the show to either take me away or give me more reasons to stay where I am."

What are the actual figures of attendance? While global statistics are not available, in our country, it is estimated that about 200,000 people each day attend a live theater production. Fifty times that number (10 million) will be watching a movie and four hundred times that number (80 million) will watch TV.

Public, ceremonial personal theatre events are dictated by existing connections between participants. For ritual events—from christenings to funerals—the audience is going to be made up largely of those who already have some strong tie to the featured subjects. Huge public ceremonies (some weddings and commencements for example) expand to include those not among the near and dear, but there is almost always a traceable connection to explain the presence of each audience member. Some are enthusiastic participants, others are only fulfilling obligations. The only element that varies is the degree to which cultures (and families within those cultures) embrace each opportunity to ritualize life events through public theatrical occasions or shun such events in favor of more private, reflective rituals.

The audience that is the most difficult to pinpoint is that for live theatre. While no absolutely reliable statistics are available, a common estimate is that less than 5% of Americans attend plays on any kind of regular basis. Live theatre audiences tend to live in large cities where there is simply greater access to a variety of live theatre companies and high quality professional work. Aside from Broadway (NYC) and the West End (London), the cities require sufficient resources to support an Arts or Community Center with space, seating, and equipment for touring productions beyond local offerings. Such audiences are often relatively affluent because ticket prices demand disposable income. Ironically, this is less true in many cultures outside our own where theatre is either subsidized by governments or is created by the whole community and therefore available to all.

Because live theatre is magical and mysterious, there are numerous small companies that defy the odds, thrive, and are in no way elitist in either content or availability. A small theatre company or community may target a specific, underrepresented audience such as the Theatre By The Blind company in New York City or the bilingual Spanish/English theatre produced in the Community Arts Center in the heart of the *barrio* in San Antonio. Depending on where you are in the world, the audience may include everyone or only a specific few.

When we talk about majority attendance in this country, what kinds of theatrical works lure U.S. audiences regularly in large numbers? There are two. The first will not surprise you. Musicals (covered in Chapter 10) are the mainstay of live theatre. When the entire community shows up, it is likely to be for a big musical. Often summer theatres are devoted entirely to them. When a touring house books shows, musical theatre will be second only to pop music concerts. At the time of this writing, there were nineteen musicals and one straight play on Broadway.

The other more surprising box office champion is Shakespeare, the single most produced playwright in the world. Almost every state has its own Shakespeare Festival, and even though they may be in remote "destination" locales, audiences show up in droves. Additionally Shakespeare is considered a draw across all spectrums of professional and educational theatre and is the only playwright likely to have multiple New York productions within any season.

These two audience favorites strike some as being at opposite ends of the cultural spectrum— from populist low-brow to elitist high-brow—but they have much in common. Audiences hope to be thrilled, and both favorites have what it takes to deliver. Both are likely to have large casts, blend intimate scenes with spectacular ones, be set in exotic, fascinating worlds and even remote time periods, and deliver sweeping pomp, spectacle, and ritual, providing a vast adventure. More importantly, both have moments when characters pour their hearts out, and both demand powerful emotional commitment from performers who need to be both big and honest. Shakespeare's speeches can have similar impact to musical numbers because the gorgeous language, poetic imagery, and musicality of his verse can stir emotions as strongly in soliloquy as they do in song.

Probably the major misconception preventing more audiences from venturing to the theatre is the belief that it is tied to a "culture vulture" perspective often placed on ballet, opera, and classical symphonies. But theatre actually embraces all cultural levels and topics. After learning more about it, you may consider joining and expanding that five percent of theatre regulars.

Audiences impact film in ways such as box office figures and whether or not we are subjected to a series of sequels. But at any individual showing of a film, nothing that happens alters what comes out of the screen. As a live theatre audience member, however, your laugher, gasps, sighs, and weeping all affect the performance. From something huge like a standing ovation to the subtle effect of looking out on a sea of smiling faces, the actor is changed by you through connection and communion.

SUMMARY

Theatre's unsung heroes are neglected when it comes to attention, but the jobs have deep challenges, satisfactions, and employment potential. The producer must manage the business end. The technical director (TD) is probably the most essential link between the ideas of the planning team and their realization, holding together all concrete and practical aspects of production. The stage manager (SM) is the glue that binds the daily running of rehearsals and ultimately performances, calls the shots, and at a crucial juncture in the process, takes over for both the director and TD. Many shows require special skills and equipment, so experts are brought in. Perhaps one team of crew members constructs a show and then another team altogethr runs it in performance. These two groups may be entirely separate entities. The PR person has the challenge of making sure all potentially interested audience members know about the show, and all potential long-range supporters and investors feel connected to the theatre company. The House Manager (HM) takes care of all the business "out front" while the SM monitors onstage and backstage activities. The audience is the essential final ingredient. While media and personal audiences are vast, only a small percentage of the population makes live theatre a regular, constant part of their lives.

SUGGESTED ASSIGNMENTS

1. Next time you attend a play, notice how well or poorly managed the production is. Were any cues confusing? Did light, sound and set changes happen fluidly? Were there any obvious errors?

2. Notice the same for the house management. Did the show start on time? If not, was there an obvious good reason such as a last minute line of people wanting tickets? Were ushers available to help you? Could they actually answer questions? Did the intermission last the amount of time the program said it would? Were you effectively warned in time to get in your seat for each act?

3. How demanding was this piece of work to produce and run? Were the demands placed on those backstage, onstage, and front of house significant? If yes or no, what evidence do you have for this conclusion?

4. What constitutes an effectively promoted production? Begin to notice posters, flyers, ads, and feature stories and make comparisons among your local theatre groups as to which are more and which are less effective at getting the word out.

5. What skills do you possess that could be called upon by a theatre with special production needs?

6. As you examine the program, ask yourself how well put together it is to serve your theatre experience? Is there enough information to divert and entertain you while you wait for the show to begin? Are there any questions that could have been answered in program notes but are not?

7. Examine the list of staff members. Do you feel that you now understand what each person on that list does? If a crew seems very large, can you determine from the performance itself why so many people seem to have been needed? Are there any positions still unclear to you?

8. As you imagine yourself taking part in a production, where do you see yourself fitting in, provided you have more training and experience? Are you absolutely a potential performer, or would you find a more comfortable niche among those less publicly exposed?

9. The next time you experience theatre with music, consider what the event would have been like without it, and evaluate the degree to which the musician's involvement enhanced or distracted from your engagement in the event.

10. Can you tell, as you look around at a performance, the demographics of this theatre's audience? Are they an older, more formal crowd, or are they young, hip, and incredibly eclectic? From the nature of the play itself and the season of which it is a part, can you find a reason for the nature of the audience?

SUGGESTED ACTIVITIES

1. Individual—Interview a music, fight, or dance director and report on the specific contributions they believe they bring to any production.

2. Group—Volunteer as a group to help with the promotion of a production about to open. Meet with the publicity director who may eventually assign you places to put up posters and may also involve you in other aspects of publicity.

3. Long term—Meet with a TD at the start of production and once a week throughout rehearsal. Identify specific challenges at the beginning and how these change as the show gets closer to opening.

4. Large group—Select a production or film the entire class has seen. Divide the class into five groups each of which is charged with coming up with a strong argument why the role of the producer, dramaturg, TD, running crew or publicist was the most important element. Have the teacher select the team with the strongest argument.

KEY WORDS AND IDEAS

Producer

Artist Director

Managing Director

Music Director

Fight Director

Choreographer

Production Coaches

Dramaturg

Technical Director

Stage Manager

Shop Managers

Construction Crews

Running Crews

Public Relation or Promotion Director

House Manager

HOW DID THEATRE EVOLVE?

At various locations around the world, theatre often developed in astonishingly similar ways. This section will explore how Indian, Greek, Chinese, English, Japanese, French and African theatres each found their own strong, early voices Other early global developments are explored: The nature of theatrical space (for various cultures) when performance was almost exclusively outside and its impact on script content and the theatrical event and performance space once theatre moved inside.

HISTORICAL PARALLELS

Europe **Origins**	Asia	Africa
GREEK TRAGEDY/COMEDY (500bce)	INDIAN SANSKIT DRAMA (700-200 bce)	"FUNCTIONAL" COMMUNAL DRAMA
CONQUEST AND RETREAT MEDIEVAL MYSTERY/ PASSION DRAMA (900-1400)	CHINESE ZAJU (XIGU 1) (900s) JAPANESE NOH (1350s)	ENTER ISLAM (700s)
RESURGENCE OF POPULAR DRAMA ELIZABETHAN DRAMA (1590s)	JAPAN- KABUKI (1600s)	COLONIAL IMPACT (1600s)
ELITISM ENGLISH RESTORATION (1660) FRENCH NEOCLASSICISM COMEDIES (1660s)	INDIAN KATHAKALI (1650s) S CHINESE KUNGU (XIGU 2-1644)	SUBMISSION/ SURVIVAL
RETURN OF THE PEOPLE ENGLISH GEORGIAN COMEDY Late 1700s	CHINESE JINGUJU (BEIJING OPERA) (XIGU 3) SPECTACLE (1790)	THE AMERICAS

EARLY BRILLIANCE

CONTENTS

THE CHART preceding this chapter shows us how theatre has swung back and forth from an inclusive event involving the entire community, to a restricted luxury for the elite few, and back again to embrace the people, in what may be an inevitable pendulum as part of its evolution. It is fascinating how often the same swing of the pendulum was occurring in separate parts of the world.

As we progress to the theatre that follows the path of "early brilliance" in various regions of the world, we will be able to see the continued influence of the Indian, African, and Greek worldview on their respective parts of the world. Rather than repeat those ideas, we only point out critical changes or divergences in thought that influenced the theatre of a particular place and time.

FIRST SCRIPTED THEATRE: INDIAN SANSKRIT DRAMA

Sanskrit dance drama was formalized in written form around 2,600 years ago. It flourished as an oral tradition for centuries before that and lasted until at least the 1200s. Its influence continues today. Sanskrit reflects the worldview of the Hindu culture and its prevailing attitudes.

World View

Time

For the Hindu, time is an eternal cycle with infinite wheels of experience coexisting in celestial harmony. The passage of time as an illusion and this life is only one incarnation of the infinite cycles of the soul. In one of the most influential epic stories, *The Mahbarhata*, a god asks a great hero, "What is the greatest wonder of the world?" With the lives of his four brothers at stake, this calm and wise hero correctly answers, "The greatest wonder is that death is everywhere, we see it every day and yet we each live as if death will never touch us."

Space

The Hindu view of space is infinite with coexisting worlds and planes of existence. The very wise, brave, or holy may venture into these alternate spaces, but most common folk will only know this space. Perhaps in a future life, they will be able to explore others.

Values

The Hindu value system is expressed through four great works called the *Vedas*, describing a male-dominated system, celebrating the victory of gods over demons, describing the creation of humanity, and establishing codes for behavior. The *Vedas* encourage physical strength, courage in battle and skill with weaponry, but also the pursuit of peace, serenity, and happiness in the mind. Rash behavior is discouraged, love is central, and men must protect and cherish women. Family is essential. The many gods and demons of the cosmos provide daily temptation and redemption. Both evil and good are necessary for the harmony of creation. The ultimate destination of each soul is Enlightenment, perfect peace and happiness. With Enlightenment comes release from the eternal cycles of time and space, birth and rebirth, into oblivion.

Structure

The caste system: *Brahmin* (priests and teachers), *Kshatriya* (rulers and warriors), *Vaishyas* (merchants and farmers), and *Shudras* (servants) is difficult for Westerners to grasp. In spiritual terms, each soul is bound to seek harmony and enlightenment and each caste is responsible for the well-being of other castes. In actual social reality, caste evolved into a complex and sometimes cruel system that allowed great luxury and pleasure to a few and hardship and hopelessness to the many. Skin color became a caste symbol, lighter skin indicating higher rank. The system continues to haunt India today, though exploitation of the lowest born, the Untouchables, is now technically illegal. Women were submitted to fathers, then husbands, to brothers, uncles or other male relatives. And yet, in Sanskrit drama, women are often central figures, objects of love and devotion, powerful figures that change the nature of the world.

Pleasure

From its first contact with Western civilization, India offered pleasures and mysteries that intrigued and beguiled the traveler. The land itself ranges from the majesty of the Himalayan Mountains to the tropical forests. Spices, silks of every hue, teas, exotic music, and sensual dance provided physical pleasures. Romance and heroism, sacrifice and victory are the core of the great epic stories. Pleasure comes through kindness, humility, duty, love, and correct behavior.

The Senses

All the senses engage in the Indian experience. Incense, spices, teas, and perfumes tease the sense of smell. Vivid silks, tropical flowers, and soaring architecture delight the eye. The warm humidity of the monsoon season on the skin, the textiles designed for clothing and lounging, the inescapable insect life of the tropics—where does it end? Always present are the ever ringing of bells, and the tinkling of gold on ankle, wrist, neck and ears.

Beyond India

About 556 BCE, Siddhartha Gautama, a young man of the warrior caste left his life of riches and power and set out to find the meaning of the suffering he saw in the world. After six years of training with spiritual masters, he sat under a tree and entered a state of profound meditation until he achieved Enlightenment. He then began a lifelong journey of teaching. He became the Buddha and began the spread of the ideals of Hinduism and Buddhism through vast reaches of the Asian continent.

The Drama

While the oral tradition is the starting point for much great drama, the recording of two epic stories and one book of rules—all three grounded in antiquity—still influence Indian theatre today. Sanskrit tradition says that the gods invented theatre and gave it to humans through an ancient sage whose name was Bharata. Bharata transcribed the will of the gods into the *Natya Sastra*, a thirty-seven chapter detailed description of theatrical presentation. The author and its date is the subject of much debate. Bharata Rami (who, like Homer, may have been one or many oral storytellers) created the current form of the *Natya Sastra* between 200 BCE and 200 CE. Essential components include:

1. Dance, music, and story are inseparable,

2. Language is poetic and lyrical,

3. Performance is danced and gestured, expressive and abstract.

4. Costumes, make up, and masks delineate character types from peasants to gods, from clowns to heroes,

5. Drama reflects the natural order, harmony, and justice of the cosmos.

Author's Insights

Annie: Recent research in the preservation of oral narratives supports the idea that a single performer can indeed memorize that much material and later have it transcribed, despite the fact that it would take weeks if not months to recite all 100,000 verses. The skill required of the storyteller is almost unbelievable.

The *Natya Sastra* outlines theatre spaces, training of performers, and "appropriate" material for performance. The two great epics, *Ramayana* and *Mahabharata*, to this day provide source material for most Indian theatre and film. *Mahabharata*, the better known of the two, is an epic poem that has 100,000 stanzas. It begins before humans became corrupt through idleness and prosperity and began to disrespect the teachings of the *Vedas*. It is the story of two great families, one with five brothers, and the other with 100 brothers. Though cousins by birth, the two families are torn apart by jealousy, greed, and betrayal. The five brothers are heroes, sons of gods, possessing amongst them all that is good. Their 100 cousins are the sons of a blind king who cannot rule because he cannot see. Sages, visionaries, gods, demons and spirits are active characters. After many adventures, the families fight a great war, and the good brothers defeat their evil cousins.

The *Ramayana* is an epic, much longer than Homer's *Iliad* and *Odyssey* combined, although not as long as the *Mahabharata*. When a wicked demon-king steals Sita, the beautiful and devoted wife of King Rama, the king gathers an army of monkeys under the guidance of the white monkey-god, Hanuman, and they embark on a quest to rescue her. After ten years of adventure, they are reunited.

Each of these two major epics contains philosophy, articles of faith, testimony to human folly and greatness, and discussions of the nature of existence. Their influence can be seen and felt to this very day.

Styles

Sanskrit dramatists found many points of attack. Most blended the comic and serious, with every character type included. The clown figure is often central, as a comic counterpart to the hero. The often-flawed hero must suffer and learn to succeed. Sanskrit never separates the sacred from the profane or the comic from the cosmic. Love and restoration is the unifying principle. Romance and Heroic Quest are the two dominant the themes. The concept of tragedy is absent. This does not mean that no suffering, death, or loss occurs. Rather, since this life and these trials are part of the great harmony, the chance of rebirth and redemption follows suffering and death.

As Sanskrit drama spread across the Indian Empire, the Sanskrit spoken language fell into disuse, becoming the language of poets and scholars. Audiences spoke no Indian languages, yet everyone knew the stories. As time went on, the plays evolved into an increasing visual form.. Performers danced, gestured, and spoke Sanskrit while a narrator, translated into the language of the audience. Music and dance provided universal languages that crossed cultural boundaries.

The Playwrights

The "Big Three" classical Sanskrit playwrights are Shudraka (dates unknown), Bhasa (c. 275–c. 335) and the most honored of them all, Kalidasa (third century) who is credited with writing the "perfect" play.

King Shudraka's play, *Mriccha Katika* (*The Little Clay Cart*) is a complicated ten-act love triangle. It is the story of Charudatta, a Brahmin (priest), who falls hopelessly in love with a beautiful courtesan who in turn is in love with a poor merchant. After many trials and tribulations, Charudatta is about to go to the gallows, but the plot against him is discovered in time and balance is restored.

Bhasa's most respected work is *Svapna Vasavadattam* (*Vasavadatta's Dream*), which tells of King Udayana, a ruler pressured by his minister of state to marry the daughter of a powerful ruler to strengthen his reign and protect his kingdom. The King, however, is too devoted to his wife to consider such a marriage. Instead the Queen, ready to sacrifice her own happiness to save the kingdom, stages her death in a palace fire, and then secretly returns to wait upon the new queen and be near her husband.

The most revered of the three is Kalidasa, whose *Abhijnana Shakuntalam* (*The Recognition of Shakuntala*), called by some Indian scholars the "perfect play," tells the romantic story of King Dusanta, who falls in love at first sight with Shakuntala, a beautiful maiden he meets while hunting in the forest. She returns his love and they agree to marry, but burdened by a strange curse the king forgets her as soon as he returns to his palace. Time passes and Shakuntala leaves her family and in the journey loses the ring the king gave her as token of their marriage. Rejected at the king's palace, she soon gives birth to the king's son. Magically, the ring is found, the gods restore the king's memory, and, to borrow a Western phrase, they all live happily ever after.

The Theatre—From Temples To Village Squares

In the theatre "handbook," the *Natya Sastra*, the stage space is outlined in detail. The appropriate space for the great epic dramas is the temple, featuring marble-pillared halls with large sweeping roofs. The building is rectangular with separate entrances for men and women. Between the two entrance doors stand two large copper drums.

As the Sanskrit drama spread across Southeast Asia, many smaller communities didn't have ornate marble temples, but tried to adhere to the basic teachings of the "handbook." A rectangular area was marked in a central location such as a market place or simple place of worship. Even today the large sweeping roof (even if it's made of canvas or palm fronds) protects the playing area. The audience might get drenched but not the actors! This basic style of theatre space spread throughout Asia, and we find remarkable similarities to theatre spaces in use today.

Theatre Conventions

The multitude of nonrealistic conventions in Indian dance drama can be daunting. Among the most obvious and unfamiliar are:

- **Masks/Makeup/Costume**—a traditional mask or makeup and costume identifies instantly each *type* of character. Heroes wear certain colors and makeup while villains wear others. Demons and gods use masks, in styles dictated by tradition for easy recognition.

- **Dance and Gesture**—the performer moves and gestures in abstract rather than realistic ways. The actor learns each step, finger gesture, and expression of face or body to communicate *essence* rather than every day *reality*.

- **The Narrator**—Narrators, or bards, sing, chant, and describe in local dialects the details of the story.

- **Music**—Music, inseparable from the dance drama, employs instrumentation, key, rhythms, and tempos to express meaning.

- **Time/Length of Performance**—Sanskrit drama can last several days or even weeks. In many parts of the world, performances start at sunset and continue all night, taxing the strength and endurance of both performer and audience.

Decline and Rebirth

Over the course of centuries, the Indian Empire declined, Sanskrit language died out even among the aristocracy, and masses of peoples previously conquered by India re-embraced their native forms of theatre. By the tenth century, setbacks in China and other areas of the Far East drove the Indian Empire back into the region it now occupies in South Asia.

Sanskrit drama survived in many new forms grafted onto local performance traditions. From Malaysia to Japan, for example, puppet theatre was and is enormously popular and distinctively regional. Yet, the puppets themselves look suspiciously like the imperial kings and queens of old India, and the stories tell of love, valor, and heroism.

In folk drama throughout the region, local and Hindu deities melded as did theatrical spaces and the model of Sanskrit drama. Dance and music continued to be inherent, as did the essentially optimistic point of view. With the spread of Buddhism, ideals of time as illusion, cosmic justice and redemption, duty and family, and love as the path to happiness continued as the dominant values. Each community grafted in local gods and demons, native languages and musical styles, and local conventions of mask, makeup and costume. Sanskrit drama provided the foundation for much of Eastern theatre.

Influences on Theatre Today

To see the influence of Sanskrit today, we can look at the Western musical, 20th century anti-realism movements in Europe, and the booming film industry of India, dubbed "Bollywood." Though the Western musical theatre as we know it today is only about 100 years old, the path from Sanskrit drama to the American musical is long and winding through centuries of adaptation and change. Yet, we today (just like the audiences of ancient India) love the beauty and power of music, dance, and story blended to tell us of love found, lost and re-found, heroes who suffer, struggle, and win, and villains who seem to prosper but pay in the end.

In non-realistic theatre styles of the last century, Western theatre artists have drawn experimental forms directly from the influences of the Far East. Samuel Beckett, a giant in twentieth century Western theatre, experimented with language and gesture as pure symbols, going so far as to compose plays entirely without words. Before him, August Strindberg, a nineteenth century master of non-realism, attempted to address the cosmic mysteries of love and pain, birth and death, and even used Hindu symbolism and deities in several of his works.

Films embrace the pageantry, magic, and sheer theatricality of Sanskrit drama. Rent a movie made in "Bollywood" (a media-invented term that is half-derisive and half-respectful) and let the beauty wash over you, noting the classic conventions. Such Chinese films as *Hero* or *House of Flying Daggers* reflect regional variants, but romance, heroism, magic, music, and stylized dance and movement are at their heart. Next, we will look at three descendants of Sanskrit theatre as they developed in Asia: China's first popular operas and Japan's *Noh* and *Kabuki* theatres.

THE FIRST CHINESE OPERA: ZAJU (*XIQU* 1)

Sanskrit drama was serious theatre for serious people, satisfying the need for ritual and continuity, but what about the need for sheer exuberant fun? An extraordinary form of theatre emerged in China in the 900s called *xiqu*. Chinese language symbols do not invite exact phonetic transcription, so English translation invariably results in multiple spellings, but *xiqu* can be broken down as *xi* (pronounced *shee*)—theatrical entertainment, and *qu* (pronounced *chyoo*)—music or tune, so it means "tuneful theatre." (A capitalized name indicates the name of its city or region of origin; if not capitalized, it's a general label.) Later, we will describe *xiqu*'s current manifestation (Bejing Opera or *Jingju*) but here is where it all began.

World View

Early China embraced values different from the *Vedas*. The sense of time, space, pleasure and the senses remained Hindu/Buddhist, but the teachings of Confucius (551–479 BCE) created a most striking contrast between Indian and Chinese values. The *Analects* or rules of Confucianism also stand in deep contrast with Western thought, which was developing at the same time.

Confucius was born into a time of war and chaos. In response, his vision emerged as a path to order and benevolence. Each individual owed absolute obedience to the hierarchy of family and empire. Those in power must rule with benevolence (kindness) and justice in exchange for this obedience. Filial piety, or the near worship of parents, grandparents, and ancestors, created a society in which the needs of the individual were unimportant when in conflict with those of the family, community, or government. Adoption of the analects resulted in a less chaotic society, but during some periods the rules were use to enforce stifling conformity and control. The thirteenth century Mongol or Yuan dynasty was one such era.

Zaju, the first form of *xiqu* (and thus *xiqu* 1), emerged in the 900s during the Sung dynasty but its peak popularity occurred during the rule of the invading Mongol Emperor Kublai Khan in the thirteenth century. Perhaps in response to the severity of Mongol rule, this form of theatre is one of the lively arts. Vivid and alive with spectacle, the plays of the Zaju also served as forums for political thought. Many deal with social injustice and the suffering of the masses, using myths and legends as subject matter to conceal their political agenda.

The Drama

Guan Hanqing was the founder of Zaju and the author of sixty-seven plays, eighteen still performed in contemporary *xiqu*. His works focus on the darker aspects of life, yet with a sense of possibility. He wrote about historical peasant rebellions and common people of history or legend who rose up against their fate. *The Rescue of a Courtesan* depicts a prostitute willing to take up cudgels in a just cause. She is sympathetic, intelligent, and courageous. In *Snow in Midsummer*, he wrote about a girl named Dou E who becomes the target of a local tyrant's lust. When she refuses to marry him, she is falsely charged with murder and convicted. Before her death, Dou E predicts snow in midsummer and a three-year drought—both of which happen. Years later, cleared of the charge, her final words endure: "Those who are kind are poor and die young, while evil-doers enjoy wealth and longevity. Heaven and earth both bully the weak and fear the strong, not daring to go against the flow."

Under the Khan regime, Guan Hanqing and his fellow dramatists suffered severe oppression. But as Huo Jianyi, a modern scholar states, "It is worth recalling that although the Yuan rulers and the . . . scholars were at opposite ends of the social scale, and waged life and death struggles, they all had the same eventual destination—the grave. Yuan Zaju has, however, survived to this day."

According to historical records, 450 Zaju plays were written during the period. To date, 160 texts survive. Many of these scripts turn up again in *Kunqu* or *xiqu* 2, forming a quarter of that theatre's repertoire.

Styles

This theatre is based on comedy, drama, music, and dance, interspersed with clowns and acrobatics, highly physical, and filled with spectacle. Zaju is definitely popular entertainment as it embraces juggling, puppets, tumbling, jokes, and riddles—and of course, lots of songs. The more farcical productions had "rude comic effects," including farting and burping. A head clown served as troupe director for companies of four to seven actors. This director (*ts'anchon*) might also have served as master of ceremonies and lead musician onstage. Sometimes he was called "the bamboo stick," a label referencing his baton.

The Theatre

Stage Spaces: The Continued Influence of Sanskrit

One of the Zaju plays that survived is *A Country Bumpkin Knowing Nothing of the Theatre* by the Yuan dynasty poet Du Renjie. It describes a Zaju performance through the eyes of a farmer coming to the city for the first time. Between this text and the stage demands of others, we can begin to imagine the Zaju theatre space

As in Sanskrit, performances would be on a stage open on three sides, with a ground area to stand surrounded by raised seating and possible balconies. Since companies would also tour, these theatres were often mobile. A wooden fence covered with colorful banners surrounded the theatre, recreating courtyards in much the same way Elizabethans would later take a familiar space to create theatres such as the Globe.

At one point in the late 1200s, Zaju grew to have such popular support that a single amusement park (think early Disneyland) in a northern capitol city, Keifeng, had up to fifty Zaju theatres, one housing at least a thousand people. Areas in large cities featuring Zaju theatres called "tile districts" were often huge fenced enclosures with flags and banners flying high above them.

Theatre Conventions

In Zaju, conventions of Sanskrit theatre and local custom blended, incorporating local gods, demons, heroes, and myths.

Dance and Music: Zaju was representational rather than realistic. Dance and music were essential. Scholars believe women were professional performers. The lead actor or actress would sing, while secondary characters would speak.

Makeup: Flamboyant makeup was used as a masking technique to identify character types. The clown, for example, wears black and white stylized makeup. Character types include heroes, honest women, and *jinn*, a term used for both clowns and devils.

Spectacle: As the play progressed, interludes of acrobats, magicians, and musicians provided entertainment between acts. Even the most serious plays included elements of farce and magic. *The Country Bumpkin* ends with the sight of the farmer running around the stage to find a toilet and, when he can't find one, leaving in disgust.

The Zaju theatre ended 600 years ago. Its vibrant appeal lives on in the texts and in its influence on today's Beijing Opera. But as Zaju was disappearing, a deeply insular and elitist form of theatre was developing across the sea in Japan.

JAPANESE MEDIEVAL AND RENAISSANCE THEATRE

Noh

World View

During the twelfth and thirteenth centuries, Japanese culture emerged as a distinct entity after centuries of Chinese domination. Many Chinese influences ran headlong into the native religions of Japan (particularly Shinto, a form of nature worship) and the theatre and performance arts enjoyed by the common folk. By the fourteenth century, the royal families were still practicing Chinese arts in their centralized palaces, but in the countryside, warriors ruled under the code of the samurai. During the height of the samurai period, *Noh* drama evolved and of course the majority of plays focused on the exploits of warrior heroes. *Noh* evolved as a surprisingly restrained and even fastidious art, considering it came out of a world of chaos, bloodshed, and war. You can go to Japan today and see a *Noh* drama performed. It is the oldest continuously performed drama in the world.

The Drama

We credit one father/son team with the creation of *Noh*. Kanami, a professional actor, began training his son, Zeami, at the age of six to follow in his footsteps. In 1374, the shogun (head samurai warrior) ordered the two to appear in a command performance. The shogun was so impressed that he took them into his service. Kanami, a skilled musician, composer, and playwright, began the work of refining *Noh* performances, which had been a hodge-podge of song, dance, bits of story, juggling, gymnastics, and stilt walking, like Zaju. He gathered stories, songs, and epic poems about the warriors and heroes of the past and structured them into the elegant dramas of the mature *Noh* theatre. Zeami continued his father's work, writing about 240 of the surviving plays, all now designated as national treasures.

Styles

Noh drama is ceremonial, mysterious, and tragic. Impregnated with Zen Buddhist concepts, it focuses on symbolic images and the struggle to escape the realities of time and place. Shinto beliefs also play a role as ghosts and gods haunt the stage while mortal men struggle to understand the mysteries of life.

The plots are slim. The focus is on the precise, choreographic musical notations and vocal inflections. The protagonist is the *shite*, meaning the doer. He may be a god, a ghost, or an animal, but most often is a legendary warrior. Always played in masks and costumes, tradition dictates every detail of this role to allow instant identification of the character. Questioned and challenged by secondary characters who may be ministers, commoners, or priests, the *shite* responds at length, defending, explaining, describing events, or chastising the others.

The Theatre

The stage is an 18-foot square of highly polished cypress (see Chapter 5 for a diagram). A bridge, the *hashigakari*, extends from the right side of the stage, connecting it to the actor's dressing area. All entrances happen on the *hashigakari*. Three pine trees precisely placed along the bridge, and a single pine tree painted on the back wall of the stage form the visual design.

All actors in the *Noh* drama are male. On stage with them and in full view of the audience are four musicians playing a flute, a small drum, a large drum, and stick drums. A chorus of six to ten singers lends vocal accompaniment to the actors and musicians.

The *Noh* drama is essentially unchanged from its development 600 years ago. Its appeal has fallen and risen over the centuries, but never faded completely. A highly revered art form today, it holds a special appeal to the intellectual and the connoisseur. Interest and attendance is on the rise again. Perhaps its grace and beauty, its ephemeral dream-like quality, and its stately ancient conventions provide a welcome respite from the hectic pace of modern life.

Kabuki

World View

The Tokugawa shoganate ruled Japan with a feudal military dictatorship from 1603 to 1868. The Tokugawa family inherited a world of civil war and provided the first centralized stability in many years. While the essential Japanese worldview prevailed, the political situation changed radically. At first the people appreciated the peace and order brought by the Tokugawa. They imposed a strict class hierarchy, with the samurai at the top, followed by farmers, artisans, and traders. Taxes set in 1603 did not account for inflation and decreased in actual value with every generation, leading to confrontations between noble but impoverished samurai and prosperous peasants. Barred from *Noh* by tradition and inclination (who wanted to watch boring samurai strutting around a bare stage?), the common folk turned to the *Kabuki* theatre. *Kabuki* is one of the most exciting and spectacular of theatres still performed around the world today.

The Drama

In 1603, a shrine dancer in Kyoto, set in motion a series of events that led to a new form of theatre that defied the refined dignity of *Noh*. Izumo-no-Okuni, the outrageous and eccentric female dancer, performed in a temple wearing a blend of male garments and a wooden cross around her neck. Her adaptation of religious dance (*numbutsu odori*) included an erotic interlude. Her audience called her *kabuku* and *kabukumono*, meaning weird and flashy, which would be true of such a show even now.

She soon had a crowd of followers who capitalized on her innovations and expanded on them. All-female dance companies began performing stories and the term *kubuku*, meaning "askew," described the cross-gender extravaganzas in which women played both male and female roles. The government soon issued a decree banning women from the stage in the interests of public order. Since the show must go on, men began playing women's roles, forcing a concentration on the skill of the actor that continues in the *Kabuki* theatre to this day.

Unlike *Noh*, *Kabuki* drama was committed to an ever-changing repertoire of plays. Each company had a team of professional playwrights, and new plays evolved based on the needs and fashions of the day. The plays are epic, and play fast and loose with history and historical personages. *Kabuki* involves lightning-fast costume changes, freezes and poses, juxtaposed with rapid, energized moves. The actor always comes first in Kabuki, so the play must offer opportunities for performers to "strut their stuff." There are eighteen famous classic *Kabuki* plays, together called the *juhachiban*, and over 200 plays in all. Performances always rely on dance, music, and elaborate vocal effects. A guiding principle is *yatsushi*, in which the old story is presented but at the same time modernized and parodied. Famous characters may appear in outrageous modern garb and predicaments.

Styles

Two main types of plays are histories called *jidaimono* or "period things" and domestic plays called *sewamona* or "common things." Most involve conflicts between love and duty, and they often end in suicide. Always highly emotional, the plays appeal to passions more than intellect. They are also very long. Audiences expect to spend the whole day in the theatre, so playwrights use every trick in the book to keep them happy.

Kabuki is popular because it deals with the joys and sorrows of common people living in a remote and fascinating past. It blends tragedy, comedy, realism, and romanticism into one performance. *Kabuki* delighted the common folk with a more spectacular and accessible style, often gaudy and always exhilarating. By 1700, the basic conventions of *Kabuki* were in place, and the actors were the center of its appeal.

The Theatre

Stage Spaces

The *Kabuki* stage evolved from the influential *Noh* stage. Over time it changed, most importantly with the extension of the bridge (*hanamichi*) through the audience to the back of the theatre and a small room for the actors—popularly known as the "hen coop." This convention made the actor/audience relationship much more direct and intense by bringing them into the same space.

The *Kabuki* stage uses a ninety-foot proscenium opening, and actors make important entrances on the *hanamichi*. The chorus (*jorjuri*) sits upstage on a raised platform. The traditional stage is made of cypress scrubbed with bean curd, resulting in a surface which greatly aids movement. A pull-curtain (*hiki maku*) is standard, although revolving stages, lifts, and other spectacular effects occur in view of the audience. Entrances and exits happen from the audience's left, traditionally believed to be superior to the right. Those entering on the *hanamichi* are of high rank, or are in some way due serious attention.

Theatre Conventions

The theatrical conventions would remind us of Sanskrit and *Noh*. Music follows Asian traditions in notation, key, and instrumentation. We would probably not see a narrator as the plays needed no translation.

No film star of today commands a more adoring and loyal fan base than the *Kabuki* actor in Japan does. The strange paradox is that at first actors were also at the bottom of the social ladder. They were outcasts with no civil rights. Adored by the public and scorned by the government, *Kabuki* actors closed ranks and became self-governing within the restrictions of their class. Eleven families produced all of the *Kabuki* actors. One current star of the *Kabuki* stage is a direct descendant of the "first family" of *Kabuki*, the Danjuro family. That first Danjuro actor, Ichikawa (born in 1660), perfected the *aragoto* style of performance, which translates variously as "thundering," "rough" and "ruffian stuff." The other major style of performance, *wagato* means "soft." To this day, only the master actor of the family can hold the name Ichikawa Danjuro, whether he is the son, adopted son, or most talented pupil of the Ichikawa who came before.

There are infinite rules each actor must know, explaining their long and arduous training period. An *onnagata* is seated a half pace behind an actor in a male role, and an actor always faces the audience for an important speech. Male characters always start with the left foot, females with the right. They seek great beauty of stage picture; each scene ending with a striking pose. Stopping frequently to pose (called a *mie*) is preceded by energetic motion and then offset by the sudden stillness. This convention crystallizes the striking contrast within the form, between intense drama and utter tranquility. Acting style veers from the stylized (*jida-mono*) to the realistic (*sews-mono*).

Music and percussion fully support the actors. Ceremonial music involves stick drum and wooden clappers, special effects (*geza*) music and *shamisen* and flute and *de-bayish* or song and chant music to accompany actor's recitation. Convention dictates that the flute can bring back departed spirits.

Decline and Rebirth

Although *Kabuki* has seen its share of hard times over the centuries, like *Noh* it clings tenaciously to life. The form changed continuously until after World War II when it froze for about thirty years. Now the leading *Kabuki* artist, Ennosuke Ichikawa III, is again stretching the limits, reviving lost traditions of clowning and audience interaction, and adding new and spectacular stunts, and all-woman companies are the rage.

Sadly, the theatre that evolved for common people has become prohibitively expensive to produce and attend. Corporate sponsorship is necessary to cover costs, and the most common *Kabuki* audience today is a group of business VIPs. On the upside, international attention paid to touring *Kabuki* troupes and renewed national interest in preserving the spirit of *Kabuki* makes its continuing survival certain.

American actors rarely perform *Kabuki* scripts, but the style can be used to mount Western scripts, especially Shakespeare and Greek tragedy, which involves a mixture of drama, poetry, music, and dance. *Kabuki* and Shakespeare share sweep, grandeur, and sheer size. For Shakespeare scripts involving magic, storms, and high ritual (*The Tempest, Macbeth, A Midsummer Night's Dream, King Lear* and *Titus Andronicus* among others), the form offers an ideal way of handling these elements through striking theatrical conventions instead of high tech. A forest suddenly created and dissolved by *koken* and a wind by swirling chiffon is a simple, highly theatrical possibility.

As the early brilliance of theatre in the East spread and adapted to the currents of change, Western theatre was experiencing its own burst of brilliance, also adapting and evolving through high and lean times. We will turn now to the some of the most famous and influential Western theatres, starting with the Greeks, and ending with the English Renaissance and its most favored child, William Shakespeare.

FIRST SCRIPTED WESTERN THEATRE: THE GREEKS

Between the first major drama festival in 534 BCE and the defeat of Athens in 404 BCE, the theatre soared to greatness. Only *three percent* of all drama written in that century remains: thirty-three tragedies, eleven comedies, and one satyr play. Yet that three percent has affected Western theatre to this day. To understand their enduring influence, we again begin with the culture itself.

Time

Greeks perceived time as linear, starting with a creation point and moving forward toward an inevitable end. Unlike Hindus or Buddhists, the Greeks saw themselves as connected to the past and future. A Greek stood firmly in the present where active participation in civic life was a primary duty. The plays of the fifth century BCE explored historical events, but they taught appropriate behavior in the present.

Space

Greek civilization evolved on a mountainous peninsula, surrounded by seas filled with thousands of islands. Each city-state or *polis* (small by today's standards) considered itself an independent state only loosely connected by language and history to the others. Many Greek citizens never left their city of origin, and so on a global scale, their sense of space was finite and limited. A small island could encompass the known world.

However, the Greek sense of space encompassed the soul and mind as well as the body. The physical world was but one portion of a vast universe with the gods above and the underworld below. Yet, like time, space was finite, and their great philosophers demanded evidence of the senses before accepting traditional or religious claims.

The average Greek experienced the most important events of his life in public. He was an active citizen and aired his views in public forums. His private life remained enclosed behind walls (as were the women, by the way, except for concubines). He had to earn and keep his place in public venues for his life to have any real importance.

Values

Essential values of Greek society are reflected in the words patriarch, warrior, intellectual, balanced, and service. Only a *citizen* had value or power in a Greek city. Citizenship was usually a birthright, though an outsider might earn it, and only men received it.

A citizen's first duty was as an able warrior and participant in his city's defense. His second duty was to his companions, the mentors of his youth, and his brothers in a battlefield. His third duty was to his family.

A citizen received an education in logic, mathematics, and rhetoric (the art of public speaking). Concepts of justice (*dike*) as a preordained, inescapable path, virtue (*arête*) as excellence within one's social context, fate (*moira*) as one's impersonal allotment in life and God (*theos*) as a higher power beyond the power of death were central in education. Balance was crucial and valued in every area of life. Worship should be balanced with ecstatic mystical experience. Power balanced mercy, and rational balanced the irrational citizen. Being too much of any one thing made one the object of ridicule and ostracism.

Structure

The social and political structure of Athens in the fifth century BCE is concentrated on Athenian democracy that divided citizens into four categories based on wealth. It was a direct democracy rather than a representative one. The two relatively minor sectors only received voting categories after approval by the two richest. The hierarchy was inflexible, preordained, and determined at birth. Ancestry, wealth, and gender determined one's place on the social ladder.

In times of war, civil liberties could be curtailed. When the Golden Age of Greek drama began, Athens was at the height of her glory, wealth, and power but had endured nearly half a century of war with Persia. During the lifetimes of two of our major playwrights, she fought a ruinous civil war with her rival Sparta that lasted over 20 years and ended with her defeat. Perhaps the plays turned to the glories of the heroic past because the present was such a dangerous and uncertain time.

Pleasure

The Greeks took pleasure in everything from intellectual debate to riotous farce. A satyr play, a bawdy, sexual mockery, always followed the serious, poetic thoughtfulness of the great tragedies. Pleasure came from balance, order, and symmetry—harmony with the natural world.

The ideals of male and female perfection were strong, athletic, statuesque, and proud. The Olympians are models—Aphrodite, Eros, and Apollo in particular. Yet, Dionysus, the newest and most dangerous god, was dark with exotic eyes and lithe, sinuous limbs. He *defied* the ideal and many thought him the most beautiful.

Athenians surrounded themselves with beauty in the form of art, sculpture, architecture, poetry, philosophy, and ceremonies—always with music and dance. The drama has rarely received such support before or since. Greek citizens worshiped the poet's gift.

The male physique defined pure physical beauty. A male's first sexual experience was likely to be with another male, forming a bond that would last for the rest of his life. We know very little about the lives of Athenian women, though we know that half the Greek pantheon of gods was female, and they represented powerful, intelligent, and emotional figures. Athens took Athena as its namesake and personal deity, yet real women lived hidden from the day-to-day life of the city.

The gods are all too human, combining all fevers and jealousies of mortals with superhuman powers and immortality. Zeus, the strongest god, was best able to manage his large and difficult family. Two of his sons, Apollo and Dionysius, reflect the opposite extremes of pleasure to the Athenian mind. The saying, "All work and no play make John a dull boy" sums up the Apollonian/ Dionysian balance. Apollo brought peace, music, and rational thought, while Dionysus brought ecstasy and horror, vitality and savage destruction. He was the patron god of the theatre and wine. His grandmother initiated him into the secret of women's mysteries. Worship of Dionysus was pure release of inhibition, resulting in a union with nature and the creative force. He offered wine and sex as paths to ecstasy. He was the only god to rescue and restore women instead of diminishing or raping them.

The Senses

Greeks were highly visual and auditory. Their city was designed to delight the eye. The natural beauty of sea, sky, and mountains inspired much of their writing. Beauty and grace in the human form delighted them. They saw beauty everywhere and worked hard to change or destroy anything ugly or out of balance.

They were oral in their communications and ceremonies. Music, chant, and poetry were designed to be *seen* and *heard*, not read in silence. In fact, one went to the theatre to hear a play as well as see one, a tradition that continued through Shakespeare's era nearly 2,000 years later.

The Drama

Sources

The sources for most surviving tragedies are the epic poems of Homer, *The Iliad* and *The Odyssey*, which carried forward the history of ancient civilizations that had colonized the country as early as 1500 BCE. Like Sanskrit dramatists, playwrights in Athens had a rich storehouse of material. For centuries, scholars believed that the stories were myth, invented by oral storytellers and eventually recorded around the eighth century BCE. We know now that historical truth grounds these stories while mythic truth adds magic and mystery. The great tragic playwrights took episodes from their Golden Age when men and gods walked the earth together, in combat and communion. The comedies, on the other hand, were about everyday events in the city, with subjects fresh from current gossip. The past held a sacred place in the minds of Athenians, while their own "modern" world deserved mockery and laughter.

The Iliad tells the story of the Greek war against Troy. (The recent film *Troy* took major liberties with the story.) Two brothers, Agamemnon and Menelaus, kings of separate cities in Greece, marry two sisters, Clytemnestra and Helen. For whatever reasons, Helen ends up in Troy with Paris, one of the sons of King Priam of Troy. The whole family of the gods gets involved, taking sides, fighting each other, making bets and toying with the humans and heroes (demi-gods or mortal offspring of a god/human coupling) until full-scale war breaks out. The war lasts ten years until the trick device of the Trojan Horse finally ends it in favor of the Greeks.

The Odyssey is the story of Odysseus, one of the heroes of the Trojan War, as he tries to make his way back home afterward. Again, the gods and goddesses of Olympus can't agree on his fate, and he and his men are tossed about the Aegean Sea for another ten years encountering powerful, seductive, and destructive forces. Back at home, his wife, Penelope, kept the home fires burning for twenty years while trying to fend off nasty suitors who claimed that her control of all of Odysseus' considerable wealth and property had nothing to do with their desire to marry her. She proved faithful and her husband returned triumphant and, as far as we know, they all lived happily ever after.

The Homeric epic story called the Theban Cycle relates the story of the founding of the city/state of Thebes and the crimes of its first kings, including the rape of a child and incest, resulting in generations of cursed and tortured offspring and the eventual destruction of the city.

These sagas, involving the rise and fall of great powers, dynastic crime and punishment, sex, power, greed, and vengeance proved fertile fields for the tragic playwrights to plow. Drawing tales from a long-ago age distinct from the day-to-day suffering of real life allows the aesthetic distance necessary for rational discourse. At the same time, the extreme nature of the characters' behavior ensures emotional impact and willing suspension of disbelief.

Styles

We are fortunate that one of the great philosophers of Western thought became interested in theatre and created a sort of *Natya Sastra* handbook about the great tragedies of Athens. Aristotle wrote his *Poetics*, an analysis of the art of tragic drama, in the century after the "golden age" of Greek tragedy, and his work is a source of much of our knowledge. In the *Poetics*, he mentions a second work on the nature of comedy, but sadly, that is lost.

We do know is that tragedy and comedy were distinct and separate, performed at different festivals at different times of the year. We have no reason to believe that a tragic playwright competed with a comic or vice versa. Yet that constant striving toward balance between the dark and light, rational and irrational, timeless and the everyday is reflected. Tragic playwrights finished their trilogies with a satyr play that satirized their own efforts, and comedy could be savage and dark behind the mask of a simple sex farce.

According to Aristotle, the ideal tragedy focused on a great man, a hero who, while attempting to serve the community, commits a grave error. In time, he sees his mistake and recognizes the solution. Aristotle preferred plays in which recognition comes too late for change. Throughout the play, the chorus represents the community watching and commenting on the choices of the hero, with their survival at stake.

The only remaining comedies are all by the same playwright, Aristophanes. They are satire and farce, and often mock the behaviors of Very Important People, criticize the government and "fully explore" the erotic. From a few remaining fragments, a shift toward domestic comedy seemed to follow, so the satire/sex farce is now known as Old Comedy and the domestic romantic comedy is called New Comedy.

The Playwrights

TABLE 7.1 — THREE PLAYWRIGHTS STAND AS THE GIANTS OF TRAGIC DRAMA

	Aeschylus	Sophocles	Euripedes
Dates	525–456 BCE	496–406 BCE	484–406 BCE
Plays	90	123	92
Extant	7	7	18
Victories	13	24	4
Died at age	69	90	78

Aeschylus lived long enough to remember tyranny but died in a democracy. His contributions included:

- introduced the second actor
- reduced the chorus from 50 to 12 members
- invented the trilogy
- made the dramatic part of the performance as important as the choral
- wrote the most magnificent choral odes
- developed wildly effective satyr plays

He was the author of our only complete trilogy, *The Oresteia*, in which, he recounts a particularly nasty episode from *The Iliad* but in a way that affirms and re-affirms the concepts of faith, justice, and Athenian law, considered by Aeschylus to be a gift from the goddess Athena.

We honor Sophocles for:

- introducing the third actor and later the fourth (*Oedipus at Colonus*),
- increasing and standardizing the chorus at 15 members
- discovering serenity in tragic vision
- adding subtlety and suppleness to drama
- discovering the power possible in quiet moments and internal conflict
- achieving the most poignant and moving of climaxes
- developing the arts of plot and characterization
- developing scenes into full acts with choral divisions
- providing the model for Aristotle's definitions of classic drama

Some Western scholars call his Oedipus the King, "the perfect tragedy." His *Antigone* is probably the most widely produced Greek tragedy in our time.

Euripides, the youngest of the three, is known for:

- increasing the number of characters and roles (but not actors)   ≠ (masks)
- showing that drama can focus on the individual and on specific social questions
- developing interest in abnormal psychology and its origins
- disconnecting the chorus from the main action
- combining realism and pathos in one event
- breaking traditions, embracing controversy, innovation, courage and independence

Medea, a strange and empathetic story of a woman who kills her children to punish their father for the crime of casting her aside, and *The Bacchae*, his chilling look at the fate of man who interferes with the worship rites of Dionysius are his most frequently produced plays today. *The Trojan Women*, dealing with the aftermath of that event is considered by many to be one of the greatest anti-war plays ever written.

Aristophanes (c. 448–385 BCE) is our master of the Old Comedy. Of his forty documented comedies, eleven remain today. He sharpened his wit on political figures, philosophers, military leaders, and his fellow playwrights. Absurd, fanciful, angry, and sometimes downright raunchy, his plays stand in testimony to the Greeks' willingness to laugh at themselves and each other. His comedy *Lysistrata*, where women decide to withhold sex from their husbands until they end the war, is considered by many to be another of the greatest anti-war plays.

The Theatre

Spaces

By the fifth century, the basic standard for the Greek theatre space was set, though scale and grandeur would grow in the centuries to come. Productions were in the open air before a crowd of up to 30,000 seated on stone bleachers in a hollowed-out hillside surrounding two-thirds of the stage. In front of the stage, a circular area called the *orchestra* was the performance area for the chorus. Behind the stage, the *skene* or scene house provided three entrance/exits and a changing room for the actors.

Conventions

Some of the conventions of Greek drama are going to be strangely similar to those of Sanskrit. Why? No one knows. Maybe actual contact between the two traditions occurred. Maybe these shared conventions arise out of the shared human need for ritual and ceremony. Our evidence about Greek theatre conventions is thin, based primarily on pottery drawings and the texts themselves. Some of the likely conventions include:

Masks: When actors put on the mask, they assume the power of the god and that of other actors who have taken on this character before. There are only seven surviving vase paintings known to show fifth century masks. They are softer, more natural, and less tortured than our earlier impressions. The mouths are slightly open. Their expressions have endlessly shifting meanings. Comic masks are not very different from what we think of as clown masks today—with buffoons, gluttons, and lechers as ridiculous then as now.

Dance/Music: Both were central to production. Many scholars believe that the entire performance was more like watching a dance and listening to songs than like realistic behavior, with constant ritualized movement and chanted speeches. Instruments most employed were the lyre (the definitive Greek instrument with up to seven spun-silk strings struck with a plectrum, sometimes using a turtle shell for sounding board), the alous (a double- or single-reed wind instrument spanning three octaves) and percussion (cymbals and drums). What emerges is a sound of haunting simplicity.

Chorus: Perhaps the strangest convention in Greek tragedy, to *us*, made it more moving and involving for the original audience. Unlike the narrator in Sanskrit drama, the chorus and chorus leader are the ideal spectators for the event, representing *us* while the heroes struggle through their trials. The chorus expresses the conventional attitude of an average citizen of this community, to introduce new characters and question them, admonish or chastise characters behaving inappropriately, offer comfort and sympathy to characters who are victims, explain puzzling events, establish facts and clarify motives. They may pray, lament, celebrate, contemplate or share ironic observations. They have a group identity, but each member also has a single identity, not unlike a contemporary chorus for musicals.

Length: Surviving scripts are generally *much* shorter than those of India. The theatre *event* might have taken all day, beginning at dawn, and ending with evening, but they produced four plays during that day. The comedies of Aristophanes are also quite compact, generally lasting much less than two hours in modern productions.

The Unities: Although later Europeans would become ridiculously enamored with Unities, the idea behind the word comes from Aristotle's study of plays he liked best. He felt that time, place, and action meld into a believable whole. So, unlike Sanskrit with epic adventures spanning decades, Greek plays tend to take place in "real time," located in a single place, and they tend to tell one story about one event, usually starting near the end (a late point of attack) so that all necessary action can believably take place in the time allowed.

Decline and Rebirth

By the end of the fifth century BCE, the glory days of Athenian drama had passed. Greece continued to be the home of beauty, philosophy, and devotion to the arts, but within fifty years of the deaths of Sophocles and Euripides, she ceased to exist as an independent state, conquered first by the Macedonians and then the Romans.

The Romans were the great "borrowers" of Western history. They happily copied anything they found useful or attractive, and one of the things they found attractive in Greece was theatre. They built huge theatre spaces that copied the Grecian style but dwarfed them in size and grandeur.

They copied the tragedians too, and at least one playwright, Seneca (c. 3 BCE–c. 65 BCE) achieved a stature that has endured. He wrote dark tragedies, and is considered one of the primary influences on the Renaissance tragedies of Shakespeare and his contemporaries.

Comedy, on the other hand, was not only borrowed but in some ways redefined in the hands of one Roman comic playwright, Plautus (c. 254–184 BCE). Adapted from Greek New Comedy, his plays avoided the critical, satirical tone of Aristophanes, but instead featured middle- and lower-class characters and were written in the language of the common people. He created stock character types like the braggart warrior and the old miser that we will see returning to the European stage a full 1500 years later in the works of Shakespeare and Moliere.

With the fall of the Roman Empire, Western civilization and the theatre entered a period of long decline and stagnation. Actors and playwrights disappear into the wilderness. The tradition of bards, troubadours, and poets who returned to the oral traditions of their ancestors, is our only evidence of their survival and our continued need to create performance art.

Theatre in the Middle Ages

Throughout most of Europe during the centuries following the destruction of the Roman Empire, the primary authority was the Catholic Church. In the beginning, in the fourth century, the Church outlawed theatre—and with good reason. Christians had been a target of mockery in the "entertainments" of the late Empire, sometimes sold into slavery and forced to perform, sometimes killed outright as the audience cheered. A long period of dormancy follows, and not until the ninth century did we find our first scrap of evidence that the Church began to use theatre as a means of teaching biblical ideas to their largely illiterate converts.

Virtues	Vices
Love/Charity, *Caritas*	Lust, *Luxuria*
Hope, *Spes*	Gluttony, *Gula*
Faith, *Fides*	Avarice/Greed, *Avaritia*
Temperance, *Temperantia*	Sloth, *Acedia*
Justice, *Iustitia*	Wrath, *Ira*
Courage, *Fortitudo*	Envy, *Invidia*
Wisdom, *Sapientia*	Pride, *Superbia*

By the thirteenth and fourteenth centuries, many European towns held annual festivals that included performances of stories from the Bible. Sanctioned by the Church, though sometimes grudgingly, trade groups organized these pageants, with each in charge of one section of the story. Our documentation of these events is spotty, but clearly, competition between guilds led to some spectacular effects and occasional episodes of secular humor. Many included *allegory*, the use of characters that represent one of the seven vices and virtues (see table). Others drew from the Bible and transformed the whole into a long series of wagon/theatres. Each wagon or "station" told one part of the biblical story, from creation through redemption and/or damnation. Damnation stations provided opportunities for creative pyrotechnics and fierce competitions for the "Hell's Mouth" project occurred.

Though these events were not a return of professional theatre, they eventually evolved into and influenced the next period of truly exceptional Western theatre—the Renaissance, a period of shining rebirth called the Elizabethan Age.

ELIZABETHAN DRAMA

After the brilliance of the ancient Greeks, over 2,000 years passed before unquestioned greatness returned to Western theatre. Plague, war, and famine wiped out much of the Europe's population and, for a time, theatre itself. Then a mighty England emerged as ruler of the known globe, and the English language exploded with over 10,000 new words added in less than a century. Neither before, nor since has a language grown so astonishingly fast. Drama is where the new words soared.

The term Elizabethan refers to the reign of Elizabeth I (1558–1603), but includes both her father's life and the two monarchs following her—in other words, the influences before and after her. Because her father (Henry VIII) broke with Rome and created his own church, Elizabeth, at her coronation, became both head of state *and* head of the church. She had no higher allegiance than her own vision. While the Renaissance began in Italy, in an emancipated England it flourished.

Strongly influenced by the rediscovery of classical Greek and Roman texts, the worldview of Elizabethan England was similar to that described earlier in this chapter. Here we will deal with only those elements that were different from the classical worldview.

World View

Much like Athens of the 2000 years before, the English of the late sixteenth and early seventeenth centuries believed they could do no wrong. Drake's voyage around the world, Raleigh's exploration of North American, and an astonishing naval victory over the Spanish, who had previously claimed title to the greatest naval fleet in the world, seemed like miracles. Elizabethans had already found "more things in heaven and earth" than ever previously dreamed. They regarded the world as *theirs*.

While providing an important backdrop, Elizabethan times are not what most of the plays are about. Many playwrights opted for choices that were more exotic. Living in an extraordinary world, they often placed their plays in worlds that exceeded even their own. Understanding this style means entering the *imaginary* lives of the writers, beyond their day-to-day existence.

Time

Like the Greeks, the Elizabethans experienced time as linear and finite. Creation led to an inevitable Armageddon. Unlike the Greeks, they left much of the past in the land of "bad old days" and forgot about it as much as possible. During Elizabeth's long reign, people could remember with vivid detail the civil wars and murderous religious conflicts of the previous decades. People opted to not focus on the past however. It was merely a catalyst to the future. The Elizabethan was optimistic, forward-looking, and ready for whatever came next. Unlike Greek plays where the future is so painful as to be almost unendurable, Elizabethan plays end with a strong sense of the *next* scene, be it a wedding celebration, reunion feast, or funeral procession to occur offstage. Even a painful ceremony promises to bring a "brave new world" with it.

Space

The Elizabethan sense of space was not fundamentally different from that of the Greeks. However, the known universe was growing and shifting under their feet. A new world had been discovered, a round world at that. The telescope challenged the immutibility of heaven itself. The English renaissance man needed his sea legs to maintain his balance. They saw the cosmos in much the same way as the Greeks, with Heaven above and Hell below. Another small nation, they too turned to the sea that surrounded them and gave them room for expansion.

Values

Elizabethans considered themselves one tiny step below the angels in the great chain of being. The majority practiced a Protestant state religion all but Catholic in its ceremonies and liturgies. New disturbing sects (Puritan, Calvinist, and Anabaptist) held secret services and Elizabeth turned a blind eye. No one wanted more blood shed over religious doctrine. After decades of bloody conflict and shifting official faiths, many Elizabethans turned to secularism. The classical humanists of Greece and Rome became their models. For all their optimism, they knew that life was short. The average life expectancy was twenty-seven years—with sixty-five percent dying by the age of sixteen.

Structure

Life is based on a belief in a great chain of being, moving from God on down to Satan. Each species had a natural leader. The body had three monarchs: liver, heart, and brain. The world consists of four ruling elements: earth, water, air, and fire. The chain with each link is as follows:

1. God—perfection

2. Angels/ether—pure understanding

3. Stars—fortune

4. Elements—being

5. Man—feeling and understanding

6. Animals—sensation

7. Plants—growth

8. Metals—durability

9. Demons—temptations

10. Satan—eternal damnation

Man is in the middle, without perfection or durability, but central to the chain. The chain was immutable and eternal, dictated by God. At the top of the human chain sat the monarch and the royal family, followed by aristocrats (both spiritual and secular), and so on down the chain. As the individual's place on the chain was ordained, mobility was not encouraged. Change threatened the order of the universe. If the country suffered under a mad or evil monarch, that was God's punishment to be endured. Although less cosmically enforced, the hierarch extended into the community and the family.

Pleasure

For the wealthy, life was regarded as a banquet of activity with feasting, dancing, and riding for hours on end. Splendor was sought everywhere and all were heavily bejeweled. Dark silks and velvets reflected and absorbed light, like the lining of a jewel box. Brighter colors flashed through slashed openings or from attached precious stones.

Nothing was vulgar, crude, or unseemly if it done with great accomplishment. All courtiers could write a sonnet, sing a madrigal, play a lute, declare a position, and ride a horse with considerable skill. Much like a Sanskrit ideal, the perfect Renaissance man was a warrior, scholar, philosopher, and poet. Humor was often bawdy and lewd. One needed to be sharp of mind, quick of tongue, lively of spirit, and graceful in movement.

Almost any event could be cause for celebration. Since life was so short and the end could come at any moment, life was devoured. Never squeamish, some public entertainments—cockfighting (two fighting cocks let loose in a ring), baiting (diverse dogs let loose on a chained bear, bull, or badger) or public executions (hangings, beheadings, and burnings) were quite bloody and very popular. Yet one of the most loved pastimes of all was going to the theatre with one-tenth of the population attending public performance regularly and a similar number at private ones.

Senses

Even Cher could not eclipse a resplendent Elizabethan lord or lady making an entrance, both in personal adornment and sense of self. In modern productions, only a few comedies are likely to be costumed in authentic Elizabethan garb because the extravagant padding, called "bombast," makes today's actors resemble hockey players. One of the most outrageous clothing elements was the codpiece, which began innocently as a practical triangle to fill the crotch area between the tops of men's hose, tied to the waist by points (strips of fabric or ribbon). Codpieces developed, however, into ostentatious, extravagant works of art, often stuffed, and sometimes slashed, bejeweled and bedecked. Capes of various kinds, long, short, draped, or stiff, were hugely popular.

Every well-educated person in this period could sight-read music, often printed on a grand scale so several singers may read it at once. Minstrels were common at court and countryside. Extraordinary music pervaded daily life, from glorious sacred madrigals to bawdy tavern rounds. Composers worked in all forms. Thirty-two of Shakespeare's thirty-seven plays have direct references to music.

Dancing moved from a loosely organized activity on the village green to an art practiced at court under the tutelage of experts.

Heavy perfume, sauces, and fabric and rich, dense, voluptuous sensations were all valued as were individuality, virtuosity, zest, and a sense of adventure.

The Drama

The era was named for Elizabeth and spans several monarchies, but Tudor, Elizabethan, and Jacobean drama—all related styles of drama—are named for the monarch in power. Tudor plays (named for Henry Tudor, Henry VIII) evolved in the universities and broke from the control of the church. They mark the transition from medieval to renaissance drama and showed from the start that English drama would not be constrained by European classical rules.

The plays included elements of morality play and farce, and ignored the unities of times, place and action. While not graced with the beauty of language and depth of character of their descendants, they re-introduced secular and mythological stories, and set the stage for the brilliant playwrights to come. Elizabethan drama shines as the pinnacle of the era. All forms of genre, poetry, source material, and theatrical effect blaze out of these scripts. Jacobean drama is much darker and more cynical. As England careened toward yet another civil war, dramatists focused their gaze on the life of the common people of London, creating grim and compelling glimpses into the subdued mood that followed the zest of Elizabeth's long reign.

Early Tudor drama owed much to both medieval and classical models. *Ralph Roister Doister* (c. 1545) by Nicholas Udall and *Gammer Gurton's Needle* (c. 1552) first combined elements of classical Roman comedy with native clowning. Almost unreadable by today's standards, they preceded the work of a group of men associated with acadamia, the self-proclaimed University Wits, including

John Lyly (*Endimion*), Robert Greene (*Friar Bacon and Friar Bungay*), and Thomas Kyd (*The Spanish Tragedy*).

No one showed greater promise than the brilliant young Christopher Marlowe. Writing about heroes whose very greatness leads to their fall, he wrote in blank verse "with a rhetorical brilliance and eloquence superbly equal to the demands of high drama." The son of a shoemaker, he was educated at Cambridge and might have challenged Shakespeare as the greatest Elizabethan playwright if he had not been murdered in a barroom brawl at the age of twenty-nine. His grand tragedies include *Tamburlaine the Great* (1587), *Dr. Faustus* (1588), *The Jew of Malta* (1589), and *Edward II* (1592). Notice how quicky he wrote, as a professional on a very limited income. He also wrote pamphlets, poetry and song lyrics, in between plays that command universal respect 400 years after his death.

The Elizabethan dramatists (see chart) lived and worked in the shadow of the greatest of them all, William Shakespeare. Born in 1564 the son of a tanner from the village Stratford-upon-Avon, he was forced by youthful indiscretion into marriage and fatherhood by the age of nineteen. He later hitched his wagon to a theatrical star and went to London where he lived and worked well into his forties. He eventually returned to Stratford, living as a prosperous land owner until his death in 1616. No Western playwright commands so much adoration, attention, criticism, and continued production as he. His poetry soars even when his plots are trifling, and his works soar to the heights and plunge to the depths of human experience. He is often called the "greatest playwright who ever lived." He wrote romping farce (*Comedy of Errors*) and agonizing tragedy (*Romeo and Juliet* and *King Lear*), shimmering romance (*As You Like It* and *Twelfth Night*) and challenging experimental forms that defy labels (*MeasureforMeasure* and *All's Well that Ends Well*). Other playwrights who gained some success and popularity at the time include George Chapman (*All Fools*, 1599; *The Gentleman Usher*, 1606; and *Bussy D'Ambois*, 1607), and Ben Jonson, Shakespeare's friend and rival (*Volpone*, 1606 and *The Alchemist*, 1610).

The Jacobean playwrights (named for King James I, Elizabeth's successor in 1603) created plays with increasingly sensational bouts of violence and mayhem. Lacking the stature of Marlowe and Shakespeare, they made up for it by entertaining audiences with buckets of gore. Their plays (even the comedies) tend to be horrific, obscene, and deeply cynical. Sadly, their plays offer us a more realistic view of seventeenth century London than the beautifully fictional worlds of Shakespeare. Thomas Middleton, Phillip Massinger, and Beamont and Fletcher, Thomas Dekker, Thomas Middleton, and John Webster represent the best of the Jacobean playwrights.

The Theatre

The Elizabethan Playhouse: enclosed but yet not indoors

Located on the south bank of the Thames River, the Elizabethan theatres shared their neighborhood with other shady (but very popular) entertainment venues such as brothels, taverns, and baiting pits. The open courtyards of inns, where carriages pulled in off the street to deposit passengers and cargo, provided the models for both the theatres and baiting pits. Open to the sky, using only natural light, the theatres were enclosed.

The Globe Playhouse had a great, open stage near forty feet wide and twenty-nine feet deep, with up to seven entrances and exits, where every corner of one's field of vision was filled with up to 3,000 spectators, none farther away than sixty feet and some close enough to touch the actors. Most productions made no attempt to suggest locale. Scenes overlap, with actors exiting while others enter. The robust enthusiasm and active interaction of a modern rock concert or athletic event comes closest to that passing between Elizabethan actor and public. The reverent, intimidated audience at a Shakespearean performance now is remote from the spirited original.

Plays and Playwrights

Below are scripts most likely to find life in a modern production. Almost any play by Shakespeare is more likely to enter your life than any single script by any other writer of the period. Do not discount his brothers, however. Some genuine thrills and chills exist in the rest of Elizabethan drama. **Note**: Naturally, the lives and works of these artists overlap, so keep in mind that the following chart denotes the period of their best work or of their strongest association.

In 1642, the English Civil War between the monarchy and its supporters and the Puritan army of Oliver Cromwell, broke out. Although the age of English dramatic greatness waned prior to the war, theatre came to an abrupt end in 1642 and would not be seen on the English stage again until 1660.

TABLE 7.2 ENGLISH DRAMATISTS

Tudor Dramatists	Elizabethan Dramatists	Jacobean Dramatists
John Lyly	**Francis Beaumont/John Fletcher**	**John Ford**
Endimion 1591	*The Knight of the Burning Pestle* I607	*'Tis Pity She's a Whore* 1625
Robert Greene	*The Maid's Tragedy* 1610	**Thomas Middleton**
Friar Bacon and Friar Bungay 1591	*A King and No King* 1611	*The Changeling* 1623
Thomas Kyd	**Thomas Dekker**	**Thomas Heywood**
The Spanish Tragedy 1592	*The Shoemaker's Holiday* I599	*A Woman Killed with Kindness* 1603
Christopher Marlowe	**Ben Jonson**	*The English Travellor* 1638
Tamburlaine the Great 1587	*The Alchemist* 1610	**John Webster**
Doctor Faustus 1588	*Bartholomew Fair* 1614	*The White Devil* 1608
The Jew of Malta 1588	*Every Man in His Humour* 1598	*The Duchess of Malfi* 1612
Edward II 1590	*Volpone* 1605	**Cyril Tourneur**
	William Shakespeare (see Chart 2)	*The Revenger's Tragedy* 1607

TABLE 7.3 WILLIAM SHAKESPEARE (DATES ARE APPROXIMATE)

Comedies	Tragedies	Histories	"Other"
Comedy of Errors 1590	*Titus Andronicus* 1590	*Henry IV* Part 1 1597	*All's Well that Ends Well* 1604
Taming of the Shrew 1591	*Richard III* 1592	*Henry IV* Part 2 1598	*Measure for Measure* 1604
Two Gentlemen of Verona 1593	*Romeo and Juliet* 1594–6	*Henry VI* Part 1 1590–1592	*Pericles* 1608
Love's Labor's Lost 1594	*Richard II* 1595	*Henry VI* Part 2 1590–1592	*Cymbeline* 1609
A Midsummer Night's Dream 1594	*Julius Caesar* 1599	*Henry VI* Part 3 1590–1592	*The Winter's Tale* 1610
Merry Wives of Windsor 1597	*Hamlet* 1601	*King John* 1596	*The Tempest* 1611
As You Like It 1598	*Othello* 1603–1604	*Henry V* 1599	
Much Ado About Nothing 1599	*King Lear* 1605	*Henry VIII* 1612–1613	
Twelfth Night 1600	*Macbeth* 1605		
	Antony and Cleopatra 1606		
	Corialanus 1608		
	Timon of Athens 1605–1608		
	Troilus and Cressida 1602		

First Theatre in Africa

When discussing theatre in Africa we must be clear about key issues:

1. It is a vast continent with distinct nations, languages, histories, and traditions. We will focus on the West African culture of Yoruba, but include variables when possible.

2. The oral tradition was and still is central to the theatre of much of sub-Saharan Africa. This means that dating the first play or playwright, even identifying dates of origin, is meaningless.

3. Much of the research about African theatre traditions is highly controversial. When scholars disagree vehemently, we will attempt to honor their points of view.

As with Sanskrit and Greek theatre, we will begin by discussing the Yoruban world view, relying on the scholarship and life experiences of West Africans such as internationally acclaimed playwright/scholar, Wole Soyinka (winner of the Noble Prize for Literature), and griotte/scholar, Adaora Nzelibe Schmiedl, and actor/scholar Charles Dumas.

Time

Think of the Yoruban sense of time as a lake. All time exists simultaneously. One's life is a drop of water in that lake. All that has been, is, and ever will be co-exists in the lake of time. The lake of time encompasses four states of being: the unborn, the living, the ancestors, and the gods. As all four states of being exist in simultaneous time, communication is possible and sometimes required. Remember the story of Ogun and his fight to re-unite with the living, his effort and sacrifice broke the barriers of time and space that kept the gods apart from the people.

Space

Like time, space is fluid in the Yoruban spiritual view. Time and space unite; you go to the burial grounds and have conversations with the dead, not metaphorically, but literally. Space is the distance you must travel to meet with the unborn or the gods.

In the prosaic world of day-to-day life, space is the defined first by the home, then by the village, then by the whole of Africa. Archeological evidence reveals that as long as 4,000 years ago, Yoruban traders and merchants were traveling from the far north in Egypt to the most southern tip of Africa in what is now called South Africa. But the family home in the village of their birth was the central space where work, play, learning, and teaching took place.

Values

Unlike both Indian and Greek culture, the Yoruban community did not define itself by warrior values. The epic stories passed down through the generations did not glorify an ancient time of wars and heroes. Instead, the people of West Africa valued family, community, and peaceful consensus. This is not to imply that violence never occurred, only that the communal history celebrated peaceful resolution of conflict.

The ancestors were worshipped, the elderly respected, and children cherished. The concept of "it takes a village to raise a child" was (and is) a working reality in West Africa. Resources were shared; gift giving and receiving was a part of daily life. The gods, spirits, and demons that shared time and space with the living were consulted, appeased, and exorcised through communal effort.

Structure

The elders, who consulted, debated, and argued with each other until they reached consensus, led the community. A single leader usually made day-to-day decisions, settled disagreements, and navigated social interactions. But this position was earned and could only be kept by consultation with the elders. Age was the defining organizational model, with those who survived childhood and adulthood into their elder years moving up in authority through the years. Each child learned the history and lessons of the community through the traditional theatre events that were literally a functioning part of each day. The faster they learned, the sooner they would achieve respect and authority within the communal structure.

Pleasure

Nothing gave the Yorubans more pleasure than their children. In fact, barrenness was so feared that a large percentage of the stories, rituals, and remedies contained within the communal memory were devoted to its cure. The birth of a healthy child was always a cause for celebration. Celebrations and feast days marked each stage of life. The survival of the child concerned all of the community.

Dance, music, storytelling, and theatre were deeply honored pleasures, in part because they were communal by nature and in part, because they were simply so much fun. The arrival of a griot or griotte was a cause for feasting and celebration. The preparation of the evening meal was a time for teaching children and entertaining adults through these performance arts. At the end of a hard day's work, the adults took turns and competed with each other while the children looked on and waited for the day they could tell the next story or act a part in the next performance.

The Senses

The natural world strongly shaped Yoruban sensory experience. Though their travel took them to the pyramids of Egypt and the great cities of Mali, they did not create artificial edifices that blocked out the natural surroundings. They lived fully in the environment, creating works of art that reflected that world without attempting to change it or perfect it. The sights, sounds, and smells of the world were perfect as they were, as the gods made them. To attempt to correct or defy the natural world would be a disrespect to the creator and to the gods and spirits who inhabited and sustained the world.

The Drama

Because Yoruba's traditional theatre is quite distinct from the formalized drama of India and Greece, we have to explore the form from a new perspective. The "text" of the plays resided in the communal memories of the people. This is not because the people of West Africa had no written language. (How could they carry on international trade without some means of record keeping?) It's because the source, style, and *function* of theatre was so different from the other cultures we've discussed.

The Source

The source of theatre was very simply the memory of the people. No one has attempted to date the beginning of the theatre in West Africa because the stories go back to the "time before" and the "time to come" and contained the history of the people through hundreds of generations. The *Ogun Mysteries* (see Chapter 2) were only one part of an enormous body of work carried forward generation after generation.

Styles

The style of the West African drama is linked to its function. Its function is linked to the event. Sometimes the function is educational (which does not mean entertainment is neglected!). An individual volunteers to tell a story. She may then select younger people to play out the parts in the story. A young person may then be challenged to tell a new story, and he can choose to play all the parts himself or recruit others to perform. This kind of theatre is an ongoing part of daily life. One didn't buy a ticket, go to a theatre, sit in a seat in the dark, and watch others perform a play. The entire community participated, playing audience one moment, actor the next, and narrator the time after that.

Comedies, tragedies, ghost stories, history lessons, and moral lessons can be combined in endless variety. Though less formal than some of the styles we have looked at, never think that this is a free-for-all improv either. The child learns from the adults, the adults learn from the elders and those who are gifted in their dramatic abilities are honored. Making it up as you go along, violating the communal memory or deciding to "correct" a narrative is simply unacceptable. Since everyone participates, everyone also feels free to critique the performance.

Three stylistic tendencies emerge (though not without debate):

1. West African theatre strives to interpret reality, rather than realistically represent it.

2. West African drama offers its audience a quality called *efe*, translated as indulgent enjoyment. The suffering of a King Lear or a Greek tragic hero, even in a performance of one of those plays, must reflect the African sense of forward-looking, solution-seeking positivism and joy.

3. The drama must not only allow or encourage audience response, but must demand audience participation.

The Theatre

As noted above, very little in Sanskrit or Greek theatre prepares one for the traditional theatre of West Africa. The theatre space is anywhere, anytime, everyday. From the kitchen to the market place, the world itself is the stage and life itself is the drama. The conventions depend entirely on the function and nature of the event. We can safely identify some tendencies:

Allegory—the use of symbolic characters that have become associated with certain human qualities. For example, many plots feature Rabbit, a trickster and thief, who can illustrate the canny solution to a problem or the punishment coming to the thief.

Mask/costume—in sacred events, gods, spirits and demons are performed in masks and costumes designed to bond the performer to the character. These masks and costumes are deeply spiritual artifacts that allow transcendence between the living and the ancestors, the unborn and the gods.

> **Kole Omotoso,** *Nigerian theater artist*
>
> "The streets of my home town . . . in Nigeria, constituted the ever-moving theatre in which my eyes first saw the rituals of my Yoruba culture, history, and rituals."

Music/dance—both are central to any performance event. The accomplished performer uses song, dance and strongly percussive, polyrhythmic music to build tension and release tension.

Call And Response—the actor expects the audience to vocally support the performance. Community involvement is so important, only by hearing the shouts and praises of the people can the actor feel secure. Silence is very bad news. Shouted criticisms and corrections are worse. The performers often talk directly to the audience, and, unlike most Western theatre, they expect the audience to talk back.

Optimism—however sad or harrowing a plot may be, the resolution is usually profoundly optimistic. Since the universe is operating in simultaneous harmony, even death is a transition from one plane to the next. (Despite centuries of colonial oppression, this profound faith that things are moving in the right direction continues to inform modern African drama.)

Decline and Rebirth

Enter Islam

Traditional theatre in North Africa almost (but not quite) ceased to exist with the invasion of conquering Arab armies bringing Islam and a new dominant culture to the region. Today only a very few hidden sanctuaries of indigenous African populations can be found (and finding them is not for the the faint of heart or weak of body). Islam arrived in Egypt in 640 BCE and in Egypt we can most easily trace Islamic influences because of the wealth of source material.

Although Alexandria fell to an Arab army in 640 BCE, transformation did not occur over night. Islam encourages tolerance of other faiths, so as its empire exanded, conversion was not the first priority. For the next two hundred years, in fact, the official religion of Egypt was Christianity. Ultimately, conversion did take place and the performance traditions of nomadic Arab tribes melded with ancient Egyptian styles.

The Arab traditions included the importance of bards who retained the tribal history and interpreted all important events. Music and dance flourished as performance arts that functioned as part narrative and part abstract expression. Egyptian tradition centered round religious and seasonal celebrations, marking community-wide participation in and observance of key events. Huge elaborate processionals were performed, often on the Nile River, the life-blood of Egyptian culture. Islamic rulers encouraged the continuation of these age old festivities and added about fifty Muslims festivals to the calendar, including the Muslim lunar New Year, the birth of Mohammed, and the feast of Ramadan.

By the Middle Ages, thirteenth and fourteenth centuries, travelers to Egypt reported seeing dancers, storytellers, bards, and even trained fleas and camels as an on-going parade of performers. They also reported finding shadow puppets, imported from Asia, but given a distinctively Egyptian flavor. The first recorded shadow puppet play, *Ajib wa Gharib*, is a comedy satirizing both performers and conmen, perhaps universally suspected of being the same thing. Later shadow puppet plays supported the birth of the Ottoman dynasty and even told stories of the Crusades.

The Arrival of Europeans

The arrival of European colonizers and missionaries deeply affected the traditional theatre of West Africa. In their attempts to exploit and "civilize" Africa, Europeans imported Western theatre traditions and styles as well. For centuries, traditional oral theatre was displaced from the center of the community, replaced by Western institutions. It did not die out completely though. It continued in the memories of the communities, in the lessons taught to children by their elders through song and dance, and in performances conducted away from the disapproving eyes of the colonizers.

SUMMARY

Early theatre moves through some remarkably similar patterns of emphasis in cultures widely separated and without direct interaction. These can be divided into three periods: 1) Origins,

2) Conquest and Retreat, and 3) Resurgence of Popular Drama. Beginning with highly spiritual and profound Sanskrit and Greek dramas, important principles are established for the theatre as a force in all our lives. Theatre is used to explore the major questions about the meaning of life itself. There is then a period of less brilliant, but intriguing theatrical productivity around the world, in some cases being used to indoctrinate, in others simply to have a wildly good time. Late in the sixteenth century, Elizabethan drama, led by Shakespeare, burst upon the world with a sweeping energy not unlike that of Japanese *Kabuki*. Suddenly theatre not only embraced all the people but also captured imaginations in tales of power, wonder, and adventure. Early African theatre was unlike anything found in Asia or the West. Grounded in a unique perspective, it pervaded everyday life, from the simple kitchen stories at the end of a workday to the high ritual ceremonies invoking the protection of gods. Islam brought a new set of aesthetic values that gradually blended with local customs, resulting in theatre unique to North Africa and grounded in the traditions of the bard, dancer, singer, and shadow-puppetry. European colonization and slavery beginning in the sixteenth century and continuing for centuries, nearly doomed Africa's theatre.

SUGGESTED ASSIGNMENTS

1. What do you find most and least similar about the earliest periods of recorded drama?

2. Why do you believe theatre moves in and out of brilliance at various times?

3. Is there any possible explanation for similar events occurring in theatrical communities with no direct interaction?

4. What characteristics would you pick to distinguish European, Asian and African theatre during their early periods of development?

5. What can you identify as the concerns of early drama, no matter what the culture? How many of these concerns are still major for all of us, and which seem to have receded with time?

6. To what extent do you believe early prevailing cultural standards and beliefs limited or set up free theatrical expression?

7. What would you identity as the greatest similarities between theatre BCE and our own, and the greatest difference between them?

8. How would you answer Question 7 for the years 1590–1620?

9. Which cultural values seem to have most separated parts of the world in terms of their theatrical expression? Where do you feel there is the most potential to meet in accord?

10. Which of the earliest theatrical achievements have had the most profound influence on theatre today?

SUGGESTED ACTIVITIES

1. Individual—Chose one ancient tradition from any part of the world and gather any visual, written, or recorded images that you can find. Present this to your class, or create a "montage" that shares and preserves your findings.

2. Small Group—Choose a topic of interest to the group (greed, lust, politics, dorm food, roommate troubles). Elect a griot, bard, or storyteller. Rehearse a performance with other group members playing roles as the storyteller narrates or sings the tale.

3. Long-term—Outline key events in your life that involve a spiritual, cosmic, or social concern of magnitude. Develop a means of dramatizing those events into one essential story line. Choose a Western, African, or Asian tradition to provide the style of storytelling used.

4. Large Group—As a community, create a traditional dramatic celebration. Decide what issue to address, what style to use, and what conventions (music, dance, puppets, and masks) to use. Decide how the audience will actively participate. Try your best to create the whole event.

KEY WORDS AND IDEAS

Sanskirt

Siddharta (Bhudda)

Vedas

Bharata

Mahabharata

Ramayana

Shudraka, Bhasa, Kalidasa

Natya Sastra

Xiqu

Zaju

Dionysus

Apollo

Homer, *The Illiad, The Odyssey*

Aristotle, *The Poetics*

Aeschylus, Sophocles, Euripides

Aristophanes

Plautus

Yoruba

Allegory

Simultaneous Harmony

Noh

Kanani/Zeami

Shite

Hashigakari

Danjuro Family

Jidaimono

Sewamona

Onnagata

Aragoto

Wagato

Hamanichi

Great Chain of Being

Shakespeare

The Globe

FROM ELITISM BACK TO THE PEOPLE

D URING THE seventeenth and eighteenth centuries, theatre went through a strange pattern. At first, new forms that welcome audiences of all classes continued to develop. Then a middle exclusivity phase restricted theatre to courtiers and aristocrats. Finally, there was a sense that enough was enough! People burst back into the theatre and have remained there ever since.

Noh, which had been a wild and giddy variety show performed in market places and town squares, became, by the seventeenth century, the exclusive domain of the warrior samurai class with common folk not invited—not that they were all that interested in the now slow-paced drama utterly disconnected from their lives.

By the mid-seventeenth century, the people's theatre of Shakespeare and his contemporaries had also been taken over by elitist aristocrats, who not only didn't welcome the commoner, but used them as the butt of their jokes.

During the same period, the rollicking, flamboyant Zaju of China evolved into Kungu. Confined to the imperial courts, this formalized and elitist theatre lost its former connection to the folk drama that had inspired it.

Meanwhile, in Africa, the long and interminable domination of European colonial powers discouraged the traditional theatre of the people and drove it underground, while European imports were performed for the governing elite.

In spite of these strange parallels in history, the people's need and desire for theatre never died, as it never will. New invigorating and accessible forms saved theatre from becoming the dull plaything of the rich and famous. In this chapter, we follow this pattern in Asia, Europe, and Africa. We look at the elite theatres of the Chinese Kungu and the Indian Kathakali, and the people's theatre of the Jinguju (Beijing Opera) of China. We examine elitist theatres of the English Restoration and the French Neoclassicists, followed by the European people's theatre of the Commedia dell Arte, the genius of Moliere, and the return of the middle class in English Georgian dramas. We introduce the most enduring form of Western theatre, the melodrama, which is as popular today as it was over 150 years ago. Finally, we look at the continued suppression of traditional theatre in Africa and discover the ways that people kept their inherent love of performance alive. (The chart preceding Chapter 7 provides an overview of these historical phenomena.)

CHINESE OPERA (XIGU 2)—KUNQU

Kunqu (pronounced *kwin-chu*) replaced the earliest form of Chinese opera, Zaju, by the end of the Ming dynasty (1644) as the center of imperial power moved from the south to the northern provinces. Unlike Zaju, with its ribald, acrobatic clowning, Kunqu (Songs of Kunshan, its town of origin) is stately, poetic, and genuinely aristocratic. It quickly gained favor in the imperial court. Refined and subtle rather than obvious and exciting, it is more of an exotic delicacy than a sumptuous buffet.

Kunqu evolved during the Qing Dynasty (1644–1912), which was founded by the Manchu, the second ethnic group to rule the whole of China, after the native Chinese Ming which gave us Zaju. The last feudal dynasty in the country's history, the Qing led imperial China to its zenith of power and influence, but its rulers were autocratic and despotic, persecuting many intellectuals, and banning or destroying works that did not meet their approval. In this atmosphere of strict feudal control, Kunqu evolved under close supervision of imperial agents. Concurrently, the educational and social level of those in the theatrical profession rose, and theatre actually received scholarly support. This combination brought new status and respect, but also limited contact between the most brilliant practitioners and the people.

The Drama

Based on the Kun melodic system, Kunqu (sometimes spelled K'un ch'u) depended on a small orchestra of wind and percussion instruments, with the flute used for primary accompaniment. Its language, neither Kunshan dialect nor standard Mandarin, is an artificial stage language, written in eight tones (all Chinese dialects use tone as well as pronunciation to indicate meaning) making composition of the libretto highly complex. Authors continuously had to refine libretto and music until the two fell into "harmony." Since Kunqu play creation presented such a challenge, almost all playwrights were poets whose work today stands as examples of high Chinese literature.

Kunqu evolved out of very early regional musical styles. It was not until the Qing Dynasty that the court musician Wei Liangfu codified a new style of delicate singing called "water mill tunes." He and his collaborators standardized rules of rhyme, tones, pronunciation, and notation, which helped this regional form become a national standard. By the end of the sixteenth century, Kunqu had spread across China and became the most prestigious form of Chinese drama for the next 200 years, during which nearly its entire repertoire was created.

Though basic rules of musical form were established by 1530, it was not until the famous playwright Lian Chenyu used its music as the foundation for his play *Laundering the Silken Yarn* that Kunqu was elevated to the status of "Official Melody." Collaborative teams of poets, scholars, musicians, and artists then created new compositions. In its own fashion, Kunqu was as much courtly theatre for courtiers as was English Restoration comedy, requiring an aristocratic appreciation for nuance and a literary finesse that makes it somewhat inaccessible to many audiences.

Styles

Kunqu scripts have complicated rules of versification and their formality suits classical plays. None have military themes. Two styles of text form the script: arias and prose. Arias—elaborate and complex poems of high literary quality—are sung and accompanied by the orchestra. Prose is neither spoken nor sung, but chanted in stylized fashion. Sometimes, the two are performed simultaneously, with one actor singing an aria and the other chanting a prose response.

The Theatre

Theatre Spaces

As in all traditional Chinese theatre, Kunqu uses minimal stage scenery. Stages are flat and bare allowing for full expression of dance and movement by the actors. No curtains or "sets" hamper the flow of movement from place to place or from time to time. These pieces were performed in the imperial courts rather than separate theatre buildings. As in Shakespeare's theatre, Kunqu performers conjure time and place by appealing to the imagination of the audience through poetry, music, and gesture.

Conventions

The Actors

Like the Sanskrit theatre convention, Kunqu theatre relies on abstract and symbolic movement, dance, and gesture. Actors assume statuesque postures that change for each word or beat of the dialogue. Because there is a movement for every shift in verse, the association between dance and poetry grew even stronger than in the past. Some theorize that the term "foot," eventually employed to describe a single unit of verse in the West as well, originated from the idea that a Kunqu actor would be likely to shift the placement of the foot at each rhythmic transition in the dialogue.

The meaning and accessibility of Kunqu performances rely on the use of well-defined character types. The chart below identifies the four major types (men, women and clowns or *jinn*) and the subcategories of each. Stylized movement associated with each role constitutes an art form in itself. These same character types occur in the wildly popular Beijing Opera discussed later.

Male—*Sheng*	Female—*Dan*	Painted faces—*Jing*	Clown—*Chou*
Lao sheng = older men	*Lao dan* = older women	*Wen jing* = civilian	*Wen chou* = civilian clown
Xiao sheng = young men	*Qing yi* = strict morals	*Wu jing* = martial arts	*wu chou* = warrior
Wu seng = martial arts	*Hua dan* = young woman		
	Wu dan = martial arts		

Costumes and Props

The costumes are elaborate, exaggerated versions of dress worn during the Ming Dynasty and do not attempt to fit the time or place of the action. In many roles, the actors wear robes with extremely long white sleeves called "water sleeves," which essentially serve as props to emphasize the performer's movements. One sign of an accomplished Kunqu performance is skilled water sleeve manipulation.

Few props clutter the Kunqu stage. A chair and table might appear, but rarely. Props might help identify characters. For example, a young man with peonies on his robe might indicate a playboy, and an actor carrying a magnifying glass might indicate social blindness. A Buddhist nun always carries a feather duster to ward off evil spirits.

Influences

Many audience members found (and still find) Kunqu just as baffling as some in our culture find opera and classical ballet. Concurrent to this exclusive form, a more popular theatre of the people called Clapper Opera developed in many regional cities. The name comes from a loud clapping of drumsticks on wooden blocks. It would be another century before the most famous Chinese Opera (Jinguju) or Beijing Opera evolved, combining elevated and accessible theatre into an indelible form.

Despite the challenges of Kunqu, it is still a dynamic form in modern China with six currently active professional companies, each consisting of 600 to 700 performers, musicians, and related support personnel. Each has its own school for training future performers. Many of the performance traditions and texts of Kunqu contributed to the evolution of Beijing Opera, when the theatre moved out of imperial courts and back to the people.

INDIAN KATHAKALI

Long after its demise, the influences of formal Indian Sanskrit dance drama lived on, giving inspiration and fire to a form of popular drama known as Kathakali (meaning "story play") which evolved in the rural villages of the southern province of Kerala in the mid-1600s. Kathakali has clear connections to classical theatre, but it is also designed to delight the commoner and today has become the most internationally familiar style of Indian dance drama.

The Drama

Based on stories from the *Ramayana* and the *Mahabharata*, the two great epics that inspired Sanskrit, the repertoire consists of about fifty plays. These plays feature kings and heroes in the constant struggle between good and evil, gods and demons. Their mood is mysterious, cosmic, and often frightening. Though the good wins in the end, the power of evil forces is fully realized.

The Theatre

Theatre Spaces

Kathakali evolved as open-air performance, performed on a sixteen foot square framed by four poles, one at each corner. A single, large, oil flame issues from a metal cauldron placed in front of the playing area. Traditionally performed at night, the sense of mystery and shadow of Kathakali is enhanced by this fire. Costumes and extreme makeup identify character types and add to the mystery and suspense in the flickering light of the oil flame.

Theatre Coventions

The Actor

A distinctive feature of Kathakali is that the actors remain mute. They communicate through gesture and mime as a small chorus of two or three singers forcefully underscore their movements. Training is long and arduous, beginning around age ten and with actors often not achieving mastery until they are in their forties. Extraordinary and powerful movement skills are required. Kathakali involves great strength and majesty, alternating huge leaps with perfectly still poses. The eyes express forceful emotion. One custom is that of placing of a tiny pepper seedpod in each eye, turning the actor's eyes blood red while doing no lasting harm. Demons roll their eyes to the extreme left and right as counterpoint to their wildly gesturing hands. According to Asian theatre scholar, A. C. Scott, "The use of such devices adds a particular dramatic emphasis to the charged silence of the actors, who are no longer human beings but dream characters from another world, the gods descended to earth."

Created by and for the common people in rural towns in southern India over 300 years ago, Kathakali, is internationally known and respected today. Its continued popularity is a testament to its power to lift audiences out of day-to-day lives and transport them to a place of magic, mystery, and suspense.

CHINESE *JINGUJU* OR BEIJING OPERA

One of the most famous and beloved of Eastern theatres was founded in 1790 during the reign of the Qing Emperor, Qianlong. *Jinguju* or Beijing Opera restored theatre to the common folk after the aristocrat *Kunqu* excluded them. During frequent hunting expeditions in south China, the emperor developed an interest in local operas. In 1790, to celebrate his eightieth birthday, he summoned opera troupes from different localities to perform for him in the capital. Four local opera troupes of Anhui Province came to Beijing. They amazed the imperial court with their combined singing and dancing supplemented by acrobatics and martial arts. In 1828, a troupe from Hubei Province came and frequently performed with the Anhui troupes, absorbing tunes of the Hubei local opera while drawing from the best of Kun Qu, QinQiang, Bang Zi and other local operas. By about 1850, the two singing styles blended to form a new genre, known as Beijing Opera. It quickly developed during the reign of Qianlong and the notorious Empress Dowager Cixi, the imperial patron, and eventually became accessible to the common people. With the exception of a thirteen-year hiatus during the Chinese Cultural Revolution, Beijing Opera has been in continual production ever since.

The Drama

From its beginnings, Beijing Opera encouraged constant development of new plays. Drama usually explored stories of legendary heroes or military feats. Using an extravagant performance style, the plays depict larger than life heroes overcoming "monsters" that threaten the people. This dynamic theatre form never catered to strict rules. Audiences expected innovation and risk-taking. Most texts drew inspiration from well-known tales, such as the Monkey King, the Water Margin, and the Romance of the Three Kingdoms, along with countless well known Chinese fairy tales and legends. Adventure, romance, and mortal combats feature strongly in the traditional texts.

The Theatre

Theatre Spaces

At first, the imperial courts controlled performance spaces, limiting allowed theatres to those of the Emperor. As a result, many actors would sneak away and bribe court officials to allow them to perform in courtyards and inns among the common people. In time, the court relinquished the strict controls, and the Opera bloomed into almost any performance space of adequate size. The stage was usually bare with no limit in space, time, or action. The actors' footwork, gestures, and body movements symbolized the actions of opening a door, climbing a hill, going up stairs, or rowing a boat. When a girl did needlework, she had neither needle nor thread in her hands. Four generals and four soldiers could represent an army of thousands.

Theatre Conventions

The Actor

Beijing Opera was a comprehensive performance combining music, singing, dialogue, pantomime, acrobatics, and martial arts. Actors had to meet more requirements than those for other performing arts, usually taking more than ten years of training to learn singing and acrobatic skills. Until very recently only men performed. They were chosen very young to specialize in male (*sheng*), female (*dan*), painted face (*jing*), or clown (*chou*) roles. Very few actors mastered more than one type of character role.

The music of Beijing Opera uses typical Chinese musical instruments, including the two-stringed fiddles, reed pipes, mandolin, lute, drums, bells, gongs, and hardwood castanets. As in Kunqu theatre (see chart), character roles in Beijing Opera are divided into four main types. *Sheng* is subdivided into *lao sheng* (middle-aged or old men), *xiao sheng* (young men) and *wu sheng* (men with martial skills). *Dan* is subdivided into various *Qing yi*, a woman with a strict moral code; *hua dan*, a vivacious young woman; *wu dan*, a woman with martial skills; and *lao dan*, an elderly woman. *Jing* are usually warriors, heroes, statesmen or demons and can be further divided into *wen jing* (civilian type) and *wu jing* (warrior type). *Chou*, recognized at first sight for his special make-up (a patch of white paint on his nose) is subdivided into *wen chou* (civilian clown) and *wu chou* (clown with martial skills).

Face Painting

In Beijing Opera, facial painting, which is applied to *jing* roles only, shows the character's age, profession, and personality by using different colors: red for loyalty and uprightness; black for a rough, stern or honest nature; yellow for rashness and fieriness; white for a cunning and deceitful character; gold and silver for gods and demons. Over one thousand painted facial patterns are used. Each actor is challenged to make subtle and interesting changes within the fixed facial pattern.

Costumes

Costumes impress audiences with their bright colors and magnificent embroidery. Some used in present performances resemble the fashion of the Ming Dynasty (1368–1644). Colors indicate social status—yellow for the imperial family, red for high nobility, red or blue for upright men, and white for old officials. A student usually wears blue, a general wears padded armor, and an emperor wears a dragon robe. Besides gorgeous clothes and headdresses, jeweled girdles for men and hair ornaments for women are also used.

Considered today a national treasure in China, Beijing Opera has become not only a true people's theatre but also an international ambassador to the rest of the world. It is one of the best-known and beloved forms of theatre. The use of pantomime, gesture, and symbolism overcomes language barriers. Amazing acrobatic and martial artistry combined with passionate and heavily percussive music delight the eye and the ear. Stories are universal, and the appeal has endured for 200 years.

ENGLISH RESTORATION

While the death of Shakespeare alone did not send the English theatre into a state of mourning, his demise coincided with a downward spiral from theatrical greatness. Politics replaced art. Those for and against the monarchy struggled for power. The extravagant and decadent Charles I was executed in 1649 after a long and bloody civil war, proving that Parliament strongly disagreed with him on the question of the divine right of kings. Oliver Cromwell and the Puritans took control, establishing the Commonwealth under which a repressive, joyless atmosphere pervaded. Theatre was officially called corrupt and eventually outlawed in 1652. With Cromwell's death, the Puritans were no longer strong enough to control the Loyalists. Charles II, who had been living in comfortable exile in France, was invited back to reclaim the throne for the Stuart dynasty. After years of self-denial, there was a longing for diversion and indulgence, and what followed was the reign of a king far more wild and corrupt than his father ever was.

While many dismiss the theatre of this era as trivial, seldom in Western history has drama been the instrument for such a strict distinction between social classes. It is an example of Western theatre gone berserk in celebrating one class and ridiculing all others. We might call this "country club theatre" written by, played by and presented to the elite in exclusive environs, safely remote from the ill-informed and unwashed masses.

Fundamentally grounded in Western worldviews, some peculiar points of view evolved in England under the rules of Charles II and his cronies. The Restoration worldview is one in which the lives of the audience, and the plays created to entertain them are virtually inseparable. Theatre became the playground of Charles and his cronies (famous or infamous for their insatiable appetites), and the meeting place for those wannabe's seeking to get closer to the wealth, power, and freedom of those at the top of the food chain. In fact, according to many diaries of the time, a better show was going on in the audience than onstage.

World View

Time remained linear, but the connection to anything but "now" was lost. A man's history and legacy faded into "whatever," as long as he had the style, wit, and line of credit to compete in the social whirl of Restoration London. All focus was on the moment. Forget the past (with the exception of course of grudges and vendettas) and defy the future. The "restored" aristocracy endeavored not to think about time. Children were entirely absent, and the elderly were included only to mock or to overcome.

Space also shrunk—restricted to the fashionable precincts of London. The city provided all worthwhile amusements. One maintained a country home, but seldom used it except as a place for sport. Aristocrats removed themselves from nature in all matters. Their hedges said it all; they were painstakingly shaped into domes, hearts, and diamonds, rather than left as simple vegetation. Nature needed to either be ignored—or altered.

Values underwent a profound shift to individual gratification. No longer concerned with state or family, courtiers enjoyed life much like a banquet—more enjoyable if nibbled than if devoured. Wit, beauty, money, and youth offered the ticket to the inner circle of power. Satire, mockery, and profound cruelty reigned, creating a vicious but pretty world.

Structure and hierarchy returned to a Western model of monarch, the brief period of the Commonwealth was no more than a political blip on the royalist screen. Royal privilege and absolute license were reflected in the authority of fathers in the families. Theatre mocked all but the young and beautiful. Tensions between wild young men (and women) and the all-powerful fathers played out again and again. Fathers controlled purse strings and arranged marriages to strangers for their offspring; the father's arrival in town caused dismay in many a Restoration character.

The elite grew into true slaves to fashion. Any lapse brought mockery and rejection. Failure to keep up regarding fashionable food, author, color, or sexual shenanigans cut the offender from the herd. Every costly plaything went out of style before it was paid for and a new toy had to be bought to stay in the game.

The Drama

Restoration comedy reveled in repeating the same essential plot. The elegant but poverty stricken young man of fashion pursued a beautiful, witty young lady either to steal her virginity and dump her (just for fun)—or to marry her and steal her fortune (also just for fun). Frequent use of second and third plot lines allowed playwrights to mock the lower classes, the overly serious, the Puritans, the Irish, or the country gentlemen.

The Playwrights

Playwrights pushed the boundaries of propriety, many writing plays that would shock a modern audience in their sexuality and promiscuity. Since the audience was limited to the fashionable elite new plays were needed every few days. Only two theatres operated in London, so a decent playwright (or a sufficiently witty/dirty one) could make a reasonable living cranking out formula plays on a regular basis. Playwrights only got paid if the play ran for a "third night" and most did not.

Some playwrights wrote comedies that stood the test of time as examples of universal humor, but most sunk into well-deserved obscurity. Below is a list of playwrights who worked above the vulgarity and elitism of the era. Their work is still produced on the modern stage.

(**Note:** Aphra Behn was the first woman to make her living as an playwright in England, and she would remain one of the very few, proud, and brave women who attempted and succeeded at playwrighting until well into the twentieth century):

Aphra Behn—*The Forced Marriage, The Town Fop,* and *The Rovers*

George Etheridge—*She Would If She Could* and *The Man of Mode*

William Wycherly—*The Country Wife* and *The Plain Dealer*

William Congreve—*The Way of the World* (perhaps the masterpiece of the era.)

The Theatre

Theatre Space

The two licensed theatres were intimate and small. The apron, an extension of the stage floor beyond the proscenium arch, was the invention of this time period. It was used constantly as a special space to allow the actor closer proximity to the audience. All entrances were made through stage doors built right into the proscenium arch. All scenery was relegated to the upstage area, which was employed for little more than background decoration. However, a new set of scenery was costly and provided a reason to advertise a play. Many diaries refer to trips to the theatre to see the new "scenes" meaning the painted backdrops—not the scenes created by playwrights and actors. But the actor, and particularly the first actresses on the English stage, were fully, closely scrutinized and even joined onstage.

Theatre Conventions

The Actor

The Restoration actor, though not as restricted as in the theatre of Asia, was certainly cast according to type. Some men played "bad boys" or rakes, others played buffoons. Some women played ladies of seductive wit, others played prudes. Character names revealed a dominant characteristic such as, Sir Clumsey, Constant, Lady Fanciful, Lady Fidget, Horner, Loveless, Manly, Pinchwife, Lord Plausible, Lady Pliant, Scandal, Mr. Smirk, Snake, Sparkish, Mrs. Squeamish, Lady Wishfort, or Witwood. Each character had a function (gallant, rogue, prude, fop, courtesan, wit, cuckold, gossip, plain citizen, wooer, philandering wife, rich uncle, jolly old knight, country bumpkin or city sophisticate) that followed a tradition. Calculated nonverbals (sighs, vaguely stifled yawns, laughter, subtle purrs, growls and even hisses) embellished verbal contests. Language was elevated, and the use of euphemism rose to a high art.

It is a rare Restoration play that does not at some point feature the leading lady in male disguise, called "breeches" roles, so that all may see her hips, calves, and ankles.

The veil and mask existed in words, looks, and moves, though characters might use an actual mask, the vizard, to hide their identity during clandestine encounters. The fan sent a series of provocative messages and the Restoration actress needed to be a mistress of its use. Seduction was a game of skill, intended for the masterful. Intrigue, flirtation, nibbling, tasting, and testing were delights which made life tolerable—playing, without innocence, being bad boys and girls. The words *naughty* and *saucy* came into widespread use.

The audience came to the theatre as much to be seen, hunt for prey, socialize, and pass the time as to see the play. The Restoration period was relatively short-lived, having passed its heyday with the death of Charles II, and faded as the throne was occupied by more serious-minded monarchs. By 1700, the raucous and racy comedies fell into disfavor, and the Georgian dramas that followed would appeal to a much broader audience, bringing the middle class back into the fold. The days of theatre by, for, and about the English aristocracy drew to a close.

Restoration comedy did influence the subsequent arch and wicked drawing room comedies during a number of eras. Certainly the privileged, self-absorbed, and often cruel characters of Oscar Wilde and Noel Coward are reminiscent of that era. To this day, the heartless, devastating wit may show up in any number of plays as a kind of Restoration ghost. The acrid comments often attributed to Truman Capote and the sort of character which Hugh Grant specializes in (*Bridget Jones* and *American Dreamz*)—the heartless but charmingly clever roué—all owe something to this form of theatre.

FRENCH NEOCLASSICISM

"Neoclassicism" refers to a renewed interest in classical Greek and Roman works. The movement stimulated architecture, painting, sculpture, clothing, and even garden design. An emphasis was placed on balance, harmony, elegance of line, and dignity of design. None of this was a bad thing, but in the realm of theatre, the Academy took things a bit further. The French theatre of the seventeenth century, except for the singular genius Moliere, became so caught up in rules and regulations that playwrighting became a sort of academic exercise. The common people had little interest in the intellectual elitism of neoclassicism, and today the plays seem so mechanical, so devoid of emotion or pleasure that they are seldom produced with any success.

The Académie Français was established in 1635 as the intellectual caretaker committee of French language and literature—and its primary aim was to protect them from corruption and foreign influences. The Academy also became the style-police in dramatic literature. New plays had to be submitted for approval before they could be produced. Censorship of content was part of the process, censorship of style also began to stifle the creative imagination of artists. They began treating the *Poetics* by Aristotle as a rule book rather than the analytical survey it was. In time, they began to make up rules that Aristotle wouldn't have recognized. Below is a list of just a few of the restrictions placed playwrights.

1. The Unities: From Aristotle's logical sense that a play should have a beginning middle and end, the Unities became absolute rules. The action of the play had to take place in a maximum of 24 hours, using only one location and telling one story on a classical theme.

2. Genre: Comedy and tragedy were strictly separated with tragedy being the higher art. Comedy had to be in prose, tragedy in verse. No exceptions!

3. Verisimilitude: "Believability" dictated no flights of imagination, no mysterious or unexplained events. Characters had to be consistent at all times. The tempests, witches, wars, voyages, and magic of Shakespeare's best plays would never have gotten past the Academy. Dramatic conventions, like asides, violated the sense of "sentimens forcez," or unnatural sentiments, as such events couldn't happen in real life.

4. Decorum, a sense of dignity and restraint, had to be employed. Even agony and ecstasy must be confined within restrained poetic language. The rational was to be celebrated; the irrational eliminated.

5. Act structure required a strict rationale for the progression of the plot, taking Aristotle's affective structure analysis and formalizing it into a restrictive list of rules.

Two playwrights achieved enduring respect under the stringent guidelines of the Academy. Pierre Corneille (1606–1684) whose masterpiece tragedy, *Le Cid* (1637) made him the darling of the Academy and the literary elite of Paris. He had a long and distinguished career, focusing thematically on the repression of passion in favor of duty. His old age was marred by bitterness after he was eclipsed by the rising star of Jean Racine (1639–1699). Racine achieved fame and fortune with his third tragedy, *Andromaque*, which he wrote when he was only twenty-eight years old. Considered a masterpiece, it earned him the patronage of King Louis XIV. Such plays were designed to please the intellectual elite of Paris and are seldom produced today—they are more often studied as literature than as theatre.

The forms of theatre that brought the common person back into the fold began first with Commedia dell'Arte and Moliere in Europe, then the Georgian comedy in England, and finally melodrama.

COMMEDIA DELL'ARTE AND MOLIERE

Commedia Dell'arte (comedy of artists) is a colorful and extremely theatrical art-form based on the interaction of traditional stock characters in improvised scenarios that facilitate a comic plot in order to arrive at a humorous climax. It originated in streets and market places of the early Italian Renaissance, though its roots can be traced as far back as Ancient Greece. These Italian street-performers wore masks with exaggerated comic features to complement their physical and acrobatic skills. In time, they teamed up with troupes of actors, often with traveling stages, to establish commedia as a genre in its own right by the mid-1500s. The troupes lived a gypsy life, traveling from town to town and using the whole family in the company. Many believe that commedia troupes were the first to use women to play women's parts, because Mom and Sister had to earn their keep too.

Troupes performed for all social classes. Language was no barrier, and with their skillful mime, stereotyped stock-characters, traditional lazzi's (signature stunts, gags and pranks), masks, clowning, improvised dialogue, and broad physical gestures, they became widely accepted wherever they traveled. The tradition spread all over Europe. In France, many of the scenarios were scripted into commedia-style plays. In the mid-seventeenth century, the commedia influence met with the comic genius of one man, Jean Baptiste Poquelin Moliere, easily the second most-produced playwright in the West and most scholar's choice for second greatest. While Shakespeare was surrounded by a half-dozen other brilliant writers, Moliere stands alone. Like Shakespeare, he stole or borrowed plots everywhere, using them merely as something on which to attach his ideas. Also like Shakespeare, he embraced characters from the aristocracy all the way down to country bumpkins, sometimes making the play *about* the bumpkin. And like Shakespeare, he died in his fifties after creating over thirty plays, working primarily with one established company under royal patronage. Both were investors in, or part owners of, their companies, and both were actors: Moliere even acted on the night of his death in 1673 playing, ironically, the title role in *The Imaginary Invalid*. No one in his time and place touched his genius. And *absolutely* no one shares his particular voice. Today, the world famous Théâtre Français is rightly called The House of Moliere.

Three important influences make Moliere's work unique:

1. Moliere managed to work within the Neoclassic framework and still write comedy. He was the first to give comedy true respectability, raising it to the level of esteem previously reserved for tragedy. He managed to create subtle nuances in an art form normally thought of as loud, broad, and indelicate. He surprised audiences with the idea that comedy could actually be polite. He created social satire as we know it today. He managed to get his audience to laugh at itself while being admonished.

2. Moliere also wrote out of the Commedia tradition that employs the very broadest comic and improvisational ingredients in performance. At one time, Moliere's company shared a space with theirs. Moliere observed and used the great precision of the Italian commedia performers, carefully refining it and giving it sophistication.

3. Moliere was strongly influenced by Louis XIV, a monarch with an incomparable ego and great love for pageantry, laughter, and dancing. After first performing for the twenty year-old Louis at the Louvre on October 24, 1658, Moliere spent much of the rest of his life creating plays, interspersed with music and dancing, featuring His Radiance, who loved to make guest appearances.

Imagine a contemporary playwright managing to draw from vaudeville and the circus in order to serve the whims of a major tycoon who believes himself the center of the universe, honoring the strictest etiquette books and most repressive lobbying groups, and still writing strong satire in the process. This was the genius of Moliere. His company, first called the Illustre Théâtre, knew humble days touring the provinces and he never lost the common touch. His comedies remained human and universal despite his elevation to courtly status and they account for his continued and constant production over the last 300 years to this day.

GEORGIAN COMEDY

Moliere, the Restoration playwrights, and the Georgians all wrote variations on a style called Comedy of Manners. While the Restoration theatre involved elegant corruption, its two closest relatives were considerably more wholesome. Both Moliere and the Georgians were interested in not simply what behavior *works* but what behavior was morally *right*. They were interested in the overall good of society as much as in the individual. They found in this struggle of self *vs.* society a strong source of laughter. The Georgians followed the Restoration by nearly a hundred years, during which time enough sweeping changes had taken place in the world to bring about a distinct type of comedy involving the middle class. The Georgians could be called the grandchildren of the Restoration. A little embarrassed by their profligate ancestors, they became *very* concerned with what is proper and much less concerned with aristocratic privilege.

The population of England nearly doubled between 1650 and 1800. The most procreating group? The Middle Class. Powerful citizens who were neither upper class nor lower class emerged. They struggled to design their place in society, embracing some aristocratic and some lower class virtues. An astonishing number of inventions and discoveries made the world and wealth more immediately accessible. The word that sums up Georgians' view on life is *benevolence*. All felt obliged to improve morals and manners—and to enlighten those less fortunate. God was seen in material terms, rather than spiritual—the main engineer who designed the universe, set its laws, and started it running. The wealthy and successful business man was favored by God. They called their own era, "The Age of Enlightenment."

A hearty sort of eroticism existed, although a clear separation was made between women of quality and tarts. A woman's purity became the "jewel in her crown," but more than that, a mere hint of sexual scandal could ruin a woman literally for the rest of her life. Adultery was no longer a fit subject for discussion. The middle class Georgians spent a good deal of time moralizing and attacking the morals of others, but they were not without a sense of fun. Diversions included horse races, fox hunting, and golf. Gambling became so popular that even at a ball a gaming room was provided for those who preferred the table to the dance floor. Prize-fighting was the sport of choice for young dandies. Ladies did not participate in any outdoor sport except shopping.

The Drama

The comedies of the period often drip with cloying sentimentality, but two writers represent the period's true strengths. Richard Brinsley Sheridan and Oliver Goldsmith both reacted against the treacle of the times and in so doing reflect the best of the times.

In 1772, Goldsmith published his famous "Essay on Theatre," which decried sentiment and cried out for "laughing comedy." He did more than criticize. The next year, he produced what he demanded in *She Stoops to Conquer*. That play had so little in common with others of the time that only through the influence of the powerful and popular Samuel Johnson was it produced at all. It, along with Sheridan's plays *The Rivals* and *The School for Scandal* define Georgian theatre for modern audiences. Both placed more emphasis on character than did the Restoration writer, but retained some of the biting wit. They identified the difference between real and feigned virtue. By our standards, there is plenty of sentiment left in both playwrights' work. Goodness is inevitably rewarded and gentility supported.

The Theatre

Theatre Space

The performance space expanded considerably. Huge new theatres reduced the apron, and lighting was much improved. The actors moved upstage, creating a much larger distance between actor and observer. Scenic wonders evolved with many cutout set pieces and much painting that actually had something to do with the time and place of the play. Sets became lavish, like the middle class homes of the audience.

The Actor

Georgians felt big and expressed it through their clothing. They wore ribbons, lace, big wigs, heavy padding on the hips, and big hats with plumes and flowers. The look was large and pale with powdered wigs, pastel garments, and a human silhouette sometimes nearly as wide as it was high. An actor had to be able to maneuver artfully in clothing that might have weighed as much as twenty pounds. They also had to master the intricacy of "manners," a mind-boggling and constantly changing pattern of social behaviors designed to distinguish class difference.

A wife functioned as a primary showpiece for her husband's wealth, so the finer and more elegantly dressed she was, the richer he was considered to be. The stereotype of women fainting emerges from this period, not as a result of their "weakness," but because the corseting allowed only shallow breathing and impaired circulation. Maneuvering in panniers (hip extensions created by padding under the heavy skirts that at their extreme extended as much as three feet on either side) required short mincing steps. Language was consciously simple and direct. Decorum was important, but so was a collective need to drop pretension and "speak clearly."

Music and Dance

Music in the form of interludes (played between scenes and acts) became common, and all performers needed to be familiar with the latest dance crazes like the Waltz. Couples embraced and did turns about the room for the first time. Moralists were quick to point out the danger of a dance which allowed young women to be grasped by their partners, thrown into the air and twirled about. Another similar and even livelier partner dance, the Polka, became popular.

Masking

While the wearing of literal masks declined in popularity, the new social mask of choice was Middle Class Respectability. A solid, outward show was employed, with lewd and power-mad impulses carefully concealed and/or suppressed in favor of good-hearted decency. The theatre re-enforced the primacy of the human mask of decorum over the magical masks of the theatre.

MELODRAMA

The century following the Georgians was so dominated by one woman and her large family that it is referred to by her name, Victoria, Queen of England and Ireland and Empress of India. Her reign, the longest in English history, spanned most of the nineteenth century, and her values were embraced across Europe, America, and the colonies.

The Victorian era saw the triumph of the middle class over the landed aristocracy. Respectability became the all-powerful goal. Take the social constraints of the Georgian era, multiply by ten and you've got the Victorian age.

Increasingly complex social rules defined Respectability. All the money in the world couldn't buy it. Only years of careful and painstaking social climbing, never taking a misstep, and never taking eyes from the prize could achieve that goal. Even those who were considered respectable lived in a precarious state of rigid, social order. For women especially, restrictions were intense, and the price to pay for defiance was very high.

The melodrama was designed to soothe and reassure the middle class, to keep telling them, "Yes, everything is right with the world, and you are right in everything you do." Evil was punished, goodness rewarded; wealth was a sign of God's favor and poverty a sign of His disfavor. Manners and social positioning were essential to an orderly universe. Melodramas were written with predictable structures and themes. Designed to appeal to emotions, not intellect, they promoted the status quo. A middle-class matron could be moved to gasps of fear, tears of pity and groans of horror by melodrama and then go home content and a bit smug, assured of her well-earned superiority and God-given purity of mind and heart. In a society completely ordered around convention rather than honesty, the melodrama evolved using the conventions below:

1. Plots involved a good man or woman tempted or tormented by villainous forces. For a young man, it might have been alcohol, dishonesty in business, or a woman of bad reputation. For a woman, it was usually her virtue under siege. After lots of action and emotion, the plot was eventually resolved with the salvation or ruination of the protagonist. If temptation was resisted, a happy ending, and if not . . . .

2. Good and evil were simple and uncomplicated. The hero was all good, the villain all bad. No complexity of character or motivation muddied the melodramatic waters.

3. Class distinctions were strictly adhered to. A servant could never be a lady. A street urchin would never rise to servant class. An outsider trying to "pass" as a lady or gentleman of the middle class was the worst of crimes.

4. Action/adventure required big scenery and big theatres. In one American melodrama called *Under the Gaslight*, the heroine was thrown into New York harbor, rescued her friend from an onrushing train, broke free of a burning shed by using an ax, and fought off a midnight attack in her boudoir by the villain.

5. Music was an important component (it's the "melo" part of melodrama). Music underscored action sequences, raised tension, identified character types, lapsed into love songs, and kept the emotions swinging from one extreme to the other.

The popularity of melodrama has never waned though it was often disparaged by the elite. We still love to believe that good overcomes evil; we are always right and the opposition is always wrong. In media theatre in particular, the action film is often just a big, expensive, violent melodrama. The *Star Wars* epic and the *Lord of the Rings* trilogy, for example, are comforting to us because of their clearly defined good and evil characters and the eventual triumph of good. On a more miniscule scale, melodrama thrives as soap opera.

AFRICA—DIASPORA

One of the enduring legacies of European involvement in Africa is the Diaspora (the "scattering") brought about by the hunger for free labor in the New World. Whole communities disappeared into holds of cargo ships to be sold in the Americas. Many survivors, both those taken into slavery and those left behind, lived as shell-shocked remnants, struggling from one day to the next. What the colonizers and missionaries didn't succeed at destroying, the centuries of Diaspora nearly did.

But the essential strength and optimism of African culture did not die. In the Americas, theatre helped transplanted slaves survive. Traditions of storytelling, dance, music, and narrative lived on, nourishing and refreshing a people pushed almost beyond endurance. Elements of African theatre lived on in American and Caribbean descendants of slaves, giving rise to the American musical theatre, Caribbean dance and music, and a tradition of telling stories and using theatre to create hope, change, optimism, balance, and proportion.

In 1801, the first European style theatre was opened in Africa in the Cape of Good Hope, and 1866 is the year in which the first European style play was performed by Africans. None of these in any way acknowledged African tradition, but rather simply imposed Western concepts. The colonizing nations of Europe met during 1884–1885 at the Berlin Conference, where they simply carved Africa into chunks and devoured it. Those "nations-states" still endure, but with the same critical problems now as then. Some have as many as 250 tribal nations within their borders, others have only two or three. Each tribal nation speaks a distinct language making national and even regional theatre almost impossible. The only shared language is that of the oppressor, often English or French. Theatre, which had always functioned as an active mechanism of justice and social cohesion, no longer worked in "nations" that weren't nations. Much of contemporary suffering in Africa traces its roots to, on the one hand, the forced separation of families and communities from the same nation, and, on the other hand, the forced proximity of unrelated tribal communities.

By the mid-twentieth century, as colonial empires were pulling out of Africa, a new mechanism was set in motion that nearly succeeded in destroying the traditional theatre of sub-Saharan Africa. Promising young artists and scholars were sent to Europe to be trained in Western theatre. When this educated elite returned, they were isolated from their roots, often given high-paying government jobs, writing and producing theatre for Europeans. In the meantime, the old stories and performance traditions were starting to die with the elders who carried them in their heads. Happily, many of the old stories finally began to be recorded and these now survive. Artists, scholars, and playwrights of the last two decades have re-embraced the traditions of African theatre and are finding ways to encourage a renaissance.

SUMMARY

Following the brilliance of the Sanskrit, Greek and West African classical periods, theatre went through a series of phases, moving outward toward the people, then inward to an elite circle and then outward again. Elitist forms include the English Restoration when the aristocracy took over and used the theatre as a toy, China where popular opera was confined to the aristocracy Kunqu, and France, where the Academy applied strict neoclassicism that stifled creativity. As always, the people simply developed new forms for themselves: the Kathakali in India, Commedia in Europe, and regional operas in China. Enduring theatre for the people evolved: the Beijing Opera, the plays of Moliere, the Georgian comedy of England, and the melodrama.

SUGGESTED ASSIGNMENTS

1. What cultural factors may have contributed to theatre being widely available or entirely exclusive at various points in history? Can you predict any trends based on historical evidence presented here?

2. What do you find most similar about theatrical activity during each period in this chapter? Given that the cultures identified here were separated by vast distances and had minimal interaction, what may explain similar theatrical trends?

3. What would you say made each culture unique or distinct from the others? What characteristics would you pick to distinguish European, Asian, and African theatre during these developments?

4. Why is it so much more difficult to pin down changes in Africa during this time?

5. The Chinese Opera moves through three very distinct phases. What distinguishes each and what ties them all together?

6. How did the concerns of drama change from those identified in Chapter 7 to this later period? Which of these Chapter 8 concerns remains an important part of theatre? Have any receded with time?

7. To what extent do you believe early, prevailing cultural standards and beliefs limited or set up free theatrical expression within each culture during this period? While we do not know enough about theatre outside our own culture to identify influences, we can do so with English Restoration, Moliere, and English Georgian Comedy. How has each of these theatrical forms influenced contemporary theatre and film? What are examples of works that might never have existed without their influence?

8. The English Restoration inspired all devastatingly witty drawing room comedy from the plays of Oscar Wilde to *Will and Grace*. What else?

9. Moliere and the commedia tradition have inspired satire, improv and target theatre generally. What are some examples?

10. The Georgian comedy is ancestor to the sitcom. The path from *She Stoops to Conquer* to *Everybody Loves Raymond* is fairly direct. What are the essential characteristics of middle-class comedy and how have they evolved?

SUGGESTED ACTIVITIES

1. Individual—Compare the visual extravagance of Beijing Opera with Restoration or Georgian period dress. Explore the worldview that encouraged such "large" characterizations on the stage.

2. Small Group—Choose any play you have studied together and prepare to produce it in a style covered in this chapter. Assign someone to direct, design costumes and scenery, and act in the play. What happens when you shift your chosen play into one of these grand styles of theatre?

3. Long term—Do the above small group activity as an individual project. For example, choose a play and decide to do it as Beijing Opera. Gather or create images and ideas to present to your class as if you were "selling" this idea to a board of directors or artistic director.

4. Large Group—Seek out an opportunity to see a type of theatre (or a film like *Farewell, My Concubine* or *Casanova* that is set in a long ago time) presented in this chapter. Most campuses have cultural celebrations, visiting performance groups, and foreign film events. Period plays may be playing on your campus this term. Early in the semester share your suggestion, vote as a group on which event to attend, then set out to experience something that may be new or unusual as a group.

KEY WORDS AND IDEAS

Theatre for the Elite

English Restoration: Charles II, Comedy of Wit

Chinese Kungu

French Neoclassicism: The Academy, Corneille, Racine

Theatre for the People

Indian Kathakali

Commedia dell'Arte and Moliere: Louis XIV, satire

Back to the People

English Georgian Comedy: Sheridan, Goldsmith

Chinese Jingujo, Beijing Opera

Melodrama: Queen Victoria

How Does Theatre Vary?

REALISM

CONTENTS

B Y THE LATE 1700s, the Neo-Classical movement was losing ground. Strictly ordered works depicting the ideal rather than the natural were declining in appeal. While melodrama would continue as a popular genre, new voices and experiments in form were about to transform the theatre from conformity to challenge.

GLOBAL IMPACT OF EUROPEAN WORLDVIEW

In this chapter, we look at realism as a style of theatre and at forms of selective realism called romanticism and naturalism. These styles, first created in Europe and America, had enormous impact on theatre throughout the world, even in places where traditional theatre had never for a moment attempted to depict gritty day-to-day life. So why the global impact? Colonialism. By the nineteenth century, most of the known world was under the control of European and American powers. The old saying, "the sun never sets on the British Empire," was true. France, Germany,

Spain, and Portugal had colonial empires nearly as vast as the English did. Nineteenth century Western ideals infiltrated these far-flung areas of the world and few places escaped the "gift" of European civilization. Along with armies and governments, colonists imported every possible aspect of daily life in their attempted to transform ancient cultures into mirror images of their own.

NINETEENTH-CENTURY CHANGES

Political rebellion was rampant in Europe of the nineteenth century. The American Revolution of 1776 was only the first in a series of revolutions aimed overthrowing monarchies and ensuring the rights of the common person. In 1789, the French began one of the longest and bloodiest revolutions, culminating in the Terror when the revolutionaries began killing their own in a cycle of manic violence. Belgium, Italy and the German provinces all revolted against their monarchies in 1848. The philosophies of democracy the were growing stronger each year, but the price was often bloodshed and suffering.

Revolutionary thinking in science and philosophy fed those in economic, social, and political arenas. Four of the most influential reformers were Comte, Marx, Darwin, and Freud. All were the product of earlier innovations including the development of "scientific method," which argued that knowledge grew out of a process of observation, hypothesis, and analysis. Unlike many Victorians, these men did not look at the world around them and assume that "all was right with the world"—they saw a world that needed changing.

Auguste Comte (1798–1857), a French philosopher, was the founder of modern sociology. He became convinced that the application of scientific methods to social concerns would result in the beneficial moral and intellectual reorganization of society, He rejected all ideas of God or metaphysical explanation, believing that scientific method could result in the perfection of human society. This theory deeply influenced the development of realism.

Karl Marx (1818–1883), in partnership with Friedrich Engles, created a revolutionary philosophy called "scientific socialism," which he articulated in his famous work *The Communist Manifesto*, in 1848. Marx believed that human history was organized around a system of exploiters and the exploited, oppressors and the oppressed. He believed that only revolution would overthrow the capitalists who profited from the labor of the working class, now mired in poverty. Then, a new classless society could emerge in which all were equal, but only organized violence could displace those in power. His vision of a society with no preferential "birthright" had a profound effect on political and literary developments.

Charles Darwin (1809–1882) was perhaps the most influential thinker of the period. His book *Origin of Species* (1859), published after twenty years collecting data, argued that species evolve through variation and natural selection ("survival of the fittest") and that humankind evolved from lower life forms. He sighted the two primary factors influencing evolution as *heredity* and *environment*. The theory of evolution challenged every traditional belief system, including biblical accounts of creation, divine intervention, and a covenant between humans and a supreme deity. It also challenged the belief in destiny and free will ... that is, we are essentially all victims of circumstance whose choices are determined by forces over which we have no control. On the other hand, if species evolve through survival of the fittest to higher levels of the evolutionary scale, so can society. The realist movement in the drama was interested in the contrasting ideas of individuals trying to cope with environments they cannot control and society evolving into a higher state of being.

Sigmund Freud (1856–1939) was the most shocking and controversial pioneer of them all. His theories of the unconscious mind, sexuality, and repression, and dark and unconscious motivations influencing behavior were frightening to the Victorian middle-class mindset. He attacked the very heart of respectability, appearance, and female "virtue" (lack of sexuality) that ordered the Victorian world. His work would also help revolutionize theatre.

These revolutions, occurring throughout Europe and America, led social themes and scientific inquiry to the theatre. By the mid 1800s, the extravagant characters, repetitive plots, and callow insights of melodrama were losing interest for young theatre artists raised in an atmosphere of revolution. Romanticism grew out of the turbulence of the late eighteenth century, and evolved side by side with melodrama. Romanticism was a call for change! A group of young writers searched for a new theatre espousing the rights of the individual, the glory of nature, and the power of emotion.

ROMANTICISM

The segue from full-blown melodrama to realism comes through the transitional movement called romanticism. In this style, feelings are more important than thoughts. Anything natural is good. Appearance means nothing; emotional truth means everything. A true hero, forced to stand outside society, lives life as passionately and fully as it should be lived. Beyond mere earthly life lies a higher truth, found through art and feeling. Happiness is to be pursued in the realm of the spiritual. The sublime in nature and art are to be worshiped. Everything exotic and picturesque has value. Even something ugly and grotesque has worth if it stimulates powerful response.

The hero often needs to die by the final curtain after following his heart in an uncomprehending world too full of reason, machines, and rules, a world spoiled by moving too far away from its natural state. Still, to die and leave the physical world is not too great a price to pay for being true to oneself.

Ironically, much of Asian theatre had for centuries embraced many of the production components taken on by romanticism, but without its agenda.

The Look

The Romantic works could be as grand and sweeping in scope as the biggest opera or musical. Large casts and spectacle were common. Settings were often long ago and/or far away. While Romanticism was influential in bringing historical accuracy in costuming, the look is likely to be *flamboyantly* historical. The vision of nature tended toward glorious sunrises and tornados, not just a blah day with a few new weeds in the garden.

This theatre style sympathized with the paintings of Caspar David Friedrich, John Constable, J. M. W. Turner and the famous Hudson River School of dramatic landscape painting. A romantic hero need not be beautiful but should somehow be extraordinary. His lady, his most ardent love, must be beautiful, passionate, and ready to die for love and freedom.

The Sound

Romantic plays used verse or poetic prose on a grand level, with a great variety of expressiveness. Freewheeling, lengthy, and passionate speeches were common and demanded a large vocal range as well as a delivery that could be defiant and sentimental without becoming strident and cloying. Language reflected the music of Frederic Chopin, Franz Liszt, Richard Wagner, and Pyotr Ilyich Tchaikovsky; and the poetry of Percy Bysshe Shelly, William Blake, and George Gordon, Lord Byron.

The Acting

Pulling off Romanticism required great bravado and expressiveness. Actors needed a willingness to hit operatic heights. Acting was tour de force, bravura playing, both soulful and expansive. Training in classical ballet and great beauty of tone helped. This was full-blown drama, and it was not for those who tended toward half-hearted attacks or who giggled easily.

Early Major Works

Major playwrights of this genre were Friedrich Schiller (1759–1805), an early pioneer, and Johann Wolfgang von Goethe (1749–1832), both German. In France, Victor Hugo (1802–1885), wrote *Hernani* (1830), so controversial it led to rioting in the theatre between Hugo's supporters and the Classicists, both groups having filled the theatre at the express invitation of Hugo himself.

Goethe's most famous play, *Faust* (1808), is episodic and vast in scope as the old tale of a learned man who sells his soul to the devil is retold to explore the Romantic vision of redemption through human struggle. This play covers many years of the protagonist's life as he travels all over the globe and even into the realms of supernatural beings.

Even Henrik Ibsen, considered by many the Father of Modern Realism, dabbled in Romanticism early in his long and prolific career. His plays, *The Vikings of Helgeland* (1858), *Brand* (1866), and *Peer Gynt* (1867), followed the Romantic manifesto in using the historical epic, vast scale, and unrestrained passion to underscore the quest of the individual to find a place in a corrupt world. Unrestrained by the rules of neoclassicism, the Romantics often created works that were almost impossible to stage, but they broke free of the rigid guidelines that were stifling dramatic creativity throughout Europe.

Media Romanticism

Our current, disillusioned age tends to not be receptive to romanticism and its flights of fancy. *Moulin Rouge* is the most recent film to embrace the conventions of the form, including the dying tragic heroine, even daring to take them over the top. Some claim that musicals (such as *Miss Saigon, Les Miserables* and *The Phantom of the Opera*) are now the almost exclusive purveyors of this form. Many films tend to some degree to romanticize the human experience. Romantic comedies, melodramatic romances, some soap operas, and so-called "chick flicks" include some of the elements but in watered-down form. But who knows? We may see a full-blown revival once audiences get bored with postmodern skepticism.

REALISM

Freud's work on the clinical analysis of personalities, Ibsen's scripts of carefully crafted social import, and Stanislavski's acting system all reflect an interest in seeing life portrayed onstage as it is lived offstage. The Moscow Art theatre named its Fourth Studio "The Realistic Theatre." For the first time in history, plays did not focus on people who were exceptional by title, power, beauty, intellect, or eccentricity of personality. For the first time, characters onstage could be people next door.

Realism is the dominant form of Western theatre, based on nature and life without idealization or distortion. While the term did not emerge until the 1850s, all periods *thought* they were doing realism in a way because the performances onstage reflected the way each period saw itself—not necessarily the way that people really looked or lived, but their collective self-concept. Every period has its own vision of realism. That vision can look quite "unreal" from the perspective of time.

Call for Change

Like most theatre movements, realism begins with a manifesto or a call for changing the status quo, proposing that it was time to reject the impractical and visionary drama of the Romantics. Instead, theatre should show how everyday people react to their environments. Characters should be multi-dimensional, internally motivated, and believably portrayed. Plays need to explore relationships onstage through psychology, environment, and the five senses. Only drama that has direct relevance to the life of the viewer has genuine *meaning* to the viewer. Enough plays about kings and lords, rebels and visionaries. What about grocers? We all experience social and domestic problems and the stage needs to illuminate them.

The Look

Conscientious effort at accuracy is made in all scenic elements, allowing some editing of irrelevant details and some partial or skeletal sets. Settings look like modifications of actual locales. An attempt is made to create the feeling of a real living space, with considerable use of props. Largely through the influence of Emile Zola, the box set develops, though sometimes several settings are represented with a cinematic overlapping of action. Costumes and properties try to be true to both historical period and character personality. Movement is true to life, which may mean it can be hesitant, unobtrusive, and occasionally random. Movement strives to appear motivated and honest. The advent of photography inspired the look of the staging.

The Sound

Realistic plays revolutionized the sound of theatre through the use of pauses, nonverbals, incomplete thoughts and informal sentence structure—all the characteristics of speech on the street or in the home. Scripts are prose, barely heightened from normal conversation. They reject any hint of declamatory artifice in delivery while maintaining clarity. Suddenly characters speak as people speak and the audience is astonished.

The Acting

Performers need a capacity for "public solitude" (behaving in front of others as if they are actually alone so that we really feel we are eavesdropping on their lives) and a strong sense of natural interaction with other actors, props, and setting. They must have a strong believability and the ability to tap internal resources in order to find truth. Stanislavski's system was developed to assist realistic portrayal. Actors need an eye for contemporary detail, shading, and nuance. No ham acting allowed. At the same time, they must have emotional availability and the capacity to play with depth of feeling at will.

Major Early Plays and Playwrights

The earliest and most influential playwrights were Henrik Ibsen, Anton Chekhov, and George Bernard Shaw. Their looks into real lives behind social masks were extremely controversial and almost universally loathed by the Victorian middle class. But their work set the world on fire for young people, social reformers, and progressive thinkers and became the groundwork for the dominant style of Western theatre today.

Norwegian Henrik Ibsen (1828–1906) was probably the most influential figure in modern theatre. Over his long career, he worked in many styles, including romanticism and non-realism. But his realistic period from 1877 to 1890 produced plays that sent a tidal wave through the smug conventions of Victorian life. Deeply affected by the revolutionary developments he witnessed, Ibsen chose to see drama as a means for social change. He tore the mask off the middle-class to reveal the suffering and corruption just beneath the surface. He wanted his plays to change society for the better.

In his first realistic play, *A Doll's House* (1879), he takes a scathing look beneath the surface of the perfect Victorian family. His heroine, Nora, a mother herself, is little more than a child having transferred her dependence on her father to her husband. She believes that he will protect her and defend her at any cost, as she has tried to do for him. When she learns that he is more concerned about social appearances than the truth, her disillusionment is so profound that she decides to leave him and learn to live as an adult. In what has been called "the door slam heard around the world," the play ends with Nora's exit, leaving her befuddled husband behind. This play was so controversial it was banned in his native Norway, creating a firestorm of angry criticism from audiences and critics alike. His response was the second of his realist plays, *Ghosts* (1881), inspired by the idea of what became of the woman who *didn't* leave her husband, who stayed no matter what he did because social convention demanded it. The play features a mature woman with a grown son, who, only after the death of her abusive husband, begins to think for herself and regret the wasted years of her marriage. Tragedy envelops the family as the ghosts of the past are revealed as destroyers of the present.

Because Ibsen's stated intention was to change society, his plays are called social realism. Anton Chekhov, a Russian writing nearly twenty years later, created four masterpieces of modern realism. But with the winds of the Russian Revolution already blowing, his plays seem gentler, more nostalgic than Ibsen's as though he knew that change was coming for his characters whether they were ready for it or not. *The Seagull, Uncle Vanya, The Three Sisters*, and *The Cherry Orchard*, all look into the quiet desperation of Russian society. They are not scathing criticisms but rather compassionate glimpses, reminders that privilege does not necessarily mean happiness. Characters find their lives restricted and their options limited. Their wealth is fading away and their social worlds shrink day by day. Chekhov himself was dying of tuberculosis as he wrote his final plays. Is it possible that he sensed that within only thirteen years, his families and their kind would all be swept away in the Revolution?

George Bernard Shaw (1856–1950) was more closely allied with Ibsen's approach than with Chekhov's, bringing Ibsen's "obscene" realism to England. A socialist, Shaw wrote to criticize society and inspire change, sometimes through charm and wit, sometimes through savage satire. His early plays were first published in an anthology he titled *Plays Pleasant and Unpleasant* (1898). Among the "pleasant" plays was *Arms and the Man*, a charming, witty attack on the glorification of war. Among the "unpleasant" was *Mrs. Warren's Profession*, a scathing look at Victorian hypocrisy about prostitution. In his long career, Shaw produced many volumes of work, both fiction and nonfiction.

Following in the footsteps of these three great innovators were some of the giants of American theatre: Eugene O'Neill, Arthur Miller, Lillian Hellman, and Tennessee Williams. These in turn inspired the contemporary works of Wendy Wasserstein, Michael Weller, Lanford Wilson, Marsha Norman, Tina Howe, A.J. Gurney, Aaron Sorkin, Beth Henley, and August Wilson.

Media Realism

Most dramatic cinema attempts realism. When receiving negative reviews, films are most often criticized for their lack of reality or believability. The slow demise of the traditional sitcom probably has something to due with increasing discontent with how different most of them are from the lives of viewers. The last great hit in this category, *Everybody Loves Raymond*, never strayed from the everyday family conflicts experienced by much of the viewing public. While television comedies will probably revive in some form, they will also likely need to reinvent themselves.

Our vision of what is "real" changes with time. Some films of the 1940s and 50s, thought then to be gritty in their realism, seem overwrought now—too much dramatic background music, too much overtly tortured acting, and too much telegraphing of danger. We have grown far more critical than prior generations of any onscreen behavior perceived as inauthentic. James Dean remains an icon of realistic performance to this day with only three films as proof.

If a film departs from real life in a genuinely imaginative way, it will attract attention, and theorists are always predicting the death of realism as passé. But the reflection of our own lives, minus the mundane distracting details, is a subject of which we never tire. Each of the films up for Oscars in 2004 (*Ray, Million Dollar Baby, Sideways, Aviator* and *Finding Neverland*) qualify. The last also incorporates elements of Romanticism.

NATURALISM

Call for Change

For artists of naturalism, realism only *begins* to oppose artificial theatricality and does not go far enough. It chooses which elements of life to present, often suggesting solutions to social problems. What is needed instead is stark reality with no compromise—life with details, including the ugly, distracting, and irrelevant. The keys to all truth are scientific method and scrutiny. Individuals cannot be responsible for what they do because heredity and environment overwhelm them. Plays should be more human and less social in orientation. No characters are specifically sympathetic; they just are. Plays do not need to progress rapidly or have clear climaxes. Endings can be pessimistic, ironic, cynical, and even disappointing, like life. Actors should *live* the life of their characters onstage rather than just *playing* them.

In the 1870s, French writer Emile Zola (1840–1902) coined the phrase "slice of life" (perhaps realism was merely a bite or sip of life) and wrote *Therese Raquin*, the first naturalistic drama. His introduction for that play was the complete manifesto of the movement. His work depicted society in minute, often sordid detail.

August Strindberg (1849–1912), the Swedish playwright who later rejected naturalism, wrote two influential naturalist plays, *The Father* and *Miss Julie*. He also refused to beautify human behavior and never suggested an alternative to the pain and misery of life. In *The Father* (1887), he dissects a family in crisis as the parents tear each other apart emotionally over the fate of their only child. Strindberg believed that men and women were destined to mortal combat and the play ends on a disturbingly unresolved note of agony. Equally, in *Miss Julie*, class struggle and sex intersect in a fatal combat between a young upper class woman and her father's servant. Another servant simply observes, expecting nothing but disaster and being glumly content when it occurs. No solutions, no happy endings, no chance at redemption, Strindberg's naturalist plays are dark and disturbing but powerfully real.

Andre Antoine (1858–1943), the director and manager who founded *Theatre Libre* or "Free Theatre" which was devoted to naturalism and became the model for experimental theatres around the world. His absolute commitment to minute detail and refusal to cater to entertainment values had a huge impact on much of Western theatre, in part by making all realize how much they had been selecting and omitting from performance.

The movement had a decidedly pessimistic tendency and rarely focused on the positive details that are every bit as "natural" as the dark side. And some would claim that some choices among the natural are essential for a work to be called art. Perhaps the pioneers of naturalism are dancing in their graves over the current glut of reality shows on TV. Eventually, filmmakers adapted the detail necessary for naturalism, but its impact remains in the theatre today.

Image statements might include: "warts and all," "don't look away," "all are victims," "the uncensored mind," and "who needs an ending?" This is theatre as eavesdropping on the dark side of human nature. Naturalism is the alley behind realism's street.

The Look

Phenomenal set detail may be employed so that water will run and stoves will cook and, in a famous Antoine production, real flies buzz around real beef hanging in a meat market scene. A highly contained box set is likely. Real clothes are better choices than costumes, which will require minutely accurate detail to pass. No gels and no make-up are preferred. The environment is a major character. It has more influence than any human does in the play. Movement needs to seem spontaneous. The fourth wall is very much in place and the audience is never acknowledged. Actors are less likely to cheat out to the audience or use open turns, are more likely to turn their backs to the house and generally drop theatrical conventions in favor of accuracy. All movement aims to come from inner experience.

The Sound

Speech may be muffled or even mumbled if it is true to character. Language is basic, gritty prose, often lower class in syntax. Conversations do not necessarily go anywhere. Snatches of dialogue may be lost or drowned out by background noise or distractions. Just as very few of us in life say exactly what we mean, characters tend to circumvent and talk around their issues.

The Acting

Naturalistic acting needs great subtlety and a complete lack of artifice. The performer must have a willingness to drop charm, charisma, and the need to command an audience. A simplicity that belies technique is essential. It is much more difficult for most actors than it first seems, because we are so accustomed to editing or exaggerating ourselves for performance. A complete concentration and absolute ability to play *in* the moment and to go *with* the moment is needed. A deeply rooted psychological comprehension of character is essential as well as strong empathy and ability to play the complexity of personality. There are no "stars" in naturalism, so a strong sense of ensemble or group consciousness is needed along with a willingness to "let it all hang out." An actor referred to his role as a "scratch and itch and belch and fart" part. He meant Naturalism.

Media Naturalism

Robert Altman's film, *Shortcuts*, contains countless naturalistic moments including a man urinating facing the camera instead of turning away, a wife squeezing a pimple on her husband's neck, a phone-sex employee who is actually a housewife changing her baby's diapers while panting to her customer and a "naked bottom" scene (played by Julianne Moore) not remotely sexual. The character has an argument with her husband while expecting guests—she spills wine on her skirt and takes it off to rinse and blow dry while the argument continues. At one point, he stops the fight to say, "You're not wearing any panties!" She rolls her eyes and the fight goes on.

One of the most vivid touches of naturalism in television history took place in the classic 1970s TV series, *All in the Family*, when the sound of Archie Bunker flushing the toilet was heard. This was not a naturalistic show, but that was a naturalistic moment. When a flush is heard on network TV, we think about all the offstage noise and life-sounds usually edited in performance. When *Rosanne* was first broadcast, audiences realized that it had been a long time since they had seen anything but tidy kitchens and svelte families on the tube.

Naturalism has largely been circumvented in recent years by documentaries and reality shows. It is much easier to show real life detail than to create it. For both fictional and actual filmed events, there is a tendency to locate the action in areas of poverty and crisis. Ghettos, housing projects, hospitals, prisons, areas of extreme poverty, drug abuse, isolation and danger are often chosen. The life that is sliced is rarely one viewers would choose to live.

COMPARISONS OF REALISTIC FORMS

These plays share a concern with telling the truth, but it is not the same truth. Their time, space, values, structure, pleasure, and senses are distinct.

TABLE 9.1

	Romanticism	Realism	Naturalism
Time	Anytime, even imaginary Epics, perhaps covering lifetimes.	Present or recent past. Usually a period of a few days or weeks.	Present or recent past. Contained with scenes or entire play in actual time.
Space	May be exotic, elaborate, fanciful, or vast.	Seem like actual living spaces but angled for sight lines, moderate detail.	Total, detailed recreation of actual settings, working plumbing.
Values	Free-wheeling emotional expression.	Solving problems	Life unedited, complete truth.
Structure	Unpredictable, epic	Well-made play with clear progressin from definite start to finish	"Slice of life"
Pleasure	Wild, over-the-top, fantastic adventures.	Honest, frank portrayal with some discretionary editing for taste.	Unedited, even conspicuously perverse, clinical, even mundane detail.
Senses	Extravagant visuals, bright, varied, larger than life, speech may include poetic tones and extravagant language.	Appearance of life, everyday speech pattern but with sharper diction and intent.	"Warts and all," common speech, including mumbling incomplete thoughts.

Of course, whatever choice the producers make, it may entirely change on a dime, depending on who is cast.

John August, *screenwriter*

"I just saw a woman driving a van with a man desperately holding on outside. As a screenwriter, I said to myself, 'If you put Will Ferrell in the role, it's a comedy, Hugh Grant and it's romantic comedy, Sean Penn and it's a dark thriller.'"

TWENTIETH-CENTURY MASTERS

This look at some American masters of realism in the twentieth century is by no means a complete accounting, nor did these playwrights limit their work to realism. Nevertheless, their plays have become standard works in the American repertoire and enjoy global respect as well. We discuss Eugene O'Neill, Tennessee Williams, Lillian Hellman and Arthur Miller below.

Eugene O'Neill (1888–1953) is regarded by many as the foremost American playwright. The son of an actor, he walked away from the theatre at a young age and spent years as a seaman, prospector, derelict, and newspaper reporter—all experiences he would use later in his plays. His realistic works depict the lives of the down and out, bordering sometimes on nihilistic despair. He won four Pulitzer prizes (including one for *Beyond the Horizon*, his first full-length play) and was awarded the Nobel Prize for Literature in 1936. His last two plays, *Moon for the Misbegotten* and *Long Day's Journey into Night*, are strongly autobiographical, focusing on the difficult and tempestuous relationships in his immediate family.

Tennessee Williams (1914–1983) was born Thomas Lanier Williams in Columbus, Mississippi. His realism is more closely aligned with that of Chekhov than Ibsen in that it is lyrically poetic. His plays are delicate, about fragile and lost souls. Often nostalgic, his early (and most successful) plays look at lives of faded beauty and faded hopes. Two of his masterpieces are *The Glass Menagerie* and *A Streetcar Named Desire*.

Lillian Hellman (1905–1984) was a political activist whose plays are remarkable for their tightly woven plots and her ability to explore depths of psychological weakness, while maintaining sympathy with flawed characters. Her political leanings were socialist, and she traveled the world as an outspoken critic of fascism and the oppression of minorities and women. Her most frequently produced plays are *The Children's Hour*, a study of the destructive power of greed, corruption and bigotry set in a girl's boarding school, and *The Little Foxes*, the story of a family of ambitious, unscrupulous and cruel siblings who stop at nothing to achieve success.

Arthur Miller's (1915–2005) work was social and political, as was his life. His most famous and enduring plays focus on the struggles of the common man to find a place in a world dominated by commerce and industry. His long life and career spanned most of the twentieth century, and his masterpieces include *All My Sons*, the story of a man who sold defective airplane parts to the American military during WWII; *A View from the Bridge*, an exploration of immigrant poverty and despair set in the Red Hook district of New York City's harbor; and *Death of a Salesman*, a modern tragedy blending expressionism and realism focused on the life of a little man overwhelmed by the failures of his life.

Realism is of course a distinctly Western concept and most indigenous theatre in other parts of the world is far removed from the form. Its impact on world theatre, however, was profound, not in changing homegrown theatre elsewhere but rather in its universal importation and presentation as an alternative. Ironically, when other cultures present works common to our culture, they most often represent two extremes, the comparatively brutal honesty of realism and the fanciful extremes of the musical.

SUMMARY

During the nineteenth century, neoclassicism faded, and the new melodrama was busily appeasing the middle class. The works of Compte, Marx, Darwin, and Freud triggered radical changes in politics and thought. Theatre artists searched for new ways to address a rapidly changing world. The Romanticists looked back to nature for solace, creating epic dramas about the struggle of individuals to free themselves from the corrupting forces of society. Early Romanticist playwrights included

Goethe, Hugo, and the first plays of Ibsen. Realism attempted to change society for the better by focusing on cause and effect and the influences of heredity and environment on behavior. Ibsen, Chekhov, and Shaw were early masters of this style. Naturalism takes realism one step further, sparing nothing, and offering no solutions. Zola, Strindberg, and Antoine were early champions of naturalism. Twentieth-century American masters of realism include O'Neill, Williams, Hellman, and Miller.

SUGGESTED ASSIGNMENT

1. Since realism now dominates as a form, why do you think the world seemed to get along fine without it for so long before it evolved?

2. Which of the four "great thinkers" (Comte, Marx, Darwin, Freud) identified in this chapter do you think has the greatest impact on your own view of the world?

3. Why is it that for over two thousand years, playwrights seemed unconcerned with writing about the average person?

4. Of recent theatre or films you have attended, which came closest to pure realism?

5. The same for romanticism and naturalism?

6. What is the most naturalistic detail you have experienced as an audience member?

7. What has been the most sweeping, romantic moment you have experienced in the theatre?

8. Consider someone writing or directing the story of your life so far. Which of the three (realism, romanticism, naturalism) would be likely to be chosen for the style or treatment? Why?

9. What is it about the playwrights identified as masters of the past century that seems to distinguish their work from that of their contemporaries?

10. Do you determine any trend in films at present to favor one of the three forms examined in this chapter?

SUGGESTED ACTIVITIES

1. Individual—Identify a moment of importance in your own life. Think about your story as a Romantic epic, a Realist social drama, and a Naturalistic "slice of your life." How does it change the meaning of this event to look at it through these three different lenses.

2. Small Group—Choose a world news event of interest to you and prepare a naturalistic docu-drama report of it for presentation to class. Then dramatize the event by applying Romantic or Realistic selectivity to it. Which style best represents the story you really want to tell.

3. Long term—Follow an event unfolding in the world around you, whether that is your personal drama or the global stage. Keep a journal in which you try to report just the facts, naturalistically, then render it as social realism intending to solve a problem. Finally, see what happens if you set this event on the epic stage of the Romantic vision. Does your participation in the event change depending on your approach? Does the outcome or meaning of the event change?

4. Large Group—Watch a news story together and determine if it is being reported in true "slice of life" fashion or not. Are parts of the story actually dramatized as Social Realism? Does any part of it seem to follow the ideas of the Romantics? Should news reports include anything but the facts?

Key Words and Ideas

Auguste Comte

Karl Marx

Charles Darwin

Sigmund Freud

Romanticism

Johann Wolfgang von Goethe

Victor Hugo

Realism

    Henrik Ibsen

    Anton Chekhov

    George Bernard Shaw

Naturalism

    Emile Zola

    August Strindberg

    Andre Antoine

Twentieth-Century American Masters

    Eugene O'Neill

    Tennessee Williams

    Lillian Hellman

    Arthur Miller

STYLIZATION

CONTENTS

I N *realism*, behavior comes close to what we believe to be our own. *Stylization* is the process of taking a play beyond reality through distortion, exaggeration, or some other stretch of convention. The more "stylized" a production is the more conventions it asks its audience to embrace. This chapter examines the "styles" that emerged as a result of crucial world events. It also examines our most highly stylized and popular entertainment, the musical.

Although realism is often serious, even grim in its examination of life and society, there is an optimism embedded in the way it advises us to look at things objectively, ferret out problems, and search for solutions. It suggests we might evolve into something better, fairer, and more humane. Realist plays often challenge our sense of the world around us by saying, "You think you know what it's like out here? You don't. Let me show you." Realism seems to imply that if we understand the problem, we may be moved to address it, if not politically, at least in our own hearts.

HOLOCAUSTS—THE WORLD AT WAR

World events in the first half of the twentieth century made many doubt the rational and scientific approach to solutions. In 1914, the assassination of an Austrian duke and duchess in Sarajevo ignited the first global war. Europe, its colonies around the world, and the United States became involved. New technologies (including chemical and biological weapons, air bombing, and tanks) made death and destruction possible on an unprecedented scale. The final toll was 8.5 million killed, 21 million wounded and 7.5 million prisoners or missing. During the final months of the war, the Russian Revolution sparked a civil war that wreaked devastation on a population already suffering. It ended with the establishment of the first communist government in the world, and sent the Imperial powers of Europe into a dither. On October 28, 1929, the U.S. stock market collapse triggered a global economic depression that would last for almost a decade.

By 1936, Hitler was elected to power in Germany, and the first assaults on neighboring countries began. By 1940, the world was again involved in war. This time the destruction was even more devastating. By 1945, 35 million had died globally along with another 10 million in concentration camps. In Hiroshima and Nagasaki, a new weapon of unbelievable force was unleashed, the first and (so far) only use of nuclear weapons. Suddenly it was clear that the human race now had the technology to destroy itself. Tension filled the decades that followed as the Cold War led Soviet and American governments to stockpile world-annihilating supplies of nuclear weapons. One wrong move by one very human leader and it could have been the end of everything.

The holocausts of the first half of the twentieth century had a profound impact on the worldview of the survivors. Science and technology had failed to make the world a better place, only creating killing machines that were more efficient. The idea of society moving toward a more just and humane system was fragile. Many theatre artists did not escape the overwhelming sense of despair. For them, realism with its basis in science, reason, and optimism no longer made sense. They began to create theatre reflecting the world as they experienced it.

This chapter examines various movements away from realism as well as the contrast between theatre that reflects our experience directly and that in which the world is stylized or altered.

ANTI-REALISM

Throughout the twentieth century, realistic and anti-realistic theatre have had an often uneasy and sometimes downright hostile relationship. The objections to realism included its emphasis on heredity and environment as controlling factors in human existence that at that time seemed too limited. Realism did not account for spiritual and cosmic forces and tended to discount ineffable, deeply personal experiences and moments of magic. Faith in the ability of science, technology, and reason to guide the evolution of society in positive directions seemed, to many, unsupportable.

THE "ISMs"

There is a tendency to name styles of theatre by adding the suffix "-ism" to its root name as in expression*ism* and symbol*ism*. We will continue this tradition. The progression of "Isms" over a period of 200 years, including those we have already identified, looks like this:

1. **Romanticism** early 1800s
   Explore history and destiny against all odds, idealize nature and reject corrupt society, epic in scope.

2. **Realism** 1850s+
   Just tell the truth in the hopes of making the world a better place.

3. **Naturalism** 1873+
   Reveal everything, warts and all. Don't expect things to change.

4. **Impressionism** 1874+
   Theatre should attempt to capture the moment through feeling, mood, and atmosphere. A higher world, artificially created and emotionally sublimated, is ideal.

5. **Symbolism** 1890–1920
   Poetic, dreamlike theatre seeks the profound or mysterious in life. Mood and atmosphere are far more important than plot or action.

6. **Expressionism** 1910
   Life is seen through a single set of subjective emotions. Theatre should be forceful, urgent, and emotionally charged.

7. **Futurism** 1910–1930
   The actor is a machine subjugated to totally integrated theatre. Reject the past and glorify progress. Anticipate a great industrial future!

8. **Dadaism** 1916
   Contradict all expectations. Nothing is sacred. Theatre should take a nihilistic approach to life and a revolutionary attitude towards art.

9. **Constructivism** 1921–
   Build a story, don't tell it. Sentimentality and individual feeling have no place here. It is time to strip away theatrical illusion and show the bare bones.

10. **Surrealism** 1924
    Freed from morals or esthetics, the artist is finally capable of creation. Theatre artists should seek spontaneous creation without interference from reason. Insanity is often true sanity.

11. **Didacticism** 1927–
    Narrative theatre should be for the intellect rather than the emotions, also called Epic or Brechtian theatre.

12. **Absurdism** late 1940s–
    Theatre must reflect an irrational world where truth is unknowable and life is nonsensical. Understanding is impossible. Sudden changes are what life is about.

13. **Feminism** late 1960s–
    Women have a voice, too long neglected and pushed inside, which must be released and heard through theatre that is by, for, and about them.

14. **Postmodernism** 1980s–
    Play with the past without nostalgia for it. Theatre should juxtapose the new and the old, one masking, disguising, or hiding itself within or behind the other.

We deal here with six Isms that have most influenced theatre styles.

Symbolism

Poetic, dreamlike theatre seeks the profound or mysterious in life.
　　Developed in France during the later years of the nineteenth century, symbolism profoundly influenced writers in England, Ireland and America such as Edgar Allen Poe, James Joyce, William

Butler Yeats, and Eugene O'Neill. Belgian Maurice Maeterlinck (1862–1949), is a pre-eminent symbolist playwright, and was influenced by the French poets Stephane Mallarmé and Paul Verlaine. Paintings by Paul Gauguin, Henri Rousseau, Henri de Toulouse-Lautrec, and Giorgio De Chirco reflect the basic values. Adolphe Appia and Max Reinhardt explored these values in theatrical lighting and set design. Wagnerian opera tried to fuse all the elements (music, dialogue, color, light, shape, and texture) in performance.

Call for Change

Let us turn our backs on objective reality and move strongly into the subjective and intuitive. Mood and atmosphere are more important than plot or action. There is no need for characters to have personalities of their own since they are symbols of the poet's inner life. Something onstage is not necessary a *clear* symbol, which the audience will recognize, but rather is symbolic of the author's *consciousness*. Suggestion is more powerful than explicit representation. Theatre should seek the profound and the unfathomable. Life shown in realism should be either changed or transcended. The autonomy of art frees it from any obligation to deal with social problems in political terms. Art needs to move beyond the real and into the truth.

Symbolists argue that realism misses the ultimate experiences of life, the immediate, unique, emotional response of the individual to an event. Language is the primary tool, de-emphasizing scenery, action, and character. The primary theorist, Stephane Mallarmé, felt that drama was "a sacred and mysterious rite which, through dream, reverie, allusion, and musicality, evokes the hidden spiritual meaning of existence."

By challenging the stilted, domesticated, scientific philosophy of the realists, they provided inspiration to others whose work could be poetic and popular, non-realistic and accessible.

The Look

Repeated symbols include water (symbolizing both life force and death), light and dark, bizarre juxtapositions, projected light, and mood music. Movement may be enigmatic. Static poses may alternate with ritualized, frenzied, and whirling ones. The space may be undefined, and dreamlike, full of shadows, mists, and possibly mirrors. Costumes, often draped and gauzelike, draw on wide ranging tribal and cultural influences. Much modern dance, in the Isadora Duncan tradition, relates to symbolism.

The Sound

Strong emphasis is placed on the voice and its music. Mixed metaphors abound. New Age music suits symbolist production. Dialogue may be full of mysterious references, perhaps simple nouns with adjectives rather than complete sentences. Lines are likely to be rhythmic, poetic, with hypnotic use of cadence and intensity to build emotion.

The Acting

Performers need to be able to function on a high level of abstraction and to play situations associated more with dreams than waking experience. The ability to play larger than life, to personify a single quality or trait, and to function sometimes like a puppet are all essential. Clarity, practicality, definition, and making it easier for the actor and the audience need to give way to a willingness to distort and exaggerate for effect.

Early Works

Andreyev, Leonid: *He Who Gets Slapped*

Maeterlinck, Maurice: *The Intruder, The Blind, The Bluebirds*, and *Pealeas and Melisande*

O'Neill, Eugene: *The Emperor Jones* and *The Hairy Ape*

O'Casey, Sean: *Within the Gates*

Strindberg, August: *The Dream Play*

Wedekind, Franz: *Springs Awakening*

Jarry, Alfre: *Ubu Roi*

Wilde, Oscar: *Salome*

Futurism

The actor is a machine subjugated to totally integrated theatre.

In 1909, Italian poet Filippo Tomasso Marinetti (1876–1944) wrote an impassioned manifesto on the front page of an important Parisian newspaper, outlining the tenets of futurism. Beginning as a strictly literary movement, it quickly spread to visual arts and music as well. The movement ran from about 1910 to 1930, and influenced Italian fascists. Eventually, Eugene Ionesco employed some of the techniques as does Performance Art today.

Call for Change

Reject the past. Glorify progress. Anticipate a great industrial future! Theatre needs to give expression to the energy and movement of new machinery. Technology can rescue it from a deadly museum-like atmosphere and literary, logical bias. Machines and wars can be a source of great beauty. War is, in fact, the world's hygiene, cleaning out unfortunate vestiges of the past. Barriers between arts, actors, and audience need to be smashed.

Futurists deplored any veneration of the past, seeing it as a barrier to progress. Marinetti wrote in praise of fast cars as a new ideal of beauty, wanting museums and libraries torn down because they only had value for the old and the dying. No futurist was over forty. Their ideal man was an aggressive young warrior, deploring the past and charging full steam ahead into the future, apparently without women. The movement, though it did not produce any great plays or playwrights, influenced future anti-realist artists by promoting modern technology to create multimedia performances, encouraging direct confrontation between audience and performer, advocating fresh untried approaches to the arts and breaking down barriers between the arts.

The Look

Actors often move among the audience. Simultaneous events take place in various parts of the performance space. Kinetic sculptures, utilitarian objects, leather, chains, steel and cement, multimedia, high-tech, multiple focus and simultaneous action may be used. Costumes with straight lines, metallic surfaces and loose fit, turn the human silhouette into a mechanical one, although face, arms, and legs are often left uncovered. Actors are integrated into the setting, which may be controlled or street theatre. The look is macho-mechanical.

The Sound

Language is blunt, simple, direct, masculine, and militaristic. Lines may involve ideological diatribes, manifestoes, shouting, and mechanical noises, delivered in presentational fashion. Sound can be just noises. "Music" may be created out of sirens, machine guns, and other war sounds.

The Acting

The actor, the director's robot, may be asked to perform in a highly geometric, machine-like fashion. Strong masculine attacks, along with the stamina to endure sustained violent, high-energy, repetitive sequences are important. Highly developed technical skills, great patience, and letting go of the desire to portray realistically are needed along with the ability to eliminate the actor's own idiosyncratic behavior in favor of total integration into surroundings.

Early Works

Balla: *Disconcerted States of Mind*

Canguillo: *Detonation*

Marinetti, Filipe Tommaso: *Feet*

Settimelli: *Sempronio's Lunch*

Dadaism

Contradict all expectations.

Dadaists also rejected traditional forms, but were stunned and dismayed by the outbreak of war and declared the world insane. They sought to infuse their art with calculated madness, discord, and chaos.

Inspired by the writings of Franz Kafka, the movement was conceived in Zurich by Tristan Tzara and, led by Hugo Ball, spread to France. Dadaism, itself defies the keeping of records, so its progress was only randomly transcribed. The Dada Gallery was established in 1916, and the ideas were prominant until 1922. More a means of creating a theatrical event than for writing scripts, Dadaism did not produce a body of work. It tends to be favored at private entertainments or Happenings.

Dada art reflects the belief that the world makes no sense. Rather than talk about chaos and madness, Dadaists performed it. Often conflicting performance events occurred simultaneously, like the futurists, employing multimedia and audience confrontation, but with new technology and warrior mentality.

Call for Change

Nothing is sacred! Theatre should take a nihilistic approach to life and a revolutionary attitude toward art. Anti-art is the way to think since "creative" acts are worthless. Audiences should be infuriated, enraged, and moved beyond rationality to passion. Destroy all elements of the past. All beliefs have no reason. The future smacks of death, so the moment is all that matters. Spontaneity is the closest anyone can come to creating—the more shocking the better.

The Look and Sound

Space tends to be vast, bare, un-localized, and abstract, but may be buried in irrelevant items. Dialogue may be incongruous, full of non-sequiturs, shouting, singing, berating, gibberish, and obscenities. Laughing at the audience is a common mode of attack.

The Acting

An ability to improvise aggressively is essential, as is the actor's willingness to humiliate himself and others. An imaginative sense of what will strike others as obscene and sacrilegious helps. Audacity and a confrontational, defiant nature are needed.

Early Works

The concept discourages scripting. Some elements appear in these works:

Weiss, Peter: *Marat/Sade,*

Stoppard, Tom: *Travesties,*

Shepard, Sam: *Unseen Hand,*

Cummings, E. E.: *Him*

Stein, Gertrude: *Four Saints in Three Acts*

Expressionism

Life is seen through a single set of subjective emotions.

The expressionism movement originated in the paintings of Auguste Herve, exhibited in 1901 under the title *Expressionisms*, and eventually influenced all the arts. The term describes work that vigorously reflects the mood or inner life of either the artist or the object portrayed.

Expressionists believed that fundamental truth lies within the soul, spirit, and vision of the individual. Reacting strongly against an increasingly mechanized world, they felt that external reality must be shaped into harmony with our interior life. In some ways, the expressionists bridge the gap between the realists and the anti-realists. They rejected the heredity/environment argument of the realists but embraced their desire to shape and improve human society. The expressionists embraced many stylistic ideals of the anti-realists while rejecting their elitist lack of concern with the lives of average people.

Shared qualities of expressionist theatre are:

1. Rather than a linear, cause-and-effect plot, the play will center around a theme, idea or motif.

2. The action often takes the form of a quest in which the protagonist searches at various "stations" for what is often a vague or illusive prize.

3. The action is often cyclical, reflecting a pessimistic view of the human condition.

4. Characters represent types rather than individuals (often having no names other than the Student, the Husband, or the Prostitute.).

5. Often a Christ-like protagonist is slowly destroyed or absorbed by a mechanistic, materialistic world.

6. Distortion is found in every element, portraying a personal rather than "objective" vision of reality

7. Dialogue is often short, simple, and staccato with gesture and pantomime used to communicate emotional intensity.

The influence of the expressionist movement was so profound that finding contemporary drama without some element of expressionism is difficult. Whenever we see a work in which what the mind knows is more important than what the eye sees, we are experiencing its influence.

Call for Change

Most other Isms are too passive and specialized. We need theatre that is forceful, urgent, and emotionally charged, capturing the inner struggle each of us goes through spiritually in order to develop into The New Person of the future. Nightmarish, anti-industrial, deliberate distortions of reality are ways to deliver a harsh truth. Dreams are a major source of truth. Portrayal of the dreamlike state may illuminate life so that the subjective can be objectified. The real heroes are hidden among the common workers, stifled by a system that is dangerous, dehumanizing, and deadly. The values of the older generation are useless. It is time for fresh subjectivity that mirrors inner psychological realities instead of outer physical appearances. It is time to get serious.

The Look

Moody, atmospheric lighting dominates. Diagonal lines, leaning panels, sharp angles, colored light, and nightmarish images may be employed. Walls may slope, windows and doors may re-form, and dark shadows may be juxtaposed with shafts of bright light. Platforms, ramps, scaffolding and unexpected elements (such as a trapeze) may enter the playing space. Geometric images dominate. Movement may involve stark groupings of actors and choreographed histrionic business. Actions may be fragmentary or disconnected. Some use of masks and Asian stage technique may be employed. Costumes and props may be grotesquely exaggerated.

The Sound

Explosive language is employed with a startling contrast between lyrical passages and staccato, almost amputated dialogue. Full range of sound including non-human noises, shouting, chanting, and barking may be used. Like the movement, dialogue may be repetitious and mechanical with tempos shifting dramatically.

The Acting

Highly theatrical, sometimes flagrantly presentational playing representing the subconscious and the spiritual is required. Actors need to be able to portray volatile emotions as well as an alienated state of abstraction. They may be asked to work in two extremes, sometimes removing a human quality (such as greed or lust) from their characterizations and at other times to become these same qualities incarnate.

Early Works

Capek, Josef and Karol: *The Insect Comedy* and *R.U.R.*

Kaiser, Georg: *From Morn to Midnight*

Rice, Elmer: *The Adding Machine*

Shaw, Irwin: *Bury the Dead*

Strindberg, August: *The Road to Damascus* and *Ghost Sonata*

Treadwell, Sophie: *Machinal*

Absurdism

An irrational world where truth is unknowable and life is nonsensical

Absurd is used here in a broader, sadder sense than "ridiculous." It is derived from the original musical term for "out of harmony." While absurdist plays were written in the 1940s, Samuel Beckett's *Waiting for Godot* (1953) was the first major success. Philosophers Albert Camas and Jean-Paul Sartre began to influence the thinking of playwrights. Their philosophy of Existentialism called for using *will* instead of *reason* to deal with problems arising from a hostile universe. Continental Europe had experienced great devastation, massive human, economic, agricultural and architectural loss, fatigue, and disillusionment. Memories of the concentration camps and gas chambers were vivid. This was the canvas for Absurdism.

Silent film comedians of the period (Buster Keaston, Charlic Chaplin, Keystone Cops, and later, Laurel and Hardy and the Marx brothers) employed absurdist elements, with their characters often existing in a nightmarish black and white world beyond their comprehension. The movement was most popular in the 1950s and 1960s, but absurdist elements are present today in some of the works of Sam Shepard, David Mamet and David Rabe.

Call for change

Understanding is impossible. Space, linear time, and conventional structure are abandoned. All laws of probability and physics are suspended. Since he is in a state of moral paralysis, man's ONLY freedom is the exercise of his conscious mind. There is no light left in the universe. There is only metaphysical anguish. Life has lost reason. Man has lost touch with his roots. Existence is useless and meandering. Laughter is a coping tool, often the only coping tool for dealing with deep pain. It is difficult to communicate with others, so we need to fill time, as if life is spent in a waiting room with no inner office, with playing games, jokes, dances, songs, silly routines, or escapes. Plots are often circular (everything that happens has happened before) with the play ending exactly where it began.

The Look and Sound

Plays may be realistically mounted so that absurdity comes out of setting up false expectations or may be staged in a cartoon-like way. Since humans, animals, and objects are interchangeable in this world, they may be given each other's qualities. Characters may be complex and multi-dimensional or completely stereotyped. Casts are mostly small and effects minimal. Speech is disconnected, non-communicative, and rambling. People never seem to listen to each other. There are rushes of sound following by unexpected and sometimes interminable silences. Just as a mood appears to establish itself, it changes.

The Acting

An ability to make rapid-fire changes and come up with surprising use of pauses and silence is essential. Having many voices and attacks, high energy and imagination are important. Movement demands may include acrobatics, silent film technique, song and dance, vaudeville, circus tricks and quick breaks between presentational and non-presentational audience relationships. The capacity to be real and unreal is in sharp juxtaposition. It is no accident that a major Broadway revival of *Waiting for Godot* featured three of the world's most brilliant clowns: Robin Williams, Steve Martin and Bill Irwin.

Works

Albee, Edward; *The American Dream* and *The Sandbox*

Beckett, Samuel: *Waiting for Godot, Krapp's Last Tape, Happy Day's, Engame, Footfall,* and *Act Without Words*

Camus, Albert: *Caligula*

Genet, Jean: *The Maids, The Balcony, Deathwatch,* and *The Blacks*

Ionesco, Eugene: *The Bald Soprano, Rhinoceros, The Chairs,* and *The Lesson*

Kopit, Arthur: *Oh Dad, Poor Dad, Mama's Hung You in the Closet and I'm Feelin' So Sad, The Day the Whores Came Out to Play Tennis,* and *Chamber Music*

Pinter, Harold: *The Dumb Waiter, The Birthday Party, The Caretaker, No Man's Land, Old Times,* and *The Homecoming*

Pirandello, Luigi: *Six Characters in Search of an Author*

Sartre, Jean-Paul: *No Exit* and *The Flies*

Shepard, Sam: *Buried Child*

Didacticism

Narrative theatre for the intellect, rather than the emotions. Also called Epic or Brechtian theatre.

Erwin Piscator conceived of the idea of a "proletarian drama." Bertolt Brecht became the movement's main theorist and dramatist. He developed a dramatic economy, simplicity of language, mature vision, and depth of expression seldom seen on the stage before. He refined his work through his own company, the Berliner Ensemble. He defined "delight" as *the pleasure that comes from discovering new truths about yourself and the world*, which he called the perfect reconciliation between teaching and pleasing. His theories have been subjected to many conflicting interpretations but continually stimulated directors throughout the world.

Call for Change

Theatre should make you think and act. The stage is meant to narrate (not embody), to demand decisions (not feelings), to communicate knowledge (not experience), to present arguments (not suggestions) and to appeal to our reason (not instincts). Actors should *present* characters instead of inhabiting them. Audiences should stay aware that they are watching a performance instead of losing themselves in the lives of the characters. "Alienation" (*Verfremdung*) destroys theatrical illusion by frequently interrupting the action, so the audience can remain emotionally disengaged and capable of viewing the work intelligently. The *subject matter* is what is alienated. (The term does not mean to be "offended" or "angry." The original German word, *verfremdung*, means to see things in a new light, to step back and look again at what has become familiar.) Audiences should feel they have the power to change society if it is not working. Critical watching discourages passivity. Drama should deal with a human being caught in the midst of social or political conflict. The best theatre spreads social ideology. Naturalism is rejected, because it fails to portray man within the general landscape of the whole society. Other forms of theatre encourage audiences to idealistic attitudes with no relevance to real life. *Gestus*, the key word for the concept, involves the revelation of a relationship by deed, word, or look. Some movement of the body, tongue, or eye can suddenly illuminate connections between people. This is achieved through productions with a loose, narrative form and numerous, separate episodes sometimes presented in the past tense.

The Look

A proscenium space is preferred with a blank screen used to project images. Signs may describe scenes before they happen and thereby remove suspense. Auditorium lights may be left on. Conspicuously, theatrical props (such as a paper moon) may indicate time. Scenery is likely to be Constructivist—simple stairs, scaffolding, possibly revolving stages. In our era, any constant reminder (cameras, amplification, and multiple screenings) that the event is a theatrical one and not real life may replace traditional choices. The movement runs the spectrum from realistic to highly stylized. Changes in time and place are frequent and abrupt.

The Sound

Clear, distinct, often harsh, and strong language is employed. Dialogue is mixed with narration and vaudeville-like singing interludes. Instead of intensifying emotions, music is used to neutralize them, the opposite of its usual function in theatre. Dialogue may be blunt and colloquial, full of both malice and wit. Strident prologues and epilogues are common. Direct address of audience is frequent, and a wide range of dialects may be employed.

The Acting

Actors must have the capacity to step in and out of character, to comment and "demonstrate" character with some flexibility. Training in mime, clowning, and Asian acting techniques is recommended. Brecht recommends that actors develop the ability to think of their characters in the third person and to "quote" the behavior of the character with the same immediacy as someone who has experienced an accident and now feels compelled to recreate the event for listeners. The distancing therefore is by no means the dropping of commitment.

Works

Brecht, Bertolt: *Mother Courage, Good Woman of Setzuan, The Threepenny Opera, The Caucasian Chalk Circle, Gallileo*, and *The Resistable Rise of Arturo Ui*

Kipphardt, Heinar: *In the Case of J. Robert Oppenheimer*

Tabari, Goerge: *Brecht on Brecht*

Weiss, Peter: *The Persecution and Assasination of Marat/Sade*

Media ISMs

Expressionism has its greatest presence in film because one of great gifts of cinema is that it can take us completely inside the emotional state of a character, seeing, hearing and feeling exactly what that character is experiencing. Probably the most expressionistic instances are in horror films where camera angles, lighting, focus and soundtrack all escalate the terror a character experiences, and we are terrified too. Some watered-down elements of Futurism exist in action movies, more so in the arcade games based on them. Dadaism is such a live event that it defies transfer to film and is most often manifested in strident rock performances where audiences are confronted and even vilified. The common vision of reality has moved in the direction of Absurdism in recent years as the world seems to have grown more incomprehensible and laughter seems the only way to deal with it. So without there being a distinctly absurdist film movement, there are likely to be sequences in many films that embrace absurdist elements. Didacticism may be employed in certain educational or training films, but is almost unheard of in fictional cinema where dispassionate objectivity is the last thing a filmmaker wants an audience to experience.

MUSICAL THEATRE

There is no more popular form of contemporary theatre in America than the musical. The vast majority of plays on Broadway are musicals. The chances are great that your first exposure to live theatre was a musical produced by your high school, a local community theatre, or possibly a professional touring production. Why do they play to packed houses every day around the world? Probably because they have the capacity to powerfully stir our emotions to the fullest heights. Can you think of a single, major public event in which music is not a crucial ingredient, whether it is one of celebration or mourning? The impulse to break into song and dance when feelings are so strong that they need some expression, even explosion, is one we all understand deep in our bones.

Origins

Music has always been a vital part of theatre. Most Asian performance, Greek tragedy, and Shakespearean comedy all have elements of song and dance. But the peculiar combination of light opera, ballet, musical hall, the minstrel show, and vaudeville that we now call the musical has only been around for about 150 years and is a distinctly American contribution to world theatre. The first musical is actually believed to have been an accident. A play called *The Black Crook* was playing in New York in 1866. By itself, it was a lackluster melodrama. However, a French dance company found itself stranded in New York, and the producers decided to add their songs and dances to the show to give it some oomph. Audiences were suddenly enthralled by the combination. This may seem amazingly simplistic but it turns out that with alarming frequency a mediocre script, with tunes and lyrics, might just be more than the sum of their parts.

While the musical flourished on the New York stage, it is important to acknowledge the British contribution of the light operas of Gilbert and Sullivan, which demonstrated that a story and music could make a delightful combination. French and Viennese composers, Jacques Offenbach (whose *Orpheus in the Underworld* introduced the world to the can-can!) and Franz Lehar (*The Merry Widow*), did the same.

The most significant early geniuses of musical theatre were Victor Herbert, whose early hits, *Babes in Toyland* and *Naughty Marietta*, and George M Cohan's *Little Johnny Jones* were not only tremendous theatrical successes but contributed songs that became popular on their own. These include *Ah Sweet Mystery of Life*, *I'm a Yankee Doodle Dandy*, and *Give My Regards to Broadway*.

The twentieth century saw two major phases in the development of musical theatre, first comedy, and then drama. At the start of the century, the musical comedy flowered. This format usually involved a madcap, zany plot, lots of young love, choruses featuring lovely chorines never wearing more clothing than was absolutely necessary, jazz or ragtime orchestrations, and tons of dancing with almost always a big, climactic tap number or maybe a half dozen of them. These were mindless, cheerful celebrations with many memorable songs, the best by George Gershwin or Rodgers and Hart, which are still beguiling us today. There were also notable all-black musicals during this period, including *How Come?*, which introduced the Charleston, the dance craze that virtually defined the 1920s. This form of musical, while moving out of dominance, has never really left us as evidenced by the recent success of *The Producers*.

The second dramatic phase is considered to have begun with *Showboat* in 1927, a musical which dealt with racial issues in a serious and profound way. The other major, serious work of this period was Gershwin's *Porgy and Bess*, which while actually an opera had considerable influence on musical theatre with its powerful, moving lyricism. In 1940, Rodgers and Hart's *Pal Joey* shocked theatergoers with a gigolo central character, an intellectual stripper, sexually candid lyrics, and a far more adult perspective than audience were used to. The following year, *Lady in the Dark* dealt with psychoanalysis! Then there was no turning back.

While the works of Rodgers and Hammerstein may seem relatively tame today, it is important to realize how often they were the first to push the musical into dealing with important social issues. Before their production of *Oklahoma!*, dance was primarily a diversion. Suddenly, it was used to tell the story and to explore character's darker emotional states. The play dealt with significant conflicts between settlers, featured a very troubled major character, and involved an onstage killing, formerly an unheard of event in a musical. Their subsequent musicals took on subjects such as physical abuse, racial prejudice, and cultural ignorance.

American dominance of musical theatre faded away during the seventies. The hits of French composers Alain Boubli and Claude-Michel Schonberg (*Les Miserables* and *Miss Saigon*) and the British phenomenon Andrew Lloyd Webber (*Jesus Christ Superstar*, *Evita*, *Cats*, *Starlight Express*, *Sunset Boulevard*, and *Phantom of the Opera*) are still playing decades later in theatre around the globe. Lloyd Webber has never been as popular with critics as with audiences. Many denigrate his work as derivative, some even suggesting he just revises Puccini opera scores, but the public remains enthralled.

The role of the critic's darling goes to American Stephen Sondheim, the most respected composer/lyricist now working. He writes music and lyrics and does both with a complex brilliance, head-and-shoulders above his peers. Each of his works (*Company*, *A Little Night Music*, *Sweeney Todd*, *Sunday in the Park with George*, *Into the Woods*, *Assassins*, and *Passion*) has pushed the boundaries of musical content with ambiguous, adult thought and an almost total disregard for the traditional happy ending. His music is so complex that actors are often warned not to attempt it at auditions because few accompanists can successfully sight-read it.

Unfortunately, his box office record reflects the fact that many audiences find his work too challenging, ironic, and downright melancholy.

Landmarks

In addition to the events above, several creators and musicals took the form to new heights and raised the bar for all who followed.

West Side Story

This contemporary *Romeo and Juliet*, with warring gangs, a Polish Romeo (Tony) and a Puerto Rican Juliet (Maria), put dance at the very center of the theatrical event, no longer secondary in any way and every bit as important as the music. Jerome Robbins elevated the potential of musical dance forever.

My Fair Lady

After countless musicals got along with meager books or highly watered-down versions of classics, Alan Jay Lerner took Shaw's brilliant original *Pygmalian*, pared it down without in any way diminishing its power, and most importantly, wrote lyrics that matched the wit, intellect, and style of the original. Suddenly the song could be as brilliant intellectually as it has always been emotionally.

Cabaret

This show evolved the concept musical to new heights, creating a total environment, which dominated the action. In the original production, slanted mirrors above the action always reflected the audience. Recent revivals recreated the entire Kit Kat Club so audience members feel they are there in a here-and-now way, intimately engaged.

Company

While every Sondheim show is to some extent a landmark, this was the first to tackle the issue of committing to one partner for life with all the problems involved in that commitment. It could be called the first truly grown-up musical, and it eliminated the chorus (group numbers involve the principal performers), opening up a world of possibility for the small musical.

Conventions

How do musicals compare with other forms of theatre we have studied?

Time

Most musicals are set in some kind of "ago" or in a timeless, encapsulated world. They run long compared to straight plays, often three hours or more with one intermission and the first part somewhat longer than the second. Musicals move swiftly between songs and generally cover a short period of time. Characters rarely age. They may, however, come to a standstill, plot-wise, when the need to sing and dance pops in or a character needs at least five minutes to tell us how wonderful it is to have met "a girl named Maria". At the other extreme, musical numbers can allow time to race forward as when Eliza's weeks and weeks of elocution lessons in *My Fair Lady* are condensed into a single song.

Space

Musicals generally play in large proscenium houses (most Broadway theatres seat 1,000 or more), which can accommodate large casts and audiences. Yet unlike straight plays, they are hardly restricted to within the proscenium arch. In *Cats* and *The Lion King*, animals actually roam the aisles; in *Peter Pan*, he flies out over the audience; and in *Phantom of the Opera* a gigantic chandelier does the same. At the end of the show-stopping, first act number, *I am What I am* in *La Cage Aux Folles*, the drag-queen singer whips off his wig and storms angrily down the aisle and out of the theatre. In fact, performances often move back and forth between ignoring the audience in a representative way and then turning to them either in asides or to share big presentational musical numbers.

Values

The majority of musicals come down on the side of celebrating life, cutting loose, not wasting precious moments, and getting back in touch with your joyous child. The song mentioned above is about coming out of whatever closet anyone may be trapped inside and joining life. Those that deal with social issues come down squarely for tolerance, forgiveness, and fighting bigotry at all costs— and all but the most somber favor the impulse to party.

Structure

Most have a healthy balance of ballads, character songs, solos, duets and big group numbers. There is a recognizable, internal structure that often separates a show tune from the kind of pop music on the charts. It is very rare not to have a major musical moment just before intermission, and frequently this is reprised somewhere in the second act. If the entire cast is not singing the final number, it is very unusual.

Pleasure

While many of us may burst into song and dance when hearing good news, we are usually talking a few bars of music and a little gyrating step at tops. And in life, we just do this in happy times. In a musical, both good news and bad can send you off for verses and up onto tables, and those around you may just suddenly feel the same way, singing your words and dancing your moves with you in perfect synchronicity.

Senses

Musicals are often a feast for the eye and ear by means of color, fabric, dazzling movement, and glorious sounds from orchestra and singers. Even though we don't get to go up onstage (usually) and dance with the cast, we feel as if we have because the empathy component is so strong. And while some songs require magnificent voices, it would be a mistake to assume that you have no future in musicals if you can't sing. Many of the major stars are marginal singers at best. Lauren Bacall has twice won the Tony Award for best actress in a musical, and she has about four notes. What is required is an oversized, exuberant personality that can fill the theatre with contagious energy and "sell" a song.

Contemporary Forms

Rock Musicals

Hair made history for more than its nude scene (or for that matter the moment when a nearly-naked actor swings on a rope into the audience to land on the arms of the seat of an elderly female patron and asks if she wants to look down inside the front of his loincloth). It brought rock into legitimate theatre. *The Who's Tommy* was a major hit of this type, and *Rent* has already become a theatre classic. Jonathan Larson's stunning work takes Puccini's nineteenth century opera, *La Boheme*, into contemporary New York's East Village and a world of HIV and homelessness.

Black Musicals

Shows featuring and exploring the lives of African-Americans have become a regular part of the theatre scene. *Sophisticated Ladies* (the music of Duke Ellingston), *Ain't Misbehavin'* (the music of Fats Waller), *Eubie* and *Bubbling Brown Sugar* (Eubie Blake) all work with small casts and dynamic musical talent. Another classic is *Dreamgirls*, which deals with a girl group much like the Supremes but also explores Black culture of the era.

Family Musicals

The Disney franchise has almost single-handedly turned what used to be largely an adult outing into a theatrical event, which embraces the presence of children. While some parents have always brought their offspring to the theatre, it was generally an invitation to enter their world rather than vice versa. Disney has systematically taken their hit animated musical films and converted them to live theatre. While their *Beauty and the Beast* is a fairly straightforward recreation of the film as closely as can be done in a live space, Julie Taymor's brilliant reinvention of *The Lion King* is a totally new experience with genuinely unexpected connections to both Asia and Africa, universal myths, stunning puppetry, mask, prop work and dazzling theatricality. She draws on the genius of the world—African masks, Javanese rod puppetry, Balinese head-dresses and South African Xhosa click language—to produce a theatre experience so stunning that if you have not yet seen it, expect your breath to be taken away and for your eyes to probably not remain dry.

Postmodern Musicals

Economics have recently made it necessary for small musicals that would formerly have played themselves out Off-Broadway to move On instead, since a large house is increasingly essential for recouping investments. While a big risk with many failures, this has also resulted in delightful, miniature works reaching a much larger audience, none more so than the 2004 Tony award winner for Best Musical, *Avenue Q*. In true postmodern fashion, this show does not go for big, socko emotions, but rather charmingly reflective ones and affectionately juxtaposes the old and the new. *Avenue Q* is a young adult version of *Sesame Street* with Muppet-like puppets among the major characters. TV screens at either side of the stage often feature exactly the kinds of graphics used on the original. The show is both tender and sassy. The opening line of the first song, *What do you do with a B.A. in English?*, engulfs the audience in laughter since so many have found out they need to ask themselves that question. There are also lots of racy dialogue and one very explicit scene of a night of Muppet carnality.

Media Musicals

Musicals were, for much of the early part of this century, a major part of going to the movies and were probably defined most vividly by all those Fred Astaire and Ginger Rogers madcap, dancing delights. The definitive musical created entirely for film is *Singing in the Rain*, and the defining number is the title song with Gene Kelly splashing merrily through wet streets. Broadway hit musicals used to be filmed almost as a matter of course and most did excellent box office as films.

But the skepticism and even cynicism of our current age has not been entirely receptive to song and dance. There was a long, dark period between the last truly successful musicals, *Cabaret* and *Dirty Dancing*, and *Chicago*, which for the first time in many years knocked it out of the park. Granted, *Chicago* itself is skeptical and cynical, but the success was almost entirely because the director Rob Marshall found a way to take a big splashy musical into the mind of its central character, so numbers emerged from her imagination and fear instead of out of air. He also connected the musical rhythms to visual ones so that there was a constant pulse to the film. The adaptation of *Phantom of the Opera*, while opulently produced, was considerably less successful. Not only does this work have fewer ideas, but it is a largely theatrical event with many moments of "I can't believe they did that live!" On film, all these special, spectacular effects are expected, even commonplace.

Also, musicals were big before music videos, which now often tell stories and provide similar diversion in a fraction of the time. It seems as if traditional musical theatre will continue to thrive far more live than in celluloid recreation in our culture. However, in contemporary India, over 800 films, many of them musicals, are produced each year, making that country by far the world's leader in musical production. Bollywood directors Bimal Roy, Mehboob Khan, and Gugu Dutt are as famous as any Western auteurs. While certain characteristics of their particular musical form can be traced all the way back to Sanskrit, it is the Urdu Parsee theatre of the 1930s that is often sighted as the start of the phenomenal interest in the form in India.

And we must remember that almost all non-Western theatre has always been (albeit with unique conventions) musical, given the importance of song and dance to the theatrical event. By the same token, it has also almost all always been "stylized" in the sense that it was and is far removed from our concept of realism.

SUMMARY

In the aftermath of devastating events in the first half of the twentieth century, the theatre began exploring new ways to present its ideas in styles we have come to call the "Isms." A variety of influential, though short-lived movements like Futurism, Dadaism, and Symbolism, evolved simultaneously. Among the most important and influential of the isms are Expressionism, which lets the playwright's subjective view of life be expressed; Didacticism, or Epic theatre, defined by Bertolt Brecht as "theatre of the intellect meant to teach and stimulate political and social action" and Absurdism, a reaction to the holocausts of the Second World War, in which all meaning is ludicrous and the only appropriate choice is to laugh. One of the most popular and well-known styles of non-realistic theatre is the musical, an American contribution to world theatre. With its beginnings in vaudeville, burlesque, the minstrel show, and light opera (operetta), early musicals tended to be light, comic, and heavily dance-oriented. Rodgers and Hammerstein were important in bringing ideas more serious to the musical. Stephen Sondheim is the reigning king of the American musical though many of the biggest hits now come from England in the works of Andrew Lloyd Webber and others. Musicals by and about African-Americans have experienced a renaissance, and the post-modern mood is being captured by fresh new talent often working on a smaller scale of production.

SUGGESTED STUDY QUESTIONS

1. How did the crucial changes in the world during the first part of the last century make realism seem less than adequate for expressing universal concerns?

2. Which of the Ism's do you believe have had a lasting impact on theatre and film, and which have faded after their initial impact?

3. For which of the Ism's do you feel the closest natural affinity? Which expresses a view of the world that is somewhat akin to your own? If you were to put together a personal manifesto, how would you alter that of the Ism's to suit your beliefs?

4. Conversely, which of the Ism's do you find most removed or outside your own thinking? What do you find off-putting about this theatre form?

5. With greater and greater frequency, plays and films that are basically realistic are being infused with elements (or at least sequences) of Absurdism. Why do you feel this is the case?

6. In your own experience as audience member, what have been the five non-realistic productions you have seen that have had the greatest impact on you?

7. Why is it that musicals seem to stir up and excite the emotions of audiences more than any other form of theatre?

8. How is it that audiences often are challenged by trying to adjust to strange, new theatrical conventions yet have no difficulty accepting those of musicals, even though it could be argued that those of musicals are the strangest conventions of all?

9. Why is it that musicals, once a mainstay of films, faded from popularity? What circumstances may be making them ripe for a comeback?

10. Given the current trends identified in musical theatre, what would you predict might be the next direction musicals will go?

SUGGESTED ACTIVITIES

1. Individual—Write six lines of dialogue that represent to the best of your knowledge symbolism. Do the same for Futurism, Dadaism, Expressionism, Didacticism, and Absurdism.

2. Group—Divide the task above among individual members of the group. Have each writer "cast" your interlude with others in the group, rehearse briefly and present them to the class.

3. Long term—Re-imagine each of the plays you are studying or attending this term as one of the featured Ism's. What would be the primary changes involved and how would this impact on audience response?

4. Large group—Agree on a play or film everyone knows well. How would it be adapted to become a musical? Hold a competition for best song title and song description. Extra points for actually singing a snippet of your imaginary song. Audience votes for winning entry. Variation: Have groups compete for solos for individual characters (such as Darth's Lament, Chewboca's Ragtime, or Yoda's Rap).

KEY WORDS AND IDEAS

Symbolism

Futurism

Dadaism

Expressionism

Didacticism

Absurdism

The Musical

    Origins

    Early Masters

    The Mature Book

    Experimentation

    Landmarks - *The Black Crook, Showboat, Oklahoma, West Side Story, My Fair Lady, Cabaret, Company, Hair, Rent*

WHERE IS THEATRE NOW?

CONTEMPORARY VOICES

CONTENTS

WHILE Broadway remains a powerful force in mainstream theatre, it is no longer the primary source of new and challenging work. Of the nine non-musical plays presented there last season, only four were new ones. Broadway has become primarily a haven for musicals and revivals of tried-and-true straight plays. There is little commitment to innovation. The exciting new play, surmounting all the financial and critical pressures involved in finding a home in the Great White Way, is an increasingly rare phenomenon.

It's time to turn our attention to the rest of the country and a number of formerly under-represented contingencies. Amazing theatre is being done everywhere, with many innovative attempts to redefine the theatre experience itself. Today's theatre challenges our very sense of what it means to go to the theatre and what we expect to take away from it. Some of these innovations have highly select and narrow advocates, but others have received far-reaching validation. Sometimes combinations of old ideas have resulted in a new theatrical experience.

Before we can understand what is happening now, we need to see how it got that way.

ETHNIC THEATRE IN AMERICA

Long before Caucasian Europeans brought theatrical forms to this continent, there was North American indigenous theatre. Native American theatre in various forms existed before other races even visited this continent, and Mexican theatre in the Southwest can be traced back over 400 years. Over the years, as various other ethnic groups arrived, a number of immigrants created productions based on customs from their homelands. Many others, particularly Jewish immigrants from both Eastern Europe and Russia, became integrated into the fabric of mainstream American theatre.

The view of minorities expressed in "white" theatre, however, was not always welcoming or respectful. Until the civil rights movement in the 1960s, underrepresented peoples' lives were rarely accurately portrayed, if indeed they were portrayed at all.

> **C.W.E. Bigsby,** *theatre historian*
>
> "In mainstream theatre, they were effectively excluded from national myths which turned on white supremacy. They found their own lives reflected, if at all, only as stereotypes, as comic caricature or simply villains. In the central plot of American history— the invention of the nation— they had been presented as either merely observers or dangerous impediments."

Fortunately, one of the results of the political activism of the 1960s was a surge of ethnic pride beginning with Black Americans but spreading quickly to include all Americans of color. Forty-some years later, the result is now a genuine rainbow coalition theatrical scene.

Ethnic theatre groups have formed over the years for five pervasive purposes:

1. At first, theatre was a way for minorities to cope with their confusion regarding the language and culture of mainstream America until they were able to assimilate or at least comprehend the culture around them. It pulled them into a place of comfort in the midst of myriad, unfamiliar stimuli. It provided that campfire around which we can all gather to tell our stories and feel we are not alone.

2. Theatre also acted as a way of keeping alive memories of homelands left behind. It helped traditions to stay constant and renewed. In a way, it represented a tangible means of transporting the old country to the new. The magic of performance allowed memories to deepen and traditions to go beyond ceremonial ritual into fully acted stories that were told again and again.

3. Eventually, ethnic theatre became politicized. Theatre became a means of protesting mistreatment and exclusion, of demanding equity. New plays served as a rallying point where rage and hurt were turned into something powerful and focused in order to bring about change.

4. After the first wave of protest, ethnic theatre also evolved into a way of showing audiences outside these cultures what it was like to be part of them, revealing lives those outside had rarely experience firsthand. Allowing audiences into the daily struggles of minorities gave them opportunities to not only appreciate cultural distinctions but also to be reminded of the ways in which we are all essentially the same.

5. Finally, as new American identities inevitably emerged, some drama became about the unique predicament of having ties to another country while being very much based in this one, for example, being neither Asian nor mainstream American, but distinctly Asian-American. As new generations within each culture had no actual firsthand experience of the motherland, it became ever more important to deal with the phenomenon of being bi-cultural.

Below are some of the beliefs, customs, and conventions that distinguish various ethnic theatre productions. There will be many exceptions to these generalities, but when a play or production strays from these standards, it is almost invariably because of mainstream influence. We present the theatre forms in their most extreme and uninfluenced contexts.

William S. Yellow Robe, Jr, *playwright*

"My parents both asked me if I was serious about the kind of writing I was doing. When I said yes, they each gave me courage and strength by saying in slightly different ways "You'd better leave, then. Because there isn't anything for you here on the rez.' They were right ... Now after writing thirty plays, I have only one regret, that Stanley and Mina Yellow Robe never had a chance to see them."

Native American Theatre

Actual records of Native American drama emerged out of a period of almost astonishing repression followed by neglect. The first collection of plays, *New Native American Drama* by Hanay Geogamah, was not published until 1980. Nothing comparable to events described in Chapter 2 (*Wiping Away of Tears*) continued into the past century, but pressure to curtail drama still came with official sanctions.

Marsh Cassady, *theatre author/editor*

"Often the government, in the form of the bureau of Indian affairs, banned religious dramas such as the Sun Dance, common to all Northern plains tribes. In 1923, the government even limited "Indian dances' to one a month and declared that only those over the age of fifty could participate."

General characteristics of indigenous American Indian theatre include:

1. Stories are not necessarily linear stories and are often not told chronologically. There may be no specific beginning, middle or end.

2. Drama is not necessarily based on a clearly defined conflict but rather on dance, rites, celebrations and spiritual beliefs being explored.

3. Audience and performers are not separated but considered a single, unified element.

4. Rather than specific settings, performances are likely to take place in a dimensionless sacred space.

5. Theatre is likely to reflect the values of the specific tribe presenting the performance, not necessarily aspiring to universal connections.

Prominent companies have included the Native American Theatre Ensemble, which has presented productions Off Broadway. Other influential, early regional companies included the Santa Fe Theatre Project at the Institute of American Indian Arts, the Navajo Theatre and the Thunderbird Company in Ontario.

In 1975, three sisters, Lisa Mayo, Gloria Miguel and Murial Miguel, wanted to create theatre free of "grandmothers and medicine women." They formed a group called Spiderwomen, named after the Hopi household god, Spider Grandmother Woman, who taught her people the art of weaving; the group calls their technique "storyweaving." Their first production to achieve widespread attention was *Women and Violence*, which weaves stories around a tribal leader who fights for his people's rights while ironically brutalizing the women in his own life. Spiderwoman's work is notable for handling highly serious subjects, sometimes using slapstick humor.

Another defining production has been *Black Elk Speaks*, produced by the Denver Theatre Center, a collaborative effort between Native Americans and company personnel. Focusing on a healing vision, experienced in 1863 by Nicholas Black Elk, this was perhaps the first mainstream production to honor the culture's emphasis on vision, spirit, and transformative dreaming.

Hispanic Theatre

We can actually trace early Spanish speaking performances to Southeast America (in what emerged eventually as Miami) in the late 1500s, but the earliest professional productions in the Southwest were first recorded in the early 1800s. Actors from Mexico and Spain toured coastal cities in southern California and northern Mexico, and then the companies migrated to Texas. Hispanic theatre companies were common throughout this region during the nineteenth and twentieth centuries, performing the classic plays of Pedro Calderon de la Barca and Lope de Vega as well as new works. El Teatro Campesino, the Farm Workers Theatre, which emerged in 1965, was probably the single most noteworthy producing group of the past century. It developed several works that advanced it from grass roots evolution all the way to Broadway. El Teatro's founder Louis Valdez created theatre for and about migrant workers and went on to great acclaim for plays such as *Zoot Suit* and his film *La Bamba*.

Louis Valdez, *playwright, director*

"In a Mexican way, we have discovered what Brecht is all about. If you want unbourgeois theatre, find unbourgeois people to do it. Our theatre work is simple, direct, complex and profound, but it works."

Cuban American theatre evolved in Tampa in the 1890s. Those who had emigrated from Cuba during its War of Independence created theatre specifically for newly established populations in Florida. Two forms of popular theatre that continued to thrive were Spanish zarzuelas, a form of melodrama, and Cuban *teatro bufo*, a vaudevillian blend of stock characters in farcical context with much music and dance. After the Cuban revolution of 1959, another huge surge in immigration to the U.S. resulted in plays dealing with the problems of adjusting to life in a new culture. A major step was taken in 1966 when Cuban-Americans and Puerto Ricans formed International Arts Relations (INTAR) to develop indigenous new works.

In the 1930s and 40s, both Emilo S. Belavel and Rene Marques had their work successfully produced. The Spanish Civil war resulted in a considerable increase in immigration to New York, resulting in a parallel increase in both conventional theatre companies and *teatro* popular, a form of street theatre concerned with social justice.

Jose Rivera, *playwright*

"All my family, my siblings, mother as well as my abuelo and abuelita tell stories and that is where my plays start. We embellish, we lie, we fib, we fabricate, we alter, we amend, we misconstrue, we misremember, we misstate—we do everything a good journalist is not supposed to do. That's what makes it art."

Nilo Cruz's play, *Anna in the Tropics*, won the Pulitzer Prize in 2002. Playwrights whose works have received prominent productions include Eduardo Machado, Maria Irene Fornes, Josephina Lopez, Carlos Morton, Omar Torres, Yvette Ramirez, and Jose Rivera.

African American Theatre

In some sad way, it is possible claimed that the theatre of Black Americans began on the slave ships where they were often forced to sing and dance. In the early 1800s, a phenomenon called the minstrel show featured not only white actors in blackface but black actors in blackface as well! The brilliant Shakespearean actor, Ira Aldridge, unable to find suitable work and support in the U.S., moved to Europe where racism was less prevalent, toured England, Russia, and Poland to great acclaim and never returned. The African Grove Theatre (1820–1827) founded by William Brown and James Hewlett presented Shakespeare and original works but was closed seven years into its work due to attacks by white audience members.

In the 1920s, a movement called the Harlem Renaissance resulted in numerous theatre companies exploring the nature of African-American Life. The custom of blackface by white musical performers and the perpetuation of stereotypes were slow to dissolve however. The latter was perhaps most vividly represented by the play *The Green Pastures*, a well intentioned and at the time much-honored work, which featured a heaven entirely populated by "Negro" residents. Langston Hughes' *Mulatto* was probably the more noteworthy effort by a Black playwright in the 1930s.

SOME AFRICAN AMERICAN THEATRE FIRSTS:

James Hewlett 1820	first black actor to play Othello
King Shotaway 1825	first play written and performed by African Americans
Bob Cole 1897	founder of the first black repertory company
A Trip to Coontown 1898	first black musical comedy
In Dahomey 1902	first Broadway production in which black actors appeared without burnt-cork make-up, speaking with a dialect and wearing fashionable clothes
Paul Robeson 1943	set still unmatched record for longest run (296 performances) as Othello
Gold Through the Trees 1952	first play written by a black woman to be produced Off-Broadway
Lloyd Richards 1959	first black director on Broadway

The landmark production of a Black playwright was Lorraine Hansberry's *A Raison in the Sun*, which achieved extraordinary success in its Broadway run and subsequent filming. The play, revived to great acclaim, consistently sold out performances (perhaps in part because of the presence of P. Diddy in a central role) in 2004. This is probably the most successful play to date at letting audiences outside the culture appreciate differences, while being astonished at how much we all share.

Clearly, the civil rights movement influenced a great expansion of African-American theatre to include regional companies throughout the nation. A landmark shift came with the Ford Foundation's support for the Negro Ensemble Theatre in the 1960s. Amiri Baraka (formerly LeRoi Jones) wrote confrontational plays such as *Dutchman* and *The Toilet*, powerfully confronting the origins of racism. In 1970, Charles Gordone won attention and the Pulitzer Prize for his powerful and clearly titled *No Place to Be Somebody*. Other landmark works were created by Adrienne Kennedy, Lonne Elder III and Ntozake Shange, whose magnificently poetic (she calls it a choreopoem) *for colored girl who have considered suicide when the rainbow is enuf* continues to move audiences with a very specific treatment of women of color that speaks to women everywhere. This script is often cited as the first hip-hop creation.

A phenomenon from the 1970s the present is the Black musical, starting with *Purlie* and moving thorough *Bubbling Brown Sugar, The Wiz, Ain't Misbehavin', Dreamgirls, Sophisticated Ladies, Five Guys Named Moe* and *Bring in 'Da Noise, Bring in Da Funk* just to name a few. George C. Wolfe has produced some of the most powerful and intriguing scripts, including the last title above, but most vividly *The Colored Museum* where, in eleven exhibits of African-American life, he satirizes both black stereotypes and those fall into them—and in other exhibits he strongly defends his people. One Segment satirizes *Raison in the Sun* for the types (a strong, faith-based matriarch and her ever-blaming, never-accountable, male offspring) that have subsequently been perpetuated, challenging his audiences to move beyond type to full humanity.

Highly respected contemporary writers include Suzan-Lori Park, Regina Taylor, Charles Randolph-Wright, Kia Corthron and their predecessors, Alice Childress, Ed Bullins, Leslie Lee, and Charles Fuller. Recent distinguished achievements include the Pulitzer prize in drama for *Topdog/Underdog* by African-American playwright Suzan-Lori Parks and the National Black Arts Festival, under the leadership of Stephanie Hughley, finding a permanent home in 2002, in Atlanta.

August Wilson, *playwright*

"Last year I said, 'Man, I don't wanna write no play.' And I was so glad when it was over. But now I'm, "What's next?' I have lots of new ideas for what I call "a dramatic and poetic, cultural history of black America.'"

The most highly acclaimed playwright was unquestionably August Wilson who died in late 2005. The winner of seven Drama Critics Circle Awards, he would probably be most critics' choice for the leading American playwright of the late twentieth, early twenty-first century. He completed an almost Shakespearean cycle of plays, depicting the African-American experience over each decade of the past century.

Phylicia Rashad, *actor*

"August's plays were a haven for disregarded souls. He saw greatness, beauty, and ability in the lives of the people he wrote about, and he was acutely attuned to their individual rhythms, not just of their speech but also of their souls.'"

AUGUST WILSON'S TWENTIETH CENTURY

1900s *Gem of the Ocean* (premiered 2003)
1910s *Joe Turner's Come and Gone* (premiered 1986)
1920s *Ma Rainey's Black Bottom* (premiered 1984)
1930s *The Piano Lesson* (premiered 1987)
1940s *Seven Guitars* (premiered 1995)
1950s *Fences* (premiered 1985)
1960s *Two Trains Running* (premiered 1990)
1970s *Jitney* (premiered 1996)
1980s *King Hedley II* (premiered 1999)
1990s *Radio Golf* (premiered 2005)

Most of his plays are set in the Hill District of Pittsburgh, the slum community where he was born in 1945. His genius expands this neighborhood to become Black America itself.

Asian-American Theatre

The voices of Asian-Americans were the last of these cultures to be fully heard in the U.S. Even the Federal Theatre Project of the 1930s, which provided opportunities for other ethnic minorities, neglected the Asian-American voice.

For many years, Asian characters in professional American productions were portrayed by non-Asian actors. The Broadway musical, *Chinese Honeymoon* (1902), had an all–white, British cast. Comedies and musicals of the 1950s (prominently *Teahouse of the August Moon*, *The King and I*, and *South Pacific*) all featured non-Asian performers in key roles. However much we may now regard their work as naïve or reductive, Rogers and Hammerstein, were in their time, among the only writers focus on issues confronting Asians and to create characters that moved beyond un–dimensioned stereotypes. In casting the film roles of these shows, often just being a person of color seemed enough. For example, Rita Moreno, a Hispanic, is cast as the Asian, Tuptin, in the film *The King and I*. There are countless, ludicrous examples of Hollywood actors impersonating minority cultures (both John Wayne and Rock Hudson made appearances as Native Americans), but the defining gross–out, racial-slur performance of all time may be Mickey Rooney's take on Mr.Yamaguchi, in full buck teeth and wildly exaggerated accent in *Breakfast at Tiffany's*, released in 1961. A major Hollywood film could still be produced with no attempt to even cast an actor of color in an Asian role, much less one culturally appropriate.

Karen Hue, *playwright*

"In *Yasuko and Young S-S-Samurai*, I wrote a farce about a reluctant samurai trying to convince a dewy-eyed maiden that gutlessness is next to godlessness in a country rife with honor, hara kiri and Hondas … I think it is time to explore the history of Asians in America in a comedic way."

Again, credit is due to Rogers and Hammerstein. Their 1958 musical, *Flower Drum Song*, was a historical landmark in featuring an all-Asian cast and was adapted from a novel by Chinese-American writer, C. Y. Lee. Sadly, it was not an artistic success. Recently, David Henry Hwang, author of *M. Butterfly* has updated the book of this musical for contemporary production.

Two landmark events occurred in 1965 and 1973. First was the formation of the East West Players in Los Angeles, wherein actors of Korean, Japanese, and Chinese heritage combined their resources. This company presented both mainstream Western works and adaptations of the works of Asian novelists. Second was the Asian-American Theatre Workshop (with founding directors Frank Chin, Janis Chan and Jeffrey Chin) which developed the first major play by an Asian-American, *Chickencoop Chinaman* by Frank Chin.

While *M. Butterfly* remains the best-known work by and about Asian culture, such writers as Jenny Lin, Velina Hasu Houston, Elizabeth Wong, and Philip Kan Gotanda have also risen to prominence as playwrights. And new perspectives are always on the horizon.

Non-Asian writers and directors, including Bertolt Brecht and Antonin Artaud, have long incorporated. Asian theatrical techniques into their work. More recently, French director Ariane Mnouchkine and English director Peter Brook have been responsible for exposing American audiences to Asian forms.

Trends

The last forty years have seen an incredible surge in grass roots, multicultural theatre. In a media-dominated society, it is fascinating how often live theatre has been chosen as the medium of expression. Scholars of international theatre have designated our country as the most prominent laboratory for cultural hybrids and convergences in the theatre. Often the introduction of very old theatre customs into a new context results in amazingly vigorous writing and in finding new ways to tell stories.

The plays often take us into the houses and families of peoples previously viewed by the nation at large only when urban violence has erupted after total failure to comprehend the conditions that escalated into that violence. Theatre has provided a way for cultures to dig in and re-establish old identities in new settings, but also for cultural blending, fusion, and the discovery of newly forged identities. We are clearly becoming a culturally pluralistic society, and the sooner dramatic works speak to all races the better. It has given us ways to reach across cultures and to provide empathy and understanding of how we are different and yet the same.

NON-SCRIPTED THEATRE—IMPROVISATION

While there are no scripts in the oral storytelling tradition, there is an effort to keep the thread of the event the same from generation to generation. Variances seep into the material as it moves from one narrator to another or from one region to another. Another kind of unscripted theatre has become incredibly popular in the last decade—improvisation.

Beginning with the legendary Second City company in Chicago (which has launched the careers of a number of Not Ready for Primetime players on Saturday Night Live) and fanning out across the country, many communities and colleges support improv troupes, and the activity is a standard part of actor training. Comedy Sportz, combining theatre with the rules of an athletic event, has franchises all over the country. Clubs that used to feature musicians and stand-up comedians are now likely to have improv evenings as well. Cast members from the improv TV show, *Whose Line Is It Anyway?*, had a successful national tour performing live last season. The appeal of this format *is* much like that of watching an athletic event, especially a fast-paced sport like basketball, where there are constant surprises and the energy and focus can change in an instant.

Few activities are as liberating as improvisation. It channels playfulness and helps renew a sense of spontaneity. It aims at tapping into intuition and knowledge that does not rely on reason or rational processes. It can help sharpen insight and the capacity for guessing accurately. It can help participants dare to decide quickly and dive in, without wasting time speculating or reflecting unnecessarily. All of us would like to make better decisions faster, without mentally debating an issue to death.

Improv Ground Rules

While seemingly freewheeling and open, improv has a number of rules to give it structure. The wilder and more freewheeling the game is, the more important are those rules that keep it from chaos. These are the areas of agreement:

1. **Always Saying Yes** Everyone needs to accept whatever another actor brings into the scene as true. No one says no. All new information is accepted.

2. **Just Doing It** All participate without instantly evaluating and judging. This is exploration without judgment. Actors listen and respond spontaneously.

3. **Staying Honest** Performers, for the most part, play to solve the problem, not find clever lines or cute endings. The more ridiculous the situation ends up being, the more it needs to appear to be taken seriously. Actors who always crack themselves up do not thrive in this form.

4. **Staying in the Game** All remain fully involved until the session is over, either because the situation has revolved itself or because a coach calls an end to it. Actors do not step outside the action or drop your concentration. Side-coaching is accepted without breaking focus and all live in the moment.

5. **Giving Up Control** Actors need to resist preconceptions or the desire to plan ahead. No one person tries to run the scene or dominate others. They are not playwrights, but rather people in a predicament.

Once actors have the basic outline, questions and discussion stop. Improv never bothers with excessive exposition, starting in what might normally be the middle of the scene, instead of the beginning. Props are kept to the barest minimum possible. Answers are kept short and sweet with lots of chances to stop and listen. Scenes work best if kept physical and active, with more action and less talk. When at a loss for words, they turn to their senses. How to do they feel? What do they smell? Taste? Hear? See? Nothing that happens is regarded as a mistake, just an interesting turn of events. All try to keep filing away twists and turns in the scene for possible later connections as these elements might emerge again.

Improv is also used in connection with scripted works as part of the rehearsal process. Actors might improv the first time their characters meet or various events referred to in the script but which happen offstage. A cast may create a party where they attend as their characters or an interview show where characters are questioned. Being able to stay in character outside the script makes performing scripted lines all the more comfortable.

Playback Theatre/Therapy Theatre

Playback performers use a somewhat more serious use of improv, where an audience member may be asked to tell a story from his own life. Actors quickly assume various other characters and play it back, so the storyteller has a chance to actually view a crucial life event and have it take on greater meaning. These events are entertaining but also profoundly illuminating for those whose stories are chosen. Since the participants have only the basic outline, it is astonishing how frequently they capture the events in a way that is moving and meaningful, to not only the featured subject but to all present and sharing.

In counseling, particularly in group therapy, participants may be asked to recreate painful moments in their lives with others in the group acting as other participants. Since these encounters sometimes paralyze the "actor" from acting her life with freedom and creativity, the reenactment can sometimes be cathartic and freeing. If she was unable to say something important back during the actual event, being able to say it now, even in this acting environment, is sometimes liberating.

Often the issue is to some extent resolved, and there is no need to confront the offender. The power of theatre is present in that almost anyone can stand in for the offender, and the mere act of much-needed confrontation being acted out is often quite enough. However, if the patient/actors do feel the need to pursue confrontation in order to experience closure, they now have the confidence of rehearsing what they wish to say in this improvisational context. Such exercises are also sometimes part of actor training, being based on the belief that actors who deal with their traumatic encounters and move on will have more emotional availability and confidence to tackle challenging roles and the competition inherent in the profession.

THEATRE FOR JUSTICE

Augusto Boal

While theatre is often intended to divert and entertain as a more polished version of dress-up and let's-pretend, it can also be used in addressing serious social issues and in bringing about needed changes in lives. While many companies deal with societal issues, Augusto Boal has been more influential than almost anyone in bringing theatre, and particularly improv, into the realm of social-consciousness, providing tools for change. For him, acting has a double definition. It is not just about performing but also about taking action.

He has developed methods for combating oppression through theatre. His work breaks down barriers between actors and audience. Observers become active spectators, whom he calls "spect-actors," offering ideas, even stepping into roles. Boal uses theatre to confront problems, with particular emphasis on those (sexual harassment, homophobia, racism, etc.) where one group oppresses another.

Boal sees theatre as a forum designed to analyze problems (usually of the misuse of power) and to explore group solutions. Seeing a problem enacted and debated and then seeing solutions enacted can have a high and lasting impact. He has established numerous participatory companies that develop community-based performance for those engaged in the struggle for liberation. Most are called Centers for Theatre of the Oppressed (CTOs). The work is a blend of developed scripted work and improvisation. Activities are of three kinds:

Forum Theatre

Short scenes represent unsolved problems of a community. Audience members are invited to suggest, interact, and enact, sometimes by replacing characters in scenes and improvising new solutions. Sometimes the "problem" scene (often called the "anti-model") is presented once, then again (possibly speeded up) until someone yells, "Stop!" and steps in. It may be repeated several more times as others step into the role of protagonist. The events are presided over by someone called the Joker, so named for the joker in a pack of cards—not because she will play jokes on participants. The Joker defines and enforces the rules of the game in the manner of a stage manager/referee. A Joker may often stop a scene saying, "That's magic," meaning that the actors have contrived a solution that does not involve step-by-step problem solving but rather the waving of a wand or incredible good fortune.

Image Theatre

Bodies and tableaus are used to sculpt events and/or relationships. Human forms are employed to create images, helping participants explore power relations and collective solutions. As much as possible, the process is done without words, though it may begin with an individual recounting a personal story of some kind of oppression, or a group discussion on the issue that will be explored. Titles are suggested, and then individuals mold participants, like clay, to form an intense, visual representation of the power relationships, and other tableaus are created to change the status quo. Two major tableaus emerge: one the Real Image of things as they are now and the other the Ideal Image of things as they could become.

Invisible Theatre

As in Forum Theatre, rehearsed scenes are used to stimulate action. In this case, however, they are performed in public spaces for an unsuspecting audience that does not recognize the event as theatre. In addition to the actors in the scenes, others may infiltrate the crowd as provocateurs, stimulating debate and discussion. For example, a scene is created and rehearsed regarding a cross-dresser. The actors go into a store and one of the men tries on women's clothing. Another actor responds by being overtly appalled at what he is doing, while another defends his rights. Everyone present is drawn into a discussion about the parameters of individual rights.

The three techniques may overlap, and all of Boal's processes share three characteristics:

1. Problems are always presented in an objective form, without the suggestion of a solution in the initial scene.

2. As solutions evolve, the issues always move outward, to include a larger group, rather than inward to individual or smaller ones. The oppression is examined in a larger context.

3. Debate or discussion never stays for long in verbal exchange or what Boal calls "radio forum." Instead, participants are frequently asked to stop talking, get up and express their intentions or interventions in theatrical forms. Actors need to be extremely comfortable with improv, socially and politically aware, able to play opposing points of view without bias, and be *dialectical and free of narcissism, with a strong sense of give and take.*

Actors comprise only part of those who participate. Social service workers, labor and union organizers, educators, and community activists may be involved. It employs classic improv techniques as well as those of Sociodrama and Playback theatre. Those learning Boal's techniques will all have the tools, in whatever community they might find themselves, to offer the art of acting as part of a solution, making a huge contribution to that populace. The techniques are equally useful for solving problems within an acting environment or theatre company, where power issues often abound.

PERFORMANCE ART

This often-electrifying theatre form rejects plot, character, suspense, and sometimes even theatres in favor of other spaces such as art galleries. Most portray a striking set of experiences, usually around a central theme, with a huge emphasis on set design, music, dance movement, and improvisation. Sculpture, lighting effects, poetry, and painting may also be involved. Some consider it a descendent of Dadaism (see Chapter 9), and the influence of the ideas of Jerzy Grotowski and Antonin Artaud are clearly present.

Big names include Laurie Anderson, Richard Foreman, Robert Wilson, Martha Clarke, Ping Chong, Meredith Monk, Tim Miller and Michael Counts, Annie Miller and Guillermo Gomez-Pena. Groups specializing in this form include the evocatively named Electronic Disturbance Theatre, Guerilla Girls, the Poetry Slams, and the Survival Research Lab.

Robert Wilson often works with Suzushi Hanayago, a *kabuki* and *noh* expert, so his works reflect an Asian sensibility, including a slow, deliberate tempo. Michael Counts does produces massive undertakings in his warehouse.

Performance art is likely to experiment with multimedia and projections, reducing both the quantity and specific detail of constructed scenery, though with a powerful visual impact. The presentations are often, though not always, highly personal and confrontational.

Whereas others in this group direct, but do not necessarily perform and often work with a large group of actors, Laurie Anderson is a solo performer and therefore provides a segue to our next category known for its stunning imagery and strange electronic sounds. During a performance she will sing music of her own composition, speak—a variety of voices, though not necessarily characters—play the violin, keyboard, guitar, and operate electronic equipment, producing both visual and sound effects.

Because you don't have to try to follow the story, performance art is both intellectually challenging and yet comforting. You are free to find your own way into the experience.

SOLO PERFORMANCE

From Hal Holbrook's *Mark Twain Tonight* to Lily Tomlin's *Search for Intelligent Signs in the Universe*, the one-person show has been a main feature of professional theatre for years. In the 2005 season alone, Jackie Mason, Billy Crystal, Dame Edna and Whoopi Goldberg all filled Broadway houses. Most, however involve playing a character and/or making humorous observations. They are (reletively) safe. What is newer, however, is an intensely confessional, autobiographical form of solo work characterized by such performers as Eric Bogosian, Anna Deveare Smith, Karen Finley, Sherry Glaser, Danny Hoch, John Leguizamo and Mario Cantone.

The most vivid example may be Sherry Glaser's *Family Secrets* where she plays five characters: herself, her mother, father, grandmother and sister. The secrets are often about sex, religion, mental illness and birth, and they are both funny and painful—sometimes at the same time.

WOMEN'S THEATRE

Many playwrights who were largely neglected during their time of creation are now being rediscovered and acknowledged in revivals—and some are being acknowledged for the first time. One of the most prolific writers of the Restoration theatre was Aphra Behn, all but ignored by history until a recent exhuming of her works. Zoe Atkins, Rachel Crothers, Sophie Treadwell, and Susan Glaspell are other women's voices of past generations that are now being heard in productions. Going even farther back is the person believed to be the first known woman dramatist, Hrosvitha (935–975), a German abbess who was so taken with the Roman comedies of Terence, though worried about their potentially immoral influence, that she converted the ideas into six rhymed Latin plays about Christian martyrs or chaste women whose chastity is unsuccessfully challenged. Only recently has one of our "founding mothers," Mercy Otis Warren, received acknowledgement for her plays, including *The Adulateur* (1772), and *The Defeat* (1773). These were considered major propaganda efforts in encouraging patriots to pursue the American Revolution.

It is increasingly acknowledged that women's voices, previously pushed inside, must be released and heard. Less than fifteen percent of plays are written by women, and less than one-fourth of the roles in plays are for women. Old plays are being re-examined, and new works are being generated from a feminist perspective.

Many regard Nora (in Ibsen's *A Doll's House*), walking out the door and leaving her family as the first step for the movement in theatre.

At this writing, the most widely known work is probably Eve Ensler's *The Vagina Monologs*. Each play, it its own way brought forth subjects formerly thought unsuitable for mainstream theatre and demonstrated otherwise. Writers who have achieved major success creating plays specifically focused on women include Marsha Norman, Wendy Wasserstein and Beth Henley. Others with similar focus in their work include Tina Howe, Constance Cogden, Paula Vogel, Naomi Wallace, Theresa Rebeck, Caryl Churchill and Lisa Loomer. Deconstructionist production, performance art, choral plays and dramatic collages are also common forms.

Ntoake Shange, *playwright*

"I found God in myself and I loved her. I loved her fiercely."

More and more productions are carefully considering women's perspective and voice. There are likely to be more women in any cast as all roles are re-examined and alternative casting (gender blind or gender bending) is considered, and there are likely to be a larger number in key staff positions as well. A huge power has been untapped.

GAY AND LESBIAN THEATRE

Those dealing with issues of sexual orientation also began to find a voice after the first stages of the civil rights movement. However, there has always been some debate about how to define this category. Is the presence of a gay character sufficient? How many need to be in a play? Must they be sympathetically portrayed? Does it include work of gay playwrights who do not necessarily present gay characters? Does the play need to have a serious, political agenda or can it be merely satiric or hilarious? Some feel the category should disappear as characters of all variants of sexuality are integrated into the total theatrical scene. While the term "gay" is often used as an umbrella, the theatre association employs the designation LGBT (Lesbian, Gay, Bisexual, Transgendered) to designate its forum devoted to issues of members with these sexual orientations.

From the seduction of Pentheus by Dionysus in Euripides' *The Bacchae* (405 B.C) to the relationship of Achilles and Patroclus in Shakespeare's *Troilus and Cressida* (1601), both homo-erotica and gay characters existed long before it became a politicized theatre movement. A long tradition of cross-dressing and drag has been part of the theatre scene for centuries and across cultures.

In twentieth century U.S, Lillian Hellman's *The Children's Hour* (1934) was the first commercial play to explore the possibility of a lesbian relationship, albeit in such a way that a central character (Martha) shoots herself over her guilt about her feelings for her female roommate.

Mark Crowley's *The Boys in the Band* (1968) was a landmark play and film in portraying a significant segment of gay culture with empathy. Ironically, the play generated a great deal of criticism in the gay community itself due the self-hatred experienced by several of the major characters. Nevertheless, it was considered a milestone in getting large numbers of audiences to experience a deep, emotional connection to gay characters.

Gay activism is often traced to the fighting back of patrons of the Stonewall Inn in Greenwich Village against police officers attempting to close the bar in 1969. Many consider this the official beginning of the contemporary gay rights movement.

Gay companies such as The Glines (New York) and Theatre Rhinocerus (San Francisco) formed in the 1970s. Charles Ludlum founded the Ridiculous Theatre Company after 1967. He was the author of such plays as *Camille* (1973), *Bluebeard* (1970) and *The Mystery of Irma Vep* (1984) and performer, often in drag, of several roles in each of his plays. After his death in 1987, he was succeeded by Everett Quinton. Charles Busch has also written and starred in similar drag vehicles such as *Shanghai Moon*.

Harvey Fienstein made a significant impact as both playwright and star of *Torch Song Trilogy* (1981), and the book author to the musical *La Cage aux Folles* (1983). Fienstein is currently known primarily as a performer, recently essaying Edna the mother in *Hairspray* as well as Tevye in a Broadway revival of *Fiddler on the Roof*.

In 1978, A Gay Theatre Alliance was formed among various regional companies, some of the foremost being TOSOS (The Other Side of the Stage) and Triangle (Boston), Diversity (Huston), Lionheart (Chicago), Alice B.(Seattle), The Glines, The Meridian Gay Theatre, The Stonewall Theatre (New York) and Rhinoceros (San Francisco).

The AIDS crisis reached epidemic proportions in 1980, leading eventually to what are sometimes referred to as "The AIDS Plays." These include *The Normal Heart* by Larry Kramer, and *As Is* by William Hoffman, both first produced in 1985. Later plays include *Before it Hits Home* by Cheryl West, *Love! Valour! Compassion!* by Terrence McNally, *Baltimore Waltz* by Paula Vogel, and both *Jeffrey* and *The Naked Truth* by Paul Rudnick. Some would place Tony Kushner's *Angels in America* (subtitled "*A Gay Fantasia on National Themes*"), as an AIDS play, though it deals with so many other issues so eloquently that it is the choice of many as the single the best play of the 1990s.

Lesbian troupes, such as Split Britches, emerged in the 1980s and an important historical moment was the founding of the WOW (Women's One World) in 1981. Landmark productions include *Last Summer at Bluefish Cove* by Jane Chambers (1980), and *The Well of Horniness* by Holly Hughes (1985). Lesbian companies have included Red Dyke Theatre (Atlanta), The Lesbian-Feminist Theatre Collective (Pittsburgh), and the WOW Café (New York).

In the 1990s, the advent of the Queer Theory movement rejected sexuality labels of the kind we are discussing here. It proposed that secular and gender identities are largely socially—rather than biologically—constructed so that broad terms such as "homo or heterosexual" or even "man or woman" are insufficient to describe individuals. It instead tends to look at what is "queer" (meaning strange or different) in any behavior that does not fit within rules.

On a more basic level of public awareness, tolerance has been a long, slow journey. Yet, there has probably been no single more distinct sign of widespread acceptance of non-straight characters in drama than the 2005 Oscar nominations. The two leading contenders for best actor each played a "gay" character, one historical and one fictional, and one of the nominees for best actress played a "transgendered" male in the process of "regenderfication."

MOVEMENT/DANCE THEATRE

The director/choreographer has always been a major force in groundbreaking musical theatre productions. Jerome Robbins, Gower Champion, Bob Fosse, Michael Bennett and Tommy Tune all demonstrated that when one brilliant mind guided both acting and dance, there was a far more organic and totally integrated sense of dance emerging out of character need and of flawless transitions. A number of artists in recent years have taken this combination a step further to create a new form of theatre.

With *Contact*, multiple award-winning Susan Stroman created what was called a dance play. There are no songs, no original music and very little dialogue. Dance tells the three stories. Mathew Bourne reinvented the ballet *Swan Lake* as a homoerotic dream with the swans being played by muscular men with bare chests and buzz cuts. He also reinvented the opera *Carmen as Car Man: An Auto-Erotic Thriller*, a bloody, violent, loud, rampantly sexual, dance theatre experience. While innovative, each may have been influenced by earlier, similar adventures on the parts of Pina Bausch and Martha Clarke. In these works, dance is not a supplement or digression. It is the very center of the experience.

Both *Stomp* and *Blue Man Group* have similarly set audiences afire with enthusiasm using movement and no dialogue. These projects share with performance art a rejection of traditional story and character in favor of pure kinesthetic impact. *Stomp*, created by English percussionist/ composer Luke Cresswell and actor/writer Steve McNichols, uses garbage can lids, brooms and other common objects instead of drums and creates athletic, rhythmic theatrical excitement. Three men with shaved heads all painted shiny blue in *Blue Man Group* have captured the imaginations of audiences across the country, including Las Vegas where more traditional fare is generally expected. When it came to New York, *Blue Man Group* started as street theatre, moved into a small off Broadway space and gradually moved up to major runs in big cities, TV appearances and major concert halls. Almost impossible to describe, the shows involves homemade instruments, food fights, extravagant clown routines, marshmallows, audience cue cards and very risky audience interaction, so think carefully if you care invited up onstage.

Liebe Wetzel, *director/devisor*

"Why devise now? Why not now? The world hungers for original, immediate emerging work that is fresh and vibrant."

DEVISED WORKS

Collaboratively created ensemble pieces have increasingly attracted both professional and academic communities. Any member of the team might be involved in researching, collating, writing, experimenting, and decision-making. Instead of beginning with a play, this process may begin with a problem or a topic of fascination. All participants gather materials, have constant input, and are always part of the process. Devising may also begin with an existing piece of literature, ready for reinvestigation and rediscovery, or with a body of literature around a central theme. In most instances, an effort is made to translate literary text into physically active, theatrical interpretation. It is as if these documents, after years of silent reading, long for a fuller life and are released in the theatre.

Mary Zimmerman, *director/devisor*

"The real reason I devise theatre, instead of working from a completed script, is because I believe in the unconscious, and I believe in the will of certain texts (great pieces of literature not yet scripts) to reach the air and our need to submit to them in a way that I find ravishing."

Some projects begin with an issue of concern to the collaborators who then generate a combination of existing and original material. To devise is "to invent, contrive, to plan, to scheme, to form in the mind by new combinations of ideas." It may involve classic or traditional materials, songs, themes, current events, news reports or repeated historical phenomena. The final product may include personal testimony, agit-prop sketch work, and improvisational sequences. In these instances, the performance may feel like a giant collage. An increased sense of ownership is one of the big pay-offs for participants.

Perhaps the best-known devised work of recent years is the Tectonic Theater Project's *The Laramie Project*, under the guidance of Moises Kaufman, which took available printed materials and testimony regarding the Matthew Shepard murder and created a riveting theatre experience. Many of the original collaborators have recently created *The People's Temple*, which first opened at the Berkeley Repertory Company in May 2005. It focused on the Rev. Jim Jones–led mass suicide of 914 American religious cult members in the Guyana jungle. You may not know about either of these events, but at the time they occurred, they dominated the news for months. *Variety* described the latter as "a news event of so high a profile that public awareness was compared to that following Pearl Harbor or the Hiroshima and Nagaski bombings." These were each aberrations in terms of what we believe about ourselves, and the devised productions sought wisdom, insight, and closure.

John Schmor, *director/devisor*

"On student-devised projects, the director is required to commit to the project as it develops, which demands a position of faith instead of privilege."

Peter Buckley, *director/devisor*

"In theatrical terms, devising places the actor in a central role in the creative process—that of a creator as opposed to an interpreter of someone else's creativity."

Devising is a complex and labor-intensive process requiring considerable time, effort and patience. Prominent figures in the professional world include Leive Wetzel, of Lunatique Fantastique, Crystal Brian of The Lost World, Norma Bowles of Fringe Benefits Theatre, Lieibe Wetzel of Lunatique Fantstique, John Schile of the Dell'ArteCompany and Stacy Klein of Double Edge Theatre. But devising has, in the opinion of many, found its most appropriate home in educational theatre, where it provides an opportunity for student actors to find a voice.

REGIONAL NON-PROFIT THEATRE

In 1965, there were only four professional regional theatres in the United States, operating year round, with their own staffs and a season of plays. In 2006, there are over 400! Every major city in the country has its own resident company. What happened? One of the motivating factors was the non-profit designation that allows funding resources (grants, foundation, corporate, and private donation support) beyond box office receipts, giving theatres tax exemptions. While this made it financially viable, there was clearly a nearly universal desire to move out of being "the boondocks," where very cool New York productions occasionally toured, to being a place where theatre originates and thrives.

Some of the most successful include:

Boston:	The American Repertory Theatre
Chicago:	The Goodman, Second City and Steppenwolf
Los Angeles:	The Mark Taper Forum
Louisville:	The Actors Theatre of Louisville
Minneapolis:	The Guthrie Theatre
New Haven:	The Long Wharf Theatre
Seattle:	Seattle Repertory Theatre, The Intiman, Empty Space and ACT
Washington DC:	The Arena Stage

These theatres have local loyalty and often produce original scripts that may eventually make it to New York or Los Angeles, or be optioned for films. But they are just the big guns. This means that wherever you live, there is probably a major, professional company doing very sound work and, perhaps even more importantly, discovering new works each year. There has been a tremendous change in energy as communities no longer have to wait for Broadway shows to make their way across the country but instead may have their own homegrown plays make their way to Broadway. In addition to resident regional companies, there are now over 100 Shakespeare Festivals in the United States.

INTERNATIONAL CONTEMPORARY THEATRE AND FUSION

We have focused largely on traditional theatre forms, however, the format of Western drama has influenced a number of global playwrights, and sadly, so have some of our customs of repression. Numerous Asian countries have developed censorship boards, and in 1998, the Chinese government shocked the world by canceling a much-anticipated American tour of the Chinese Opera, *The Peony Pavillion*, judging it too erotic and not genuinely representative of *xiqu*.

The Market Theatre of Johannesburg continues to offer theatre that formerly confronted Apartheid and now confronts its aftermath. The most prolific and eloquent spokesman regarding this issue is a white man, Athol Fugard, who wrote six other apartheid plays beyond *Master Harold... and the boys*, and whose works, *Valley Song* and *The Captain's Tiger*, deal with the efforts to heal after a long term of injustice.

Wole Soyinka of Nigeria, often jailed for his political activism and now in political exile in our country, has nevertheless created scripts which could never be produced in his own country but which deal with government corruption, inept officials and other forms of post-independence chaos.

> ### Roslyn Sulcas, *journalist*
>
> "Despite South Africa's peaceful transition from the apartheid regime to democracy in 1994, the country is still dealing with the difficulties of racial integration, a population ravaged by AIDS, domestic violence, high unemployment, and an elevated rate of violent crime. The performance arts are a world unavailable to millions who live in poverty."

In Ghana, traditional African theatre blends with modern techniques and content in a growing phenomenon called the Concert Party. In a Concert Party, the traditional Joker or *Ananse* (the spider) has evolved into a character known throughout the country as simply "Bob" after the first master performer. The Concert Party melds traditional stories and storytelling techniques with ragtime music, minstrel show, tap dance, black American sea shanties, and stand-up comedy. Famous Concert Party performance groups include The Two Bobs, The Axiom Trio, Bob Cole's Dynamic Ghana Trio, and the Fanti Trio. The evening usually consists of music performance and comic plays, generally performed by three men who compose the most common form of the Concert troupe. As the play titles suggest (*The Jealous Rival* and *The Ungrateful Husband*, for example) one member of the trio always needs to specialize in "drag" or cross-dressing roles.

In Ghana, as throughout Africa, women are creating powerful new opportunities for their voices to be heard, often in issue-based theatre. AIDS and malaria epidemics cause stress within families particularly borne by the women. New plays and performance styles address those stresses in new ways. Women shout, fight, and hurl insults at their abusers in ways unheard of only a decade ago. Single motherhood creates another economic and familial stress factor finding outlet in new theatres. Emerging playwright Tess Onwueme may have said it best when she remarked about the growing feminist movement in African theatre, saying simply, "Who can silence her drum?"

In Niger, Hausa theatrical troupes are moving slowly but inevitably toward a re-emergent national theatre. The typical Hausa troupe features thirty to forty members, the majority of which are young to middle aged men. In this predominantly Muslim country, where seclusion of women is still the ideal, each troupe now attracts five to ten women to its membership. Most are young unmarried women who leave the troupe when they marry, creating a constantly changing pool of actresses. This pool may yet stabilize though, as one Hausa actor expressed, "Kansu ya hwara waiwaiye (they are beginning to awaken)." Hausa plays develop around a theme just as the devised works described earlier do. Themes may be historical, religious, or political, but they always represent something of immediate importance to the community. The plays expose wrongdoers, suggest solutions, and, uniquely, let the criminals know that the community is on to them. This is theatre at its most immediate level of community involvement: sometimes scathing, sometimes risky, often comic, and always personal to the audience.

The term **total theatre** is used to identify a contemporary mix of Western and traditional African ritual performance. This theatre renews a connection with Africa's past, honors those cultural heritages long suppressed, and confronts important political issues. It also holds accountable European intervention. In presentation, it fuses the two dominant theatre forms rather than choosing between them.

Wei Hai-Ming, *actor*

"Beijing Opera portrays beauty. Western drama depicts life." When Ms. Wei portrays Lady Macbeth in the adaptation Shakespeare's *Macbeth*, renamed *The Kingdom of Desire*, she emphasizes vicious words with lashing movements of her dress, moving it so her train is like the tail of a snake. Wei Hai'Ming as Macbeth does not just do battle. He back flips from the top of a ten-foot wall. The blending of conventions is breathtaking, and everything old becomes new.

Fusion, a term for blending theatrical conventions from different cultures into a single production, is an exciting and probably inevitable result of our becoming a global culture. The most noteworthy directors fusing international concepts into their productions are Peter Brook and Ariane Mnouchkine. We focus on her because she has received less recognition. Mnouchkine, artistic director of the Théâtre du Soleil, is particularly known for blending Eastern production traditions and Western texts. She searches for a new language of theatre and blends influences of Artaud, Brecht and improvisation. She has brought North African Islamic fundamentalism to an innovative production of Moliere's *Tartuffe*, which is already a study of religious hypocrisy. She has directed four Asian-themed (Cambodia, India, Tibet, and China) plays by Helene Cixous. She constantly finds ways to use the old to illuminate the new. *Drums Along the Dyke* is based on His Xhou's 400-year-old work on the relationships between humans and nature. It employs masked actors manipulated like puppets. In the original ancient Chinese, characters try to contain rampaging rivers. But she uses a decision to flood many farmlands without warning the inhabitants.

One of the most vivid current examples of fusion is in the work of the Contemporary Legend Theatre of Taiwan, which has taken the plots of major works of Shakespeare (*Hamlet*, *The Tempest*, and *Macbeth*) and ancient Greek tragedy (*Media* and *The Oresteia*) and placed them in the form of Beijing Opera. They perform in Mandarin verse with (when touring the West) English subtitles. While both forms employ verse and a relatively sparse stage, the differences provide considerable fusion excitement.

In the media world, a powerful new overlap between China and the West amounts to a steady stream of re-makes of Asian language films (such as *The Ring*, *The Grudge* and *Dark Water*), a new international profile for Chinese actors such as Ziyi Zhang, Michelle Yeoh and Gong Li, far more worldwide distribution of Chinese films, and Western masters acknowledging inspiration from the East. At this writing, Martin Scorsese is filming *The Departed*, based on a trilogy of Chinese gangster films. Quention Tarantino honors Chinese director Wong Far as his primary artistic influence. As *Variety*, with its antennae always out for industry trends, put it: *"There has been much jumping over the Great Wall."*

ORAL TRADITION AND SHRINKING TONGUES

While the oral tradition continues to thrive, the languages in which stories are being told and enacted are shrinking in number. There are approximately 6,800 languages in the world, but 3,000 have the same risk factor as endangered species since only living adults and no children speak them. At least 400 languages can, within the last century, be classified as dead. The Apache tribe has a language that, at this writing, has only three living speakers. Busuu, the old language of Cameroon, can be spoken by eight citizens. At the present rate of demise, ninety percent of existing languages will probably disappear within in the next 100 years.

After this happens, what languages will dominate? Will English be the global language? Possibly, but it is not certain. At present, over a sixth of the world's population speaks Mandarin Chinese. English is actually a slow second, followed by Hindi and Spanish. It will be interesting to see how the oral tradition develops, as there are fewer languages to speak.

SUMMARY

In the U.S, a large shift in theatre has resulted in New York no longer being the center of creativity. An increase in grass-roots performance is evolving, either through various ethnic contingencies or from regional repertory homegrown companies. Carefully scripted theatre has been increasingly suspended for improvisation, which is not only a major, diverting entertainment but also a tool for bringing about social (and personal) change. Language-centered theatre has sometimes been supplanted by productions based almost entirely on movement and non-verbal communication. Non-dramatic source material is increasingly adapted and developed to become devised theatrical works. All other art forms and various adjustments to the traditional theatre experience may be present in performance art. Globally, a fusion of traditions often makes for exciting blends of conventions and ideas from various cultures. An alarming reduction in the number of languages spoken raises questions about the future of the oral tradition. While there will always be a welcome home for a traditionally-scripted drama, there also appears to be an ever-widening welcome for more physically based and less linear experimental work, casting a wider net for new ways to create exciting theatre.

SUGGESTED ASSIGNMENTS

1. How does ethnic theatre in the U.S. differ most clearly from Asian and African theatre? How do the needs to blend cultural influences in the former distinguish it from the traditions of the latter?

2. As ethnic theatre has moved into being politicized, what patterns can be recognized in its development?

3. How is the theatre of American Indians distinct from other ethnic theatre traditions? Why do you feel this difference is present?

4. What does interest in improvisation, devising, and performance art indicate about the position of the well-made, scripted drama in theatre?

5. What do these forms suggest regarding the hierarchy or power structure of traditional theatre?

6. While improvisation can be pure entertainment, what are its potential uses of a more serious or significant nature?

7. Identify an area of controversy in your community or campus. How might the processes developed by Augusto Boal be used to help solve the problem or to bring closure?

8. What were the primary factors in the decentralizing of theatre in the U.S. and the advent of grass roots and regional production?

9. Some examples of fusion are offered in this chapter. Can you think of any other blends or juxtapositions of conventions that might make for exciting theatre?

10. Given the trends identified here, what would be your predictions regarding the next developments in live and media theatre?

SUGGESTED ACTIVITIES

1. Individual—Pick any single artist or theatre group identified in this chapter. Go online to research the topic further and to gain insights into the contributions of this person or collective on contemporary theatre.

2. Group—Using the ideas from #7 above, agree on a problem of significant enough interest to the whole group to develop it further into a theatre problem solving experience, using Boal's techniques.

3. Long term—Try to identify the not-for-profit regional theatre closest to where you live. Research its history, development, and sources of funding. If possible, interview someone on the staff regarding the challenges of running a large regional theatre under such circumstances.

4. Large group—Use a town hall format to have a public debate over which contemporary theatre movement has the greatest significance. Take volunteers to argue for each area discussed in this chapter. Vote on whose argument was most convincing.

KEY WORDS AND IDEAS

Ethnic American Theatre

    American Indian

    Asian-American

    African-American

    Hispanic-American

Improvisation

Playback Theatre

Augusto Boal

    Theatre of the Oppressed

Performance Arts

Women's theatre

Movement/Dance Theatre

Devised Works

Total theatre

Regional Non-Profit Theatre

Fusion

Wole Solynka

Ariane Mnouchkine

Spiderwomen

Louis Valdez

Jose Rivera

Lorraine Hansberry

August Wilson

Henry David Wang

Laurie Anderson

Susan Stroman

Matthew Bourne

CHAPTER

12

CRITICISM AND CONNECTIONS

CONTENTS

T HE final powerful player in a production is the critic. How powerful? We will never exactly know. Producers fear critics and hope for notices that will, as publicists say, "put butts in seats." In New York, *The Times* review alone may influence millions in box office receipts. Many theatergoers in your hometown wait to read what your local reviewers say before buying tickets. Critics certainly have influence, but increasingly, the public ignores them and flocks to a work that critics unanimously warn them to avoid. Many believe theatre critics influence attendance far more than film critics. Clearly, there are millions of moviegoers who never read reviews.

How long have critics existed? Probably as long as there have been performances. In Robert's book, *Acting: Onstage and Off*, he creates a variation on Ook's story in which Ook enthralls his cave audience with tales of dinosaurs instead of lions. After his triumphant performance and all cave couples are leaving the fire: "As Ook and his mate head off to their corner of the cave, she says to him, 'Ook, you've got it all over those dumb brutes. You're a real artist.' As another couple moves to their corner, she says, 'That Ook. Isn't he amazing? The way he got just how the dinosaur's head swings back and forth. It was perfect.' Her mate replies, 'Well, it was pretty good. Personally I wouldn't have swung my head so far. It's more of circle than a swing, actually.' And so the first actor is born. And minutes later, the first critic."

This chapter explores what the role of the critic is and what it takes to be a good one. It provides guidelines for writing an informed critical review. And it offers ways of connecting your total theatre exposure into potential future participation.

THE POWER OF LIBEL

We are all critics, and one of the great "after-pleasures" of seeing a play or film is discussing and perhaps heatedly debating its merits, often deepening our experience by each of us sharing insights the others may have missed. In any theatre department, we critics gather in small groups in the halls after an opening, debate how our responses may match or contradict those of the reviewers and generally dissect the entire event. If the reviews were mixed-to-negative, these huddles get more quiet and deep.

But professional critics are granted something called "the power of libel." Below is an excerpt from Anthony Lane's review in *The New Yorker* about the final installment in the *Star Wars* series.

> "The general opinion seems to be that it marks a distinct improvement on the last two episodes...True, but only in the same way that dying from natural causes is preferable to crucifixion."

To say that this was a "pan" would be a major understatement. If someone in life writes that you "totally suck" without any real evidence, you can sue. Imagine someone writing or reporting on your local television station that being around you was only a desperate distinction between natural death and the cross. Not so for the critic because this license is essential in a free society when evaluating art. We may sometimes hate what they say but should vigilantly defend their right to say it. We want critics that are honest. If they are, we should be tough enough to take it, whatever it is. Yet it is devastating when people suggest to thousands of readers or millions of viewers that you are unworthy. Here is a further excerpt:

> "R2-D2 and C-3PO? I still fail to understand why I should have been expected to waste 25 years of my life following the progress of a beeping trash can and a gay, gold-plated Jeeves.... But the one who gets me is Yoda. May I take this opportunity to enter a brief plea in favor of his extermination?"

You may be among viewers who love, maybe even adore, these characters and would rally to their defense. Because they are not real, they do not even have to consider suing. Also, it is not likely that *The New Yorker* reviewers or subscribers had any influence on the track record of this largely positively reviewed film, which achieved record box office figures.

NO TURN UNSTONED

Excerpts from reviews are often used in ads to promote a show. Full-page ads in the *New York Times* herald the success of the production with lavish praise from various critics presented in support. Sometimes these quotations have desperately squeezed a few positive words out of an otherwise unenthusiastic review. It used to be that only major influential publications were used. In recent years, however, publicists, when putting ads together, have been willing to cast an ever-widening net, going as far down into less prestigious periodicals as it takes. No matter how bad a film seems to be in the opinion of most, there are always raves available out there somewhere. Ads will trumpet the work, and then in very tiny print you find out this is not from *The New York Times*, but the *Ashtabula Grange Record*.

Every actor receives devastating reviews at some point for some project, and while publicists search out the ads for raves, we could also find negative responses for even generally triumphant productions. This is the nature of individual taste. The smartest actors clip out their worst reviews and sometimes even keep them in their make-up kits to keep them humble. There is also comfort—once you have been panned in a devastating, personal, and humiliating way—that it will probably never get worse than this.

Helen Mirren, *actor*

"I remember the reviewer who first panned me. And he's still out there writing—the bastard."

Almost every great actor has experienced critical devastation. Here are some classics, which the much-praised British actor Diana Rigg compiled in her book, *No Turn Unstoned*:

"Miss Hepburn ran the gamut of emotions from A to B."

"Ms. Stapleton played the role as if she has not yet signed a contract with the producer."

"Peter O'Toole (as Macbeth) delivers every line with a monotonous bark as if addressing an audience of dead Eskimos."

"Anthony Hopkin (as Macbeth) sweats apprehensively . . . and gives the impression that he is a Rotarian pork butcher about to tell the stalls a dirty story."

"Judi Dench as Regan compensates for her strong scowl with a nervous speech impediment which, no doubt, is all Lear's fault."

"Maggie Smith . . . will not let the words speak for themselves. . .and we never forget for a moment this is a performance."

"The best thing about Ian McKellan's Hamlet is his curtain-call."

"Albert Finney's Hamlet is no prince at all, much less a sweet one. More of a 'Spamlet' really."

Sometimes actors get a bit of their own back. Here is Sir Peter Ustinov on the subject of critics:

"They search for ages for the wrong word, which, to give them credit, they eventually find."

CRITICAL THREES

An alarming number of critics have training in journalism, but not theatre. The problem is that when evaluating the work of, say, costume designers, if you do not actually understand how these artists function, the challenges they face and the standard process of moving from design conferences to renderings to completion, your response is likely to be facile, shallow, and uninformed. The more knowledge a critic has about the specific demands faced by each participant, the more likelihood for an insightful response. We believe that clusters of threes can be used to determine whether critics have the necessary qualifications required to determine the quality of a theatre production.

A Critic Should Be . . .

A critic should measure up in these areas before presuming to judge the work of others and asking us to read or watch his response. Is he:

1. *Knowledgeable* Critics should know more than we do about the play, the playwright, the period or style in which it is written, other work by this author, director and major actors. They should be able to place this event in a historical and artistic context. They should have sharply tuned senses and be able to predict responses of the average viewer. They should have the writing

skills to present their ideas with precision, clarity, and wit. Reading reviews should be like reading *Consumer Reports*, where very-informed researchers tell if this product (which on Broadway can mean a $100+ memory) is worth purchasing and offer guidelines to make a wise consumer choice. Because this is theatre, they should also be entertaining, lucid, and clever.

2. *Demanding* A good critic holds us to the highest standards, calls out bad work, as well as lazy, repetitive work and never panders to mediocrity. At the same time, he honors the best. So much is produced that is unworthy. Critics need to place the blame, in the hopes that everyone will aspire to quality next time out. They also need to be reminders of the difference between dreadful and merely bad, between pretty good and superb, and provide examples for those who aspire to the latter. A critic should never pander to even the most revered writers, directors, and actors when any of them are phoning in their work. Critics are there to keep us all on our toes.

3. *Compassionate* Many critics, alas, come across as vultures, actually seeking open wounds. The best are open-minded, hopeful, empathetic, and even when needing to write potentially devastating responses, do so in a way that makes it clear how and why such inadequate work could have been avoided. They need to acknowledge how difficult some challenges are and even to honor ambitious failures for attempting to raise the bar. The best critics express their opinions with grace and are ever hopeful that the next work or next season will be better than this one.

Benedict Nighingale, *critic*

"So often criticism seems to be a courtroom in which theatre practitioners are arraigned. If that is so, then perhaps the critic should think of himself as a court record and defense attorney at least as much as a prosecutor and judge."

Critics Should Ask...

1. *What was the artist trying to do?*
   It is essential to know what was being attempted. If, for example, a production is trying to update a classic play to connect it to current political events, it is pointless to criticize it for not being traditional and conventionally classical enough. The question should be considered for both the play and the production. What did the playwright want us to think and feel, and how closely did the production adhere or diverge from these aspirations? What was each artist trying to achieve? If it is difficult to answer these questions, then a valid criticism can be made regarding a lack of clarity of intentions. It is essential to get inside the artist's aspirations before gauging success or failure.

2. *How well did she do it?*
   To what degree did the artists accomplish what they set out to do? It is quite likely that some elements of the production came closer to the mark than others did. The perspective of this question allows a clear framework, beyond the mood or inclinations of the reviewer. It forces the reviewer to get past deep prejudice. Maybe you don't really care for sentimental, madcap, mindless musicals that attempt to create nostalgia for bygone days that never were. And while it is acceptable to admit this bias, you also need to admit how well or poorly they did what they wanted to do. Were the performances convincing and compelling? Was the same true of the work of the director, designers, the stage manager, and running crew? If it was supposed to provoke outrage and debate, to what extent did it? If it was supposed to provide amusement, diversion and laughter, how well did it succeed? If it was supposed to shock us into taking social action, to what degree did it?

3. *Was it worth doing?*

Sometimes, even after the most strenuous effort is put into a theatre piece and it largely achieves its aspirations, you have to ask if it was worth all the time and effort. The critic must now consider if it is worth the price of the ticket for audiences. While the world of theatre may seem very unlike that of business, in all activities, it is essential at some point to stop and ask if the investment is worth the payoff.

Trying to connect the rhythmic elements of rap to those of *kabuki* in a production set in the 'hood, but integrating *joruri* and *koken* and hypothetically called *Gangsta Buki*, could be brilliant—or not. If, after all the fusion work there are neither insights into either theatre form, nor the birth of a new one, and, if it was not all that entertaining, then the answer would probably have to be no. However noble the intentions and the success of achieving them, there is always the lingering question of whether all this has any lasting value or reverberation. Were enough people engaged and satisfied? Were there enough new insights, moments of theatrical magic, enough gasps, bursts of applause or extended ovations to compensate for the effort on the parts of both actors and audience? Did it probe deeply enough or buoy us high enough? Would we like to do it again? Will we tell our friends that they must experience it? Many *civilians*, a term we sometimes use for non-theatre people, consider us "mental" for the amount of time and energy we are willing to devote to an event that plays a few weekends and then is nothing but a memory. So the question becomes, "Was all the sweat worth the pay-off?"

A Critic Should Ask . . .

A good critic for each production will raise the questions below. Does it have:

1. *Relevance?*

Some plays and films have no aspiration beyond a diverting good time. Critics sometimes call these films "flicks." There is nothing wrong—and a lot right—with simple diversion. But if a work is to be judged as major, even great, and presents itself with high ambitions, these questions come up: Does it relate to concerns of our culture, to issues currently being debated? Does it present these with new clarity or complexity? Does it offer any solutions or at least help bring the debate into sharper focus? Does it awaken the public to something important, help bring about an end to ignorance and offer a beginning to healing? Does it get everyone at least talking and thinking in new ways? If it is a classic, does it point out how much we are still struggling with these issues perhaps thousands of years later? When we call a play great, it usually has a resonance throughout all our lives.

2. *Humanity?*

At the other end of the spectrum, how personal is this play? How deeply does it connect, not to the political or social, but to private pain, fear, joy, disappointment, or ecstasy? Even if it chooses to savage some of us, does it seem to have any positive intentions for bringing us together after bursting our balloons? How effectively does it make each of us realize that in these private concerns, we are not alone? How much does it make us aware that the hopes, hang-ups, and conflicts we face are actually our connections in the family of humankind? How much does it help us discover, not only our connectedness, but also possible paths to move out of our personal traps? Do we feel a genuine compassion and empathy for each of the characters and through their journeys, find insights into our own lives?

3. *Excitement?*

Is this a riveting, "can't leave my seat even though I gotta pee," experience or is it easy to let go, not only during the performance but after? Does it rev-up our emotions? Excite our minds? Are we transported out of our ho-hum lives into a far more desirable or perhaps more appalling world? Were we consistently held captive or did we sometimes drift off? If the play was live, did it use the theatre space in imaginative ways to remind us why live theatre can be a far greater high than the anonymity of the multiplex? Were there genuine suspense, surprise, spectacle, and a continuous stimulation of our curiosity? Does it have resonance? To what extent were we electrified at the time, and how much does it now resonate in our lives? Are we thinking about it and reliving it in the days that follow or does it instantly dissolve for us?

REVIEWERS VS. CRITIC/SCHOLARS

The terms critic and reviewer are generally used interchangeably, but the differences between media respondents and thoughtful critical analysis are considerable. Reviewers need to rush back to their computers, pound out an immediate first response with almost no reflection. It is comparable to being handed the conditions for an improv and just going for it. Some now attend final previews of a production just to give them more time before publishing the day after opening, but if the show was in the process of still pulling itself together and there was not the excitement of opening night, did they not really miss the opening?

Others, writing for scholarly journals, have more time, not only to reflect, but to do further research before formulating a response. Publications such as *Theatre Topics*, *Theatre Journal* and *The Voice and Speech Review* actually solicit reviews that will be published long after a production has closed. These serve as historical records or archival documents rather than consumer advice since the opportunity to see the show is long past.

In dictionaries, to criticize is sometimes defined as "to find fault" but also "to understand and appraise." While the former, if witty enough, can be hugely entertaining, the latter is more likely to contribute both to those who have done the work and those considering seeing it. In Samuel Beckett's great absurdist play *Waiting for Godot*, the two central characters shout insults at each other, such as *"Vermin!,"* *"Moron,"* *"Sewer Rat,"* *"Cretin"* and finally for the topper, *"C–r-ritic!!!"*

Many theatre practitioners share Beckett's view. But we ask you, while not denying any of the above, to give reviewers a massive dose of empathy for working under such tight deadlines, rarely being given enough space in print or broadcast time to explore their responses with any degree of depth, and for rising to the challenge of trying to predict how countless others will respond when most of us are not even all that sure how our best friends will. They also need points for putting their ideas on the line and then subjecting themselves to a barrage of outraged disagreement. They function in a relatively isolated, outsider context regarding the theatre community, not invited to parties or receptions and possibly confronted and vilified when they meet theatre practitioners. The reviewer must have a strong sense of personal integrity and no real need for the affection of or even interaction with those he reviews.

Of course occasionally reviewers become celebrities in their own right, and their reviews are read as much for entertainment value as for readers to decide whether or not to see the show. Roger Ebert in film and Frank Rich in theatre have both published collections of their reviews to be savored after the fact.

WRITING A REVIEW

You may be asked to write a critical review for a class assignment or even consider offering your services to your school or local newspaper. Believe it or not, you are more qualified now than many who step up to pass judgment without a theatre education of any kind. Start by reviewing the section on Responding Fully to a Production in Chapter 1. Ask yourself which of those elements you would like to include. Then consider these additions:

If you cannot actually read the play, try to read *about* it—newspaper articles or interviews that are part of the publicity, possibly a summary of it in a study guide. Do the same for the playwright to get a sense of how this play fits into the body of her work. Examine the lobby display, which is often a source of the dramaturg's research, possibly containing fascinating quotes and insights into the culture surrounding early productions, as well as photos of other performances of this work. Read whatever notes are in the program, which are intended to help shape the experience for audience members. While it can be distracting to take notes during a performance, it is often a good idea to have a small notepad where you can jot down your thoughts at intermission and immediately after the performance while your response is fresh.

Other guidelines:

1. Assume the best of your readers. Write to them as if they are well-educated adults, people of taste and good judgment. Do not patronize them. Write up rather than down to them.

2. Be fair in your expectations. If a theatre obviously functions on a shoestring budget, complaining about a lack of opulence in the production is pointless. If they specialize in raunchy satire, why bother to make judgments of taste?

3. If you make a strong, negative criticism, supply an example or evidence to back up this assertion. Select a part of the performance where it failed and try to identify, to the best of your ability, why.

4. Write with confidence when you are quite sure that you believe other audience members would share your response, but do not hesitate to admit that your response is singular. If the show is constantly stopped by hysterical laughter and applause, but you never cracked a smile, admit it. If only you and three others were on their feet cheering at the end, admit that as well.

5. Be sure to include whatever is unusual or noteworthy about this particular production: if the setting or time period have been changed, cross-gender casting is being used, extensive song and dance has been added or a radical interpretation of a famous character is being presented. Prepare audiences who may have past familiarity with this script for what they may find unsettling. If they are to experience a musical drag King Lear, at least let them know.

6. Identify the names of the actors when describing their performances, and distinguish between actor and character. Make it clear when you are discussing Juliet as written vs. Lois Lipschitz's Juliet as presented. This also helps define your criticism. Lois may have gone beyond the character as written in terms of fiery engagement, or somehow not have measured up to the role as presented on the page.

7. Make the same distinction between the script and the actual performance. Imagine this play done in a different fashion. Try to gauge the quality of the playwright's initial effort in comparison with what the production team achieved in realizing, transcending, circumventing, or even violating that effort.

8. In keeping with other journalism standards, write in clear, vivid language with relatively short sentences and paragraphs. While responses that are more scholarly are freed from this restriction, the instant response usually needs to be sharp, short and sweet.

9. Go over the list of participants in Chapters 3–6, review the production chart, and ask if there is a reason to include or exclude any of them from mention in your review. Do not feel the need to mention everyone, but rather focus on those who showed exceptional skill or who dropped the ball in a big and unfortunate way.

10. Try to avoid pure rating phrases like "good job" and "awesome" or "didn't quite cut it," and instead specify in what way something was good or bad. A performance is awesome because the

actor takes great risks, has outrageously perfect comic timing, shows astonishing versatility, and shows incredible subtlety and nuance or perhaps outrageous theatrical bravado. It disappoints because it may be flat and unvaried, or it lacks energy and conviction, the actor is clearly miscast, the actor fails to find the character's vulnerability and let the audience in or perhaps it is awkwardly at odds with the work of other actors in the show.

11. Write as if you are discussing the play during its run and allow for change. Write about it as an ongoing activity rather than generalizing from a single performance you attended. Not "The actors never pick up their cues," but "The actors at the performance I attended, had difficulty picking up their cues, but with more performances..." allowing for potential growth rather than pronouncing sentence.

12. Be sure to let the audience know what kind of a time they will have, if they will collapse with laughter, be stunned but stimulated to think in a new way or simply diverted in a harmless way. Try to predict its experience.

13. If there are great lines in the play and great line deliveries by actors, do not hesitate to quote them.

14. Do not waste time recounting the entire plot, and do not give away surprise elements. Give us the same amount of story that might be part of a preview of coming attractions, and no more.

Authors' Insight

Robert: "I recently directed a production of *Much Ado About Nothing* where the woman playing Beatrice, a strong character, was also very physically strong (she did gymnastics on horseback competitively). At the curtain call, the last two couples came out and we had Claudio pick up and swing Hero around after their initial bows. The final couple, Beatrice and Benedick reversed this pattern as she lifted him and twirled him to great surprise, laughter, and applause. It was a delightful, final surprise for the audience. The local reviewer, while raving about the production generally, told readers about this. We could have killed her."

---

15. Try to find an opening sentence and paragraph that is striking and somehow crystallizes your response.

16. Consider putting this play in a historical context for readers, either in the history of plays like this done by this theatre, the evolving work of the playwright or even the growth of this theatre, as productions have gotten more and more ambitious.

17. If you feel great futures are ahead for any of the participants, say so. All critics have a stake in keeping theatre alive and in encouraging brilliance.

18. If you are writing for a newspaper, conclude with dates and times for the remaining run of the show and contact information for securing tickets.

PERSONAL CRITICISM

In your personal theatre, this ongoing play called *Your Life*, moments of criticism play a big part. When given and received, there is often tension, discomfort, and conflict, the very heart of drama. One of the major life-skills is to offer criticism when it is needed in a respectful way without wimping-out (not doing it at all or doing so in such an apologetic way that is has virtually no impact) or going over-the-top into explosive anger or grief (so shouting and/or tears get in the way of communicating basic information). Behavioral science has shown us that many of us (often women) quickly circumvent anger into grief and that many others (often men) do the exact opposite. Clearly, frightening, enraged shouting, and incomprehensible, inconsolable crying can stop communication. If this was not even what the person was really feeling in the first place, it gets even more complex and distracting. In the theatre of your own life, it is crucial to determine the circumstances and probably to rehearse and revise serious criticism.

Learning to *give* criticism gracefully is one of the most desirable skills in life, so is learning to *receive* it. The same responses noted above often occur. Consider first that people who do not care about you do not *bother* to criticize you. They are too busy. There is always some level of concern and connection. So try to get past the comment and into the intention behind it. Many of us find it useful to write down a particularly harsh criticism, thank the person offering it for being concerned enough about us to give it, and then go off to consider its validity. This is usually a better decision than giving in to an immediate impulse. Receiving criticism is a kind of spotlight. Many receive no attention at all. If anyone is offering you this kind of feedback, it means that you matter to him or her.

Most criticism is more successful if it is not a public performance done in front of observers, but rather given in private, so that the impact of the audience does not add to the drama.

GETTING INVOLVED

At the end of an introductory theatre class, the question invariably comes up, "Where do I go now with theatre?" For some this one course is enough. This exposure will make you a more informed audience member for live theatre and media and you are likely to get more out of future viewing experiences. It may also make you a more acute observer of theatrical elements in your own life and give you some insights into how to make these events go more the way you would like them to. Other readers are going to want to take part in some additional way and wonder how to begin.

The place to start may be the theatre departmental website, main office, or even a bulletin board where notices of upcoming auditions, opportunities to work production crews, workshops, field trips, or discount tickets are posted. Some departments have an email newsletter, highlighting upcoming activities, to which you can subscribe. Local theatre companies probably have similar resources, and the arts calendar section of the newspaper often lists auditions for productions around town.

If one or more aspects of theatre particularly intrigue you, consider enrolling in a class that focuses specifically on, for example, acting, costuming, or directing. The class you are taking now is often a kind of funnel for students to discover and then further explore those areas of theatre that especially fascinate them. Find out if there are prerequisites or an application/audition process for admission. You might also explore majoring or minoring in theatre. Most departments have a brochure or student handbook with basic degree requirements, faculty profiles, scholarship and financial aid resources as well as production requirements. Theatre is a major that usually requires taking part in the shows themselves beyond class work.

Your parents may express concern over focusing on subject that does not guarantee employment. While it is true that many theatre majors do not work in the theatre, one of the largest employment agencies in the country has found great success placing majors in other fields. This is because theatre teaches you basic skills valued in any organization: meeting deadlines, time management, working under pressure, comfort in meeting the public, collaborating, coming up with creative solutions, making presentations in a poised, dynamic way and taking initiative. Those who have studied acting have a far greater awareness of the first impressions they make, the way they look, sound, and move and the skills to alter these to suit an occasion. These aptitudes are as valued in corporate cultures as they are in the arts.

For those seeking employment in theatre, it is wise to study the full spectrum of theatre arts and to select at least three or four for specialization. Actors who only study acting do not always interact successfully during costume fittings, tech rehearsals, or promotion if they do not entirely understand how costumers, tech directors, and publicists work. Those who have studied the process of all team members have more positive, empathetic communications with each of them, enhancing the collaborative process. Some actors also limit their job options to being actor/waiters, so that when they are not performing, they are far away from the theatre environment they love. But it is not essential to divide one's time between a theatre and a restaurant. Training to be an actor, director, playwright, designer, publicist, teacher, or any number of other combinations of positions described in this book increases the likelihood of finding a place in the theatre that allows you to *be* there, in varying capacities

You may wonder after all this, how people of the theatre can invest so much time and energy into something that lasts so briefly, may be blasted with critical scorn and is regarded by much of the population as frivolous. You must understand that we consider ourselves to be (on most days when we are not just feeling overworked) the most blessed people alive. We live in a state of constant bewilderment and compassion for "civilians" who do not get to do "let's pretend," "dress up," "once upon a time," and "hey, let's put on a show" all the time. We are particularly privileged to regularly rediscover our childhood innocence, to fast forward into our deep mature peace and in-between to explore our "dark side" without ending up in jail or dead—not to mention our hero-lover-wit-wacko-genius-magic-suave-hopeless-inspired sides. We get to enter briefly the lives of almost every kind of person, and to taste every life. Those of us fortunate enough to earn our living in the theatre enter it each day full of possibility that is the same as feeling fully alive.

Arthur Miller kept a journal of rehearsals for the first production of his legendary play, *Death of a Salesman*. Here is a key entry:

"Lee J. Cobb, who was playing Willy, sat for days on the stage like a great lump, a sick seal, a mourning walrus. When it came his time to speak lines, he whispered meaninglessly. Elia Kazan, the director, pretended certainty, but from where I sat he looked like an ant trying to prod an elephant off his haunches. Ten days went by. The other actors were by now much further advanced, but Cobb stared at them heavy-eyed, morose, even persecuted, it seemed.

And then, one afternoon, there on the stage of the New Amsterdam theatre high above 42nd street, Lee rose from his chair and looked at Milly Dunnock and there was a silence. And then he said, "I was driving along, and all of a sudden I'm going off the road..."

And the theatre vanished. The stage vanished. The chill of an age-old recognition shuddered up my spine. A new human being was being formed before all our eyes, born for the first time on this earth, made real by an act of will. A birth was taking place; a man was here transcending the limits of his body and history. A mere glance of his eye created a window beside him, a touch of his hand on this empty stage made a bed appear, and when he glanced up at the emptiness above him a ceiling was there, and there was even a crack in it where his stare rested.

I knew then that something astounding was being made here. It would have been almost enough for me, without opening the play.

There is a certain amount of immortality involved in theatre, created by the knowledge the actor keeps to his dying day that on a certain afternoon, in an empty and dusty theatre, he cast a shadow of a being that was not himself but the distillation of all he had ever observed; all the unsingable heartsong the ordinary man may feel but never utter, he gave voice to. And by that he somehow joins the ages."

When the playwright Maxwell Anderson got a letter from a very discouraged young theatre artist considering giving it up, this was his answer:

"If you have truly and deeply chosen to practice this art, be totally proud of it and then, in return, make the art proud of you. If you now hesitate on the threshold of maturity, wondering what rewards are out there beyond feeding, sleeping and breeding, turn deep into this art, which has moved you so powerfully. Take what part in it in whatever way you can, as participant, spectator, secret practitioner, or hanger-on and waiter at the door. Neglect no sacrifice at your chosen altar. It may break your heart, it may drive you half-mad, it may betray you into unrealizable ambitions or blind you to financial opportunities with its wandering fires. But it will fill your heart before it breaks it; it will make you a person in your own right; it will open the temple doors to you and enable you to walk with those who have come nearest among people to what people may sometime be."

The theatre may or may not be for you. If not, we thank you for spending time with us. If so, welcome to potential torture and infinite possibility.

SUMMARY

Critics have a powerful and ambivalent role in the theatrical process. An astonishing number are not trained in the art they evaluate. Critics have the power to say things that could get others sued. We have a right to expect important credentials and insights from those whose reviews we read or watch. Those who have to write instant responses for tomorrow's paper function in an entirely different framework than those writing for scholarly journals with months of preparation. Reviewers should follow certain, essential guidelines for writing a critical response, in order to make what they say connect to a large body of potential audience members and to include all those who have contributed significantly to the production. After learning about all aspects of theatre, many readers may wish further involvement and options that are offered in this chapter. There are many ways to keep theatre part of your life.

SUGGESTED ASSIGNMENTS

1. Why is it essential that reviewers, however unfair they may be in their assessments, have the freedom to write whatever they want?

2. Why do you think actors are willing to subject themselves to the potential public humiliation of devastating reviews?

3. Examine several reviews by any critic and assess how this writer qualifies in demonstrating the qualities that we should generally expect from someone in this position.

4. What is the fundamental difference between a reviewer and a scholar/critic?

5. Write a review of either a live production or film, following the guidelines outlined in this chapter.

6. If a classmate or someone you know evaluates the same production, examine each other's responses and attempt to analyze in particular the areas in which your opinions differed.

7. What can be learned about the art of criticism in the theatre that might transfer to successfully giving and receiving it in life?

8. Identify how you think you may wish to become involved in theatre at some point in the future.

9. Why are theatre majors often successfully employed outside the theatre?

10. In spite of the hard work and often harsh responses involved, what is it that keeps theatre artists committed and involved?

SUGGESTED ACTIVITIES

1. Individual—Locate two different versions of the same dramatic work, perhaps a live production and a filmed version or two different filmed treatments. Using the guidelines from this chapter, write a review, which compares and contrasts the productions.

2. Small Group—Have each member of the group interview an actor regarding the impact that reviews have had on his or her sense of self-esteem and performances. Discuss the range of responses and where actor's opinions seem to be most strongly shared.

3. Long-term—Identify a major theatre or film critic who has worked in the field for a number of years. Examine at least ten reviews this person has written over a period of time. What patterns can you determine? What changes seem to have taken place in the critic's written emphasis and preferences?

4. Large Group—Offer a prize such as complementary tickets and engage the class in a competition to determine who can come up with the most devastating excerpt from a critical review. Note that in addition to major newspapers, almost all weekly magazines (such as *People*, *Time*, *Entertainment Weekly*, and *The New Yorker*) feature reviews that might provide your winning entry. Let the class vote to determine the victor.

KEY WORDS AND IDEAS

Reviewer vs. Scholarly Critic

Qualities of a good play:

Relevance, Humanity, Excitement

Qualities of a good critic:

Knowledgeable

Demanding

Compassionate

Three critical questions:

What is trying to be done?

How well was it done?

Was it worth doing?

WORLD OF THE PLAY CHECKLIST

1. TIME

- When in history is the play written/organized, set and performed?

- How do these time facts and choices vary and how do they interact?

- How far does this production move away from the original time period?

- How do these issues of time interact?

- How rapidly does time move for most people?

- How conscious are characters of the passage of time? Are they culturally trained to view time as linear, cyclical, or eternal?

- How do they record or note time? What is the dominant rhythm/tempo of the world of the play?

- Are these people past, present, or future focused?

- What lengths of attention span are most obvious?

- Is age revered or feared? What is the relationship between youth and maturity?

2. SPACE

- How is space defined and viewed?

- Is space only literal or do people think in terms of spiritual, philosophical, or abstract space?

- How large of a personal "bubble" do most people carry, what is the accepted comfort zone of interaction?

- Is there flexibility allowed in personal spaces?

- To what degree are private spaces respected?

- How is space violated, and what are accepted responses to personal or public "invasions"?

3. VALUES

- What beliefs are most widely shared? Which truths, ideals, and traditions are deemed to be self-evident?

- What commitment is made to these values, and what is the punishment for not sharing them?

- What is the predominant mood?

- Who are the role models or idols?

- What fantasies or ideal futures are shared?

- What is the value of money or property?

- What kind of humor is dominant?

- How is fear defined, and is it legitimized or stigmatized?

- How, and to what degree, are emotions of any kind expressed, suppressed, or repressed?

4. STRUCTURE

- What is the hierarchy of authority? Who are the leaders and who are the followers?

- Is change possible? Is authority absolute or flexible?

- What is the governance system and how entrenched it is? Is authority inherited or earned? If earned, what is the mechanism (career, physical strength, beauty, etc.) by which it can be achieved?

- What is the definition and mechanism of justice?

- How are family and marriage defined? How are they related to social structures? How open or closed are familial relationships? Do they change over time?

- To what degree is the individual free within the social and familial structure?

- To what degree is daily life formalized, and how strictly enforced are the etiquette, manners, and tastes of the individual?

5. PLEASURE

- What traits are considered beautiful, desirable, or enviable? What are the ideal male and female types?

- Is pleasure primarily sought through physical, social, spiritual, or intellectual pursuits?

- What colors, shapes, textures, or silhouettes give the most pleasure?

- Does comfort have any relationship to pleasure?

- What is the collective attitude toward sex, sexuality, and sensuality? What areas of the anatomy are considered erotic? What areas are forbidden; what pleasures are taboo? What's hot and what's not?

- What is generally accepted as "fun"? What is the perfect social occasion, vacation, or day?

- What are the shared pastimes, or hobbies? What are the favored foods, beverages, or games?
- How much flexibility is allowed for individual taste?

6. SENSES

- How do all of the above ideas become manifested in the world of the play?
- Which, if any, of the five senses is most frequently and effectively stimulated?
- What is the quality of light, sound, textures and patterns that are most prized?
- By what level of stimulation do the senses become overwhelmed or understimulated?
- When people approach one another, how close is too close; how far is too far?
- What skills does one need to maneuver artfully in this world?
- What is the relationship between degrees of nonverbal gestures and verbal skills? Is the gracefulness of speech or of movement more prized? What vocal qualities of tone, pitch, pronunciations, and dialects give the most pleasure to the senses?
- What role does music and dance have? Is the average individual expected to participate or not?
- What smells and tastes are likely to be dominant in this world? Which give pleasure, and which simply can't be avoided?
- To what degree are the people aware of the sensory world around them?

THE PRODUCTION

To what extent do any of the above influence the production itself:

1. **Time**—How long does the show run and how it is divided into intermissions? How tight or leisurely is the presentation? How often does the tempo/rhythm fall into a predictable pattern or timing? How often does it shift and surprise?

2. **Space**—To what degree may the audience be acknowledged, involved, invaded, or even invited to take part? How large is the house and what degree of adjustment needs to be made to fill it or to go down to subtle nuance based on close proximity? How does the position of audience to actor influence choices?

3. **Values**—Is this show reinforcing generally assumed beliefs or actually polarizing audiences? Is it in sync with what we now seem to consider funny or shocking or does it stun us and make us reconsider what we believe? Is it welcoming or challenging to what we have formerly valued?

4. **Structure**—Is the play taking place in a time of potential significant change in governance? How does the potential for who rules and who does not influence the action? Is the way the event is structured reflective of the structure in the world of the play?

5. **Pleasure**—To what extent is this a hedonistic or cerebral event? Do the ideas about what is pleasurable match or contradict those in our culture at present?

6. **Senses**—To what degree is this a sensual experience? How have your own senses of sight, sound, and feeling been challenged or enhanced?

RESPONDING TO A PRODUCTION

Event _____ Produced by _____
Where? _____ When? _____
Author(s) _____ Respondent _____

YOU AS AUDIENCE

How familiar were you with the text, story, or type of theatre event?

_____
_____
_____
_____

What expectations did you bring with you? Were they met or not?

_____
_____
_____
_____

What was your mood when you entered the theatre space?

_____
_____
_____
_____
_____

What kind of environment was the theatre space? Did it contribute to your comfort or discomfort? Did it seem "right" for the play?

_____
_____
_____
_____

THE STORY

What happened? (Just the basic spine of the story in as few words as possible.)

_____
_____
_____
_____

What was the central conflict?

_____
_____
_____

What was the emotional mood of the event? Did it end satisfactorily? Was the conflict resolved?

_____
_____
_____
_____

THE WORLD OF THE PLAY

(Refer to Chapter 1 or Appendix A for a list of questions to guide you)

1. **Time**—When was the play written? How familiar are you with that time period? Was the production set in the same time or was it changed? What else did you notice about time in this world?

_____
_____
_____
_____
_____

2. **Space**—Where was the story set? How familiar are you with that place or type of space? How did the performance space relate to the theatre itself? What else did you notice about time in this world?

_____
_____
_____
_____
_____

3. **Values**—Did this story affirm your own values or challenge them? What specific values were addressed?

_____
_____
_____
_____

4. **Structure**—What kinds of structure were at play in this world? Were those structures rigid or flexible? Did one or more characters challenge the structures?

_____

_____

_____

_____

_____

5. **Pleasure**—What pleasures were the characters pursuing? Were those pleasures taboo or mainstream? How much of the story was about pleasure?

_____

_____

_____

_____

_____

6. **The Senses**—What senses were stimulated in the world of the play? Did characters seem focused on any one of the senses? How were your senses touched? Did anything surprise you about your sensory experience?

_____

_____

_____

_____

_____

CONCLUSIONS

Write one or more clear and concise arguments for what you believe to be the author's intention, message, or project.

_____

_____

_____

_____

_____

WRAP UP

Discuss briefly the essence of your experience – your opinion about the production, your emotional response, and whether you would recommend it to others.

_____

_____

_____

_____

_____

_____

Sample Character Analysis

Actors may be asked to answer these questions as the character. Answering from a human being other than yourself can be illuminating and unsettling. The playwright may or may not have provided all of this information. The actor is generally asked to *investigate* (checking for facts in the text) first, and only when that search is complete, move on to *inference* (intelligent conjectures based on this detective work), and finally *invention* in order to fill in all the gaps.

Character _____ **Actor** _____

For the Play as a Whole:

Character Past

I come from

My childhood was

The experience that made the most lasting impression on me was

My five most important given circumstances are

The two most powerful members of my private audience and the reasons for this are

The most crucial event prior to my first entrance in the play is

The details of my past history with other characters in the play are

The most significant of these in terms of influencing my attitudes and behavior are

Character Present

Environment affects me most dramatically when

Other characters and/or the playwright describe me as

I describe others as

In groups, I tend to

I would describe myself as basically

My most distinguishing characteristics are

My favorite things are

The things I loathe are

My temperament could be described as

I am most interested in

I am least interested in

My physical life differs from the actor playing me in that

My vocal life differs from the actor playing me in that

I make the following discoveries in the play

Character Future

My super objective in the play is to

If this changes, it becomes

My hierarchy would include these other objectives

The obstacles I face are

The strategy and tactics I most often employ are

My three rehearsed futures are:

    Best possible

    Worst possible

    Wildest dreams come true

FOR EACH SCENE

Major outside forces influencing me are

My immediate objective in the scene is

The major obstacle I encounter is

The strategy and tactics I employ to get what I want include

OUR FIFTY BEST-KNOWN PLAYS

In our culture the following plays are so familiar that they are referenced constantly in class, auditions, and rehearsal. If you study theatre further, you will want some familiarity with this mix of musicals, Shakespeares, classic, and contemporary titles. If reading them all seems too overwhelming, many are on film. All are available as part of study guides or master plots, so that you can at least have an idea of basic story, major characters and style for each.

A Doll's House (Ibsen)

A Midsummer Night's Dream (Shakespeare)

A Streetcar Named Desire (Williams)

Angels in America (Kushner)

Antigone (Sophocles)

As You Like It (Shakespeare)

Cabaret (Kander, Ebb, Masteroff)

Cat on a Hot Tin Roof (Williams)

Carousel (Rogers & Hammerstein)

Chicago (Kander & Ebb)

Cyrano de Bergerac (Rostand)

Death of a Salesman (Miller)

Electra (Sophocles)

Fiddler on the Roof (Kander & Ebb)

Guys and Dolls (Loesser, Burrows, Swerling)

Gypsy (Laurents, Styne, Sonddheim)

Hamlet (Shakespeare)

King Lear (Shakespeare)

Long Day's Journey into Night (O'Neill)

Lysistrata (Aristophanes)

Macbeth (Shakespeare)

Medea (Euripedes)

Mother Courage (Brecht)

Much Ado About Nothing (Shakespeare)

My Fair Lady (Lerner, Lowe, Shaw)

Oedipus Rex (Sophocles)

Oklahoma (Rogers & Hammerstein)

Othello (Shakespeare)

Our Town (Wilder)

Rent (Larson)

Richard III (Shakespeare)

Romeo and Juliet (Shakespeare)

Six Characters in Search of an Author (Ionesco)

South Pacific (Rogers & Hammerstein)

Tartuffe (Moliere)

The Bacchae (Euripedes)

The Cherry Orchard (Chekhov)

The Crucible (Miller)

The Glass Menagerie (Williams)

The Importance of Being Earnest (Wilde)

The King and I (Rogers & Hammerstein)

The Misanthrope (Moliere)

The Odd Couple (Simon)

The Producers (Brooks)

The Rivals (Sheridan)

The Sea Gull (Chekhov)

The School for Scandal (Sheridan)

The Taming of the Shrew (Shakespeare)

The Tempest (Shakespeare)

The Three Sisters (Chekhov)

The Trojan Women (Euripedes)

The Zoo Story (Albee)

Twelfth Night (Shakespeare)

Waiting for Godot (Beckett)

West Side Story (Bernstein, Sondheim)

Who's Afraid of Virginia Woolf? (Albee)

COMPARING WESTERN AND EASTERN THEOTRE

While there will be exceptions to the generalizations below, these theatrical preferences tend to dominate within each culture.* Because much of African theatre is largely undocumented and widely varied, we limit this comparison to those areas of the world where established traditions invite comparisons.

1. TIME—TEMPO? RHYTHMS? AGE? POINT IN HISTORY?

Western—Plays are plotted tightly and often criticized for not moving swiftly enough to hold attention.

Eastern—Pacing is far more leisurely, less based on plot development, more given to digression and diversion.

Western—One may embark on a theatrical career even into middle age.

Eastern—Most performers are trained from early childhood, and it is all but impossible to break into the profession in another way.

Western—The vast majority of plays are contemporary, set in the time in which they are written. Even Shakespeare and other classical writers are constantly updated to "now" in production.

Eastern—Almost all are set either in the distant past or in a universally recurring phenomenon such as the shifts between seasons.

2. SPACE—BUBBLES? PRIVACY? INVASION? RELATIONSHIP TO NATURE? AWARENESS OF OTHERS?

Western—40% of world's population.

Eastern—60% so our lack of knowledge of theatrical traditions is surprising.

---

* There are realistic, linear, contemporary, and avante guarde experimental productions in Asian theatre, but they are invariably Western influenced and exceptions to the dominant theatre choices of the culture.

Western—While some plays are based on spectacle, far more often theatres attempt intimacy, trying to get audiences physically closer to the action and more involved in the internal lives of characters.

Eastern—Generally performed broadly and in a highly stylized manner that would be considered "over the top" in the West.

Western—In realistic drama, often performers ignore the audience altogether with the impression that observers are eavesdropping.

Eastern—Performances are almost invariably presentational and directly involve audience members.

Western—When audience acknowledgment is present, it may ask for participation, reaction, even entering the performance space.

Eastern—Audience is a constant present but rarely directly challenged or asked to take part in any way not already ritualized.

3. VALUES—MOOD? IDEALS? MONEY? GOD? EMOTION?

Western—Most plays are judged on how realistic or honestly they portray human experience, or how cleverly they reframe our familiar experiences. Plays aspiring to greatness are judged by what they mean or say about the lives of audience members and their potential for profound impact on those lives.

Eastern—Plays are judged for sensuality of experience, rhythm, melody, beauty of expression, and the degree to which audiences are transported and diverted.

Western—There is great interest in innovation for both performers and technicians, with new interpretations, technical advances are constantly pursued and honored.

Eastern—Highly traditional and deeply connected to religion, folk tales, and myths. Eastern theatre is slow to embrace or even respect change.

Western—A great actor is capable of emotional nuance, empathy, and striking originality.

Eastern—A great actor should be a great athlete, singer and dancer, highly respectful of those that have come before, with subtly nuanced original choices rather than revolutionary changes.

4. STRUCTURE—GOVERNMENT? DAILY LIFE? EDUCATION?

Western—Drama is a significant part of literature; plays are often read rather than seen.

Eastern—Drama is almost exclusively a total theatrical experience with few scripts published, and almost none read as part of standard education.

Western—Many actors train briefly, with no universally recognized pattern to achieve recognition, some achieving success with no formal training at all.

Eastern—Actors are often born into a theatrical family or adopted by one, then embark on an intense and standardized training based on apprenticeship and moving up through the ranks.

5. Pleasure—Beauty? Comfort? Artistic expression? Seduction? Courtship? Recreation? Participation? Consumption?

Western—Diverse theatrical forms, from naturalistic (going to the theatre to see our own lives reflected) to escapist (a fantastic better version of our lives) make for a virtual smorgasbord of choices when one decides to go to the theatre.

Eastern—A great love of spectacle dominates with brilliant colors, graceful movement, no interest in realistic portrayal, but great concern with stunningly beautiful theatricality, visual perfection and dazzling, sweeping movement.

6. Senses—Sight? Stillness? Movement? Ritual? Sound? Language? Listening? Music? Smells? Tastes?

Western—Except for musicals (and some of them are "sung through,") the text is almost entirely spoken with great effort at making the speech seem natural. Even in classical productions, great effort is made to have the elevated speech and period-style movement appear natural to the performer.

Eastern—Almost never just spoken, but sung, danced, chanted, and pantomimed; the theatrical event demands more suspension of disbelief in order to enter a highly stylized universe.

Western—The appeal is to the intellect and the emotions, with surprise often presented in plot twists, sudden reversals, disclosures, and unexpected climaxes. Audiences expect to be stimulated by ideas and/or stirred to feel powerfully.

Eastern—The appeal is to the senses. The basic story is likely to be known by the audience so surprise is in moment-to-moment theatrical delights. The event is more likely to be judged by its moments of beauty and esthetic pleasure than shocking details.

Western—Actors may rely on props or pieces of business to enhance performance but largely turn to their own inner recourses. The more classical the production, the less detail, but it is rare for a performance to be about more than the actor herself.

Eastern—Puppets, stilts, and other extravagant extensions of the actor's art, including hugely challenging, gorgeous costumes may support performances. At any moment, the individual performer may step back and allow the theatrical effect to step into focus.

MEDIA MILESTONES

FILM

1888—first motion picture camera invented by Thomas Edison

1895—first screen projection system developed by the Lumiere brothers

1903—first plot/storyline film (*The Great Train Robbery*)

1915—first major film (*The Birth of a Nation*)*

1916—1925-advent of the star system

1922—Hays Office Motion Picture Code

1927—first "talkie" (*The Jazz Singer*)

1930—establishment of the studio system

1946—top box office attendance of all time (90 million)

1948—television is marketed, competing with films

1960s—emergence of Independent film movement

1968—MPAA ratings warn and restrict attendance

1977—big budget blockbuster concept takes off, modeled on *Star Wars*

1980s—home VCRs in general release

1995—first major computer generated film (*Toy Story*)

1997—DVD introduced

1999—Netflix flat rate rental introduced

2007—D2D theatres

---

* "major" becomes term for films over 90 minutes in length

Television

1925—first TV transmission

late 40s, early 50s—television's "Golden Age"

1950—Nielsen ratings system initiated

1953—color TV introduced

1956—dominance of three major networks

1967—Public Broadcasting Act

1970—FCC's limits network prime time access

1972—cable approved by the FCC

1975—HBO available on satellite, VCRs introduced

1976—first basic cable service (WTBS)

1984—Cable acto integrates wireless technologies

1996—mergers motivated by Telecommunications Art

1998—networks lose dominance

2004—reality TV supplants scripted shows

2008—planned transition to digital TV

MULTI-CULTURAL FILM RESOURCES

AFRICA

The Swampdwellers (film of Wold Soynika's play)
VHS, #DAK762, 40 min. Insight Media

Wole Woyinka (lecture from the playwright)
VHS, #DAK1606 61min. Insight Media

Obo Koso: Nigerian Drama (excerpt from the folkloric Yoruban dance drama)
VHS, #DAK762, 28min. Insight Media

Yaaba Soore: Path of the Ancestors (exploration of mask performances in Burko Faso)
VHS #DAK1603, DVD #DAK3968, 17 min. Insight Media

Dance of the Spirits: Mask Styles and Performance (rare footage and analysis of conventions of the masked dances of Burkina Faso)
VHS #AAK762, 42 min. Insight Media

Stage Shakers! Ghana's Concert Party Theatre (documentary showing how this dynamic theatre forms incorporates fashion, music, song, dance and social issues.)
VHS #9AK1617, 90 min. Insight Media

Sizwe Bansi Is Dead (film of Athol Fugard's play about repressive laws in South Africa)
VHS #9AK312, 60 min. Insight Media

The Blood Knot (excerpts from the original New York production of Athol Fugard's play)
VHS #9AK312, 60 min. Insight Media

ASIA

Theaters of Asia: An Introduction (exploration of classical and folk drama, interviews with participants)
VHS #DAK1433, DVD #DAK3778, 50 min. Insight Media

Asian Concepts of Stage Discipline and Western Actor Training (comparisons and potential applications, including principles of t'ai chi.)
VHS #9AK684, 30 min. Insight Media

INDONESIA

Mayadanawa (Balinese puppet drama)
VHS, #DAK3643, 26min. Insight Media

Adapting Topeng: The Masked Theatre of Bali (Excerpts from Little Red Riding Shawl, combining Western techniques and mask training in Bali)
VHS, #DAK626, 46 min. Insight Media

Wayang Golek: Performing Arts of Sunda
(exploration of rod-puppet mix of storytelling, songs, and music)
VHS #DAK1602, DVD #DAK3687, 42 min. Insight Media

Wayang Kulit: Shadow Theater of Java (exploration of shadow-puppet traditions)
VHS #9AK1618, DVD #DAK3687, 22 min. Insight Media

Isle of Temples: Bali (Balinese folksongs, gamelan orchestras, and dance dramas, excerpts from Barong and Ketchak)
VHS #9AK1209, 30min. Insight Media

CHINA

What is Chinese Opera? (seven sections covering both performance and production aspects)
VHS #DAK3665, DVD #DAK3688, 33 min. Insight Media

Chinese Opera (training and performance at the People's Theatre in Canton)
VHS #DAK519, DVD #DAK3610, 30 min. Insight Media

Aspects of the Peking Opera (traditional male and female gestures and expressions demonstrated by Hu Hun-Yen)
VHS #AAK428, 15min. Insight Media

The Performing Arts in China (examination training and rehearsal methods)
VHS #9AK379, DVD#9AK3899 15 min. Insight Media

INDIA

The Mahabharata (Peter Brook's staging of the revered classic)
VHS #DAK273, 166 min. Insight Media

Sanskrit Drama (recreation of classical dance forms with performance excerpts from The Vision of Vasavadatta)
VHS #DAK317, 14 min. Insight Media

The Clay Cart (classic fifteenth century Sanksrit play in the Natyshastra style)
VHS #9AK772, 40 min. Insight Media

A Casebook of Sanskrit Theater (origins and conventions of Sanskrit theater) mix of storytelling, songs, and music)
VHS #9AK771, 120 min. Insight Media

Bhavai: Folk Theater of Gujarat (exploration of the evolution of the Bhavair of Sanskrit theater)
VHS #9AK647, 23 min. Insight Media

Mudras: Hand Gestures of Sanskrit Drama (demonstration of two major types of mudras by Mrinalini Sarabhai)
VHS #9AK508, 38 min. Insight Media

Shakuntala (Kalidasa's play produced in classic Natyshastra style)
2 DVDs #DAK3928, 120 min. Insight Media

Women Theater Activists of India (interviews with 35 women working in contemporary Indian theater
VHS #9AK934, 77min. Insight Media

JAPAN

The Tradition of Performing Arts in Japan (overview of kabuki, bunraku, and Noh with performance excerpts in each form)
VHS #DAK350, DVD #DAK3884, 35min. Insight Media

Theater in Japan: Yesterday and Today (exploration of the cultural debate regarding traditional and contemporary theatre forms)
VHS #9AK1899, 53 min. Insight Media

Sagi Musume: Kabuki Dance (performance by kabuki's greatest performer of female roles, Tamasburo Bando)
DVD #DAK3592, 70 min. Insight Media

Shiranami Gonin Otoko: The Five Bandits (tale of a notorious bandit featuring Onoe Kikugoro in both male and female roles.)
DVD #9AK3903, 102 min. Insight Media

Kamagai Jinya: Kumagai's Battle Camp (classic jidaimono work chronicling crucial incident within the Battle of Ichinotani)
DVD #9AK3833, 86 min. Insight Media

Kabuki Techniques (famous kabuki actors demonstrate the central form of motion or kata)
VHS #9AK684, 30 min. Insight Media

Kabuki Acting Techniques (two-part instruction, one on movement, the other on voice)
VHS 1) #9AK3712, 2) #9AK269 24 min. Insight Media

Kabuki for Western Actors and Directors (potential adaptation of techniques to enhance performance)
VHS #9AK688, 38min. Insight Media

Fuinkiri: Breaking the Seal (central actors of the classic Chikamatsu drama *Medio No Hikyaku* or *The Courier for Hell*)
VHS #9AK684, 30 min. Insight Media

Hiroshi Inagaki's Samurai Trilogy (epic saga of seventeenth century samurai Musashi Miyamoto)
3 DVDs #DAK3784, 300 min. Insight Media

This Is Kyogen (production excerpts illustrating the classical fourteenth century comedy involving slapstick and satire)
VHS #DAK723, 21 min. Insight Drama

Kyogen Classic: Poison Sugar (Busu) (one of the most popular plays in this form)
VHS #DAK733, 28 min. Insight Media

This Is Noh (insights into the ancient masked dance drama)
VHS #DAK1601, 40 min. Insight Media

The Style of the Classic Japanese Noh Theater (movement and dance techniques presented by Sadayo Kita)
VHS #DAK318, 417 min. Insight Media

Noh: Classical Theater of Japan (demonstration by Akira Matsui of vigorous physical movements and use of masks)
VHS #9AK271, 28 min. Insight Media

Acting Techniques of the Noh Theater of Japan (basic postures, patterns of walking and turning)
VHS #DAK623, 30 min. Insight Media

Izutsu (short version of the 600year old tale)
VHS #DAK1600, 40 min. Insight Media

Japan's Classical Noh Drama: Aoi No Ue (production of the famous classic designed to introduce Japanese traditions to Western audiences)
VHS #DAK3886, 30 min. Insight Media

Bunraku: Masters of Japanese Puppet Theatre (the story of bunraku demonstrated by two of its greatest masters)
VHS #9AK3781, DVD #9AK3810, 52 min. Insight Media

The Lover's Exile (performance of the 1711 play by the Bunraku Theatrical Ensemble of Japan)
VHS #9AK1492, 90 min. Insight Media

NATIVE AMERICA

Yes, I Am Not Iktomi (Native American humor and visual language demonstrated through the Trickster storytelling tradition)
VHS #9AK3888, DVD #9AK3900, 27min. Insight Media

Native Voices (exploration of the richness of Native American oral traditions)
VHS #9AK3889, 30min. Insight Media

Distant Voices/Thunder Words (story traditions and the influence of the natural world are illuminated by poets, writers and storytellers)
VHS #9AK1843, DVD #9AK3895, 60min. Insight Media

GLOSSARY

A

Abstraction An artistic point of view that differs from an exact, accurate representation of the object observed.

Absurdism A style of drama that portrays human existence as meaningless and language as an insufficient way of communication. It was made popular after World War II in France by major authors including Samuel Beckett and Eugene Ionesco. There are three types of absurdism: fatalist, existentialism, and hilarious.

Abydos Passion Play The earliest known example of written theatre, Egyptian.

Académie Français The literary establishment that monitors language and the arts and that controlled the dramatic literature of the Neoclassic movement.

Academy A school for special, specific instruction. A group or society of artists joined to further an artistic or literary end.

Act To perform a role in front of an audience. Also, a basic division used to separate a play into two or more sections.

Acting Impersonating and/or creating a character to perform for an audience.

Action The physical or psychological movement of actors while portraying a character in response to a given circumstance of a play that in turn affects the course of that play. In character analysis, it is the tactics available to the character in pursuit of their super objective.

Actor Manager The starring actor who is the head of the acting company that organized the production.

Actor The essential artist of the theatre, television, or film who creates, portrays and/or impersonates a character bringing life to a story through words and gestures.

Actors' Equity Association The union that represents professional stage actors. Abbreviations: Actors' Equity, Equity, or AEA.

Adler, Stella An American acting teacher and a disciple of Stanislavski who based her work in close attention to the text.

Ad lib The word or words improvised by an actor during a production usually because the actor has failed to remember his/her line after something unplanned has occurred on stage. Sometimes a playwright, especially in crowd scenes, may direct an actor to ad lib.

Aeschylus The earliest of the three great Athenian tragedians and the author of our only complete trilogy: *The Oresteia*.

Aesthetics A branch of philosophy that deals with the study of the nature of beauty.

Aesthetic Response A reaction to art that does not explore its meaning, but rather, the experience.

Afterpiece An event staged after the main production in eighteenth and nineteenth century theater.

Agent a professional who acts for or represents an artist in theatre, television, and film who in turn receives a percentage of the artist's income.

Agit Prop An abbreviation of "agitation propaganda." A form of political drama that communicates information in a simple, and entertaining way, to persuade an audience's point of view. It was first used by Marxists in the 1920s in Russia then popularized in the 1920s and 1930s in America. As a result, the phrase used to describe morally instructive drama that was unusually militant.

Agon The Greek for the word "action." Agon depicts the interaction between opposing sides in Greek comedies.

Allegory The characters representing human qualities, especially used in the Middle Ages to represent the Seven Virtues and Seven Vices in religious dramas.

Alley Theatre A long rectangular performance space that has the audience on each side.

Amphitheatre Historically a large outdoor circular theatre in Rome, originally designed for entertainment using gladiators and animals.

Amplification The magnification of sound using electricity.

Anderson, Laurie A twentieth century American performance artist and pioneer in personal intimate confessional theatre.

Antagonist The character that works in opposition to the protagonist's intention.

Antoine, Andre An early proponent of naturalism, who began the Theatre Libre, an experimental theatre which practiced strict recreation of real life on stage.

Apollo The classical Greek god representing reason and balance.

Apron The forward-most structure of the proscenium stage commonly used during the English Restoration Period.

Aragato The heightened and bombastic rugged form of acting utilized in certain Kubuki performances.

Archetypal Characters The characters who incorporate the basic nature of certain human peculiarities that allow them to vocalize across cultures and centuries. (*See also* Allegory.)

Arena Theatre A theatrical performance area that is usually circular and completely surrounded by the audience.

Aristophanes The fifth century BCE author of our only examples of Old Comedy, a classical Greek style of satire and sex farce.

Aristotle The fourth century BCE Greek philosopher, the first known Western theatre critic, and the author of *The Poetics*.

Artha Sastra The fifth set of precepts guiding the Hindu religion, which placed actors at the bottom of the social ladder.

Artistic Director A member of the producing team, usually responsible for the management of the production season.

Aside The brief lines given directly to the audience that reveals a character's inner thoughts. Commonly used by William Shakespeare, often to comic effect.

Atellan Farce A style of brief improvised theater, in classical Rome, portraying larger than life family situations and ridiculing historical or mythological figures.

Audition An event where an actor engages in the active pursuit of a role. The process can include performing a monologue, prepares scene or "cold-reading" in front of a director or casting director.

Avant-garde The experimental theatre that pushes the barrier and challenges tradition; from the French term used to describe soldiers that march ahead in the military formation.

B

Back Drop The expansive drapery or decorated canvas which furnishes the upstage or the rear costuming of a set.

Back Story The conversation about what happened to the characters before the play commenced and what transpires between the scenes and off stage. Also known as exposition.

Balcony The raised spectators' area that overhangs one-third to one-half of the orchestra.

Ballad A song about love.

Bard The storyteller, performer, and keeper of communal memory. They are primarily seen in Western and Middle Eastern traditions.

Beat The smallest unit of an actor's role set by the evolution of the character's need. A dramatic pause.

Beijing Opera A flamboyant style of Chinese opera centered in Beijing, one of the most beloved and enduring of the *xiqu* styles of Eastern performance.

Bharata Author of the *Natrya Sastra* or The Canons of Dance and Drama. According to legend, Bharata received the Canons directly from the god Brahma. The Canons describe the elements of Sanskrit and much of Eastern theatre.

Bhasa One of the three great classical Sanskrit playwrights and the author of *Vasavadatta's Dream*.

Biomechanics A method developed in Russia by Vsevolod Meyerhold to enable an actor to behave like a machine.

Black Box Theatre An adjustable theatre space that usually holds less than a hundred people.

Blackface A derogatory comic black stereotype portrayed by whites in black make-up with white circles around the eyes and mouth. It started in minstrel shows.

Black Out A speedy and total dimming of the lights on stage.

Blocking The actor's movement on stage during a theatrical piece.

Boal, Augusto The theatre artist, theorist, and the creator of Theatre of the Oppressed. He designs theatre events for the disenfranchised in order to encourage and support social change.

Book The written dialogue and plot of a musical.

Book Musical A musical with a developed story and integrated plot.

Box Office The compartment where theatre tickets are sold.

Box Set A set design commonly used in realistic plays where the interior of room has three sides represented by flats and the fourth wall is removed.

Breaches Role Any role in which a female character dresses as a man. Common in the English Renaissance and Restoration periods.

Broadway An area in the center of Manhattan where the major commercial theatre district is located on Broadway , 8th Avenue, 42nd street and 52nd street.

Bunraku The theatre originally in Japan in the seventeenth century still present today.

Burlesque Technically, any parody of a serious work of art. Specifically used in early twentieth century America to denote a form of adult variety entertainment that was a forerunner of the modern American musical.

Business The physical behavior of an actor to reveal the character.

C

Call Back After the primary audition, the director or casting director calls back actors they may be interested in for a certain role for additional readings and/or an interview.

Call Back List A list directors create during auditions to narrow down the actors they are most interested in for a certain role.

Caricature A broad, stereotypical manner of creating and/or portraying a character.

Casting Call The public advertisement, announcement, or posting of auditions for a play.

Casting Against Type To cast someone in a role that is the opposite of or a completely different "type" of who one would expect to be cast in that role.

Casting Director A professional who specializes in finding the appropriate actors for specific roles.

Catharsis The release of emotions experienced by the audience. In Greek tragedy, these emotions are specifically pity and fear. The goal of Greek tragedy is to purge the audience of pity and fear that developed during the climax of the tragedy. The term was first coined by Greek philosopher Aristotle in the fourth century B.C.

Cattle Call An audition that is open to anyone. Also known as an "open call," the audition usually brings out big numbers. As a result, actors usually receive less time to perform audition material.

Character Flaw An internal flaw that affects a character's judgment, which forces the character to make bad decisions that lead to an unfortunate or tragic outcome. Also known as "tragic flaw," this quality can be found in the protagonist in Greek tragedy.

Chekhov, Anton The nineteenth century Russian author of early realism. He worked with Stanislavski at the Moscow Art Theatre.

Choreographer The designer of the dance and movement in a production.

Chorus An ensemble, in classic Greek plays, that moved, spoke, sung, and danced mostly in unison. Their function included providing commentary and narration, serving as a character in and of itself, or representing the mindset of the general public. Originally, the chorus was a large number of about fifty men then was reduced to twelve or fifteen. As other playwrights emerged, such as Shakespeare, the chorus became a character that was portrayed by a single actor or a smaller group of actors. In musicals, it is an ensemble that sings and dances in unison or as a series of solos or smaller groups.

Classical Drama Technically refers to plays from the classical Greece and Rome periods, now often used in reference to the masterpieces of the early and late Renaissance.

Climax The point of greatest dramatic tension when the conflicts of a play all come to a head, sometimes it is the moment the antagonist is defeated and/or the highest point of excitement for the audience when watching a play.

Cold Reading The requirement of actors to read from a script with no opportunity for preparation sometimes for an audition and/or call back.

Colorblind Casting The casting of actors regardless of race or ethnic background.

Comedy The dramatic genre that is usually humorous with a happy ending.

Commedia dell'Arte Originating in Italy, one of the first true theatre movements following the religious domination of the Middle Ages. A style based in scenarios (or basic story lines) fleshed out with lazzi, improv, and topical humor.

Compte, August The nineteenth century inventor of modern Sociology and who heavily influenced the development of Realism in the theatre.

Conflict The tension between two opposing forces in a play, key to the movement of the story. It creates set backs and obstacles for the characters to overcome.

Cue Something that occurs during the play, technically, physically or orally that signals an actor or theatre technician.

D

Dada A European Artisan movement that began after the first World War and portrayed the meaningless of life. It influenced poetry, paintings and theatre.

Dance Play A theatrical piece illustrated through dance minus dialogue in which characterization, narrative, and dramatic conflict are told in choreography instead of words.

Danjuro Family The hereditary "first family" of the Kabuki theatre, starting in 1660.

Darwin, Charles The nineteenth century naturalist, whose *Origin of Species* and theory of evolution heavily influenced the development of realism in the theatre.

Declamatory Acting A form of acting in which performers use large gestures such as "sawing the air" and exaggerated motion in combination with consistently boisterous line readings. It was first articulated as a method by Francois Delsarte in the eighteenth century.

Deconstruction In literary criticism, a movement that challenges the notion of fixed meanings, as truths of dramatic text.

Decorum The suitability and desirable taste in behavior and speech.

Denouement The point of the play, usually the final scene, where the results of the climax are revealed and any loose ends are tied up.

Devised Works Theatre events developed by a group of artists in a democratic forum, often based around a theme or existing non-theatrical text.

Dialect The body of a spoken language characteristic to a region or social group.

Dialogue The words spoken by two or more characters in a play.

Didacticism A theatre style, also known as epic or Brechtian theatre, that attempts to lead the audience into an intellectual, rather than emotional response.

Dimmer An apparatus that controls the intensity of light. Run by a dimmer board.

Dionysian Relating to Dionysus

Dionysus In Greek mythology; the god of wine and merriment.

Direct address The name of the person who is being spoken to.

Director The individual who steers a printed script in a theatrical stage production.

Dithyramb In ancient Greek, a song sung to honor the god Dionysus

Documentary theatre A leftist political theatre that challenges people to consider the political body that governs over them.

Downstage The part of the stage closest to the audience.

Drama A brand of theatre that expresses a story about people, their actions, and the opposition that results.

Dramatic Criticism Writings regarding drama.

Dramaturg An expert adviser of theatre history who helps actors, designers, and directors better understand the particulars of the play.

Dress Rehearsal The last rehearsals before opening night where actors don their costumes and make-up is added.

Drop A painted canvas or large curtain hung at the rear of the stage to plant an atmosphere or specific locale.

E

Education Theatre Theatre used to teach a distinct and specific message for the benefit of the student, usually in an elementary, secondary, or collegiate setting.

Ekkyklema A wheeling cart like machine, in ancient Greek theatre, that usually carried dead characters on and off stage to illustrate violence that occurred off stage.

Emotional memory An exercise created by Constantin Stanislavski that enables an actor to obtain some type of emotional connection to the experiences and situations of his/her character by recalling his/her personal, real life experiences that have evoked a similar emotional response that the character might have at a given time. Also referred to as sense memory or affective memory.

Encore When performers repeat a performance or a portion of the performance at the request of an audience determined by the level of applause and/or cheers the audience gives in response to the performance.

Ensemble A group of actors and/or performers.

Environmental Theater Aims to eliminate the space and distinction between the actors on stage and the audience by using the total theatre space to create the environment for the production. As a result it is usually a small, non-traditional space or black box type of theater.

Epilogue A speech delivered after the conclusion of a play by one of the performers addressed to the audience.

Episodic Plot A plot connected by characters not by the usual cause and effect.

Equity Theatre Theatre company or producing organization that pays its actors according to union contract to perform in a space that seats at least 100 audience members.

Euripides The last of the great classical Greek tragedians and the author of *Medea* and *The Bacchae*.

Existentialism A post World War I movement that views the world as a godless, senseless place where human beings live in a meaningless void.

Experimental Theatre Theatre whose goals, themes, or methods differ from whatever is the mainstream of the day.

Exposition In a play, information about prior events, or events that have taken place off stage that is necessary for the understanding of the plot of the play. This overall information is usually given in the form of a narrative.

Expressionism A theatre style that attempts to expose life through the lens of the author of the protagonist as they experience it, frequently through dream and nightmare imagery. Especially anti-industrial, anti-military, and anti-urban.

F

Fade A continuous dimming of the stage lights.

Farce An extreme comic form of theatre that pokes fun at authority through visual effects and physical activity and is generally light at heart.

Feminism In theatre theory, a belief that a woman's role in theatre has not been adequately investigated.

Fight Director Choreographs any fight sequences, balancing realistic violence with safety and theatricality.

Flats A frame made of wood usually covered by fabric to create a set, particularly a wall.

Fly Loft or Flies The area above the stage where sets and scenery, when not in use, maybe hoisted out of sight by the use of counterweights or pulleys.

Focus The spot on the stage that attracts the audience's attention designated by the director.

Footlights Stage lights or light sources strategically set in between the actors and audience.

Foreshadowing A structural device in the form of a warning of impending danger, used to increase tension.

Forestage *See* Apron.

Fourth Wall A device of Realism created in the mid-eighteenth century in which an imaginary wall is placed between the actors and the audience.

French Neoclassicism An influential seventeenth century style of formal playwrighting that desired to emulate Aristotle and the Greek classical playwrights.

Freud, Sigmund The nineteenth century developer of theories about psycho-analysis and the unconscious mind. His theories heavily influenced the development of realism in the theatre.

Fugard, Athol The twentieth century South African playwright whose anti-apartheid plays got him in trouble with the authorities.

Full House An actor's dream; when the seating in the theatre has reached its capacity.

Fusion The blending of theatrical forms from different cultures into a single performance.

Futurism A movement of art which began in early twentieth century Italy and glorifies the age of mechanization and the energy of the Industrial Age.

G

Genre The division of drama used to classify plays in a certain category. Most popular categories (or genres) are comedy, tragedy, melodrama, and farce.

George II, Duke of Saxe-Meiningen A German, often referred to as the Father of Modern Directing. He developed the role of the director as a single voice controlling all elements of production.

Georgian Comedy The eighteenth century English comedy that tended to the sentimental rather than the satirical.

Gesture Any physical movement used as a form of communication. It can be accompanied by verbal communication or it can stand alone. Onstage, actors use gestures to enhance their communication and to help bring a sense of real life to a text. They can be planned or unplanned.

Given Circumstances The facts that create the world of a play or facts given by the playwright about a character.

Goethe, Johann Wolfgang von The playwright of the Romantic Movement and author of *Faust*.

Goldsmith, Oliver The eighteenth century English playwright of Georgian comedy, such as *She Stoops to Conquer*.

Greenroom A small room located backstage for actors to relax, eat, or wait for cues before, after, or during a show.

Griot The singer, storyteller, and keeper of the community's collective memory/history in traditional African theatre.

Grotowski, Jerzy The European director who used the text as a springboard for conceptualized productions.

H

Hamartia A term created in ancient Greek that is translated as "tragic flaw" or "missing the mark." Scholars suggest that it is more of an error of judgment made by the protagonist rather than a deficiency in the character's psychology.

Hanamichi In the Japanese Kabuki theatre; a long narrow pathway leading from behind the audience to the stage where actors make entrances and exits and express heightened dramatic text.

Hansberry, Lorraine The twentieth century African American playwright, her *Raisin in the Sun* was the first play by a female African American ever produced on Broadway.

Happenings Theatrical events that are unstructured, and occur outside of commercial theatre, usually on street corners, bus stops, or places where people congregate.

Harlem Renaissance Centered in Harlem in the 1920s and 1930s in which African Americans expressed themselves through a collective arts and music movement.

Hashigakari In the Japanese *Noh* Theatre, it is the pathway from the dressing area to the stage.

Hellinistic Age The theatre of the ancient Greeks during the fourth and third centuries B.C.

High Comedy Comedy composed of intellect and language, usually specific to upper class characters and interests.

Hellman, Lillian An American master of realism, her plays include *The Children's Hour* and *The Little Foxes*.

Hero The character or figure that symbolized the culture's most valued traits and is the central figure in a heroic tragedy or play.

Homer A person or persons who first recorded the ancient stories of Greece in the eighth century BCE, including the *Iliad* and the *Odyssey*.

House The seating area in a theatre

House Holder An acting company member who retains a share of the theatre himself.

Hugo, Victor The French playwright of the Romantic Movement and author of the Romanticism *Manifesto* and the Romantic play *Hernani*.

Hwang, David Henry The twentieth century Asian-American playwright and author of *M. Butterfly*.

I

Ibsen, Henrik The nineteenth century Norwegian playwright, called by some the Father of Modern Realism, author of *The Doll's House* and *Ghosts*.

Impressionism An artistic style that searches for the truth.

Improvisation An acting technique or exercise that frees a performers' imagination and allows him to create and respond without a defined script or rehearsal behavior. It can be spontaneous dialogue (ad lib) or stage business created by an actor in the moment of the performance.

Inciting Incident The event that sets the action of a play into motion.

Ingénue A role that has the following qualities: young, innocent, and pretty. It can also refer to an actress that portrays this type of role.

Inner Conflict Something that is bubbling below the surface of a character that eventually becomes so overwhelming it must be confronted.

Inner monologue An actor's internal movement of thought connected to his/her character's lines and/or situation used to enhance his/her performance.

Intermission A small pause in the action of a production where the audience is permitted to leave their seats for a short time—usually for ten to fifteen minutes.

Irony A technique of indicating through plot, character, or action an intention or attitude in direct opposition to the one being overtly stated.

J

Jidaimono A type of Kabuki play focused on history, translates to "period things."

Jing In *xiqu*, the "painted faces" roles, often depicting gods, demons, or heroes.

Jinguju Another name for Beijing Opera, the most popular form of Chinese theatre in the world today.

Jorjuri The chorus in a Kabuki play.

Juhachiban The body of eighteen classical Kabuki plays still performed today.

K

Kabuki One of the classical theatres of Japan, dating from the seventeenth century, a popular form in contrast with the elitist form of the *Noh*.

Kalidasa One of the three great playwrights of the classical Sanskrit tradition. Author of *The Recognition of Shakuntala*, regarded by Sanskrit scholars as "the perfect play."

Kanani/Zeami Japanese father/son team responsible for creation of the *Noh* drama and most of its extent texts.

Kathakali A popular form of Indian classical drama, meaning literally "story play." An intense all-night outdoor theatre event designed to evoke mystery and fear.

Kunqu A refined, elitist form of *xiqu* or Chinese opera, beginning in 1644 and still performed occasionally today.

L

Lighting Designer The artist who is responsible for creating the lighting vision of a production.

Light Plot The diagram that illustrates all the lighting instruments, how they are hung, and what areas of the stage they are focused to light.

Literary Managers Dramaturges who work for theatre companies to read, research, and evaluate the plays performed.

Long Run A continuous run of a particular production.

Low Comedy A type of comedy that relies on physical, visual, and obscene humor.

Lyrics The sung words of a song in a musical.

M

Magic if An acting exercise created by Stanislavski. When an actor asks himself "What would I do if I were in that position?"

Mahabharata One of the two great epics of Indian tradition.

Managing Director A member of the producing team, in charge of finances and budgetary concerns.

Mask Establishing a character by covering the face. Used since the beginning of theatre including Greek, Roman, and Commedia dell'Arte.

Masque Grand private theatrical entertainment created in Renaissance Italy and traveled to the courts of France and England.

Marx, Karl A nineteenth century political theorist, whose *Communist Manifesto* influenced the development of realism in the theatre.

Medium The raw material chosen by the artist as the starting place for creative activity. A painter may choose between oil and water color; a playwright between media and live theatre.

Meisner, Stanford An American acting teacher, disciple of Stanislavski, who developed a training system involving repetition exercises. "Behaving truthfully in imaginary circumstances."

Melodrama A specific type of plot oriented drama with clearly defined characters that articulates middle-class values.

Method, The A system of actor training developed by Lee Strasberg, focused on the truth of emotional memory or recall.

Miko A storyteller, performer, and shaman in traditional Japanese oral theatre.

Miller, Arthur An American master of realism, author of *All My Sons* and *Death of a Salesman*.

Mime A form of theatrical entertainment acted without words. Performers of mime traditionally use white face make-up and exaggerate their movements and expressions.

Minstrel Show A nineteenth century racist style of performance, in which white performers in blackface denigrated African American culture.

Miracle Play Medieval dramas about the lives of Saints.

Mnouchkine, Ariane A twentieth century fusion artist, director of the Theatre du Soliel.

Moliere A seventeenth century French comic playwright who transcended the rigors of neoclassic demands to create universally respected comedies of satire and manners. He was strongly influenced by Commedia dell'Arte troupes.

Mood A play's predominant attitude, particularly comic or serious.

Monologue An unbroken speech in a play sometimes directed to the audience, sometimes to another character. (*See also* Soliloquy.)

Morality Plays Late Medieval dramas intended to teach a lesson.

Motivation The conscious or subconscious reason a character determines behavior or action.

Multiculturalism The effort to achieve an inclusive society by giving equal voice and representation to underrepresented groups of people.

Music Director The person who guides the singers and orchestra through the score in a musical.

Musical A form of theatre that highlights song and dance integrated with spoken text.

Musical Comedy A form of musical theatre that has a light hearted, rapid moving comic story and integrated with popular music.

Mystery Play Plays produced during the Medieval Era in Europe that dealt with biblical stories performed outdoors. Also known as pageant plays in England, when dealing with the Crucifixion of Jesus Christ, and as Corpus Christie plays when mounted in combination with that certain festival.

N

National Endowment of the Arts An agency of the federal government that distributes tax dollars in the form of grants in order to fund cultural programs.

Naturalism A movement in nineteenth century Europe that represents realism in its most radical form and shows that nature and the social environment control human behavior.

Neoclassicism A renewed excitement in the artistic and literary philosophies of Ancient Greece and Rome and the effort to express them in a more current fashion.

New Comedy Comic dramas of Greece of the late fourth to second centuries B.C.

Noh (also spelled *no*) A classical dance drama created in fourteenth century Japan that relies heavily on tradition. This style of drama predates Kabuki.

O

Objective The desire, need, want, or goal of a character within a beat (dramatic moment) or scene that drives the action of a play.

Obstacle A challenge or anything in a play, that makes it difficult for a character to achieve his/her goal. It helps to create tension, complications, and conflict in a play.

Off Broadway The small professional theaters in New York City located outside the Broadway district. Today, it is considered a scaled-down version of Broadway. Originally it was a movement initiated in the 1940s inspired by Broadway commercialism as an outlet to provide a more experimental atmosphere for new and innovative works unhindered by commercial influences. Many American actors and directors jump start their careers Off Broadway.

Off-Off Broadway The non-traditional, non-professional theatre in New York City that displays new talent in experimental, non conventional and original work productions. This movement was created in the 1960s as a result of the commercialism of Broadway and increasing commercialism of Off Broadway.

Old Comedy Greek comic plays written in the classical period that directly or indirectly comments on the social, political, and/or cultural issues of the times. It usually filled with physical and obscene humor.

O'Neill, Eugene An American master of realism, author of *Moon for the Misbegotten* and *Long Day's Journey Into Night*.

Onnagata A male performer in traditional Japanese theatre who specialized in playing female roles.

Opening night The first full-priced performance during a run of a production open to the public.

Opera An emotionally heightened, dramatic musical that is entirely sung. It was created during the Renaissance.

Oral Tradition Theatre based in spoken word and communal memory rather than written text.

Orchestra The floor level seating in an auditorium or theatre located in front of a proscenium stage.

Orchestra Pit The area below apron of a proscenium stage. It can be the space for musicians as well as a mobile part of the stage.

P

Pageant Wagons The movable stage drawn by horses or people in which these biblical plays were mounted on.

Pantomime Silent storytelling through dance performed during the Christian Era in Roman theatre. It is also a term used in England and France to describe commedia-type figures.

Para Basis When a character in a Greek Old Comedy does a "coming forward" in the middle of the play and gives a direct address to the audience.

Parody An over the top imitation of an individual or of an artistic genre that makes it look ridiculous.

Passion Plays Plays portraying events from the passion of the Christ.

Performance Live public execution of at least partially planned behavior or action.

Performance Art An art form created in the mid twentieth century that focuses on visual expression of personal truth and a state of being, more than literal expression and telling a story. There are usually one or more performers with a blend of music, painting, dance, theatre, poetry, and visual arts in performance art pieces.

Performing Art Any form of art that relies on a live performer in front of a live audience.

Pit The space around the raised stage in the Elizabethan Theatre, in which viewers could stand to watch the performance.

Play Text A printed script containing dialogue spoken by characters that can be interpreted by actors and directors on the premise for behavior on stage.

Plot The arranged set of events in a play, and the way those events unfold to tell a story while simultaneously creating maximum dramatic impact.

Point of Attack The beginning moment in a play that starts the action of the play, chosen by the playwright out of the larger story of a character's life.

Political Theatre Theatre that expresses a certain view or opinion about current issues.

Poor Theatre Theatre that utilizes only those materials required to perpetuate the illustration of the actor.

Postmodernism A concept of the late twentieth century where relativism replaces absolute values allowing other forms of artistic expression to come to view.

Presentational The style of theatre that shows the obvious artificiality of a stage performance and does not attempt to create any type of realistic illusion. Actors may acknowledge the audience, speak to them, and even encourage them to participate.

Presentational Staging Staging that makes apparent use of the theatre resources.

Preview A free or discounted performance usually scheduled after or during dress rehearsal and right before opening night.

Producer Any individual, group, or institution, that controls the business side of a production.

Production Concept The thematic idea of a play or production

Progression The order of changes that outlines character development.

Prologue An introductory speech given to the audience before the play or a scene.

Prompt Book A book or binder with a copy of the script inside including sound and light cues, blocking and other rehearsal and performance information.

Props An abbreviation for properties, it includes set props which are items like furniture that dress the set and hand props which are any items used by the actors on stage.

Proscenium Arch The arch that serves as a frame separating the stage space from the audience area.

Proscenium stage An arrangement of a theatre area in which the audience faces the actor on any one side.

Problem Play A play that tells about a social malady so that it can be cured.

Protagonist The main actor in Greek theatre. Today, it is the central character that drives the action onward; also known as the hero.

Public Relations/Promotion The link between the production and the general public, in charge of generating attendance through advertising and other means.

R

Ramayana One of the two great epics of Indian tradition.

Rasa The producing of a fitting emotion in the audience (from Sanskrit aesthetic theory).

Realism The cultural movement that supports theatrical realism and extended the belief that these plays could be a force for social and political change. Also: realism—a form of theatre where the behavior on stage happens as it would in life.

Regional Theatre A professional, not-for-profit, non-touring theatre located outside New York City.

Rehearsal The practicing of plays in order to refine their performance.

Renaissance The "re-birth" or renewed excitement in the learning and culture of ancient Greece and Rome beginning in Italy (1450–1650) and spreading throughout Western Europe.

Repertory A decided assortment of performance pieces done by a company.

Representational A type of theatrical performance in which the actors represent real life and are oblivious to the presence of the audience.

Resolution (*See* Denouement)

Restoration A return to the theatre after the re-establishment of the monarchy in England, in 1660; noted for clever and lustful comedies.

Revenge plays Grisly dramas from the Roman era that influenced theatre during the Elizabethan period.

Revival The remounting of a play after its first run.

Rising Action The intensifying action.

Ritual A usually spiritual cultural practice involving well-defined and exact movements, music, and spoken text that serves to communicate with deities.

Rivera, Jose A twentieth century Cuban American master playwright.

Rock Musical A musical that encompasses rock and roll music.

Rock Opera A form of comedic opera that includes rock and roll music such as Andrew Lloyd Webber's *Jesus Christ Superstar*.

Romanticism A movement in nineteenth century Europe, from neoclassic formulism toward enormous passions, exotic, distorted stories, gaudy writing, and inclusive worldviews.

S

Sanskrit Drama The classical theatre of India.

Satire A type of drama that uses comedy, wit, and irony, to exaggerate and expose a certain idea; usually to reveal or express opinions about that idea.

Scene The term for the small units of a play that make up the acts of the play.

Screen Actors' Guild The name of the union that represents film and TV actors.

Script The text of a play.

Set The physical scenery for a play or scene.

Sewamona A style of Kabuki play focused on domestic issues, translates to "common things."

Shanghai Opera The traditional people's theatre centered in its namesake city that features all female performers.

Shaw, George Bernard A nineteenth century English playwright of the realist movement, author of *Mrs. Warren's Profession* and *Arms and the Man*.

Sheridan, Richard Brinsley An eighteenth century English playwright of Georgian comedy, such as *The Rivals*.

Showstopper A big musical number that receives so much applause from the audience it stops the show.

Shudraka One of the three great classical Sanskrit playwrights, and the author of *The Little Clay Cart*.

Siddharta (The Buddha) The Hindu Prince who achieved Enlightment, and was influential in the spread of Sanskrit dramatic conventions throughout Asia.

Sides Copies of the entire script or sections of the script given to actors at auditions or call backs. It can also be an actor's copy of his/her lines, cues, and blocking.

Sight Line An audience's visual boundary. Sight lines extend horizontally as well as vertically and anything beyond the sight lines is out of the audience's sight.

SlapStick A style of comedy that relies heavily if not solely on physicalization, it is very common in farce or low comedy.

Slice of Life Theatre that aims to depict natural everyday life, synonymous with pure naturalism. Slice of Life plays usually follows a character's life for the duration of the realistic time the actual play lasts. For example, if the play lasts two hours, it only highlights two hours of the world of the character.

Soliloquy A monologue in which the character speaks his or her thoughts out loud, but not directed toward any other person.

Sound Booth The area or room where the sound equipment is operated, prepared, or edited.

Soyinka, Wole The Nigerian playwright whose political plays got him into trouble with the authorities.

Spectacle All visual elements of a production. Musicals are known for using great spectacle.

Spiderwoman A Native American performance group that revitalizes the ancient stories and performance styles of their culture to address contemporary women's issues.

Stage Directions The suggested directions of a playwright included in the text of the play.

Stage Managers The person who overlooks the execution of a production. This person acts as the 'go between' for the director, the performers, and the entire production staff. The stage manager is vital to the production and works closely with the director from the beginning of a production until the end. In professional theatre it is common for directors to leave a show before the end of a run leaving the stage manager in charge of the production.

Stage Reading The reading of a script using actors with scripts in hand, few props, and a minimal to bare set.

Stanislavski, Constantin The Father of Modern Acting. He developed a highly influential method of actor training that encouraged realistic and detailed performances.

Star In a production, the actor who is usually well known enough that his/her presence brings in an audience. The star is usually paid more and may receive certain perks because of their status.

Star System A nineteenth century touring technique, in which the star or lead actor purchased the rights to a play and produced it to his or her own advantage.

Stock Characters Stereotypical characters that are usually less than three dimensional. Stock characters were created during the Italian Renaissance in the Commedia Dell'Arte. These types of characters are still popular today.

Straight Play A play without music.

Strasberg, Lee An American acting teacher and a disciple of Stanislavski. He developed a school of acting based on emotional memory or recall, called The Method.

Strindberg, August A nineteenth century Swedish playwright. Though he was an early master of naturalism (*Miss Julie* and *The Father*), he later rejected naturalism as inadequate. He pioneered Expressionism on stage (*Road to Damascus* and *Ghost Sonata*).

Subtext The real meaning and/or intention of character that lives below the surface of the actual text.

Super Objective A larger unit of an objective that embodies the major intention or desire of a character and carries him or her through all or most of the play.

Symbolism A theatre movement that attempts to capture the ineffable, mystical, and sub-conscious on stage, through poetry, repeated imagery, and avoidance of plot and action-oriented structures.

T

Table Work The initial step in the rehearsal process; actors are seated at a table and read through the play.

Tableau A "frozen moment" onstage, which usually occurs at the conclusion of a scene or as the lights dim.

Tan A female role in Peking opera.

Technical Director The head of the technical areas, including set construction, lighting and sound, and cost-effectiveness. He/she is involved in all stages of production from planning to closing night and strike.

Tetralogy From ancient Greek theatre, four plays, three tragedies and one satyr written by a single author performed in sequence for festivals.

Text The play script

Theatre A performing art comprised of a live actor, a live audience, a space, and a story or idea.

Theatre of Cruelty A form of ritualistic theatre designed by Antonin Artaud to assault spectators' sensibilities and cleanse them of those harmful tendencies.

Theatre of Dionysus The largest ancient Greek theatre capable of holding as many as seventeen thousand people. It is located in Athens,

Theatre of Identity Plays written by and pertaining to a particular culture or ethnic group.

Theatre of Protest Plays that are critical of the policies of the dominant culture and command justice.

Theatre of the Absurd A style of theatre originating from the atrocities and devastation of World War II and dramatizes the uneasiness and chaos of the world.

Theatron The seating space in classic Greek theatre, carved into a hillside.

Thespian An actor, from Thespis who was identified by Aristotle as the first Greek actor.

Three Unities The rules for writing a play concerning time, place, and action. They are derived from the Neoclassical (Western) Dramatic theory.

Through Line A constant element of an actor's role that ties all of the character's words that run throughout the scene or play. Through line originated from Stanislavski's vocabulary.

Thrust Stage The area of the theatre in which the spectators are placed on three sides of the stage.

Tiring House A three-story stage house from which the thrust stage or Elizabethan platform extended.

Total Theatre An absolute integration of all performance elements including acting, mime, music, dance, and text. It originated in Asia.

Tragedy A serious play with an unhappy ending in which the main character, or hero, elicits our sympathy through forces, or events that were out of the characters' control. It is one of the most renowned of all dramatic genres.

Tragic Flaw A fixed trait in a character that brings about his own downfall. (*See* Character Flaw)

Tragicomedy A dramatic piece that starts as a tragedy, but includes comic ingredients and ends happily.

Trilogy In ancient Greece, three tragedies penned by the same playwright and presented in one day.

Trope Song lyrics inserted to musical passages in religious services in the early Middle Ages. Structured like playlets these interpolations resulted into liturgical drama.

Turkey A play that is expected to fail.

U

Upstage The part of the stage that is the farthest from where the audience sits.

Upstaging Occurs when more than one thing is onstage at a time and one of them pulls the focus from the other. Performers can upstage each other, and lights, sound, and set pieces (including props) can pull focus as well.

V

Valdez, Luis A twentieth century Mexican American theatre artist who practices his art among the disenfranchised to promote social change and empowerment.

Values In character analysis, what a character believes to be true and important.

Variety show A performance of unrelated singing, dancing, and comedic routines.

Vaudeville A popular stage variety show in America from the 1880s to the 1930s. The performance included song and dance numbers, comedy skits, animal acts, and magic acts; a descendant of burlesque.

W

Wagato A style of performance in Kabuki theatre characterized as "soft" rather than aggressive or aragoto.

Warm-up Physical exercises used to prepare for a performance, rehearsal, or audition.

Williams, Tennessee (Thomas Lanier) A twentieth century American master of realism, author of *The Glass Menagerie* and *A Streetcar Named Desire*.

Willing Suspension of Disbelief The idea that when one comes to the theatre there is an unspoken agreement that the audience consents to allowing their imagination to give in to the circumstances of the play.

X

Xiqu "Tuneful theatre" in Chinese. The common term for all forms of traditional Chinese Theatre. Also known as Chinese Opera.

Z

Zaju The earliest form of *xiqu* or Chinese Opera, c. 900–c. 1400. A comic form of popular theatre with songs, acrobatics, clowns, and puppets.

Zanni Comic male servants in commedia dell'arte.

Zarzuela A form of court entertainment from the Spanish Golden Age that includes brief stylized musical drama, founded on mythology with showy scenic effects, motivated by Italian opera and interezzi.

Zibaldoni Writings collected by actors in commedia dell'arte, including jokes, comic business, and repeated scenes and speeches from the Italian Renaissance.

Zola, Emile A nineteenth century French theorist and playwright of naturalism. The author of *Therese Raquin*, considered by many to be the first naturalistic play.